aces & aerial victories

The United States Air Force in Southeast Asia 1965·1973

by R. Frank Futrell	William H. Greenhalgh	Carl Grubb
Gerard E. Hasselwander	Robert F. Jakob	Charles A. Ravenstein

Edited by
James N. Eastman, Jr.   Walter Hanak   Lawrence J. Paszek

The Albert F. Simpson
Historical Research Center
Air University
and
Office of Air Force History
Headquarters USAF
1976

Library of Congress Cataloging in Publication Data

Main entry under title:
The United States Air Force in Southeast Asia—aces and aerial victories, 1965–1973.

    Includes index and glossary.
    1. Vietnamese Conflict, 1961–1975—Aerial operations, American. 2. Vietnamese Conflict, 1961–1975—Personal narratives, American. 3. United States. Air Force—History. I. Futrell, Robert Frank. II. Eastman, James N. III. Hanak, Walter K. IV. Paszek, Lawrence J. V. Title: Aces and aerial victories, The United States Air Force in Southeast Asia 1965–1973.
DS558.8.U53 1976   959.704'348   76-7485

Foreword

During the war in Southeast Asia, U.S. Air Force fighter pilots and crewmen were repeatedly challenged by enemy MIG's in the skies over North Vietnam. The air battles which ensued were unique in American history because U.S. fighter and strike forces operated under stringent rules of engagement. With periodic exceptions, for example, MIG bases could not be struck. The rules generally forbade bombing or strafing of military and industrial targets in and around the enemy's heartland, encompassing the capital of Hanoi and the port city of Haiphong. These restrictions gave the North Vietnamese substantial military advantage. Free from American attack and helped by its Soviet and Chinese allies, the enemy was able to construct one of the most formidable antiaircraft defenses the world has even seen. It included MIG forces, surface-to-air missile (SAM) batteries, heavy concentrations of antiaircraft artillery (AAA) units, and an array of early warning radar systems. These elements sought to interdict and defeat the U.S. bombing campaign against North Vietnam's lines of communication and its military and industrial base. The primary mission of U.S. fighter pilots was to prevent the North Vietnamese MIG's from interfering with U.S. strike operations. This book tells how American airmen—assisted by an armada of other USAF aircraft whose crews refueled their planes, warned of approaching enemy MIG's and SAM's, and flew rescue missions when they were shot down—managed to emerge from their aerial battles with both victories and honor.

JOHN W. HUSTON, Major General, USAF
Chief, Office of Air Force History

ADVISORY COMMITTEE

I.B. Holley, Jr.
Duke University

Lt. Gen. James R. Allen
Superintendent, USAF Academy

Robert F. Byrnes
Indiana University

Lt. Gen. Albert P. Clark
USAF (ret.)

Lt. Gen. Raymond B. Furlong
Commander, Air University

Henry F. Graff
Columbia University

Louis Morton
Dartmouth College

Forrest C. Pogue
Director. Dwight D. Eisenhower Institute for Historical Research

Jack L. Stempler
The General Counsel, USAF

Office of Air Force History
Chief, Maj. Gen. John W. Huston

Chief Historian—Stanley L. Falk
Deputy Chief Historian—Max Rosenberg
Chief, Histories Division—Carl Berger
Senior Editor—Lawrence J. Paszek

Preface

Aces and Aerial Victories is a collection of firsthand accounts by Air Force fighter crews who flew combat missions over North Vietnam between 1965 and 1973. They recall their air battles with enemy MIG fighters, the difficult and dangerous tactical maneuvers they had to perform to survive, and their victories and defeats. The narratives are taken directly from aircrew after-action reports. A number of direct quotations have been altered, but only to clarify for the reader the very specialized language of their profession (e.g., code words).

The unofficial title of "ace" originated during World War I in recognition of a combat pilot who had shot down five enemy aircraft (including observation balloons). The honorific title was used again during World War II, the Korean War, and the war in Southeast Asia to recognize similar exploits. Credits for the destruction of enemy aircraft in the area are confirmed by the Air Force. The manner of awarding them, however, has varied from war to war and even from theater to theater (as in World War II). The different guidelines reflected the different circumstances in each theater and each war, and the weapons technology employed by both sides.

When the Air Force found itself engaged in aerial combat over North Vietnam beginning in 1965, it had no plan for handling claims or awarding victory credits. A year elapsed before Headquarters Seventh Air Force, located at Tan Son Nhut Air Base (AB) in South Vietnam, developed a method for awarding credits. By this time at least 16 MIG's had been downed by USAF crews. On 12 November Seventh Air Force published a regulation to govern victory credits; however, it was not until 1967 that Headquarters USAF authorized the Pacific Air Forces to publish confirming orders.

In accordance with the Seventh Air Force regulation, each combat wing or separate squadron was required to establish an Enemy Aircraft Claims Evaluation Board of four to six members. Each was composed of at least two rated officers, the senior operations officer, and the unit's intelligence officer. A crew seeking confirmation of a "kill" was required to submit a written claim to the board within 24 hours after the shootdown. The board had 10 days to process the claim and to forward it through the unit commander to Seventh Air Force headquarters, where another board was convened to review the evidence. This headquarters board consisted of six officers—three from operations, two from intelligence, and one from personnel. They reviewed the evidence and were required to confirm or deny the claim within 24 hours. Credit for destroying an enemy aircraft became official upon publication of a Seventh Air Force general order.

The criteria established for aerial victory credits were not much different from those used during the Korean War. Credit was given to pilots of any aircraft and to gunners in multiplace aircraft if they fired the weapon that destroyed the enemy aircraft or caused it to crash. While credits were awarded only for the destruction of enemy aircraft, claims were accepted for probable destruction or damage.

An enemy aircraft was considered destroyed if it crashed, exploded, disintegrated, lost a major component vital for flight, caught fire, entered into an attitude or position from which recovery was impossible, or if its pilot bailed out. The claim had to be substantiated by written testimony from one or more aerial or ground observers, gun camera film, a report that the wreckage of the enemy aircraft had been recovered, or some other positive intelligence that confirmed its total destruction. No more than two 2-man crews could be credited with downing a single enemy aircraft, thus limiting the smallest share in a victory credit to one-fourth. Every detail had to be described as clearly as possible to insure that claims were evaluated judiciously and speedily.

The war in Southeast Asia was peculiar and did not provide U.S. pilots the opportunity to amass the high victory scores that were common in World War II and Korea. One reason for this was that enemy pilots did not engage American aircraft whenever the North Vietnamese were at a disadvantage. This strategy probably was devised by their commanders in an effort to conserve aircraft obtained from foreign sources and to introduce their newly trained pilots into combat gradually. Another reason for the limited number of victories was that the enemy relied heavily upon Soviet surface-to-air missiles and antiaircraft artillery units. When the MIG pilots did scramble to challenge U.S. strike aircraft, it was to prevent the destruction of vital transportation and other war-supporting industrial facilities by American bombing planes.

Another important factor which limited U.S. aerial victories was the 3½ year standdown in American air operations over North Vietnam, which began in November 1968 and lasted (with certain exceptions) until the spring of 1972, when Hanoi launched a massive invasion of South Vietnam. Finally, the kill ratio was low because of restraints imposed on U.S. airmen throughout the war and the many intermittent halts of air operations between 1965 and 1968, whose aim was to get peace negotiations under way. As a consequence, many airmen completed their 1-year combat tours without having the opportunity to engage the enemy in the air except on limited occasions.

When President Lyndon B. Johnson announced the complete bombing halt of 1 November 1968, he placed North Vietnam off limits to fighter aircraft. At that time, the highest kill scores consisted of only two victories each, awarded to two pilots: Col. Robin Olds and Capt. Max C. Brestel. Olds shared the credits with his F–4 weapon systems officers and was responsible for the destruction of four enemy aircraft. Brestel, flying alone in an F–105, destroyed two aircraft. The Air Force thus had no aces at the time, and no crewmember approached the magic score of five victories.

After USAF operations over the North were resumed in the spring of 1972, Gen. John D. Ryan, Chief of Staff, changed the policy of dividing aerial victories between aircrew members of dual-place fighters. He announced that each member of a 2-man crew would be assigned full credit for each hostile aircraft downed in combat. The policy became retroactive to April 1965, the date when the first F–4's arrived in Southeast Asia. As a result, Olds was awarded four kills and he thus headed the victory list.

Following the Communist Easter offensive of March–April 1972, air units were ordered back into action over North Vietnam and MIG's once again came under the fire of USAF guns and missiles, enabling U.S. fliers to score sufficient victories to become aces. The Navy produced the first aces of the conflict on 10 May 1972, when Lieutenants Randy Cunningham and William Driscoll destroyed three MIG's to bring their total score to five. But the Air Force was not far behind. On the same day, Capt. Richard S. (Steve) Ritchie and Capt. Charles B. DeBellevue shot down their first MIG. Ritchie downed his fifth on 28 August, and DeBellevue followed on 9 September. Another weapon systems officer, Capt. Jeffrey S. Feinstein, became the third USAF ace on 13 October, when he scored his fifth victory.

The achievements of the fighter crews, however, could not have been accomplished without the assistance of other USAF airmen flying supporting missions. The latter included members of aerial refueling squadrons, who made it possible for the fighters to engage the enemy in the skies over North Vietnam and return safely to base. Fighter pilots also were indebted to the USAF electronic warfare crews, who jammed enemy radars and interfered with North Vietnamese fighter control. SAM-hunting Wild Weasel aircraft, flying deep into enemy territory, sought out and destroyed the SAM sites and their radar systems. Search and rescue crewmen assisted in locating and recovering downed fighter crews; unarmed reconnaissance aircraft brought back photo intelligence needed by top commanders to direct air operations; Air Force weather men provided vital information on the weather situation in the theater, which enabled Seventh Air Force commanders to decide when to launch the strike force; and, of course, USAF maintenance, supply, and other support units kept the fighter planes flying.

Individual contributors to this volume included: Dr. R. Frank Futrell, Mr. Charles A. Ravenstein,

Mr. Gerard E. Hasselwander, and MSgts. Robert F. Jakob and Carl Grubb. For other significant contributions, the writers are indebted to Mr. William H. Greenhalgh, who compiled the information on awarding victory credits. The manuscript underwent extensive editorial revision by Mr. Lawrence J. Paszek, Office of Air Force History, Headquarters, USAF, and Col. Walter Hanak, mobilization assignee to the Office. Mr. James N. Eastman, Jr., Chief, Historical Research Branch, Albert F. Simpson Historical Research Center, Maxwell AFB, Ala., supervised the work and also contributed to the editing. The task of typing the manuscript and its numerous revisions was shared by Mrs. Jane Motley, at the Center; and Mrs. Selma Shear, Mrs. Eleanor Patterson, Mrs. Elizabeth Schwartzman, and Mrs. Jewell Newman, of the Office of Air Force History.

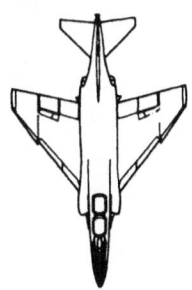
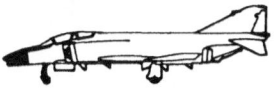

F–4C Fighter

Contents

	Page
Foreword	iii
Preface	v
List of Illustrations	x
List of Maps and Charts	xii
List of Tables	xiii

I. THE SITUATION
Dr. Robert Frank Futrell

	Page
Rolling Thunder	3
Freedom Train and Linebacker	14
Linebacker II	16

II. COMBAT NARRATIVES: 1965–1968
Charles A. Ravenstein

	Page
First USAF MIG Kills	22
Enemy Stand-Down	26
More MIG Kills	27
Operation Bolo	35
Another Successful Ruse	43
A Temporary Lull	44
Heavy Opposition Again	45
MIG Fight for Survival	48
Seven Victories in One Day	53
An Old-Fashioned Dogfight	58
Another MIG Stand-Down	64

	Page
Renewed Opposition	66
New MIG Tactics	73

III. COMBAT NARRATIVES: 1972–1973
Charles A. Ravenstein

	Page
Victories over Laos	85
Linebacker Operations	89
"Triple-Nickel" Hits Jackpot	92
MIG's Intensify Threat	96
The First USAF Aces	102
USAF's Third Ace	109
Score Two for B–52 Gunners	111

IV. THE MEN: THEIR UNITS, TOOLS, AND TACTICS
Charles A. Ravenstein
Gerard E. Hasselwander
Robert F. Jakob
Carl Grubb

	Page
The MIG-Killers	117
Their Units	141
Aircraft and Armament	155
Their Tactics	160
Glossary of Terms and Abbreviations	172
Index	179

List of Illustrations

	Page
F–4C Fighter	vii
Gen. Hunter Harris, visiting Pleiku Air Base, November 1966	3
EC–121D aircraft, providing radar coverage in Southeast Asia	5
Lt. Gen. Momyer with Col. Forrest L. Rauscher	10
President Johnson, announcing termination of all attacks north of the 19th parallel, 31 March 1968	13
An F–4C Phantom approaching runway at Cam Ranh Bay	18
Members of the first USAF flight to down MIG jets over North Vietnam	26
Capt. Cameron and Lt. Evans; Capt. Blake and Lt. George	28
Maj. Gilmore and Lt. Smith; Capt. Dowell and Lt. Gossard	29
Capt. Keith and Lt. Bleakley	30
Capt. Golberg and Lt. Hardgrave	31
Lt. Butell and Capt. Swendner; Lts. Krieps and Martin receive congratulations from Lt. Col. Leland Dawson; Lts. Jameson and Rose	32
Lts. Wilson and Richter	33
Lts. Klause and Latham, Maj. Tuck, and Lt. Rabeni	34
Col. "Chappie" James and his GIB, Lt. Evans	37
Col. Robin Olds; Lts. Glynn and Cary; Lt. Dunnegan; Capt. Raspberry and Lt. Western	42
Capt. Kjer and Maj. Anderson	49
Entrance to Ubon Royal Thai Air Force Base; Maj. Dilger, Lt. Thies, and Lt. Col. Hoyt S. Vandenberg, Jr.	52
A close-up of a MIG–17 in flight; MIG–17 recorded on the gun camera of an F–105 shortly before it was shot down on 13 May 1967	55
Maj. Hargrove, Lt. DeMuth, Capt. Craig, and Lt. Talley; an F–4C refueling	56
Col. Olds, preparing to nail four more red stars to the 8th TFW scoreboard	60
F–4D's in flight	61
Maj. Kuster and Capt. Wiggins	63
Capts. Pascoe and Wells	65
A MIG–17, trailing flames and smoke, heads earthward on 18 October 1967—a victim of Maj. Russell's 20-mm cannon; Capt. McGrath and Maj. Kirk	67
Capt. Basel	71
A MIG–17 in a firing pass at an F–105 in an air battle north of Hanoi, 19 December 1967	73
An AIM–4E Falcon missile	76
F–4D Fighter	79
North Vietnamese prepare to launch a surface-to-air missile	80
North Vietnamese pilots rush for their MIG–17's in response to alarm that USAF planes are in the area; a MIG with markings, in flight	81
A SAM photographed in flight; a North Vietnamese SAM site near Haiphong	82
A USAF Phantom falls prey to a North Vietnamese SAM	84
Col. Kittinger, released from captivity on 28 March 1973	87
MIG–21's in flight; "Triple-Nickel" Squadron's motto displayed on sign	92
An AA unit in Hanoi; a North Vietnamese SAM unit	97
Capts. DeBellevue and Ritchie, and Col. Baily with Capt. Feinstein	100
AIM–7 Sparrow, air-to-air missile	101
F–4E Phantom II Fighter	103
Capt. Ritchie displays fifth star on his F–4 to Capt. DeBellevue, Sgt. Taylor, and Sgt. Buttrey; MIG–21's at Phuc Yen	104

	Page
Capt. DeBellevue, USAF's second ace	105
Capt. Feinstein, USAF's third ace	109
A North Vietnamese SAM fired at USAF strike aircraft northwest of Hanoi; a SAM burst recorded on camera; Gen. John C. Meyer awards Silver Star to S/Sgt. Turner	112
B-52 in flight	114
Crew boards B-52	115
F-105 refuels in flight	116
The "Polish Glider," one of last Thuds in Vietnam; a MIG kill recorded on camera	126
B-52C/D bomber	141
Unit Insignia:	
Seventh Air Force; 2d Air Division; 8th, 35th, and 355th Tactical Fighter Wings; 307th Strategic Wing	143
366th and 388th Tactical Fighter Wings; 432d Tactical Reconnaissance Wing; 4th Tactical Fighter Squadron	145
35th, 44th, 45th, and 58th Tactical Fighter Squadrons	147
307th, 336th, 354th, and 357th Tactical Fighter Squadrons	149
389th, 390th, 421st, 433d, and 435th Tactical Fighter Squadrons	151

	Page
Unit Insignia:	
469th, 480th, and 523d Tactical Fighter Squadrons	153
555th Tactical Fighter Squadron	154
Sgt. Donald F. Clements and A1C Greg E. Sniegowski load an SUU-23 gun pod; Sgt. John. F. Host and A1C William B. Bokshar guide an SUU-23 into shop for overhauling; A1C Gary P. Mincer, Sgt. Vernon E. Kisinger, A1C Lonnie J. Hartfield, and Sgt. Phineas T. Barry load Sparrow missile on F-4; F-105 Thunderchiefs stand ready for night maintenance; two Sidewinder missiles mounted under wing of F-105; Sgt. James E. Faison carefully unpacks Sidewinder missile at Da Nang	158
NVN pilots discuss mission; NVN SA-2 missile unit responds to alert; NVN crew unloads a 37-mm AA Gun used against USAF fighters; MIG-17's parked on the runway of Kien An Airfield, North Vietnam	159

List of Maps and Charts

	Page		Page
Mainland Southeast Asia	xiv	Laos	86
Major Infiltration Routes (Ho Chi Minh Trail)	2	North Vietnam: Yen Bai	90
		North Vietnam: Yen Bai and Phu Tho	93
North Vietnam—Rolling Thunder Armed Reconnaissance Boundaries	6	North Vietnam: Thai Nguyen and Kep	96
		North Vietnam: Yen Bai, Phu Tho, Kep, Phuc Yen and Viet Tri	99
USAF-Navy Air Strikes, 1965–1966	8		
Route Package Areas and Operational Restrictions	9	North Vietnam: Yen Bai, Tuan Quan, Thai Nguyen, Kep, and Phuc Yen	106
Communist Thrusts into South Vietnam, March–April, 1972	15	North Vietnam: Airfields, 1973	107
		North Vietnam: Yen Bai, Thai Nguyen, Phu Tho, Kep, and Viet Tri	110
North Vietnam: Thanh Hoa	19		
Principal USAF Bases in Southeast Asia	23	Organizational Chart, 7th Air Force and 7/13th Air Force	140
North Vietnam: Yen Bai	24		
North Vietnam: Bac Giang	27	Sketches:	
North Vietnam: Dap Cau	33	Field of Maneuver	161
North Vietnam Airfields, 1967	36	Basic Escort Formation	162
North Vietnam: Xuan Mai	46	Fluid Four	163
North Vietnam: Hoa Lac, Thai Nguyen, and Kep	48	Finger Tip or Finger Four	163
		Split-S	164
North Vietnam: Vinh Yen, Kep, Bac Giang, Bac Le, and Ha Dong	51	Immelmann	164
		Scissors	165
North Vietnam: Yen Bai, Phuc Yen, Dai Loi, Bac Giang, and Yen Vien	62	Vertical Rolling Scissors	166
		High-Speed Yo-Yo and Low-Speed Yo-Yo	168
Hanoi Rail Net	70	Barrel Roll Attack	169
North Vietnam Surface-to-Air Missile Threat Areas, 1972	83	Pop-Up Tactic	170
		Wagon Wheel Formation	171

List of Tables

	Page
1. Chronological Order of USAF Aerial Victories in Southeast Asia	118
2. Alphabetical Order of USAF Fliers Scoring Aerial Victories in Southeast Asia	127
3. Units Credited with the Destruction of MIG's in Air-to-Air Combat	142
4. Aircraft and Weapons Combinations Used in MIG Victories	157

I

The Situation

Attainment of air superiority was the primary mission of U.S. tactical air power during World War II and the Korean conflict. Air superiority has been officially defined as "that degree of dominance in the air battle of one force over another which permits the conduct of operations by the former and its related land, sea, and air forces at a given time and place without prohibitive interference by the opposing force." Establishing air superiority is essential for successful land, sea, and air operations. In Southeast Asia the Communists unwisely conceded air superiority to the allies operating within South Vietnam. The air war over North Vietnam, however, was another story. There the enemy waged an all-out air defensive battle, the likes of which never before had been seen in history.

When the North Vietnamese, under the leadership of Ho Chi Minh and his military commander, Gen. Vo Nguyen Giap, launched campaigns in Southeast Asia, they started with guerrilla tactics. Ho's insurgents began their operations against the French in 1946 and 4 years later received active support from Red China and the Soviet Union. At first the United States remained aloof of the problems of Indochina but in 1950, when the Communists were so clearly in command in East Asia, President Harry S Truman then ordered materiel assistance sent to help France suppress the insurgency. However, it was too far along to be stopped. The military climax of this phase of the conflict came in May 1954, when General Giap's forces overwhelmed the French garrison at Dien Bien Phu. At the subsequent international peace conference held in Geneva, Switzerland, Vietnam was temporarily divided at the 17th parallel into a northern Communist-controlled Democratic Republic of Vietnam and a non-Communist Republic of Vietnam in the south, the latter led by Ngo Dinh Diem.

President Dwight D. Eisenhower, soon after his inauguration into office in January 1953, had committed the United States to assist South Vietnam and the other free countries of Southeast Asia to defend themselves against Communist aggression. As part of this commitment, the U.S. government sponsored establishment of the Southeast Asia Treaty Organization and provided military assistance to South Vietnam, Laos, Cambodia, and Thailand. By 1959, noting that the Republic of Vietnam was pursuing an independent course, Ho Chi Minh sent his guerrilla forces into a renewed war aimed at uniting Vietnam. Against this background, President John F. Kennedy in early 1961 increased American aid to Saigon and dispatched U.S. advisors to Vietnam. Air commando and ground force advisors sought to assist Vietnamese military forces to counter the infiltration of Communist cadres southward and the growing insurgency within the country.

During the early 1960's Washington recognized that the North Vietnamese were actively participating in military operations, both in South Vietnam and Laos. Hanoi's interference in the affairs of Laos was essential to the Communist cause, since the Ho Chi Minh trail wended its way through the Laotian panhandle into South Vietnam. Despite this knowledge, Washington officials decided that the insurgency would have to be defeated within South Vietnam and operations should not be expanded into North Vietnam. A major U.S. objective in 1961–

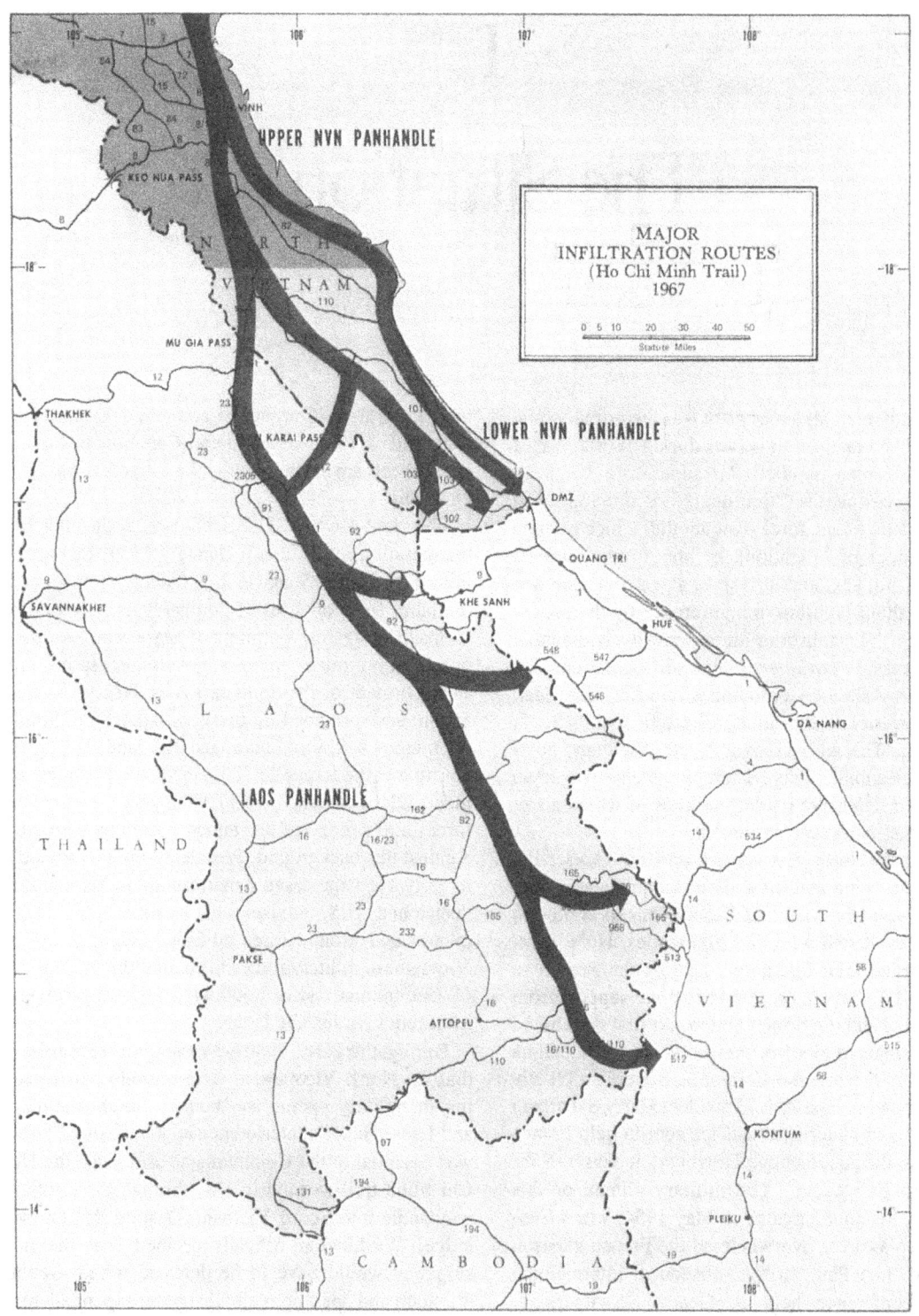

1964 was therefore to strengthen the Republic of Vietnam and to enable it to withstand the Communist guerrilla effort to topple it.

North Vietnamese strategy called for building an insurgent force in the south, then starting widespread guerrilla operations, and finally launching an all-out offensive to destroy Saigon's military forces. After December 1963 North Vietnam's rulers greatly increased infiltration into the south and, by the autumn of 1964, apparently were ready to start the final, decisive campaign. Meanwhile, on the night of 2 August 1964 North Vietnamese torpedo boats boldly attacked the U.S. Navy destroyer *Maddox* in the Gulf of Tonkin. On the night of 4 August the *Maddox* and *Turner Joy* again reported torpedo attacks. In Washington, President Johnson announced that the United States, while seeking no wider war, was determined to honor its commitments in Southeast Asia. Accordingly, on 5 August U.S. Seventh Fleet carrier aircraft attacked North Vietnamese patrol boat bases. The immediate reaction from the Communist side was to deploy some 30 MIG-15/17 jet fighters from China to Hanoi's Phuc Yen airfield on 7 August. Also, during the next several weeks, a division of North Vietnamese regulars began to deploy down the Ho Chi Minh trail in Laos heading for South Vietnam.

Against this background of a more unfavorable military situation, the U.S. Joint Chiefs of Staff drew up contingency plans for American air operations against North Vietnam. In late 1964 the Joint Chiefs recommended a "fast/full squeeze" hard-hitting, 16-day air campaign against 94 targets in North Vietnam to establish U.S. air superiority and destroy Hanoi's ability to continue to support operations against South Vietnam. However, President Johnson and Secretary of Defense Robert S. McNamara rejected the plan. They decided that bombing North Vietnam would be a supplement to and not a substitute for an effective pacification campaign within South Vietnam. According to Secretary McNamara, the basic objectives of air attacks against North Vietnam were to:

> reduce the flow and/or increase the cost of infiltration of men and supplies from North Vietnam to South Vietnam.
> Make it clear to the North Vietnamese leadership that so long as they continue their aggression against the South, they will have to pay a price in the North.
> Raise the morale of the South Vietnamese people.

President Johnson agreed with these objectives. Thus, when in early 1965 he authorized the first strikes against North Vietnam, he saw them as a demonstration of America's determination to retaliate against military targets so that Hanoi would understand that it was not immune from attack. Accordingly, the Joint Chiefs—with Gen. John P. McConnell, the USAF Chief of Staff, dissenting—directed that air operations against North Vietnam (known by the nickname "Rolling Thunder") would be limited in scope and not be a hard-hitting military campaign.

Rolling Thunder

Under these circumstances, Gen. Hunter Harris, Jr., Commander in Chief, Pacific Air Forces, proposed to strike the Communist MIG base at Phuc

Gen. Hunter Harris, Commander, Pacific Air Forces, boards his T-39 after a visit to Pleiku Air Base, South Vietnam, Nov. 1966.

Yen, situated north of Hanoi, and destroy an immediate threat to U.S. air operations. Although this proposal was not immediately approved, the Strategic Air Command armed 30 B–52's on Guam for a night strike against Phuc Yen. This air raid was to be followed at first light by tactical fighters to complete the job of destruction. However, this planned strike—initially included in the first Rolling Thunder operations order—was cancelled by higher authority. Between 2 March 1965, when the first tactical air strikes were launched, and 11 May when the first phase of operations ended, Rolling Thunder attacks were directed against military and transportation targets in the panhandle of southern North Vietnam below 20 degrees North latitude. The initial attacks were against fixed targets, but on 19 March the first armed reconnaissance against targets of opportunity was authorized.

In August 1964, on the occasion of the Tonkin reprisal air strikes, North Vietnam's air defenses consisted of approximately 1,426 antiaircraft artillery weapons, 22 early warning radars, and 4 fire control radars. This rudimentary defense allowed U.S. strike pilots to begin their attacks without great concern about enemy AAA defenses. Their initial flight tactics, however, were for those involving a nuclear weapons strike. These tactics involved a high-speed, low-altitude penetration to a target followed by a pop-up maneuver to unload the nuclear device onto the target and then to depart as fast as possible before detonation. Low clouds, often encountered en route and in the vicinity of the assigned North Vietnamese targets, justified this tactic for conventional ordnance. It became common for enthusiastic aircrews to make multiple passes on targets at low altitude. However, enemy automatic weapons and small caliber AAA soon began to take a toll of Air Force planes. It became evident that low-altitude, high-speed tactics did not provide sufficient protection for aircrews. Accordingly, USAF pilots changed their methods and ascended to 15–20,000 feet and dive-bombed their targets, thus cutting losses by operating above the effective altitude of most enemy guns. At higher operating altitudes, however, U.S. pilots sacrificed the element of surprise.

Meanwhile, with the aid of the Soviet Union and Communist China, North Vietnamese air defenses rapidly improved. By the end of March 1965 they possessed 31 early warning radars, 2 height finders, and 9 AAA control radars and demonstrated an ability to construct, occupy, and operate 85-mm radar-controlled gun positions in as few as 8 days. In the early weeks of the air war, North Vietnamese MIG pilots trained with ground control intercept (GCI) controllers, but appeared reluctant to engage in combat. But by 3 April several MIG–17 pilots were ready for action and air-to-air fighting ensued when three MIG's attacked a U.S. Navy strike force that was bombing a road and rail bridges near Thanh Hoa, 76 miles south of Hanoi. The following day, when USAF F–105's attacked the same bridge, a flight of MIG–17's was apparently vectored by GCI around USAF F–100's flying MIG combat air patrol (MIGCAP). The enemy pilots pounced upon the heavily loaded F–105's orbiting over the target waiting their turn to attack, downed two with cannon fire and escaped at high speed.

On 6 April President Johnson directed that the "slowly ascending" tempo of the Rolling Thunder operations would continue against targets outside the effective GCI range of the MIG's. But the first MIG engagement and growing enemy AAA demanded corresponding reactions. It was obvious that enemy jet pilots working with their GCI units had substantial advantages over the bomb-laden F–105's which lacked a warning system of impending attacks. To provide advance warning, in April 1965 a detachment of Air Defense Command EC–121 "Big Eye" aircraft was deployed to the theater and began flying radar surveillance orbits over the Gulf of Tonkin while USAF strikes were in progress. The EC–121's were equipped to provide "yellow" caution and "red" immediate danger warnings to U.S. pilots of impending MIG activity.

Arrival of USAF F–4C fighters at bases in Thailand promised to increase the effectiveness of MIG combat air patrols. Another USAF deployment—aimed at jamming enemy fire control radars—brought the first EB–66C "Brown Cradle" aircraft to Southeast Asia where their electronics countermeasures (ECM) equipment could be used against hostile AAA radars. Initially, these EB–66's were able to operate without difficulty over North Vietnam, but growing enemy opposition forced them away to safe areas over Laos and the Gulf of Tonkin where they would orbit during Rolling Thunder strikes.

During the week of 12–17 May 1965, while U.S. officials sought to get the North Vietnamese to begin peace talks, U.S. armed reconnaissance and strike missions were suspended. During this standdown, the Air Force evaluated the results of its air campaign. When Washington's peace efforts proved unfruitful, Rolling Thunder (Phase II) was initiated and expanded somewhat. The first target north of 20 degrees latitude was cleared for attack on 18 May. In July some additional strikes were authorized against fixed bridge targets on the northwestern rail line between Hanoi and the Chinese border. In September new targets were approved for strikes, including four bridges on the Hanoi-China rail line. The air operations into the northeast quadrant continued into October-December but were rigidly controlled by Washington. Pilots were not permitted to enter a 30-mile buffer zone along the Chinese border, or within 30 miles of Hanoi and 10 miles of Haiphong.

During the summer of 1965, MIG pilots remained in training status; there were only sporadic challenges to combat-loaded F-105 fighters. The few MIG pilots who did appear tried to use the superior turning ability of their aircraft to get into 6 o'clock positions behind the F-105's. But this maneuver worked poorly whenever used against Navy F-4B's or USAF F-4C's. On 17 June two Navy F-4B's downed two MIG-17's with Sparrow missiles and on 10 July two Air Force F-4C's—positioned at the end of a strike force—downed two other MIG-17's with Sidewinder missiles. After 10 July and through March 1966 the MIG force apparently again stood down and renewed extensive training. Enemy GCI controllers not infrequently positioned MIG's for stern attacks against U.S. aircraft, but the pilots would break off before engaging.

On 24 July 1965 Soviet-built SA-2 surface-to-air missiles, dispersed about Hanoi and Haiphong, were used for the first time by the North Vietnamese. On that day, two SA-2's were fired at a flight of four F-4C strike aircraft, resulting in the loss of one plane and damage to the other three. The following month 11 missile firings destroyed two more U.S. aircraft. The immediate reaction of American pilots was to return to low-profile missions in SAM-defended areas, approaching and departing their

EC-121D aircraft sent to Southeast Asia in April 1965 to provide radar coverage and control in areas over the Gulf of Tonkin and over Hanoi and Haiphong harbor.

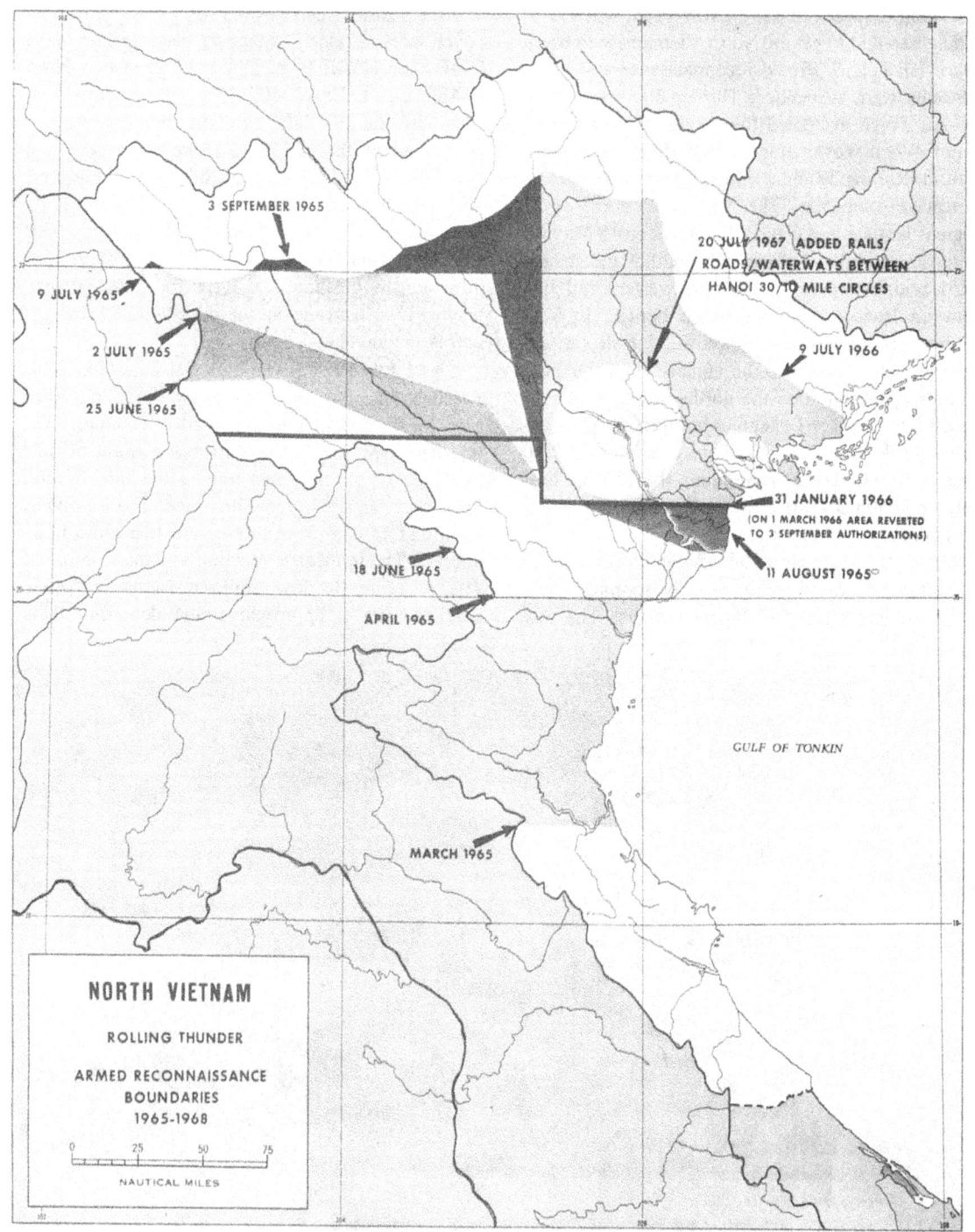

targets at an altitude of 500 to 1,500 feet. But while this return to low-altitude attack was effective against the SAM, the cure was worse than the disease since aircraft losses to other types of enemy ground fire rose sharply. It was soon clear that while the SA-2 was dangerous, it could be avoided through appropriate maneuvers if advance warning was received by strike pilots. Moreover, the SA-2 proved less dangerous than flying at low level into the most lethal part of the AAA and automatic weapons flak envelope.

U.S. flights gradually returned to 3–4,000-foot altitude and within a few months to 6–9,000 feet. Successful evasive manuevers were developed to avoid the SAM's provided the launchings were detected in time. Although losses to SAM's were not great compared to losses due to other causes, the effect of the SA-2 on strike forces was nevertheless considerable. Attacks were run in streams of four-ship flights spaced 1 to 3 minutes apart, and each flight gave little mutual support to the other. Evasive maneuvers often demanded jettisoning of ordnance. At the very least, flight and mission integrity was disrupted or destroyed when the SAM's were fired.

During the 37 days of the "Christmas Truce" (25 December 1965 to 30 January 1966), all bombing of North Vietnam ceased while the President and his aides sought once again to bring Hanoi to the conference table. When they received no response, Rolling Thunder (Phase III) was launched on 31 January and continued to 31 March 1966. In authorizing these renewed strikes, President Johnson still maintained tight control over the operations. Rolling Thunder limited strikes to lower North Vietnam and the Air Force and Navy were authorized a total of no more than 300 sorties per day.

The arrival in Thailand of F-100F aircraft (nickname Wild Weasel) equipped with radar homing and warning (RHAW) sets proved of great assistance to the strike force. This equipment enabled the F-100 crews to home in on SA-2 Fansong radar guidance signals and to mark their location with rockets for strikes by accompanying F-105's (nickname Iron Hand). The F-100F's also gave early warning of an impending SAM firing. The F-100F's and F-105's orbited the day's target and positioned themselves in order to suppress SA-2 firings that might threaten the strike force. The F-100F gave the Air Force its first real capability to detect an impending SAM launch. On 18 April 1966, with a further perfection of tactics, an F-100F launched its own AGM-45 Shrike missile against a SAM site. In May and July 1966 the F-100's were replaced by the higher performance F-105F's (known as Wild Weasel III).*

As an additional precaution to prevent enemy interference with the air campaign, during the first quarter of 1966 F-4's were employed to assist the F-105 strike force by flying MIG Screen orbits ahead of strike forces and by assisting strike aircraft in the event MIG's slipped past the screen.

Toward the end of the monsoon season in early April 1966, the fourth phase of Rolling Thunder began. All of North Vietnam, aside from specific sanctuary areas, was vulnerable to attack. The highlight of this massive new series of strikes was an attack by Air Force planes against seven major bulk petroleum-oil-lubricant (POL) storage areas in the Hanoi and Haiphong areas from 29 June to 1 July.

During these major penetration strikes, F-105's and supporting F-4C's arrived first over assigned targets and were then followed over the same route by other strike F-105's with a 3- to 5-minute separation between flights. While the Iron Hand aircraft and the accompanying F-4C's prepared to react to enemy SAM launches, the strike F-105's descended from altitude and dashed into the SAM defense ring at an altitude just above the effective height of small arms and automatic weapons fire. At the same time, an EC-121 orbited the area to provide MIG warnings while USAF EB-66's (also with F-4C cover) employed their jammers.

Perhaps because of improving weather, but more probably because of the importance of the military targets under attack, Hanoi ordered its MIG's into action. On 23 April there took place a major air clash involving two flights of eight MIG-17's, each under GCI control, which attempted to intercept the F-105's as they came off target. Instead, the MIG's found themselves engaged by F-4C's, and two of the enemy planes were downed. On 25 and 26 April, MIG-21's entered the air battle for the first time and launched a high-altitude attack against the EB-66's.

---

*Wild Weasel II was an experimental model tested at Eglin AFB, Fla.

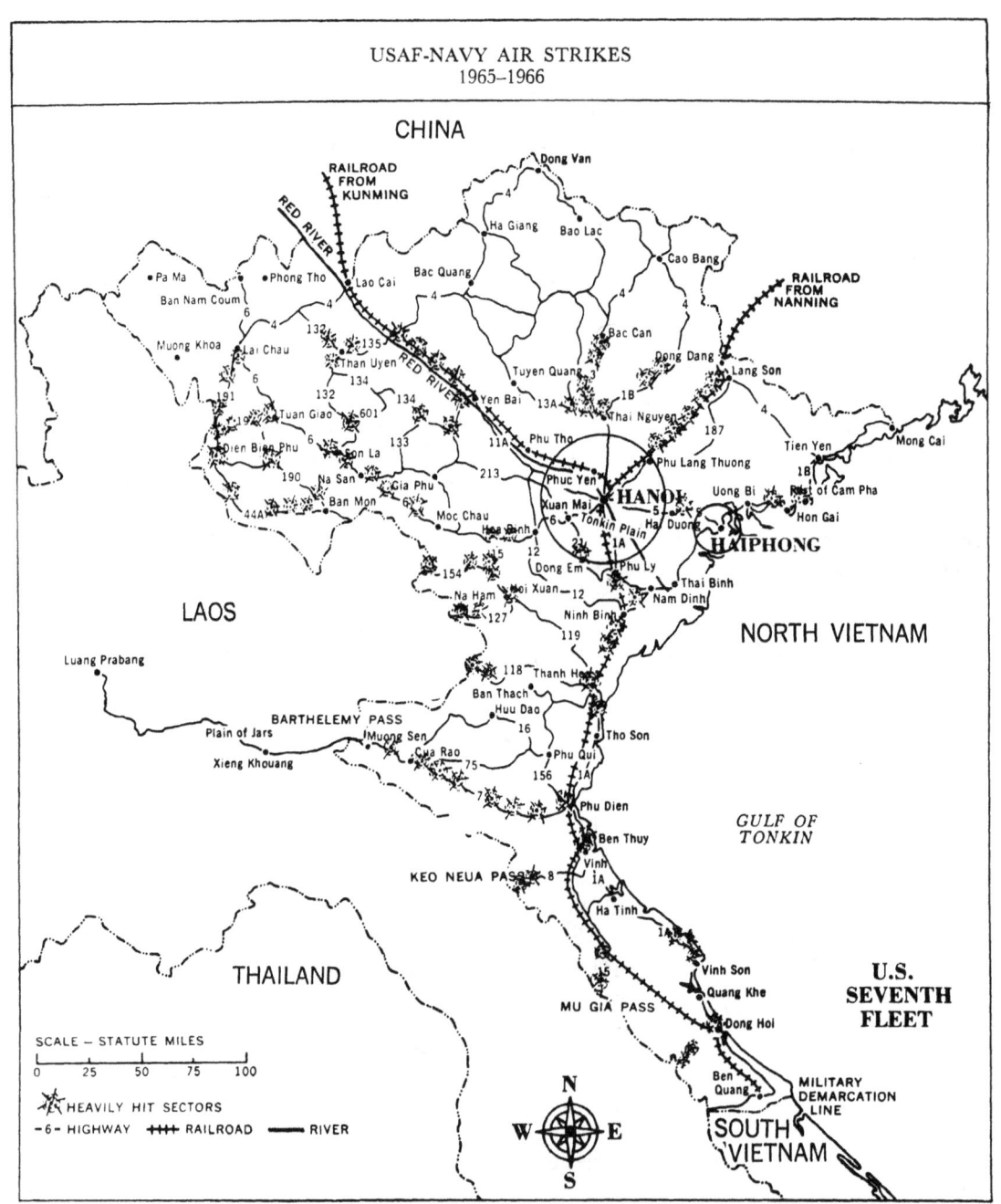

The first MIG–21 was shot down on the 26th by an F–4C flying combat air patrol when the latter scored two Sidewinder hits on the North Vietnamese aircraft. Following these losses, MIG pilots seemed reluctant to engage the large numbers of F–4C's committed in May and June. In May only one MIG–17 was shot down, while it attempted to attack an EB–66 protected by F–4's. The next month an F–105 downed another.

Although MIG pilots appeared to be unskilled in

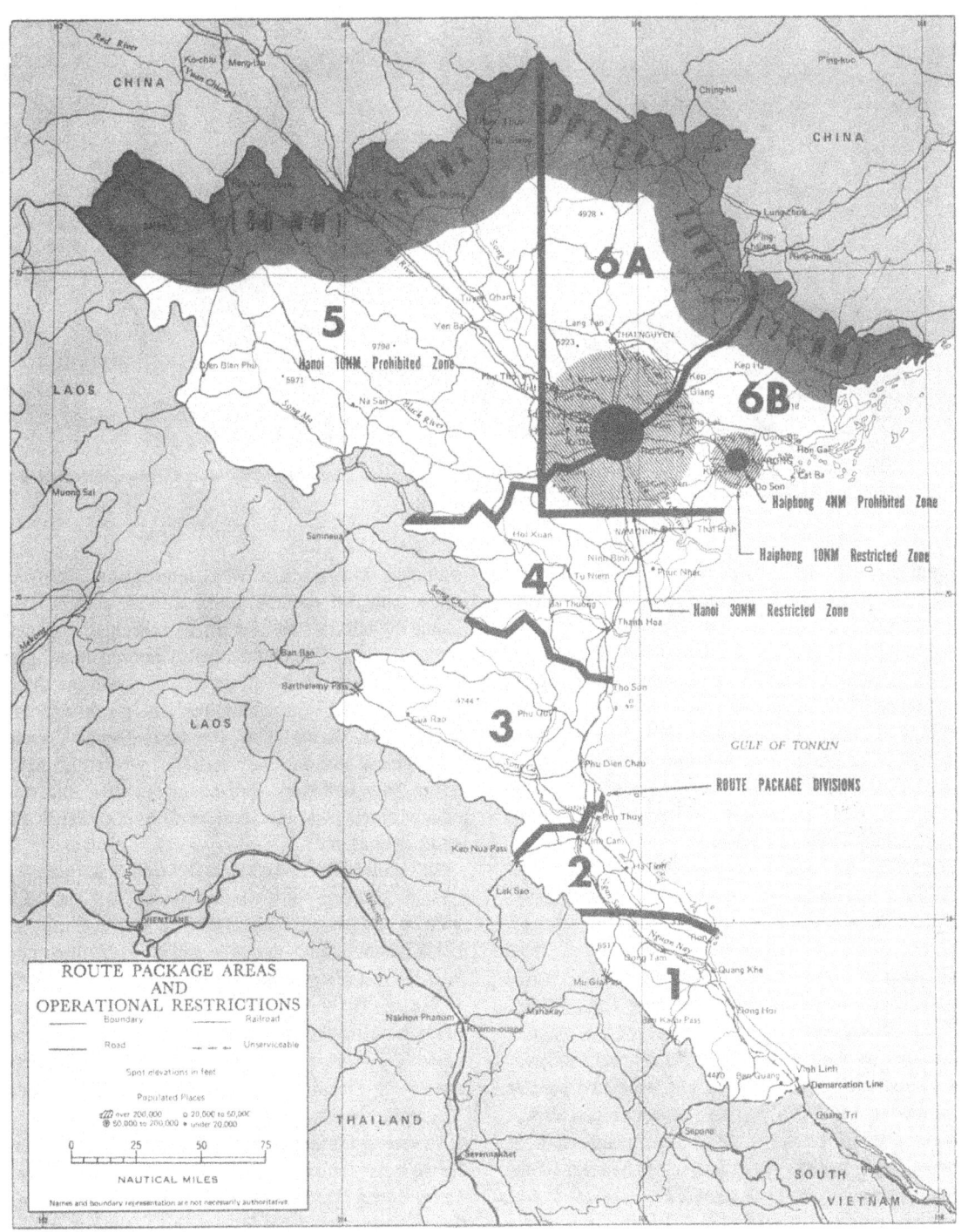

Lt. Gen. Momyer, 7th Air Force commander, flew a strike mission with Col. Forrest L. Rauscher (right), Vice-Commander of the 3d Tac Fighter Wing, to get a close look at his units in action. January 1967

aerial combat, the slowly escalating air war gave them time to mold their force into a more serious threat, a fact that became evident during the summer and autumn of 1966. The roles of the MIG–17 and MIG–21 were distinctive, the former concentrating on low-level interceptions while the latter operated at high altitude. Although some MIG's still tried to interdict U.S. strike aircraft during their bomb runs, others assumed positions to threaten American planes en route to targets. The enemy's objective was to force strike aircraft to jettison their ordnance. The MIG pilots also discovered that they could successfully out-maneuver most U.S. air-to-air missiles with a rapid turning descent, since the Sparrow (AIM–7) and the Sidewinder (AIM–9) had been designed to down bombers, and the missiles could not maneuver fast enough in a fighter engagement.

As a consequence, U.S. pilots asked that guns be installed on their F–4's. External 20-mm gun pods were mounted on the F–4C's and were first used in combat in May 1967. Until the modification was accomplished, however, MIG attacks against U.S. strike forces became quite difficult to handle. Of the 3,938 strike sorties flown (Route Packages 4, 5, 6A, and 6B, *see* Map, p. 9) during September–December 1966, only 107 sorties—or 2.72 percent—jettisoned ordnance as a result of MIG interceptions. On the other hand, of the 192 strike aircraft actually engaged by MIG's, 107 (or 55.73 percent) jettisoned their ordnance. This rather clearly demonstrated that the MIG's reduced the effect of U.S. strikes on those days when they were committed. As a solution, the Joint Chiefs of Staff had recommended that North Vietnamese airfields be struck to reduce the MIG threat. But Secretary McNamara believed that the enemy threat was not sufficient to interfere with strike operations.

In combination, MIG's, SAM's, and flak posed a difficult problem for the strike forces. Lt. Gen. William W. Momyer, Commander of the Seventh Air Force, commented that his crews were forced to fight for their lives to reach the route packages north of Hanoi. By the end of 1966, approximately 150 SAM sites provided continuous coverage of a zone extending from Yen Bai to Haiphong in the north and to Ha Tinh in the south. Pilots called this area "Slaughter Alley."

In air-to-air engagements, however, American crews held the edge over the North Vietnamese. Experienced North Korean "instructors," according to creditable intelligence sources, appeared in the North Vietnamese Air Force along with NVAF crews trained in the Soviet Union. Some 70 North Vietnamese MIG's, including about 15 MIG-21's, were based at Phuc Yen and Kep airfields. The North Vietnamese were also developing and using other fields to serve as MIG dispersal areas.

During the Christmas-New Year interlude beginning on 24 December 1966 and continuing to mid-February 1967, attacks on North Vietnamese targets were suspended for 48 hours over New Year's Day and for a 6-day period during the lunar New Year (8-15 February). On occasion throughout this period, adverse northeast monsoon weather restricted operations severely, but on some days American airmen could exploit newly-arrived electronic equipment (ECM jamming pods) to improve dramatically their operations. This device provided the U.S. strike forces with their first self-protection capability and was probably the most significant item of equipment introduced into the air war. The F-105 strike wings received their initial allotment of pods in October 1966. More time was required to equip other aircraft—including the F-4's—with the electronic countermeasure device.

Meanwhile, on 2 January 1967 the 8th Tactical Fighter Wing, using borrowed electronic jamming pods, launched Operation Bolo. In order to insure that the North Vietnamese would engage in an air battle, a force of F-4C's simulated an impending F-105 and F-4C strike. As anticipated, a large MIG-21 force, quite possibly manned by newly-trained Vietnamese pilots fresh from the Soviet Union, challenged what they thought were primarily F-105 crews. The result was the destruction of seven MIG-21's within 12 minutes of combat. There was no damage to USAF aircraft. On 6 January F-4C's simulated a weather reconnaissance mission and this lure resulted in the destruction of two more MIG-21's. Stunned by their losses, the North Vietnamese Air Force stood down for further training which extended to February 1967.

The next phase of Rolling Thunder operations—conducted between 14 February to 24 December 1967—reached a new peak of intensity as U.S. strike forces began the destruction of Hanoi's industrial base. Major power plants were knocked out, key military airfields came under attack, and systematic strikes were launched against rail transportation targets (yards and repair facilities). For the first time, targets in restricted areas of North Vietnam were approved for controlled attacks. Pilots were permitted to hit military facilities both within the China buffer zone and the "Hanoi Circle."

Although the Joint Chiefs of Staff expressed interest in setting up another MIG trap similar to Operation Bolo to further erode the morale and effectiveness of the North Vietnamese Air Force, the overriding purpose of the aerial campaign remained that of placing ordnance precisely on assigned targets with the least possible loss of American crews. MIG-killing decidedly took second place to bombing. Maj. Gen. Alton D. Slay elaborated upon this point when he stated: "Much has been written about the MIG-killing campaign . . . I will only add that MIG-killing was not our objective. The objective was to protect the strike force. Any MIG kills obtained were considered as a bonus. A shoot-down of a strike aircraft was considered . . . a mission failure regardless of the number of MIG's killed." General Momyer, in agreement with Gen. Slay, emphasized that any excessive losses of USAF aircrews could very well have led Washington officials to reduce or terminate the operations.

As new ECM equipment became available for general use, USAF strike forces were able to return to mass formation tactics reminiscent of World War II and Korea, i.e., to operate at altitudes above the range of enemy flak. When major air strikes were required, F-105 wings usually employed three four-ship flights of strike aircraft, one flight of four flak suppressors, and one flight of Iron Hand aircraft. In addition, the strike force usually was escorted by four F-4C's, which through April 1967 normally preceded the strike force by 5 minutes to "sweep" the target area of MIG's and then stand by to fly cover.

MIG operations were habitually cyclical, perhaps geared to training and definitely related to the importance of targets under attack. By April 1967 it became evident to the North Vietnamese that the MIG's would have to bear the brunt of the defense of their key military facilities. In April, May and June of that year, their airmen tried a great variety of tactics, ranging from single, apparently uncoordinated attacks to highly effective, well-coordinated group attacks involving as many as 16 aircraft. Once again the F-105's were forced to jettison ordnance and some were lost to MIG guns. In April, Washington finally authorized attacks against Hoa Lac, Kep, and Kien An airfields. The same month, F–4C support for the strike formations was doubled, with two flights of F–4C's now assigned to fly MIGCAP.

During the first 6 months of 1967—but primarily in the months of April, May and June—U.S. aircrews scored 54 confirmed MIG kills at a cost of 11 U.S. aircraft. The North Vietnamese Air Force lost another 9 MIG's on the ground during airfield strikes in April and 15 more in May. As MIG activity diminished in July, the F–4's were used to drop ordnance as well as to fly escort missions. The F–4's, which were equipped with both bombs and air-to-air missiles, were placed at the rear of the strike forces.

In August 1967 the situation once again changed when MIG–21's, seemingly flown by elite pilots, introduced a tactic that was extremely difficult to counter. The MIG–21's took off in pairs from either Phuc Yen or Gia Lam and flew at low level, keeping within radar ground clutter until they were abeam of the inbound USAF force. As a result, the F–4 radars were unable to detect the enemy aircraft. Once behind the American formation, the MIG–21 pilots fired their afterburners to climb to a high perch above the U.S. force. Then, with the aid of GCI vectoring, they would launch down at speeds in excess of Mach 1, fire their Atoll missiles (infrared seekers, similar to Sidewinders), and either zoom back to altitude or pass through the USAF formation. After one firing pass, the MIG's would separate and head for an airfield either in North Vietnam or China.

The initial success of these MIG–21 hit-and-run tactics was due in part to the fact the F–4's were being used either as strike or combat air patrol aircraft. Until the new threat was clearly analyzed, the MIG–21's operated with near impunity. But by the end of September, F–4's were positioned to guard the rear quadrants of strike forces against the MIG's. Also in late October, President Johnson for the first time authorized the Air Force to hit Phuc Yen, the major enemy base. At year's end, all jet airfields in North Vietnam—with the single exception of Gia Lam International Airport at Hanoi—had been attacked, and all but about 20 MIG's had been driven back into China. Even so, the MIG–21 hit-and-run passes continued to be highly damaging to American aircraft. To August 1967, 24 MIG–21's were shot down compared to 6 U.S. losses to the MIG–21; but from August 1967 through the end of February 1968, the score was 5 MIG–21's downed while 18 U.S. aircraft were lost to the MIG–21.

The Christmas and New Year's halt in operations (between 24 December 1967 and 2 January 1968) was shorter than before. Each cessation lasted 36 hours. The usual Tet ceasefire was cancelled because of a massive enemy offensive against South Vietnam's cities and towns. Meanwhile, the Seventh Air Force on 3 January launched another phase in Rolling Thunder operations, but strikes were limited because of adverse weather in the Hanoi and Haiphong areas. The strike aircraft were then diverted to support Marines at Khe Sanh. By late March, with the end of the North Vietnamese siege and clearing weather in the north, Rolling Thunder operations accelerated and continued until President Johnson halted all attacks north of the 19th parallel on 1 April 1968.

Until the April bombing halt, the Air Force, responding to the threat of high-speed MIG–21 stern attacks, undertook to extend its airborne GCI control into northeastern North Vietnam. It became clear that, while the EC–121's (nicknamed "College Eye" after March 1967) were able to provide general MIG warnings, something better was needed. Fortunately, the Air Force was then testing an experimental EC–121M (nicknamed Rivet Top) in the theater. This aircraft was equipped with advance airborne radar and IFF.* On 6 October, the EC–121 crew was authorized to communicate directly with strike aircraft and was able to warn F–105 and F–4 pilots of MIG's. These advance warnings of MIG's in the area proved accurate and important. They resulted in saving U.S. aircraft and crews and contributed to the confirmed destruction of 10 MIG's and probable destruction of 5 others between October 1967 and the end of March 1968.

The bombing restriction of 1 April 1968 shifted U.S. air attacks far south beyond the normal MIG operating areas. Below 19 degrees latitude, the

---

*Identification, friend or foe; a method of determining the friendly or unfriendly character of aircraft and ships by other aircraft or ships.

President Johnson, on 31 March 1968, appeared on nation-wide TV to announce termination of all attacks north of the 19th parallel.

North Vietnamese were unable to work effectively, since they had no GCI support. Some MIG's did attempt to raid southward under radio and radar silence. In one such incident on 23 May, a MIG-21 was downed by a U.S. Navy Talos surface-to-air missile. Following this, U.S. forces were instructed to "clear the air" whenever MIG's appeared over the North Vietnamese panhandle and to give the Talos "clear fire" at the target. However, the North Vietnamese seem to have soon recognized that the MIG's could not operate without their ground control. Their air threat thus dwindled well before 1 November 1968, when President Johnson halted all air and naval attacks against North Vietnam.

When he suspended air operations against North Vietnam, Mr. Johnson had received reasonable assurances from Hanoi that they would respect the demilitarized zone (DMZ) between North and South Vietnam, would cease attacks on South Vietnamese cities, and would begin peace talks in good faith. Hanoi also understood that the United States would continue to fly unarmed reconnaissance aircraft over North Vietnam and that if they were fired upon, armed escort fighters would return the fire.

When President Richard M. Nixon entered the White House in January 1969, he hoped that the peace talks under way in Paris would secure a supervised ceasefire, ensure the withdrawal of all non-South Vietnamese forces from South Vietnam, and guarantee political self-determination for the people of South Vietnam. Even as the talks continued, President Nixon directed the Joint Chiefs of Staff to expedite the military training and equipping of South Vietnamese forces to enable them to take over the conduct of the war while U.S. forces withdrew. This was his policy of "Vietnamization."

At Paris, however, the North Vietnamese refused to proceed with substantive negotiations and used the respite from air attack to develop further their military forces. The North Vietnamese Air Force extended radar control down the panhandle, establishing GCI sites at Vinh, Bac Mai, and Chap Le. By early 1972, the NVAF fighter inventory included 93 MIG-21's (some of them newer models, designated the "Export Fishbed-J"), 33 MIG-19's and 120 MIG-15/17's, for a total of 246 aircraft. Both SAM's and AAA units were deployed southward as well, and increasingly they began to fire at U.S. reconnaissance aircraft and also across the border into Laos. Between 1 November 1971 and 31

January 1972 there were 57 MIG incursions into the panhandle of Laos, where U.S. airmen continued attacks against North Vietnamese infiltration of men and supplies southward.

Under the rules of engagement which prevailed for U.S. forces between 1969 and 1971, American pilots could launch protective reaction strikes if the enemy fired AAA or SAM's against friendly reconnaissance or strike aircraft, or if USAF planes detected enemy radar signals indicating a firing was imminent. The frequency of protective reaction strikes increased in proportion to increasing enemy activity. There were 14 such strikes by F–4 or F–105 aircraft escorting reconnaissance planes in November 1971, 29 in December, 27 in January 1972, 30 in February, and 35 in March.

In Laos increasing MIG interference with USAF operations also demanded attention. As a consequence, USAF strike aircraft were sent aloft to fly combat air patrol and to serve as escorts for B–52 strikes. Additional EC–121's (with a new call sign: "Disco") and F–4D's were deployed to Southeast Asia. Special F–4D crews were designated and authorized to intercept MIG's penetrating toward Laos which had been identified either by "Disco" or the U.S. Navy "Red Crown" radar warning and control vessel operating in the Gulf of Tonkin. These actions served to check MIG activity. In February and March 1972 there were only 10 enemy penetrations, and in 13 air-to-air engagements the United States lost one aircraft while the Communists lost five.

Freedom Train and Linebacker

On the night of 30 March 1972, North Vietnamese forces commenced an all-out field attack through the DMZ into Quang Tri province. This action was quickly followed by other attacks launched from Laos and Cambodia into Kontum and Binh Long provinces of South Vietnam. Captured North Vietnamese documents reveal that General Giap confidently believed that these division-level assaults with heavy armor would overwhelm Saigon's forces, after which Hanoi could demand a ceasefire and install a coalition government in South Vietnam.

On 6 April American airmen were authorized to resume attacks (nicknamed Freedom Train) as far north as 20 degrees latitude. This operation was expanded into Linebacker I on 8 May when President Nixon authorized the aerial mining of North Vietnamese ports and a resumption of air and naval strikes against military targets throughout North Vietnam. At the same time, the President stated that the United States would halt all offensive operations when Hanoi agreed to release American prisoners of war and to accept an internationally supervised ceasefire. The Joint Chiefs of Staff gave the Seventh Air Force responsibility for attacking prevalidated targets in Route Packages 5 and 6A, the areas where the enemy concentrated his strongest defenses to protect his heartland and rail links to China.

Between the period Rolling Thunder terminated and Linebacker I operations began, USAF tactical fighter crews flying F–4's lost some of their proficiency because of a lack of aerial combat. On the other hand, their tactical fighter aircraft were now equipped with new military hardware: laser guided bombs (LGB's) for strikes, ECM chaff, and improved electronic countermeasures for tactical fighter mutual self-protection. College Eye ("Disco") EC–121's orbiting over Laos and the Gulf of Tonkin were assigned the task of controlling chaff, photo, strike, and escort flights. The Navy's Red Crown control ship in the Gulf provided additional warning of MIG activity.

Because of the strength of North Vietnamese defenses and the need to provide maximum protection to the limited number of F–4's equipped for laser-guided bombing, the ratio of support aircraft (those assigned chaff, escort, MIGCAP, SAM/flak suppression, ECM, and search and rescue missions) during Linebacker I was not infrequently as high as 5 to 1 in comparision with strike aircraft. Support forces were able to counter the extensive and well-disciplined SAM and AAA defenses, but the North Vietnamese MIG force—although still essentially limited by too few combat ready pilots—was still a serious threat.

Most MIG–21 interceptions were clearly flown by experienced pilots, who would get airborne, cruise at low altitude, pick up a lot of "smash" (speed and energy), strike from 6 o'clock with good control, excellent position, and "much overtake," and then

disengage and head for home on the deck. It was not uncommon for some of these MIG actions to last no more than 12 to 14 minutes. This gave USAF pilots very little reaction time or margin for error. In May 1972 the use of EC-121's and the Navy's control ship to alert MIGCAP aircraft of the approach of enemy planes was moderately effective. But in June and July the MIG threat burgeoned when North Vietnamese pilots launched their supersonic rear attacks. Quite often under such circumstances, the first warning of an attack was the sighting of an enemy's infrared missile streaking in. The success of the F-4's against the MIG's now was due primarily to the greater proficiency and aggressiveness of the American fighter pilots. Between February and July 1972 the Air Force lost 18 aircraft while downing 24 MIG's, but in June and July of that year air combat victories and losses were on a one-to-one basis.

Had the Seventh Air Force possessed an airborne warning and control system which could have provided "look-down" radar coverage of the target area, together with positive control over counter-air fighters, it is probable that 75 percent of the USAF losses could have been avoided. Fortunately, the U.S. Air Force, working with the Navy, developed a new command and control capability, and they refined tactics which resulted in a 4-1 ratio in favor of USAF pilots between 1 August and 15 October 1972.

As a result of progressing diplomatic talks, Dr. Henry Kissinger, President Nixon's Assistant for National Security Affairs, was confident in mid-October 1972 that peace arrangements would shortly be accepted in Paris. Accordingly, on 22 October 1972, the Linebacker I air campaign ended.

Linebacker II

Contrary to expectations, the North Vietnamese continued to drag out the peace negotiations, raising many technical objections to propositions already agreed upon. Quite possibly, Hanoi anticipated a resumption of bombing attacks in the Hanoi and Haiphong areas but believed that the impending onset of bad weather during the northeast monsoon seriously would hamper U.S. tactical fighter attacks and that its forces could ride out the strikes as they had done before. While Hanoi stalled the talks, Saigon became more rigid. "Therefore," in the words of Dr. Kissinger, "it was decided to try to bring home, really to both Vietnamese parties, that the continuation of the war had its price."

In order to convince North Vietnam, the United States on the night of 18 December 1972 launched Linebacker II, an intensive USAF and Navy day-and-night attack against electrical power plants and broadcast stations, railways and railyards, port and storage facilities, and airfields around Hanoi and Haiphong. During this daily around-the-clock operation, which lasted through 29 December with but a single stand down on Christmas Day, the Air Force employed the new A-7 and F-111 tactical fighters as strike aircraft. Also, for the first time, Strategic Air Command B-52's struck targets in the heavily defended Hanoi and Haiphong areas.

The Air Force campaign was divided into two distinct, highly compressed operations with B-52's and F-111's attacking by night and F-4's and A-7's by day. Each B-52 attack was supported heavily by other aircraft. The F-4's established chaff corridors and flew escort and MIGCAP's; EB-66's orbited for ECM jamming; and F-105's flew Iron Hand or F-105 and F-4 hunter-killer missions against the enemy's SAM complex. The F-111's were assigned specific targets, frequently airfields, with their attacks being bracketed in between B-52 waves. These new tactical fighters approached their targets at low level, made single high-speed ordnance delivery passes, and departed at low level and high speeds. Daylight tactical air included F-4 Pathfinders which provided long-range navigation/target acquisition for delivery of unguided bombs by other F-4's or A-7 aircraft. When weather permitted, F-4's equipped with laser bombs struck high priority targets with precision. The support forces for daytime strikes were equivalent to that provided for the B-52's at night. In fact, many of the support aircraft (and sometimes the same tired crews) flew both day and night missions.

The intensity of Linebacker II operations completely disrupted North Vietnamese air defenses and did not allow them to recover during the campaign. MIG fighters got airborne but flew through B-52 formations apparently without knowing what to do;

two were shot down by B-52 tail gunners. SAM direction radars were jammed successfully, but the enemy fired nearly a thousand SA-2's at the big bombers and downed 15 of them, evidently by visually sighted barrage fire. The enemy stock of SAM's began to diminish and only 15 to 20 missiles were fired at the B-52's on the night of 28 December. During the course of Linebacker II, the Air Force flew 729 B-52 sorties, 613 tactical strike sorties, and 2,066 support sorties. Twenty-seven USAF aircraft were lost, the B-52's being hardest hit with 15 losses and severe damage to 3 other bombers, all by SAM's. One SAM also downed a tactical aircraft. Three other tactical aircraft were lost to AAA and two to MIG's.

When President Nixon announced the termination of Linebacker II effective on 29 December 1972, he included the news that Dr. Kissinger would resume negotiations with the North Vietnamese in Paris on 8 January 1973. The effect of Linebacker II clearly hastened the conclusion of peace negotiations or, as Kissinger said: ". . . there was a deadlock in the middle of December . . . there was a rapid movement when negotiations resumed . . . on 8 January." On 23 January 1973, Kissinger and North Vietnam's Le Duc Tho initialed the agreement that provided what the United States wanted: a supervised ceasefire, return of U.S. prisoners of war, and political self-determination for the people of South Vietnam. "I am convinced," stated Adm. Thomas H. Moorer, Chairman of the Joint Chiefs of Staff, "that Linebacker II served as a catalyst for the negotiations . . . Airpower, given its day in court after almost a decade of frustration, confirmed its effectiveness as an instrument of national power—in just 9½ flying days."

An F-4C Phantom flies low over the South China Sea as it makes a final approach to the runway at Cam Ranh Bay air base, following a mission in Vietnam.

II

Combat Narratives 1965–1968

The first U.S. aircraft on a mission against targets in North Vietnam in August 1964 encountered only a rudimentary air defense system which did not severely impede the attack. North Vietnam possessed no jet aircraft or surface-to-air missiles and had only a crude radar system. These deficiencies were soon corrected, however, when the North Vietnamese introduced MIG–15 and MIG–17 aircraft and other defenses.

Enemy MIG's soon rose to challenge U.S. aircraft. Air-to-air warfare in Southeast Asia began on 3 April 1965, when a U.S. Navy strike force of four F–8E's bombing the Thanh Hoa Bridge, approximately 33 nautical miles south of Hanoi, was attacked by MIG–17's. One Navy aircraft was damaged during the engagement. Enemy aircraft did better the next day when an Air Force attack force, bombing the same target, was jumped by MIG–15's and MIG–17's about 76 miles south of Hanoi; two F–105 Thunderchief fighter-bombers were shot down by MIG cannon fire. Until 17 June, on which day a U.S. flight of F–4B's downed two MIG–17's with Sparrow missiles, aerial engagements had been infrequent. One month later, a flight of four F–4C's of the 45th Tactical Fighter Squadron faced two MIG–17's. Both fell victims to the deadly Sidewinder heat-seeking missiles. By mid-1965, the air-to-air contest was well underway.

The aerial battles in Vietnam bore little resemblance to the dogfights of World War II or even Korea. The equipment had become so sophisticated and the speed of aircraft so incredibly increased that it took coordination and teamwork to kill a MIG. Every air-to-air encounter involved the ability and training of many people—support personnel, ground crews, strike and protective flight aircrews, and the

airborne and ground radar operators. Unlike the air-to-air engagements of previous wars in which a single pilot pitted his aircraft against a single opponent, some modern aircraft required 2-man crews, working as an integrated and well-disciplined team.

Captain Richard S. (Steve) Ritchie, the first USAF pilot to down five MIG's in Southeast Asia, achieved this distinction as one member of a team. On his fifth kill, for example, he needed the aid of his backseater, Capt. Charles DeBellevue; he relied on the support of his flight; and he coordinated his techniques with those of the other flights in the area, as they all blended their skills for the mutual assistance necessary to fight as a team. Moreover, it would have been impossible for him to score his victories without Red Crown and Disco, the two supporting radars that pinpointed MIG's and friendlies in the skies of Vietnam. They provided Ritchie and the F–4's with flawless coordination and exact information.

How important this interaction proved to be can be illustrated in the following radio transmissions recorded in Ritchie's fifth kill. Cockpit communications are identified as "Ritchie (intercom)" and "DeBellevue (intercom)." Transmissions between Ritchie and other aircraft and radar are identified as "Buick," "Olds," "Vega," and "Radar." "Bullseye" was a reference point in North Vietnam known to aircrews and ground agencies. Bullseye located the MIG's without the MIG pilot knowing that the U.S. transmissions referred to him.

Radar:	Buick, Bandits 240/30, Bullseye.*
Buick:	Copy 240 at 30.
Ritchie (intercom):	What in the hell are they [the MIG's] doing down there?
DeBellevue (intercom):	What's our fuel?
Ritchie (intercom):	11.2.
DeBellevue (intercom):	OK.
DeBellevue (intercom):	I've got some friendlies and some MIG's. The MIG's are behind the friendlies right now.
Buick:	Buick shows MIG's 10 miles behind friendlies.
Buick:	Stand by for position.
Olds:	Olds 90 right [Olds flight is also turning toward the MIG's].
Radar:	This is Red Crown. Bandits at 253/37, Bullseye.
Buick:	Copy that.
Ritchie (intercom):	Bandits on the nose.
DeBellevue (intercom):	It looks like two of them at least.
Buick:	Buick flight, fuel check.
Olds:	Olds, 90 left.
Radar:	This is Red Crown. Bandits 252/51, Bullseye.
Buick 3 (The element lead responsible for protecting Capt. Ritchie's airplane):	Buick 4, this is 3. Can you read me? We've got bogies [unidentified aircraft] off to the left at 10 o'clock, way out.
Buick 4:	Tally.
Radar:	This is Red Crown. Bandits 251/57, Bullseye.
DeBellevue (intercom):	Roger, I've got 'em.
Ritchie (intercom):	I can't believe we're not getting a SAM [surface-to-air missile] shot at us.
DeBellevue (intercom):	Me either.
DeBellevue (intercom):	Bandits. We're running in.
DeBellevue (intercom):	He's at 1 o'clock right now. [At this point, Buick Flight is converging head on with the MIG's. Olds and Vega flights are chasing the

---

*Enemy fighters at 240° and 30 miles from Bullseye

	MIG's, ground radar is telling everyone where the MIG's are. All the F-4's are using radar, eyeballs, and everything else to try to get to the MIG's, and the MIG's are trying to run away from everyone and get home.]
Ritchie (intercom):	Keep giving it to me, Chuck.
DeBellevue (intercom):	OK.
Buick:	Disco, do you have an altitude on them?
DeBellevue (intercom):	Looks like the MIG's are 160 [degrees] from us.
Radar:	This is Red Crown. Bandits 250/67, Bullseye.
DeBellevue (intercom):	1 o'clock [the MIG's are just to the right of the nose] Two of them at least.
Radar:	Vega, they are 255/62, Bullseye.
Vega:	Roger.
DeBellevue (intercom):	Two sets looks like. Maybe 4 MIG's.
Radar:	Vega, Disco. They are 248 for 53 [miles].
Buick:	Say altitude of MIG's.
Radar:	Buick, they are 266 for 32. Heading 080. Speed point 7. [Capt. Ritchie now knows their position, heading and speed. Speed is seven-tenths of the speed of sound, or point seven mach. Now all he needs is their altitude.]
Buick:	Say their altitude.
DeBellevue (intercom):	22 miles dead ahead.
Buick:	Say altitude please.
Buick:	Anybody know their altitude?
DeBellevue (intercom):	25. We're locked. [The bandits are at] 25,000 [feet], 15 miles dead ahead.
Buick:	Buick flight, reheat. [Capt. Ritchie is now starting a climb from 15,000 feet to get up to the MIG's.]
Ritchie (intercom):	We want to get a visual first. [Because of all the friendly airplanes converging, Capt. Ritchie wants to see the MIG's before he fires.]
DeBellevue (intercom):	They are dead ahead going right to left. They're about 1130. You're in range.
DeBellevue (intercom):	Come left a little.
DeBellevue (intercom):	Come left a little.
DeBellevue:	About 11 o'clock. Three and one-half miles ahead. Turning left. 3 miles, 2½. They are off the scope. Hurry it up!
Ritchie (intercom):	I've got'em. I've got'em, I've got'em [visual].
Buick:	Buick's got a tally ho. [He sees them.]
DeBellevue (intercom):	Three miles – 3½ miles, 2 o'clock. [Capt. Ritchie is in a hard climbing turn, attempting to get behind the MIG's. He fires his first missiles, which miss.]

DeBellevue (intercom):	You got min overtake. OK, you are out of range. You are out of range. [At this point, Capt. Ritchie has turned and is directly behind the MIG's. He fired and missed during the turn, but is now accelerating and closing on the MIG's from behind.]
Ritchie (intercom):	They are 12 o'clock straight ahead.
DeBellevue (intercom):	You're in range. You're in range. Fire. [Captain Ritchie fires again.]
Ritchie (intercom):	He's conning way high [the MIG is making a contrail].
Buick:	Splash! I got him! Splash!
DeBellevue (intercom):	Good show, Steve!

First USAF MIG Kills

Air Force pilots flying missions in the northern part of Vietnam during the early summer months of 1965 had discovered a pattern in enemy air activity. This was evident in the Big Eye (airborne early warning radar aircraft) warnings, broadcasting the approach of MIG aircraft. These warnings, as noted earlier, were of two types. As the first U.S. aircraft entered the area, the first warnings from Big Eye flashed yellow, indicating that MIG's were airborne from Phuc Yen airfield. The warnings turned red as the MIG's approached within 10 minutes flight time of the attacking U.S. aircraft. Soon thereafter however, the red warning would change again to yellow. Then, as the last flight departed the area following the attack, the red warning would reappear, and the MIG's would follow the flight out of the area. The North Vietnamese timed their threats (the second red warning) so that the escorts, with a critically low fuel supply, would be forced to fly home and could not engage their MIG's. Apparently, MIG pilots could determine from their own radar equipment when the escorts had returned to base.

Pilots of the 2d Air Division recognized this pattern and decided to take advantage of MIG tactics. Having observed the same characteristics during morning strikes on 10 July, the afternoon flight planned to engage the harassing MIG's. The F-4C escort flight delayed its take-off time for this particular mission by 20 minutes and arrived in the area about 15 minutes later than the North Vietnamese normally anticipated.

Each of the four F-4C aircraft was armed with four Sparrow and four Sidewinder missiles. Major Richard Hall, flight commander, and 1st Lt. George Larson flew lead. Captains Harold Anderson and Wilbure Anderson flew in the number 2 position. The number 3 plane was manned by Captains Kenneth E. Holcombe and Arthur C. Clark, and the 4th was crewed by Captains Thomas S. Roberts and Ronald C. Anderson.* All were members of the 45th Tactical Fighter Squadron (TFS), based at Ubon Royal Thai Air Force Base, Thailand.

The flight and the refueling rendezvous were accomplished in complete radio silence. With full tanks, the four aircraft flew north at Mach .85 and at an altitude of 20,000 feet, a tactic which resembled that of the F-105 strike aircraft. The track pointed toward the target—the Yen Bai ordnance and ammunition depot. The F-4's moved in a "fluid-four" formation. Fluid-four was a tactical formation in which the second element was situated on vertical and horizontal planes to enhance maneuverability, mutual support and visibility. Aircraft numbers 1 and 2 were on the left, and 3 and 4 on the right; the two elements were separated by about 5,000 feet. Fluid-four, designed to provide complete visual coverage to the rear, became the favored formation for MIG-hunting throughout the Southeast Asian conflict. The F-4's moved randomly in both vertical and horizontal planes, maintaining the same basic formation. The second element, aircraft 3 and 4,

---

*For the sake of convenience, the narrative may, at times, make reference to these aircraft under the aircraft commanders' names. It must be realized, however, that aerial victories are achieved as a result of joint effort. Both crew members receive credit.

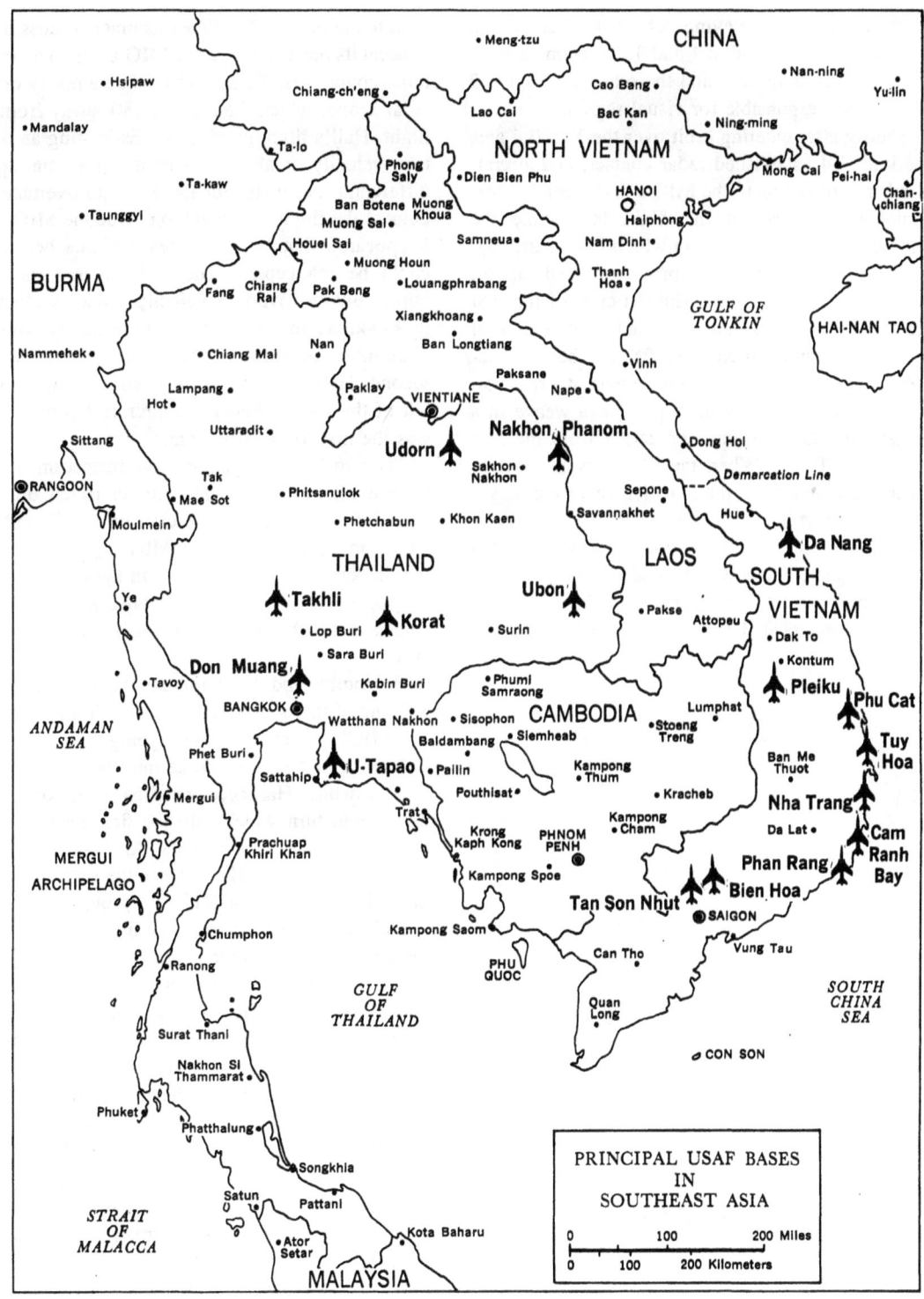

provided cover by weaving behind the lead. Radar coverage was assigned to 1 and 3, the element leaders, one searching high and the other low, while 2 and 4 were responsible for visual search.

Shortly after entering orbit over the Yen Bai area the lead F–4 established radar contact, and aircraft number 3 locked on to the MIG a few seconds later. Major Hall instructed the flight to assume the "loose-deuce formation," in which two of the four aircraft would maneuver to provide mutual support and increased firepower. While aircraft of the first element proceeded to make a visual identification of the bogey (unidentified aircraft), the second element, in order to enter the engagement at a reasonably high airspeed, flew an S-pattern (a weave in a horizontal plane) to gain separation from the first element of F–4's. When the MIG's were visually sighted and identified, the F–4 elements were only 2 to 3 miles apart instead of the desired 7 to 8 miles. A Sparrow missile, therefore, could not be launched by the second element without endangering the first.

Hall and Larsen were unaware that the other flight members had located the targets. The lead aircraft tried to maintain radio silence as much as possible to conceal its presence from the MIG's. Upon an initial radar contact, Hall's aircraft tracked a bogey on the radar scope, which then turned 180° away from the flight. Hall's flight gave chase. Estimating an overtake velocity at about 200 knots, (i.e., the speed differential necessary for the F–4's to overtake the bogies) the flight continued to pursue the MIG until it appeared that he would reach China before he could be intercepted. The F–4's then turned for home. But the overtake velocity suddenly changed to 900 knots and Hall's flight immediately returned to an intercept course. They visually sighted MIG's seconds later. Both bogies were slightly high, to the left of the F–4's. Anderson, aircraft 2 commander, was the first to identify them.

The two MIG's, flying in close formation, started to turn after the lead element but rolled out and turned toward the second element. Hall and his wingman closed left into the MIG's, jettisoned their fuel tanks, and lit afterburners in the turn. As they did so, they saw the MIG's moving up behind Holcombe and Roberts (3 and 4), also jettisoning their tanks.

Holcombe and his wingman heard Anderson's warning of the bogies, and they too lit afterburners. The MIG's swept by them dropping their tanks, but Holcombe and Roberts broke into the MIG's.

Meanwhile, Hall accelerated as Anderson started a climbing turn which split the first element. Hall also climbed to orbit the area. Anderson continued to search for other MIG's, since the flight had been briefed to look out for MIG's in groups of four.

Holcombe and Roberts broke into the MIG's, but the enemy aircraft turned very tightly behind them and fired. Both commanders saw their blasts, but there were no tracers—just "the nose of the MIG lighted up" by muzzle flashes, recalled Holcombe.

Although the MIG–17's had out-turned the F–4's, Holcombe and Roberts accelerated during their turns and gained separation. Roberts broke right in an attempt to either "sandwich or split" the MIG's. The latter occurred and one followed Holcombe, while the other chased Roberts. Once the MIG's had split, Holcombe reversed his turns several times and his MIG slid by, having overestimated his distance (an "overshoot"). Then Holcombe again reversed. His radar went out during these scissors maneuvers,

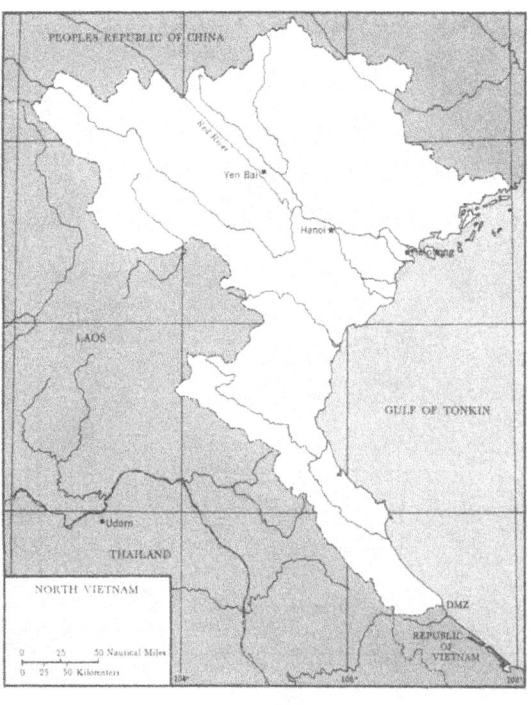

and when the MIG overshot, he decided to gain separation, executing a right roll and going into a 30° dive.

The MIG tried to give chase and ended up at 7 o'clock, three-fourths of a mile away. This gap increased to a 5-mile separation. Holcombe then executed a hard left turn into the MIG, attacking almost head-on. From the rear of his aircraft, Clark tried to advise his aircraft commander that the radar was out and to "Go heat" (he wanted Holcombe to use a Sidewinder missile equipped with the heat-seeking homing device). Holcombe misinterpreted the message as a problem in detecting the MIG on radar and told Clark to "Go boresight" (to fire the weapons visually). While the crew members tried to clear up their misunderstanding, the MIG passed very close head-on and fired but scored no hits.

Once the MIG had passed, Holcombe turned slightly left to maintain the MIG in sight and then made a very steep dive to 10,000 feet. The afterburner had been turned on in the initial break and was still operating, so the F-4's speed increased to Mach 1.3. Holcombe then initiated a high-G barrel roll with the MIG behind at about 1 mile. When the F-4 reached the 270° position, the MIG opened fire from 7 o'clock at a range of 1/2 mile, but scored no hits. As Holcombe dished back (i.e., emerged from the maneuver) the MIG again overshot and then turned, leveled, and descended toward a cloud.

Holcombe's aircraft was now between 13,000 and 15,000 feet, flying at a speed of Mach .9 to .95, with the MIG ahead. He fired a Sidewinder missile, but nothing happened. A second Sidewinder produced a large fireball at or slightly to the right of the tail cone. The third missile detonated slightly to the right of the MIG. He fired the fourth missile and again nothing happened. Neither Holcombe nor Clark saw the MIG explode, but they did see a fireball as the MIG entered the cloud. The two Andersons in aircraft 2, on the other hand, witnessed the attack and saw the enemy aircraft "blow completely apart."

After firing his fourth and last Sidewinder, Captain Holcombe broke left and intended to head for Udorn, since his fuel level had dropped to 3,000 pounds.

Meanwhile, after Roberts and Anderson in aircraft 4 broke to the right, they started to dive from 20,000 feet in afterburner and unloaded the aircraft. Roberts accelerated to about Mach 1.4 at 12,000 feet and started a "4-G pull-up" (a climb, four times the pull of gravity), to get into position for an attack.

The MIG lost ground behind him but continued to pursue. During the pull-up, Roberts lost sight of the enemy aircraft but continued his climb to 33,000 feet. By now his radar was completely inoperative. Rolling out at the top of the climb, he saw the MIG at 28,000 or 29,000 feet, falling off on its left wing into a 90° bank and then making a vertical recovery. The MIG pilot smoothly pulled out in a 20° bank and descended slightly to the left, placing himself about 4,000 to 5,000 feet ahead, as Roberts came out of afterburner.

A fall-off to the left and a turn gave Roberts an excellent firing position. As his aircraft closed on the MIG, Roberts fired a Sidewinder. It streaked past the tail and detonated about 4 to 6 feet from the left wing tip. The MIG rocked its wings several times following the detonation but remained in flight, rolling slowly to the left in a bank. Roberts fired a second Sidewinder, but since he fired hastily, it was without tone (i.e., without an audio indicator that the radar track was locked on for the missile). The missile proved ineffective. Roberts then established tone with the third Sidewinder and fired. The missile tracked well and exploded just short of the MIG's tail, but in line with it. The fireball expanded until only the MIG's wing tips were visible. He saw no debris emitting from the aircraft. After the fireball had subsided, the MIG started to discharge white smoke from its tailpipe.

Roberts continued to descend with the MIG, slowly closing distance. When the MIG reached 6,000 feet, it was 60° nose down and inverted. Since his aircraft was about to overshoot, Roberts rolled inverted, nosed toward the MIG, and fired his fourth Sidewinder. He did not watch for results, for just at that moment Anderson, in the rear, sounded a flak warning. Roberts went into afterburner and began maneuvers to evade the flak while leaving the area. Later, Roberts reported: "The MIG obviously lost sight of me. It was simple from then on."

As soon as Roberts completed his encounter, the F-4's left the battle area and rejoined about 30 miles from Udorn. The flight landed with approximately 1,800 pounds of fuel remaining aboard each aircraft.

On 11 July, Lt. General Joseph Moore, Comman-

After receiving awards, members of the first USAF flight to down MIG jets over North Vietnam whoop it up. Flight Commander Maj. Richard Hall gets a ride on the shoulders of the other flight members: (l. to r. in the foreground) Capt. Ronald C. Anderson, Capt. Kenneth D. Holcombe, Capt. Harold Anderson, Maj. Hall, Capt. Arthur C. Clark, and Capt. Wilbure Anderson.

der of the 2d Air Division, awarded Silver Stars to the men scoring these two aerial victories; the other two aircrews were awarded Distinguished Flying Crosses. This established a tradition for the tenure of the Vietnam conflict that, whenever significant aerial victories were achieved, appropriate awards would be made to the aircrews. However, while the U.S. Air Force was duly proud of its fighter pilots who had achieved aerial victories and had nullified the MIG threat to strike forces, MIG kills were not a primary objective at any time during the conflict.

Enemy Stand-Down

Sporadic encounters between MIG's and U.S. fighters occurred during the 9 months following the initial aerial victories. During this period, American crews shot down five MIG's, while four U.S. fighters were lost to the enemy's aircraft. Prior to July 1965, North Vietnam had augmented its MIG-15/MIG-17 force with modified versions of the MIG-21, which were equipped with Atoll infrared homing missiles, but they showed a marked reluctance to commit this jet fighter force to other than defensive roles. The NVN Air Force seemed more intent upon improving its electronic defenses and at the same time began a considerable expansion of its surface-to-air (SAM) sites and Antiaircraft Artillery/Automatic Weapons network. North Vietnamese MIG's were committed to lengthy training exercises against U.S. aircraft and made dry firing passes (feinting an attack) under GCI radar vectoring, but broke off before U.S. fighters could engage them.* This training period extended from July 1965 through April 1966. The integration of GCI and MIG systems produced excellent training for inexperienced NVN pilots and ground controllers in developing their intercept capability.

When aerial encounters did occur, MIG pilots effectively used the superior turning capability of their aircraft to achieve a 6 o'clock position, which then endangered F-105 strike aircraft if they slowed down to follow or turn. MIG pilots relied on turn radius and cut-off tactics almost exclusively to attain a viable combat attack capability. They usually forced F-105 aircraft to jettison their ordnance in order to take evasive action and prepare for counterattack. Against F-4's armed with radar-controlled and heat-seeking missiles, however, the MIG-17's were at a disadvantage when they employed turn radius and cut-off tactics, since under these conditions the F-4's enjoyed superiority.

U.S. air forces customarily attacked targets from high altitudes to escape small arms fire and flak. When NVN introduced surface-to-air missiles in mid-1965, this threat became significant and strike aircraft shifted to lower approach and withdrawal altitudes, since SAM's were less effective at these levels. Once beyond the concentrations of SAM sites, American aircraft would then pop up to higher altitudes and make their attack. When gunfire again

---

*Ground control intercept (GCI) radar vectoring is the electronic control of a friendly aircraft from the ground. In air interception—that is, in the contact by a friendly aircraft with an enemy aircraft—there are five phases of maneuvers: (a) climb phase—airborne to cruising altitude; (b) maneuver phase—receipt of initial vector to target until beginning transition to attack speed and altitude; (c) transition phase— increase or decrease of speed and altitude required for the attack; (d) attack phase—turn to attack heading, acquisition of target, completion of attack, and turn to breakaway heading; and, (e) recovery phase—breakaway to landing. The MIG's would break away sometime before the attack phase.

became too effective, the strike aircraft returned to higher levels where, with advance warning and time to see the missiles, the aircrews could outmaneuver them. MIG's were more of a threat at the higher altitudes, but this threat was more potential than real in 1965 and early 1966.

With the growing nuisance caused by MIG tactics against strike forces, by March 1966, the F-4's began to fly "MIG Screen" missions (i.e., protecting fighters were placed between the threat and the strike aircraft). When MIG's bypassed the MIG Screen flight, the F-4's left orbit to assist the strike force. When no MIG's engaged, the orbit was maintained until the last F-105 departed target, then the MIG Screen aircraft escorted the strike flights from the target area.

More MIG Kills

When the northeast monsoon season ended in April 1966, American activity increased against North Vietnam, and there was a corresponding reaction in MIG activity. The NVN Air Force compromised American strike missions and affected the security of strike aircraft. Seven Phantoms and one Thunderchief downed eight MIG's between late April and June, as NVN fighter pilots became increasingly aggressive.

The first encounter came on 23 April with a flight of four F-4C's of the 555th Tactical Fighter Squadron, 8th Tactical Fighter Wing, flying MIG Screen in support of Thunderchief strikes against the Bac Giang highway and railroad bridge, 25 miles northeast of Hanoi. Involved in the two MIG-17 victories were flight aircraft 3 (Capt. Max F. Cameron and 1st Lt. Robert E. Evans) and 4 (Capt. Robert E. Blake and 1st Lt. S.W. George). Four MIG-17's were detected on radar at a distance of about 15 miles, and the two forces met in a near head-on pass.

The flight lead and aircraft 2 each fired one Sparrow; Cameron fired a Sidewinder during this head-on contact. None of them made a hit. For the next 10 minutes, the aircraft were in a left-turning engagement between 10,000 and 18,000 feet. Three of the MIG's gained position on aircraft 2, one of them firing without making a hit. Cameron and Blake maneuvered their F-4's to attack the three MIG's.

"We could see little flashes of light when the lead MIG fired at our number two man with his cannon," Cameron later reported. "I quickly fired a Sidewinder missile at him, then went after the second MIG behind our flight leader's wingman."

Cameron's rear seat pilot, Lieutenant Evans, said he thought the Sidewinder went up the MIG's tailpipe. "As the MIG went down," he said, "it was falling apart and trailing thick, whitish-gray smoke."

Another MIG, meanwhile, achieved a firing position on both Cameron and Blake, but was unable to follow their climbing separation maneuver and rolled down to the right. Blake followed the MIG. "I went into a diving roll and came straight down on the MIG," he later commented. "The pilot must have seen us on his tail. He applied full power and dove toward a valley. As I came out of the roll, I fired one Sparrow. I had a bad angle on him and missed but I realigned and fired again." This one connected. "The smoke looked like taffy streaming from the rear," Blake said.

Three days later, on 26 April, Maj. Paul J. Gilmore, in the front seat of the lead F-4C, and 1st Lt. William T. Smith in the back, downed the first

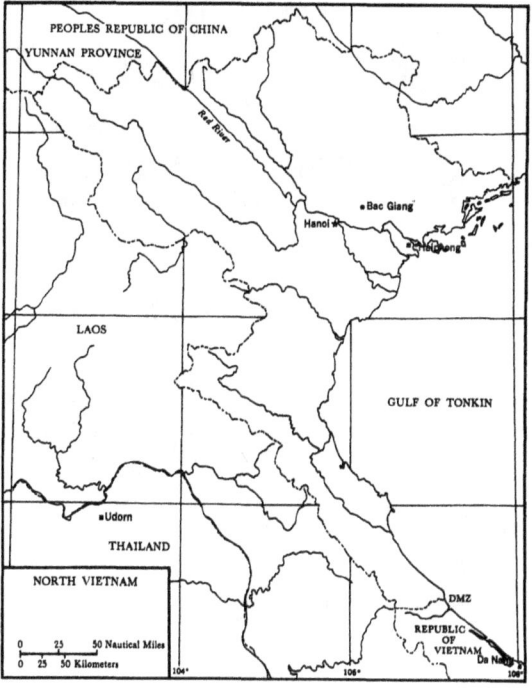

MIG-21 of the war. They were part of a flight of three F-4's flying escort for two RB-66's. Launching from Da Nang, they rendezvoused with the RB-66's and proceeded north to the Red River, where one RB-66 and one F-4 split off for a separate mission. Gilmore, flying the other F-4, and the other RB-66 proceeded northeast of Hanoi. Almost at once they spotted two or three MIG's coming high in the 2 o'clock position and closing rapidly. Gilmore and his wingman jettisoned their external tanks, lit their afterburners, and broke into a hard left-descending turn while the RB-66 departed the area.

Gilmore pulled out of his vertical reversal at 12,000 feet, with his wingman flying a tight wing position. They pulled up after the MIG's, which were in afterburner, heading northwest at 30,000 feet.

The second MIG was descending very slowly, trailing white vapor toward the east. The F-4 aircrews lost sight of this aircraft as they closed rapidly on the first, which was making gentle clearing turns as he climbed away. Gilmore had several boresight lock-ons but was out of range for a good Sparrow

Capt. Cameron (left) and Lt. Evans pose beside Sidewinder missiles upon return from their victory.

shot. At a range of 3,000 feet, Gilmore fired one Sidewinder with a good tone; he then maneuvered to the left to gain more separation and as a result did not see his first missile track.

Later, Gilmore reported that the had not realized that he had scored a victory with his first missile: "My wingman, flying cover for me, told me later the MIG pilot had ejected after I fired the first missile. I didn't realize I'd hit him the first time. My wingman wondered why I kept after him as I had hit him the first time and the pilot ejected." Because of radio difficulties, his wingman could not inform Gilmore of his success.

After his maneuver to gain separation, Gilmore pulled up behind the pilotless MIG-21 again and fired another Sidewinder without effect. He again rolled to the left, pulled up, and fired his third Sidewinder at a range of 3,000 feet. "After missing [he thought] twice," Gilmore later told newsmen,

Capt. Blake (left) and Lt. George

years in the tactical fighter business."

Phantom aircrews of the 555th TFS destroyed two more MIG-17's on 29 April, when they were flying MIGCAP for a force of F-105's attacking the Bac Giang bridge about 25 miles northeast of Hanoi. The Phantoms met four of them north of the strike area, and the F-4C crewed by Capt. William B. D. Dowell and 1st Lt. Halbert E. Gossard downed one of them with an AIM-9 Sidewinder.

The flight leader, Capt. Larry R. Keith, flying with 1st Lt. Robert A. Bleakley, accounted for a second MIG by maneuvering him into a crash. Observing the two aircraft of the other element rolling into the MIG's, Keith broke off in the opposite direction. He saw a MIG preparing to attack Gossard and quickly fired a Sidewinder to distract the pilot. The MIG then executed an evasive maneuver, but Keith followed in hot pursuit. At a distance of 6,000 feet behind the MIG, Keith's F-4 was just beginning to get Sidewinder tone. During his evasive tactics, the MIG inverted rolling to the left at an altitude of 2,500 feet. He crashed. The flight leader recalled later that the MIG pilot "either lost control of the

Maj. Gilmore (left) and Lt. Smith pose beneath the red star painted on their aircraft for downing the first MIG-21 of the war.

"I was quite disgusted. I started talking to myself. Then I got my gunsights on him and fired a third time. I observed my missile go directly in his tailpipe and explode his tail."

The two F-4 aircrews then descended to watch the debris impact. As Gilmore commenced his pull-up he spotted another MIG-21 tracking his wingman and called for a defensive split. He broke to the left and down while his wingman broke to the right and up.

When Gilmore emerged from the roll, he sighted the MIG ahead, in afterburner and climbing away. He rolled in behind this aircraft and climbed in afterburner until he was directly behind. He fired his fourth Sidewinder, but the range was too short and the missile passed over the MIG's left wing. Because of low fuel reserves, both F-4's then left the battle area. The 6-minute aerial battle was Gilmore's first encounter with an enemy plane "after twelve

Capt. Dowell (left) and Lt. Gossard shot down the first MIG-17 destroyed in aerial combat on 29 April 1966.

aircraft or attempted a Split-S with insufficient altitude."

On the morning of 30 April an element of two F-4C's (aircraft 3 and 4) were alternating with another element (1 and 2) in air refueling. They were providing rescue combat air patrol (RESCAP) for two pilots downed about 100 miles west-northwest of Hanoi. The number 3 and 4 aircraft were withdrawing from the area and 1 and 2 were returning when four MIG-17's attacked. The MIG's, under ground-control, flew out of the sun and waited until the F-4's were low on fuel before closing. They were headed directly for the Phantoms when the aircrew of aircraft 3 sighted them at a range of 5 miles. In the ensuing air battle, Capt. Lawrence H. Golberg and 1st Lt. Gerald D. Hardgrave in aircraft 4 fired a Sidewinder into a MIG's tailpipe. The aircraft exploded. The two Phantoms, then low on fuel, hurriedly left the battle area. Golberg landed at Udorn with only 400 pounds of fuel on board.*

Controversy erupted from the next USAF MIG kill, on 12 May, when Communist China charged that U.S. fighters had intruded into Chinese airspace and shot down a Chinese aircraft. China's report placed the air battle in Yunnan Province, 25 miles north of the border.

Involved in this aerial victory was an F-4C crewed by Maj. Wilbur R. Dudley and 1st Lt. Imants Kringelis, the third aircraft of a flight of three Phantoms escorting an EB-66 on an ECM mission in the Red River Valley. Four MIG-17's jumped the flight about 105 to 115 miles northwest of Hanoi, more than 20 miles south of China's frontier.

"The enemy flier seemed to be a pretty good pilot, but he made one mistake," Dudley later reported. "He apparently had a case of tunnel vision when he bore in on the EB-66 and never knew we were behind him. That was his mistake. And one mistake is all you're allowed in this game."

Dudley missed with his first Sidewinder, fired just as the MIG began descending in what appeared to be a Split-S maneuver designed to regain an offensive position. When the MIG rolled out behind the EB-66, Dudley fired a second missile. It guided up the MIG's tailpipe and the aircraft disintegrated. It spun out of control and crashed. The pilot was apparently unable to eject, for no parachute was observed. The battle continued a little longer without any further losses on either side, and the two forces then disengaged.

The first half of 1966 ended with another MIG-17 kill by an F-105D pilot: Maj. Fred L. Tracy, 388th TFW, Korat AFB, Thailand. This was the first instance in which a Thunderchief claimed a victory. A flight of four F-105's was flying an Iron Hand (SAM suppression) mission during the afternoon of 29 June when it encountered four MIG-17's about 25 miles north-northwest of Hanoi. The F-105's had just left their target when they detected the MIG's closing at 7 o'clock.

The first MIG fired, but missed the third Thunderchief which along with number 4 was breaking and diving. The first and second MIG's then pursued the lead element. The third and fourth MIG's followed, but did not take an active part in the engagement. The F-105 flight leader and his wingman had begun a left turn when the MIG's were sighted. The American aircraft went to afterburners and jettisoned their ordnance as they commenced a dive to the left.

Capt. Keith (left) and Lt. Bleakley maneuvered a MIG-17 into a crash.

---
*Flying time was about 4 minutes.

The lead MIG fired at Tracy, in aircraft 2, and made several hits. One 23-mm slug entered the cockpit and knocked Tracy's hand off the throttle, putting him out of afterburner and damaging his instruments, including his gun sight and oxygen equipment. The MIG overshot the Thunderchief and ended up at Tracy's 12 o'clock position.

Tracy fired 200 rounds of 20-mm, observing about 10 hits. The MIG rolled over and did a Split-S into clouds at an altitude of 2,000 feet. Because of the damage to this aircraft, Tracy then left the battle area, with aircraft 3 providing cover.

Cannon fire from the second MIG, meanwhile, hit and damaged the lead F-105. Aircraft 4 engaged the fourth MIG, which had joined in the battle. The lead Thunderchief pilot fired about 200 rounds of 20-mm, but scored no hits. Before departing the area, he fired a burst at the departing MIG's, and again he apparently missed.

During July, August, and September 1966, North Vietnamese MIG activity increased, and six more MIG's were downed by Air Force F-4's and F-105's. During this period, MIG-17's concentrated almost exclusively upon the F-105 strike forces. As MIG activity picked up, it became apparent that the primary objective of NVN was to prevent as many strike aircraft as possible from reaching their targets with ordnance. The MIG pilots attacked the F-105's during their bomb runs and often caused enough distraction to disrupt the attack. Once they succeeded in forcing strike pilots to jettison their ordnance, they quickly withdrew. During this same period, MIG-21's slowly began to assume most of the high-altitude intercept role.

The earlier MIG Screen flights of American F-4's evolved during this period into pure MIGCAP missions. The Phantoms kept watch for MIG aircraft and actively engaged them to prevent them from attacking strike forces. MIG pilots, however, at times out-maneuvered American air-to-air missiles.

Two MIG-21's were destroyed on 14 July by F-4C aircrews of the 480th TFS. Capt. William J. Swendner and 1st Lt. Duane A. Buttell, Jr. flew the lead Phantom, and 1st Lts. Ronald G. Martin and Richard N. Krieps the number 2 aircraft. They were part of a flight of four F-4's providing MIG cover for an Iron Hand flight of three F-105's.

Following the Thunderchiefs north of Hanoi, the Phantom flight, in a right turn, sighted the first MIG-21 in a 7 o'clock position. The F-4's jettisoned their tanks and spotted a second MIG pursuing the third F-105. Even though the second MIG closed in on the F-105, the pilot continued his Shrike launch. Captain Swendner and his wingman gave chase.

Swendner's first Sidewinder passed close to the MIG's canopy without detonating, and the MIG pilot lit his afterburner, initiating a 30° climb to the right. Swendner's second Sidewinder detonated behind the MIG, but seconds later a third one went up the MIG's tailpipe and blew the enemy aircraft into pieces.

Lieutenant Martin, meanwhile, had maneuvered behind the second MIG, which was attacking the fourth Phantom. Just after the MIG missed that aircraft with a missile and initiated a climb with afterburner on, Martin fired a Sidewinder which impacted near the right side of the MIG's tail. The pilot ejected at once.

No additional aerial victories were chalked up by Air Force aircrews until 18 August, when Thunder-

Capt. Golberg (left) and Lt. Hardgrave fired a Sidewinder into the tailpipe of a MIG-17.

Lt. Butell (left) and Capt. Swendner. Their third Sidewinder went up the tailpipe of a MIG-21 and blew the enemy aircraft to pieces.

Lts. Krieps (left) and Martin (center) receive congratulatio from Lt. Col. Leland Dawson, their squadron commander, shooting down a MIG-21.

Lts. Jameson (left) and Rose scored against a MIG-17.

chief pilot Maj. Kenneth T. Blank of the 34th T destroyed a MIG-17. A flight of four F-105's volved in an Iron Hand SAM suppression mission that day sighted two MIG-17's.

One MIG came in firing his cannon at the le Thunderchief. Flying aircraft 2, Blank maneuver into a 6 o'clock position on the MIG and opened fi with his 20-mm gun. He fired about 200 rounds at range of 400 to 600 feet before the MIG burst in flames, entered an inverted dive, and hit the groun The entire engagement took less than 2 minutes. T second MIG broke off and fled.

The first of three September MIG kills came the 16th when at least four MIG-17's were sight by a flight of three F-4C's of the 555th TFS Ubon, which was conducting a strike/CAP missi against the Dap Cau railroad and highway bridg During the air battle, the lead Phantom fired all his Sidewinders and two of his Sparrows at sever MIG's, but all escaped damage. The number thr Phantom fought with two MIG's and did not retu from the mission. First Lieutenants Jerry W. Jam son and Douglas B. Rose downed the only MIG lo by the enemy that day.

"It seemed unreal," Jameson later told newsme "I think for the first 3 or 4 minutes I didn't reali what I was doing. I was just hanging on, trying get away from a MIG that was chasing me. After I got away I started putting into practice what I had learned in training." When Jameson had tried to get behind one of the MIG's in order to fire his Sidewinders, the slower but more maneuverable MIG went into a tight turn and ended up on his tail.

When the MIG pilot began firing his 23-mm gun, Jameson put his F–4 into afterburner, turned hard to the left and then hard to the right to escape. He then jettisoned his tanks and ordnance and returned to the engagement. Another MIG was sighted dead ahead, but Jameson was unable to pick it up with radar so he could launch a Sparrow. He overshot the MIG, ignited afterburner again, made a hard right turn, and observed still another MIG at his 12 o'clock position.

"At about a mile out," he reported, "I fired two missiles. Then I turned hard to the left and back to the right again to get away from another MIG that had begun firing on me. When I straightened out again I saw debris and a man in the air."

F–105 pilots made the other two MIG kills on September 21. The two Thunderchiefs were from different wings, performing different missions. The first flight of one F–105F and three F–105D's from the 388th TFW at Korat was flying an Iron Hand mission against SAM sites in support of a large strike force directed against the Dap Cau highway and railroad bridge. Aircraft 4 sighted the MIG's visually as they closed in on aircraft in positions 1 and 2. First Lieutenant Karl W. Richter in number 3 and his wingman, flying number 4, then turned into the MIG's, which went into a left turn after failing to overtake 1 and 2. Richter got within 2,000 feet and opened fire with his 20-mm gun, hitting the first MIG, which rolled out level and then went into a hard right turn. The second MIG broke sharply to the left.

Richter's wingman shot at this MIG but did not score any hits. Both 3 and 4 stayed with the first MIG, and then Richter fired a second time. "I saw my 20-mm rounds start to sparkle on his right wing the second time I fired," Richter later reported. "His right wing fell off. As I flew past I saw the MIG's canopy pop off." The enemy pilot ejected safely as Richter and his wingman followed the MIG, watching it hit the ground.

The second flight on that day comprised four

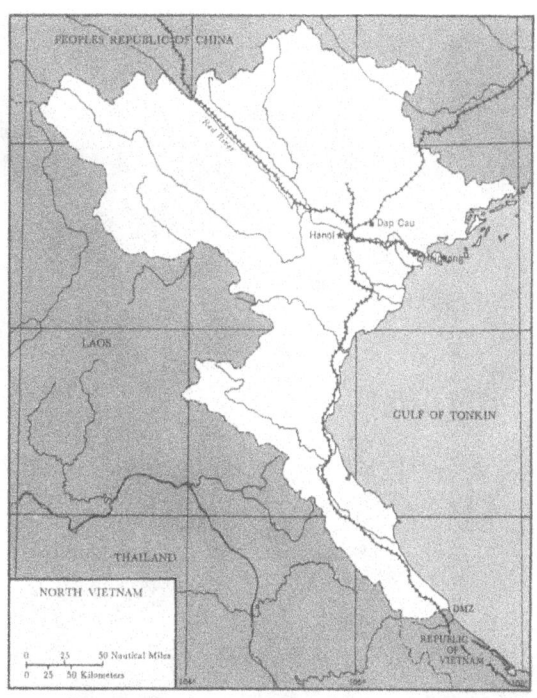

Thunderchief pilots Lts. Wilson (left) and Richter scored MIG–17 kills on 21 September 1966. Richter, 23 years old at the time, was the youngest pilot to score a MIG kill in Vietnam.

Lts. Klause (l. to r.), and Latham, Maj. Tuck, and Lt. Rabeni, in two F-4C's, shot down two MIG-21's in 3 minutes.

F-105D's of the 355th TFW from Takhli AFB, Thailand. They were flying a strike mission against the Dap Cau bridge. Within a few minutes after Richter had downed his MIG-17, this flight also sighted a MIG-17 in a 12 o'clock low position. Aircraft 1 and 2 descended to the 6 o'clock position in afterburner, leaving 3 and 4 as high cover.

The lead F-105 fired a burst of 154 rounds and damaged the MIG. The North Vietnamese pilot then suddenly lit his afterburner and pulled up and rolled left behind the F-105 lead. But, flying in position 2, 1st Lt. Fred A. Wilson, Jr. began shooting at the MIG from the 6 o'clock position.

"He [the MIG pilot] still had some fight left in him and he could have fired at the leader. I just rushed up behind him firing my 20-mm guns all the time. My sights were not even set up. I just kept firing." Wilson fired off 280 rounds, shooting off a portion of the MIG's aft section. The lead F-105 was safe, he noted. Breaking hard left, he then observed an explosion in the area where the MIG could have crashed.

Aircraft 3 and 4 in the meantime spotted another MIG. Number 3 attacked, firing 135 rounds before his guns jammed and the MIG broke hard left. No hits were observed.

The aggressiveness of MIG pilots continued unabated. Between 4 September 1966 and January 1967, with the exception of 4 days, the MIG's ascended each day. This marked the first continuous use of these aircraft for active air defense purposes. North Vietnam's intention to employ as fully as possible its MIG force to reduce U.S. strike effectiveness resulted in the loss of several American aircraft. The kill ratio was still favorable for the U.S., but the MIG threat clearly demanded special attention.

During December MIG activity further increased, particularly against Thunderchief strike aircraft, although—as earlier—the MIG pilots generally broke off engagements once the American aircraft dumped their ordnance and prepared for offensive action. Three MIG's were destroyed by Air Force crews during the last quarter of 1966, and one of these was credited to an F-105 pilot.

Four F-4C's of the 366th TFW were providing

escort for an EB-66 on 5 November when they were attacked by two or more MIG-21's in the northeastern section of North Vietnam, near Hanoi and Haiphong. The EB-66 was making its final orbit of the area and all of the escorting Phantoms were near the minimum fuel level for a safe return to their home station.

The MIG's were first detected on radar at a range of 18 miles. Shortly after the EB-66 executed a left turn, Maj. James E. Tuck, flying the lead F-4, saw the MIG's visually and called them out to his flight.

The first MIG launched a missile at the EB-66 just as that aircraft broke into a diving spiral. The missile missed. The F-4's and MIG's also spiraled down, and Tuck and his pilot, 1st Lt. John J. Rabeni, Jr., launched three Sparrow missiles. The explosion from the third Sparrow caused the MIG to flame out, and the pilot ejected.

Meanwhile, a second MIG got on the tail of Major Tuck's Phantom, and his wingman, 1st Lts. Wilbur J. Latham, Jr., and Klaus J. Klause, maneuvered to fire on it. During the execution of this maneuver, Latham saw a MIG (possibly a third one not previously observed) pull up in front of him, and he launched a Sidewinder. The missile exploded near the MIG's tailpipe, and the pilot ejected. The entire air battle lasted less than 3 minutes.

That night there was a celebration in the "Doom Club" at Da Nang's officers' open mess. These MIG kills gave the 480th Tactical Fighter Squadron its fifth aerial victory.

Maj. Roy S. Dickey of the 388th TFW at Korat, flying in a flight of four Thunderchiefs on 4 December, scored the final victory of 1966. His flight was one of several in a second wave assigned to strike a railroad yard approximately 2 miles north of Hanoi. As the flight rolled in on the target, the Thunderchiefs sighted four MIG-17's directly over the target, several thousand feet below their flight level.

As Dickey came off his bomb run, he saw one of the MIG's at a 2 o'clock position, attacking aircraft 3. He was then 2,000 feet behind and slightly above the MIG's 4 o'clock position, so he began to fire his 20-mm guns as he closed to within 700 feet. He ceased firing when the MIG burst into flames at the wing roots. The entire fuselage behind the cockpit was a sheet of flame. The MIG rolled over on its right wing and began spinning. Dickey last saw the MIG in a flat right-hand spin at 3,500 feet.

Meanwhile, another MIG had begun to fire at Dickey from the Thunderchief's 6 o'clock position. Dickey took evasive action and after entering a steep dive, leveled out at 50 feet, and lost sight of the second MIG.

Operation Bolo

MIG activity directed at the strike forces late in 1966 was unusually high and demanded measures to counteract the threat. Operating from five principal airfields—Phuc Yen (north of Hanoi), Kep (northeast of Hanoi), Gia Lam (east of Hanoi), Kien An (southwest of Haiphong), and Cat Bi (east of Haiphong)—the MIG's enjoyed a degree of immunity so long as they remained on the ground. The United States imposed political restrictions until 23 April 1967, barring strike forces from bombing enemy airfields. Assured of such immunity, the MIG's could feint air attacks against American bombing aircraft, forcing them to jettison bomb loads prematurely. But instead of confronting U.S. jets in air-to-air combat, the MIG's would withdraw and return to their safe havens. Moreover, to complicate matters, the later model MIG-21's carried radar-guided or heat-seeking missiles, which presented a direct threat to American fighter aircraft. This threat had to be negated.

With outright destruction of MIG's on the ground prohibited for political reasons, the commander of Seventh Air Force hit upon another scheme to eliminate or reduce the threat. He called upon Col. Robin Olds, commander of the 8th TFW, to launch an offensive fighter sweep of North Vietnam. Olds arrived on 22 December 1966 at Headquarters Seventh Air Force, where operation "Bolo" was outlined.

The first step was to get the MIG's airborne and then to destroy them in air-to-air combat. At the same time, it was necessary to cover the airfields and routes which they might use to recover or escape to China. The entire mission hinged on this. The execution of this plan in all its phases required a large force of F-4's to be airborne at staggered intervals.

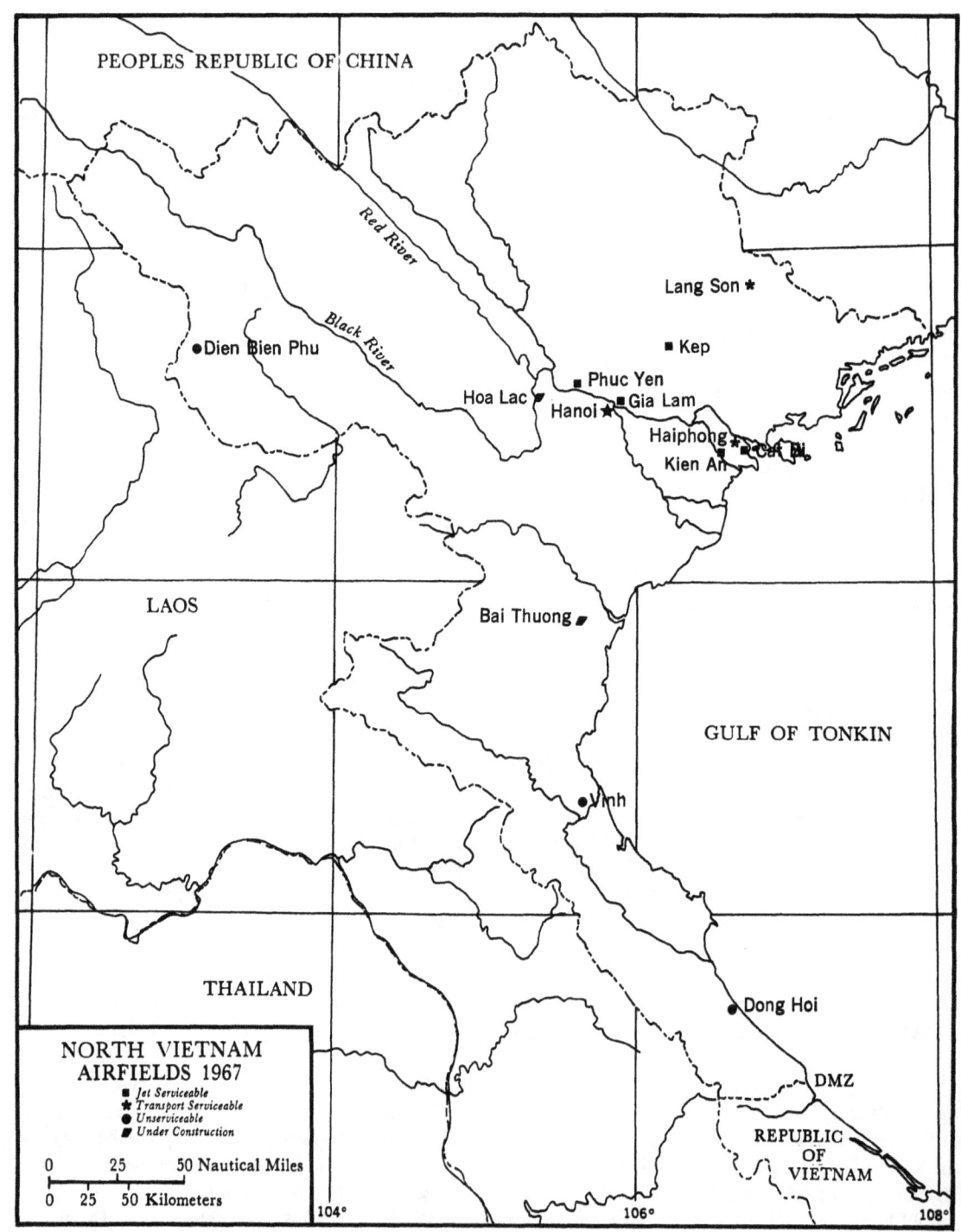

The fighter forces were drawn from the 355th, 388th, 8th, and 366th Tactical Fighter Wings. The 355th and 388th Wings, equipped with F-105 Thunderchiefs, were to fly regular Iron Hand strikes. The F-4C's of the 8th TFW became the West Force and were charged with bringing the MIG's up and covering suspected orbit areas as well as Phuc Yen and Gia Lam airfields. The F-4C's of the 366th TFW, designated the East Force, were assigned to cover Kep and Cat Bi airfields and to block approach routes to and from the north.

The West Force used an elaborate ruse to make the Phantoms appear to the enemy as an F-105 Rolling Thunder* strike force. The F-4C's used F-105 tanker anchors, refueling altitudes, approach routes, approach altitudes, airspeeds, and radio call signs and communications to simulate a normal Thunderchief strike force. This was intended to deceive the enemy on NVN radars. For this operaton, the F-4C's were also equipped for the first time with ECM pods to outwit the enemy's SAM and AAA acquisition and tracking radars.

The Bolo task force consisted of 14 flights of F-4C's, 6 flights of F-105 Iron Hand aircraft, 4 flights of F-104's and supporting flights of EB-66, RC-121 and KC-135 aircraft. Time on target for each flight was separated by 5 minutes to provide at least 55 minutes of F-4C air coverage in the target area. It was believed that MIG's could remain airborne for approximately 50 minutes and could devote 5 minutes to aerial combat.

Because of the size of the task force and the required logistical support, timing was crucial. A 24-hour standdown was required prior to H-hour. Based on this planning and on long-term weather prognostication, D-day was set for 2 January 1967. For 3 days prior to the execution of Bolo, all aircrews received special briefings. The F-4 aircrews were briefed not to attempt to turn with or to try to out-turn the MIG's.

On the 2nd, weather conditions over the target area were poor and considerable cloudiness and overcast was forecast. A 1-hour delay was instituted on the 2nd to await more favorable weather and then the mission proceeded on schedule. All other flying was cancelled for that day and all designated units went into high gear to carry out the operation.

Col. "Chappie" James and his GIB, Lt. Evans, prepare for take-off.

Each flight of the West Force was comprised of four F-4C's. Olds' flight arrived over target at 1500. The next arrived at 1505—led by Col. Daniel "Chappie" James, Jr., the 8th TFW's deputy commander for operations, and his crewman, 1st Lt. Bob C. Evans. The third flight arrived at 1510. Other West Force flights arrived later, but only the first three encountered MIG's.

The first flight over the target was given unrestricted use of air-to-air missiles, since any other aircraft in the vicinity would have to be a MIG. Olds' flight expected to encounter MIG's about the Red River or near Phuc Yen airfield. Given the adverse weather conditions, however, the NVN Air Force apparently did not expect a strike force and their reaction to Operation Bolo was much slower than anticipated. Proceeding on the preplanned route over and to the southeast of Phuc Yen, no MIG's were sighted and Olds' flight turned to a northwest heading. The second flight entered the Phuc Yen battle area minutes later. Because of the slow MIG

---

*A nickname assigned to air strikes against targets in NVN on a continuing schedule from March 1965 to October 1968.

scramble reaction, Olds' missiles-free option was cancelled in order that the flights would not endanger one another.

The cloud overcast made it impossible for the West Force to cover the airfields, which would have prevented a MIG recovery. The cloud layer also gave the MIG's an easy means to disengage from aerial combat by diving into the overcast for cover. The weather also hampered the East Force, since its primary mission was to cover the airfields. Unable to enter the battle area, the East Force sighted no MIG's.

While heading northwest from Phuc Yen, Olds' flight acquired a low, very fast radar contact at a distance of 17 miles from their 12 o'clock position. The lead was given to aircraft 3 of Olds' flight, who pursued the radar contact in a diving intercept to the top of the cloud layer. But aircraft 3 lost radar contact as the target passed under the flight. Aircraft 1, Olds and 1st. Lt. Charles C. Clifton, resumed the lead and climbed to 12,000 feet, heading toward Thud Ridge, a chain of mountains northwest of Hanoi. James' flight entered the area and reported a MIG at 6 o'clock to Olds' flight and closing. The entire battle was fought within a 15-mile radius centered on Phuc Yen airfield. For 15 minutes the Americans fought a high-speed duel with aggressive MIG-21 pilots.

Lieutenants Ralph F. Wetterhahn and Jerry K. Sharp, flying in aircraft 2 in Olds' flight reported the start of the air battle:

> Olds 03 [aircraft 3 of Olds' flight] observed one MIG-21 at 6 o'clock. Olds 01 saw one at 8 o'clock and Olds 02 saw one at 10 o'clock. Olds 01, 02, and 03 swung left and slid between the second and third MIG's. Olds 01 fired two AIM-7E's which failed to guide, while the number three MIG began sliding to 6 o'clock on the three F-4's. Olds 01 fired two Sidewinders which immediately guided on the undercast. At this time Olds 02 achieved a boresight lock-on, returned the mode switch to radar, centered the dot, and salvoed two AIM-7E's. The first was felt to launch, but was not observed. The second launched and it appeared just left of the radome. It guided up to the MIG-21 (range 1½ to 2 nautical miles) and impacted just forward of the stabilizer.

> A red fireball appeared and the MIG-21 flew through it, continued on for an instant and then swapped ends, shedding large portions of the aft section. A small fire was observed in the aft section, emitting black smoke. The aircraft went into a flat spin and rotated slowly, similar to a falling leaf, until disappearing in the clouds . . .

A left turn was continued, as Olds 01 had sighted the first MIG and was maneuvering for a shot. As we turned to approximately 250° Olds 01 began a barrel roll, and was lost by Olds 02 in the sun. Approximately thirty seconds later Olds 01 was seen slightly low at 10:30.

About a minute after the first victory, Capt. Walter S. Radeker, III, and 1st Lt. James E. Murray, III, downed the second MIG. They later reported:

> We continued the right turn to approximately 330° when Olds 03 called contact below the cloud layer. The flight then turned left and down, but the contact passed under the flight, exceeding radar tracking capabilities.

> As the flight began climbing again, Ford flight,* which had just entered the target area, called MIG's at Olds's 6 o'clock. Olds 03 observed one MIG-21 at 6 o'clock, and Olds 01 and 02 concentrated on two MIG's, one at 8 o'clock and one at 10 o'clock.

> Olds 04 then performed a high speed yo-yo which afforded us an excellent advantage on one MIG-21, who passed under us apparently tracking Olds 03. The second MIG-21 was no longer visible behind us so we dropped down behind this MIG. Initially we had a very poor Sidewinder tone. We then added some power and climbed slightly and the Sidewinder tone became excellent. The missile was fired after the radar-heat switch had been transferred to the heat position, and guided right into the MIG. It struck slightly forward of the tail, immediately resulting in a burst of black smoke and a violent tuck-under. The MIG was observed to be uncontrollable and violently falling, still trailing smoke.

> As the MIG entered the overcast, Olds lead and 02 had just completed successful attacks on their MIG's.

---

*Ford was the call sign assigned to the flight led by Col. James.

Certain MIG tactics became obvious during the air battle. Directed apparently by ground control, two MIG's attacked from the 10 and 12 o'clock position while others simultaneously were vectored in from a 5 to 7 o'clock position. The purpose of such a double attack was to force the F–4's to turn from the rear encounter, putting the MIG's originally at 10 to 12 o'clock in position for a tail-on attack. Colonel Olds describes this tactic in the report of his first MIG kill:

At the onset of this battle, the MIG's popped up out of the clouds. Unfortunately, the first one to pop through came up at my 6 o'clock position. I think this was more by chance than design. As it turned out, within the next few moments, many others popped out of the clouds in varying positions around the clock.

This one was just lucky. He was called out by the second flight that had entered the area, they were looking down on my flight and saw the MIG–21 appear. I broke left, turning just hard enough to throw off his deflection, waiting for my three and four men to slice in on him. At the same time I saw another MIG pop out of the clouds in a wide turn about my 11 o'clock position, a mile and a half away. I went after him and ignored the one behind me. I fired missiles at him just as he disappeared into the clouds.

I'd seen another pop out in my 10 o'clock position, going from my right to left; in other words, just about across the circle from me. When the first MIG I fired at disappeared, I slammed full afterburner and pulled in hard to gain position on this second MIG. I pulled the nose up high about 45 degrees, inside his circle. Mind you, he was turning around to the left so I pulled the nose up high and rolled to the right. This is known as a vector roll. I got up on top of him and half upside down, hung there, and waited for him to complete more of his turn and timed it so that as I continued to roll down behind him, I'd be about 20 degrees angle off and about 4,500 to 5,000 feet behind him. That's exactly what happened. Frankly, I am not sure he ever saw me. When I got down low and behind, and he was outlined by the sun against a brilliant blue sky, I let him have two Sidewinders, one of which hit and blew his right wing off.

The MIG erupted in a brilliant flash of orange flames. As the wing fell off, the aircraft swapped ends falling, twisting, corkscrewing, and tumbling into the clouds. No one could see if the pilot had ejected. Looking for other MIG's, Colonel Olds checked his fuel level, and gave the order to head for home when Radeker reported Bingo fuel.

Although James did not get a MIG for himself, he observed the MIG kills. He also noted the NVN tactic of double attacks from MIG's located at different positions of the clock:

At approximately 1504 hours my flight was attacked by three MIG–21's, two from 10 o'clock high and one, simultaneously, from 6 o'clock low. I did not see the MIG at 6 o'clock at first, as I had already started to counter the attack of the two closing from the front quarter. My rear seat pilot called me (very urgently), stating a MIG was closing from 6 o'clock and was in missile firing range on my number three and four aircraft. I was a bit hesitant to break off the attack I already had started on the other two MIG's, as I had just seen Olds flight pass underneath us a few seconds before and I had a fleeting thought that this was who my rear seater was seeing. However, I quickly max rolled from a left bank to a steep right and observed the low MIG as called. I called a hard right break for 03 and 04. As they executed, the MIG broke left for some strange reason, and for a split second was canopy-to-canopy with me. I could clearly see the pilot and the bright red star markings.

I immediately started a barrel roll to gain separation for attack and fired one Sidewinder. As he accelerated rapidly and broke harder left, my missile missed, but he broke right into the flight path of my number two aircraft, flown by Capt. Everett T. Raspberry. I called Captain Raspberry and told him to press the attack as the two aircraft that I had initially engaged had now swung around into range, head-on. I had a good missile growl and fired two AIM–9's in rapid succession at them. I immediately rolled over to reposition in fighting wing position on my number two, Captain Raspberry. It was during this maneuver that I saw an F–4, which was Olds lead, blast the wing off another MIG in another fight in progress a few miles from us.

I continued down with Captain Raspberry and remember thinking he was getting a little inside optimum missile parameters. He then executed a rolling maneuver, placing him in perfect position.

Raspberry was flying with 1st Lt. Robert W. Western in Ford 02 during the encounter, when they rolled in for the fourth victory in Operation Bolo:

The maneuver positioned my aircraft at the MIG's 6 o'clock at a range of approximately 3,500 feet in a left turn. I assume that the MIG pilot was not aware of my position because he rolled out of his turn, placing me in a perfect position to fire the AIM-9B. I fired the Sidewinder and observed the missile home up his tailpipe. As soon as the missile detonated the MIG-21 swapped ends and stalled out. The aircraft went into a slow spiral, falling toward the undercast.

Colonel James related what happened to the MIG:

Captain Raspberry fired one AIM-9 which impacted the tail section of the MIG-21. The MIG pitched up violently, then started into a slow, almost flat, spin. I followed in down to cloud top level and observed it burst into flames (a large explosion just aft of the canopy) and disappear into the clouds. I called Captain Raspberry and directed him to rejoin in wing position. I headed for the Olds flight fight but they had already dispensed with their MIG's and were rejoining to proceed out of the area. I covered their egress from 6 o'clock high and departed the area with them.

The third West Force flight fought in two separate engagements. Captain John B. Stone, flight leader, had monitored the radio chatter of Olds and James and had asked if his flight could assist, but he received no intelligible reply. Nearing Phuc Yen, the number 2 aircraft in Stones' flight observed MIG-21's at 3 o'clock and at a distance of 6 nautical miles, coming up out of an overcast on a heading of about 20° in an easy left turn. Because of his radio failure, however, he could not alert Stone and the other members of the flight and himself take the lead, a practice which was a prebriefed procedure for a flight member making MIG contact. Aircraft 4 also observed the flight of four MIG-21's and an additional two in trail at a distance of 2 or 3 miles.

Stone sighted two of the MIG's crossing over Phuc Yen in a 3 o'clock position about 4,000 feet below at a range of 2 nautical miles.

As Stone's flight began closing, the MIG flight leader broke left and Capt. Stone steepened his turn to follow. This placed Maj. Philip P. Combies and 1st Lt. Lee R. Dutton in aircraft 4, on the outside of the echelon, in a position where they had to go high to clear the other members of the F-4 flight, who were turning into them. Combies later described the chase and the victory:

We were flying at 16,000 feet mean sea level and 540 knots true air speed. Shortly after completing the turn to the northwest we spotted a flight of four MIG-21's in loose formation, 2 o'clock low at approximately 6 to 8 miles. Approximately 1 to 2 miles behind were two more MIG-21's, making a total of six observed. Due to their position "ahead of the beam" I wonder now if they were being vectored against us or possibly against Olds or Ford flights, who were initiating their egress from the area.

As the MIG's crossed in front of Stone, he started in on them, breaking left and down. This caused the flight to slide to the right and I, as 04, wound up high and right from the remainder of the flight. I went "burner" and held minimum "burner" throughout the initial engagement. The MIG's broke left and our flight commenced the engagement. My pilot secured, by boresight, a full system lock-on on one of the MIG's. I had selected radar and interlocks out, as prebriefed for an ACT [air combat tactics] environment. I had no difficulty in tracking the MIG. I don't think I pulled over four G's at any time during the whole battle. Using the Navy tactic of disregarding the steering dot, I pulled lead on the MIG using the reticle. When I felt I was where I wanted to be, I pulled the trigger, released, pulled again, and held. I did not observe the first Sparrow at all. However, I saw the second from launch to impact. We were approximately 1 mile behind the MIG, in a left turn, at approximately 12,000 feet at the time of launch. The second Sparrow impacted in the tailpipe area followed by a large orange ball of fire and a chute sighting.

Meanwhile, two MIG's (probably the fifth and

sixth aircraft) maneuvered to gain an advantage on Stone and his wingman, who were attacking MIG's 1 and 2 from the flight of four. One of the pursuing MIG's passed low between the two F–4's and the other fired cannon at a angle off, with no effect. Captain Stone and 1st Lt. Clifton P. Dunnegan in the lead aircraft broke right in an evasive maneuver and reversed back to the left to continue attacks on the first and second MIG's. Stone in the meantime lost his wingman, who ended up in a left barrel roll, high, where he mistakenly joined aircraft 4, thinking he had rejoined Stone. Stone again closed behind the same two MIG's and fired three Sparrow missiles. He recalls:

> I called for boresight and continued to turn to position for the kill. Due to the excessive chatter and not knowing for sure whether we were locked on, I fired three AIM–7E's.
> I maintained illumination of the target by tracking with the pipper. I planned to fire in salvoes of two. The first Sparrow was not observed, so I fired two more. The second missile detonated just at the wing root. The MIG caught fire and the pilot ejected.

Aircraft 3 had also attacked a MIG, probably the fourth plane in the four-ship flight. He had locked on at 2½ miles and launched two AIM–7's at a 1½ mile range. The first Sparrow did not guide and the second followed the MIG into the clouds. No impact was observed and this MIG could not be claimed.

Minutes later, Stone's flight had its second encounter. On a heading of about 20° Stone picked up three radar contacts 30° to his right and at a distance of 12 miles. Stone turned right to identify these contacts, but then he visually acquired two more MIG's at 10 or 11 o'clock, 3 miles away in a left turn. He turned left for position on these MIG's, intending to launch a Sidewinder, but he was unable to do so because at that moment aircraft 3 called a MIG on the tail of an F–4.

"I turned toward my 7 o'clock," said Stone, "and saw a MIG at 700 feet, firing. I initiated a hard break up into the MIG. When I reversed I could not see the MIG nor did I have my wingman. I then unloaded to make separation."

Aircraft 2 and 4 had tailed in behind other MIG's, which split, with one or more going left and down, and one going right and up. Aircraft 2, flown by 1st Lts. Lawrence J. Glynn and Lawrence E. Cary, followed one of the MIG's, and aircraft 4 followed another. Glynn fired two Sparrows at his MIG; the second one hit and the MIG exploded. Glynn flew through the debris, which caused some damage to the underside of his aircraft. The MIG pilot bailed out, thus raising the day's score to seven victories for the "wolf pack" of F–4's. Glynn then fired a Sparrow at still another MIG, but it passed about 2,000 feet in front of the enemy aircraft.

Combies and Dutton, in aircraft 4, fired two Sparrow missiles at the MIG they were pursuing, but neither missile made contact with the target. Combies then fired four Sidewinders at the MIG—two detonated near the aircraft, and as he was firing the last two Sidewinders, Combies heard a warning on the radio: "F–4C, I don't know your call sign, but there's a MIG on your tail. Break hard right!" When Combies broke hard right, he failed to see what happened to his missiles.

Glynn, in aircraft 2, spotted two more MIG's, but he could not attack because his radio was out and he did not desire to break formation with Combies. Aircraft 3, piloted by Maj. Herman L. Knapp, was the only F–4 still without a MIG victory in Stone's flight. He had attacked a MIG which had been in pursuit of Stone and fired one Sparrow as the MIG dove into a left spiral. The missile apparently failed to ignite, since it was never observed. Before the flight departed Phuc Yen, one other MIG attacked Glynn's F–4 with cannons and 8 to 10 rockets, but Glynn pulled hard left and escaped the barrage.

Without the loss of a single American aircraft, Operation Bolo had accounted for the destruction of seven enemy MIG–21's—nearly half of the North Vietnamese operational inventory at that time. Had the weather been more favorable, Olds' "wolf pack" would probably have destroyed several more enemy aircraft. Although these losses hurt the enemy, the NVN Air Force had more MIG–21's stored in crates at Phuc Yen. Operation Bolo, however, did without question establish the air-to-air superiority of the F–4C over the MIG–21. "We outflew, outshot and outfought them." Colonel Olds told newsmen following the spectacular air battle.

(Top left) Col. Robin Olds, commanding the 8th TFW, led Operation "Bolo," in which USAF Phantoms downed seven MIG-21's on 2 January 1967. Some of the crews participating appear on this page.

(Top right) Lt. Dunnegan is congratulated for one of the seven victories scored on 2 January 1967.

(Bottom right) Lts. Glynn (left) and Cary.

(Bottom left) Capt. Raspberry (left) and Lt. Western.

Another Successful Ruse

An opportunity to perpetuate another ruse presented itself a few days later, when RF-4C weather reconnaissance aircraft were forced to abort their planned weather reconnaissance missions in North Vietnam because of MIG attacks on 3 and 4 January 1967. To lure the MIG's into the air, two F-4C's on the following day flew, in close formation, a route similar to that normally flown by weather reconnaissance aircraft. The intent of the F-4C's was to deceive the enemy radar operators into believing that only one aircraft was flying a weather reconnaissance mission. The F-4C's flew above cloud formations topping out at 7,000 to 7,500 feet, but they made no radar contacts nor encountered any enemy aircraft.

Scheduled MIGCAP for an F-105 strike mission was cancelled due to weather conditions on the 6th, and the 8th TFW decided to try the ruse one more time. Capt. Richard M. Pascoe and 1st Lt. Norman E. Wells crewed the lead F-4; Maj. Thomas M. Hirsch and 1st Lt. Roger J. Strasswimmer manned the number 2 aircraft. They flew in a "missiles-free" environment, i.e., any sighting or radar contact could only be an enemy. When they encountered radar-controlled AAA near Phuc Yen, Pascoe turned on the ECM pod to deflect the radar lock and caused the flak to become inaccurate, falling either short or wide of the flight. Preplanned tactics called for an attempt to establish radar contact with MIG's, maneuver the F-4's to Sparrow parameters, (i.e., within the linear range of the missile) and then proceed from there. The ruse worked.

The flight made radar contact with four MIG's about 25 miles northwest of Hanoi, and immediately Pascoe pounced on them. Pascoe reports:

> I maneuvered the flight by use of airborne radar to effect a visual identification of four MIG-21C aircraft and fired two AIM-7 radar missiles at the enemy flight leader. The second missile struck the MIG aircraft in the fuselage midsection and detonated. The MIG-21 was seen to burst into flame and [fell] in uncontrollable flight through the clouds.

Hirsch had launched an AIM-7 at this same aircraft, but his missile apparently did not guide and there was no detonation. Pascoe continued the attack on the second MIG, which dove into the clouds. Seeing the third and fourth MIG's at Hirsch's 6 o'clock position, he barrel-rolled into them at their 6 o'clock, but they also disappeared into the clouds. Pascoe continued turning hard right, assuming the MIG's would continue their turns in the clouds.

When the third and fourth MIG's came out of the clouds in wing formation, level, Pascoe barrel-rolled left to decrease lateral separation and to drop to the rear of the enemy aircraft. But they spotted him during the roll and turned into him. As soon as he completed his roll, Pascoe put his gunsight pipper on the fourth MIG's tailpipe, switched to heat, heard a Sidewinder tone, and fired an AIM-9 to "keep their attention," even though he realized that his angle was too high. The missile passed about 300 to 400 feet behind the MIG. He fired another Sidewinder, which passed close to the MIG's tail but did not detonate.

The two MIG's reversed, and the fight degenerated into a slow-speed scissors during which Pascoe fired a third Sidewinder. It missed. The third MIG pilot seemed to realize he was getting into a disadvantageous position and left the area, but the fourth MIG continued the scissors maneuvers.

Hirsch wrote in his report about locking on to the fourth MIG at this time:

> In rolling to watch one of the enemy aircraft dive away I lost sight of the flight leader. Approximately one minute later I picked him up and saw two MIG-21's reappear from the undercast in a climb. The lead F-4 engaged the MIG's as I turned to close on them. As I approached I obtained a radar lock-on to a MIG-21 which was in a right climbing turn. As I slid in from his 4 o'clock position to his 5 o'clock, I fired an AIM-7 with full radar computing system. The MIG steepened his climb to near vertical and appeared to lose airspeed. When next observed, the MIG was in approximately an 80° nose-down attitude and rolling slowly. Just prior to entering the undercast in this attitude, both crewmembers in the #2 F-4 observed the MIG pilot eject and separate from the seat.

Because he was in a turning maneuver, Hirsch could not follow the missile's track. The AIM-7 did not seem to detonate, thus the MIG either flamed out, or the pilot lost control.

A Temporary Lull

The two MIG-21 kills of 6 January and the seven enemy losses earlier in the month dealt a serious blow to the North Vietnamese. For the next 2 months, NVN fighters showed an understandable lack of aggressiveness. The NVN Air Force was obviously stunned by its losses and entered another intensive training phase. Although American strike forces occasionally sighted MIG's in their normal operating areas, none of the MIG pilots challenged them to combat. During the latter part of January and through February and March, the northeast monsoon was in full swing. MIG activity was therefore curtailed as much by weather as by the need for additional training.

The lull in the air-to-air war was only temporary. The MIG's began to venture forth once again during March as American air strikes intensified. Although no longer rising in force, only in 4-aircraft flights, the North Vietnamese patrolled only their own bases. A few MIG-21's did attempt single aircraft attacks against American strike forces, while MIG-17's conducted their attacks on a more or less random basis, following the well-established tactic of attacking just as the strike aircraft entered into or recovered from a bombing run.

F-105 fighter-bomber pilots in March downed three MIG-17's which ventured too close or lingered too long. These were the first MIG losses since the January disasters. All three MIG's fell prey to fighters of the 355th TFW, two of them to Capt. Max C. Brestel on 10 March and the third one to the Wing Commander, Col. Robert R. Scott, on the 26th.

Brestel's aerial victories became the first USAF double kill of the conflict. At the time, he was flying the third Thunderchief in a flight of four and was tasked with suppressing flak in and around the Thai Nguyen steel mill and supporting other F-105 strike forces. Brestel relates how his two victories came about:

> We proceeded to the target via the Red River to a point north of the target, where we turned south. Numerous SAM and MIG warnings had been transmitted. Also, the 388th Wing, which had preceded us on the target, had encountered MIG's.

As the flight pulled up to gain altitude for delivering our ordnance, I sighted two MIG-21's making a pass at Col. Gast [Lt. Col. Philip C. Gast, the flight leader] from his 4 o'clock position. I was in lead's 8:30 o'clock position. I broke toward the MIG's and passed across his tail. They broke off the attack and I continued on my dive delivery. Flak was normal for the area. We delivered our ordnance as planned.

As the flight pulled out at an altitude of approximately 3,000 to 4,000 feet, Gast called MIG's at 2 o'clock low. "Let's go get them," he urged. "I'm with you," Brestel acknowledged as he spotted the flight of four MIG-17's in staggered trail heading north at approximately 1,500 feet. Behind them was another flight of four. Brestel's narrative continues:

> I observed all MIG's light their afterburners. Colonel Gast began firing at one of the first two MIG's. I observed the second two begin to fire at Colonel Gast. I called a break and closed to within 300–500 feet of the number four MIG. I fired an approximate 2½ second burst at him as he was in a right turn. I observed hits in the wing and fuselage. The MIG reversed into a left turn. I fired another 2½ second burst into him, observing hits in the left wing, fuselage and canopy, and a fire in the left wing root. The aircraft rolled over and hit the ground under my left wing. I then closed 300 feet on the number three MIG, which was firing at Colonel Gast. He was in a right turn and again I fired a 2½ second burst, observing hits in wing, fuselage, etc. He also reversed to the left and I fired another 2½ second burst, observing more hits and pieces flying off the aircraft. The aircraft appeared to flip back up over my canopy and disappeared behind me. We broke off the engagement at this time after approximately 1½ to 2 minutes of combat. A SAM was fired at us and more flak as we exited the area.

> I know I destroyed the first MIG, as I saw him crash. I did not see the pilot bail out and doubt if he was alive, since hits were observed in the cockpit and the canopy broke up. My wingman,

Lt. Weskamp [1st Lt. Robert L. Weskamp] also observed the MIG hit the ground.

I feel I also destroyed the second MIG, as the range was the same and hits were observed in the same areas, i.e., fuselage, wings, etc. Also, his last maneuver could not be considered normal. The aircraft appeared to be in a violent pitch-up or tumble and out of control . . . However, because he pitched up and over and behind, I did not see him strike the ground.

Brestel was given credit for destroying both MIG's.

The third MIG-17 destroyed during the month was credited to the 355th TFW commander, Colonel Scott, who was leading an F-105 flight on a strike mission not far from Hoa Lac airfield on 26 March. His account follows:

I had acquired the target and executed a dive-bomb run. During the recovery from the run, while heading approximately 250°, altitude approximately 4,000 feet, I observed a MIG taking off from Hoa Lac airfield. I began a left turn to approximately 150° to follow the MIG for possible engagement. At this time I observed three more MIG-17's orbiting the airfield at approximately 3,000 feet, in single ship trail with 3,000 to 5,000 feet spacing. MIG's were silver with red star. I then concentrated my attention on the nearest MIG-17 and pressed the attack. As I closed on the MIG it began a turn to the right. I followed the MIG, turning inside, and began firing. I observed ordnance impacting on the left wing of the MIG and pieces of material tearing off. At this time the MIG began a hard left-descending turn. I began an overshoot and pulled off high and to the right. The last time I saw the MIG it was extremely low, approximately 500 feet, and rolling nose down.

Heavy Opposition Again

The northeast monsoon ended, and the weather improved considerably during April. The impetus of U.S. air activity shifted northward. American strikes against key targets in the north grew heavier, smashing at the enemy's war-making capabilities in the Red River delta and harassing his northern lines of communication. Increased numbers of aircraft, modernization, new munitions, and improved tactics made these strikes more effective than ever before. Stung by these punishing blows, North Vietnam sent it's MIG's aloft in larger numbers to protect its vital resources.

MIG-17's by now had initiated a tactic which had been popular with U.S. aviators in the First World War: the Lufberry circle defensive tactic. Remaining in a continuously turning orbit to provide each other mutual defensive support, two, three, and sometimes four MIG's formed the circle. This formation allowed coverage of everyone's 6 o'clock position—the most vulnerable point. The circle could tighten, keeping the faster-flying, heavier U.S. aircraft from entering. Or, each time a USAF aircraft attempted to engage a MIG, another MIG from across the circle could go to full power and pull across the circle, thus placing itself in a firing position on the attacking American plane. American aircraft were at disadvantage because the MIG's had a tighter turn radius.

To counter the Lufberry defense, U.S. pilots learned to coordinate their attacks and to break individual MIG's out of the orbit pattern. High speed was essential for success. U.S. aircraft crews were warned not to enter a duel with the orbiting MIG's and to make only hit-and-run attacks. With this maneuver, NVN gained a means of efficiently using a MIG-17 force composed of a small cadre of experienced pilots and large numbers of inexperienced pilots.

With surplus speed, MIG-21 pilots often employed a climbing turn as a defensive tactic because of the maneuverability and climbing advantage of their aircraft. For low-speed maneuvers, they often dived in a high-G turn. With lower wing-loading than U.S. models, the MIG-21 could accomplish a much tighter turn. MIG-17 pilots also employed dives to avoid missiles, which would then impact into the ground.

The first MIG engagements in April which resulted in kills came on the 19th. The 355th TFW's fighter-bomber pilots had reason to take pride in the four MIG-17's they destroyed that day. Three separate flights were involved in a hectic afternoon of aerial combat in the Xuan Mai army barracks target

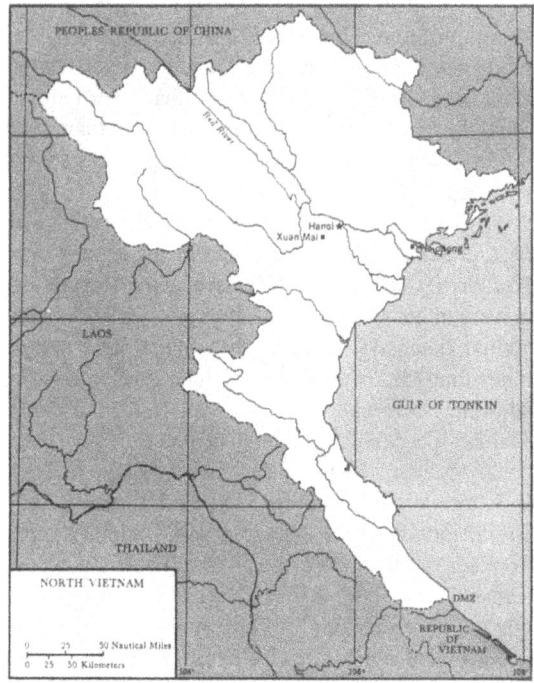

area. While several other flights had engaged MIG's they achieved no victories.

The first MIG kill of the day was recorded by Maj. Leo K. Thorsness, pilot, and Capt. Harold E. Johnson, Electronic Warfare Officer (EWO), flying in an F–105F. Thorsness' flight consisted of four F–105F Wild Weasel aircraft, each plane being manned by a pilot and EWO and being specially equipped to locate and attack SAM sites. The flight was ahead of the main strike force and was committed to suppress SAM activity in the target area. About 8 to 10 MIG–17's attacked as the flight prepared to strike a SAM radar site with Shrike air-to-ground missiles. The Thorsness flight split up into three parts: the third and fourth aircraft entered into separate MIG engagements while Thorsness and his wingman continued the attack against the radar. The time was then about 4:55 p.m. Johnson provides an account of the encounter:

> We found and delivered our ordnance on an occupied SAM site. As we pulled off the site heading west, Kingfish 02* called that he had an

---

*Radio call sign for aircraft 2.

overheat light. He also headed west, and the crew, Majors Thomas M. Madison, pilot, and Thomas J. Sterling, EWO, had to eject from their aircraft. We headed toward them by following the UHF-DF steer we received from their electronic beepers and saw them in the chutes . . .

As we circled the descending crew, we were on a south easterly heading when I spotted a MIG–17 heading east, low at our 9 o'clock position. I called him to the attention of Major Thorsness . . .

Thorsness continued the story:

> The MIG was heading east and was approximately 2,500 feet mean sea level. We were heading southeast and at 8,000 feet MSL. I began "S" turning to get behind the MIG. After one and a half "S" turns the MIG had progressed from the foothills over the delta southwest of Hanoi. The MIG turned to a northerly heading, maintaining approximately the same altitude and airspeed. Captain Johnson continued to give me SAM bearings, SAM-PRF [pulse recurrence frequency] status and launch indications as I continued to maneuver to attain a 6 o'clock position on the MIG.
>
> The first burst of approximately 300 rounds of 20-mm was fired from an estimated 2,000–1,500 feet in a right hand shallow pursuit curve, firing with a cased sight reticle. No impacts were observed on the MIG. Within a few seconds we were in the 6 o'clock position with approximately 75 to 100 knots overtake speed. I fired another burst of approximately 300 rounds of 20-mm. I pulled up to avoid both the debris and the MIG. While pulling up I rolled slightly to the right, then left. The MIG was approximately 100 feet low and to our left, rolling to the right. The two red stars were clearly discernible, one on top of each wing, and several rips were noted on the battered left wing. We continued in a turn to the left and after turning approximately 130° again sighted the MIG, still in a right descending spiral. Just prior to the MIG's impacting the ground, Captain Johnson sighted a MIG–17 at our 6:30 position approximately 2,000 feet back. I pulled into a tighter left turn, selected afterburner, and lowered the nose. I again looked at the crippled MIG, saw

it impact the ground in what appeared to be a rice field. After confirming the MIG had in fact impacted the ground I made a hard reversal and descended to very near the ground, heading generally westerly into the foothills.

Thorsness then left the battle area, but returned after refueling to provide rescue combat air patrol during the search for his wingman's aircrew. Thorsness and Johnson attacked another MIG and scored some damaging hits before they were themselves attacked by other MIG-17's. Although it is highly probable that Thorsness and Johnson destroyed a second MIG, this kill was not confirmed.

Another flight of F-105's striking Xuan Mai Army barracks entered the target area a few minutes after the Thorsness flight. This flight was soon attacked by about 11 MIG-17's. Maj. Jack W. Hunt was the first of their number to engage in aerial combat. Flying lead, Hunt missed the first MIG with an AIM-9 missile, got into another fight but missed with his 20-mm gunfire, and made his kill during his third engagement.

This time, he reported, "I observed numerous hits and flashes coming from the top of the fuselage just behind the canopy. My pipper at this firing position was just forward and a little high on his canopy. I observed no large pieces of materiel coming from his aircraft." The MIG broke hard right and down, trailing a small amount of smoke. Hunt's gun camera film pack did not operate properly, but his MIG kill was confirmed by other evidence. At the time that Hunt was preoccupied with his third engagement, the flight's number three pilot, Maj. Frederick G. Tolman also encountered a MIG-17. Tolman writes:

I closed to gun firing range, at which time the MIG broke hard left. I fired approximately 300 rounds of 20-mm at him and observed hits around his canopy section. The MIG passed by my aircraft going to my 6 o'clock position. I engaged afterburner and performed a high-climbing turn for re-engagement. Upon sighting the MIG again I noted a trail of white smoke coming from his tailpipe. He was in a climbing attitude, about 40° nose up, when I observed him, and approximately 2 miles away. I saw him roll slowly to the left and start a gentle descent.

Tolman's gun camera film confirmed his MIG kill.

The third flight encountered two separate MIG's over Xuan Mai army barracks. In the first aerial duel, Capt. William Eskew, flying aircraft 1, and Capt. Paul A. Seymour, flying his wing, each scored hits on MIG-17's, but apparently damage was not critical to either enemy aircraft. In the second encounter, while his F-105 flight was assisting in RESCAP operations for a downed F-105F, Capt. Eskew's gunfire proved fatal to another MIG-17. He provides the following account.

As we were approaching the area of the downed aircrews, Sandy 02* (an A-1E) made a desperate call for help. Sandy 02 stated that he had four MIG-17's making firing passes at him and that the MIG's had just downed his leader, Sandy 01.

I immediately headed for the area of Sandy 02. Spotting the four MIG-17's, I took my flight directly through the MIG formation in an attempt to draw them off Sandy 02 and thus allow [him] to egress the area. After my flight passed through the MIG formation at a speed of Mach 1.05-1.1, I turned back to the right in an attempt to engage the MIG's.

The lead MIG apparently decided to run for home at this time. I pulled in behind the lead MIG and fired my AIM-9B at him. My missile passed directly under his aircraft at a distance of approximately 15 feet, but failed to detonate. At this time I broke off to the left and observed my number three man—Capt. Howard L. Bodenhamer—firing at a MIG-17 while both were in a descending left turn. I saw number three score numerous hits in the left wing and wing root area of the MIG. Also, there was a second MIG behind number three, firing at him while he was firing at the MIG in front. Panda 04 was behind this MIG, firing. Behind me was a fourth MIG, and behind this MIG was Panda 02 (Seymour).

At this time the fight broke down into a Lufberry circle at approximately 3,000 feet actual ground level. The order of the circle was MIG, Panda 03, MIG, Panda 04, MIG, Panda 01†, MIG, Panda 02. Panda 02 fired at the MIG behind

___
*Radio call sign for an A-1E Flying RESCAP in the area.
†Eskew's aircraft.

me, causing this MIG to break off from the fight. I then fired two short bursts at the MIG in front of me. This MIG broke off to the right and started a gentle climb toward the Hanoi area. I pulled in behind this MIG and, at an estimated range of 800–1,000 feet, began firing. My pipper was directly on the canopy of the MIG. I continued firing to a range of 50 feet. I saw an estimated 50–75 hits on the upper fuselage directly behind the canopy.

As I passed through 100 feet, firing, the MIG started a slow, gentle roll to the left. The roll could not have possibly been an evasive maneuver as the MIG never exceeded 1½ G's and his rate of roll was quite slow. As I pulled up to avoid a collision with the MIG, he exploded directly beneath my aircraft. I saw the red fireball and was shaken by the shock. At this time I broke back to help Panda 03 (Bodenhamer) who was engaging two MIG's. Glancing back at the downed MIG, I saw the wreckage of his aircraft burning on the ground . . . I could see smoke from both Sandy 01 and the MIG. As I passed behind the MIG which was firing at Panda 03, the MIG broke into me. Captain Bodenhamer then turned and fired his AIM-9B at this MIG. I did not see the missile impact. We then broke off the fight and proceeded to an emergency post-strike refueling.

MIG Fight for Survival

MIG aircraft enjoyed particular advantages in defending North Vietnam. Unlike USAF aircraft flying far from home bases and being subjected to heavy SAM, AAA/AW, and MIG threats in NVN, MIG's operated over friendly territory close to their six primary bases. This permitted far better dispersal and spontaneous recovery in the Hanoi area. Moreover, they enjoyed relative freedom of operation, because the U.S. restricted its aircraft from bombing bases in sanctuary areas. The MIG's made the best of these advantages, and, as NVN built up its air force, USAF and USN aircraft losses increased. And as they climbed, pressure mounted amongst Americans to remove the bombing restrictions. Indeed, because of this pressure the immunity ceased.

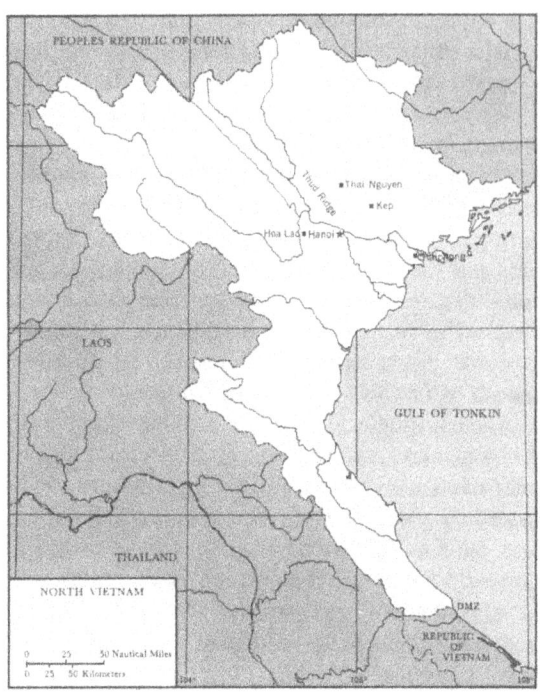

The United States finally, in April 1967, removed North Vietnamese air bases from the exemption status, and the Joint Chiefs of Staff approved air strikes against Kep and Hoa Lac airfields. Kep was probably the most active of the bases, and Hoa Lac was nearing completion at this time. Both were lucrative targets rich with MIG's. The first strike against the MIG's was carried out on 23 April followed by others. On the 23rd, USAF aircraft with certainty destroyed nine MIG's on the ground and possibly three more. Follow-up strikes on 28 April and on 1 and 3 May accounted for 20 more, although several assessments were in question. The strikes and aerial combat inflicted severe losses on the NVN Air Force, and the MIG's now struggled to survive.

The die had been cast and the MIG's had no choice but to accept the challenge. Their reaction was vigorous. During April, following the initial air strikes, and especially in May, air-to-air combat became particularly intense.

While flying an air strike mission on 23 April, three F-4C's from the 366th TFW encountered two flights of two MIG-21's each. Maj. Robert D. Anderson, aircraft commander in aircraft 3 position, flying with Capt. Fred D. Kjer as pilot, made the

Capt. Kjer (left) and Maj. Anderson. The MIG pilot they shot down never "knew what hit him."

only MIG kill during this encounter. According to the after-action report:

Chicago* saw the MIG's (two MIG-21's) turning into the strike force and jettisoned bombs and left outboard external wing tanks to engage. The MIG's were in a staggered trail formation and entered a left climbing turn to a general heading of west. Chicago was unable to turn tight enough to decrease angle-off and reversed to the right to rejoin the strike force.

The flight immediately sighted two more MIG-21's in staggered trail passing off the right wing. The MIG's entered a right climbing turn at max[imum] power. Chicago 01 began a right turn, attempting to set up an attack on the lead MIG. The other MIG was in the contrail level at this time in a left turn. The missile fired from Chicago lead was tracking the MIG when both went into a cirrus cloud.

Chicago 03 continued accelerating to attack the other MIG. With the pipper on the MIG, a boresight radar lock-on was obtained and then a full system lock-on. At this time the range was marginally close for a successful Sparrow shot. A climbing turn to the outside was initiated and the pipper placed again on the target. The radar was still locked on.

*Radio call sign for the flight.

One missile was fired that left the aircraft going slightly right of the MIG-21, but guided back to the target, striking the MIG in the right aft fuselage. A large explosion was observed and fire and fuel began streaming from the MIG. It continued the left turn and bank increased until inverted and the plane went straight into the ground. The MIG was hit around 32,000 feet. No chute was observed prior to aircraft impact, approximately 16 miles northeast of Thai Nguyen.

"The one thing I learned," Anderson later commented, "is that you can't afford to be complacent up there. You have to keep looking around. He [the MIG pilot] thought he was out of the fight, home free. He made no evasive maneuvers. I don't think he ever saw me or knew what hit him."

Three days later, on the 26th, the 366th destroyed another MIG-21—this one was hit by Maj. Rolland W. Moore and his pilot, 1st Lt. James F. Sears. They were flying the lead aircraft in a MIGCAP flight dispatched to cover a large F-105 strike force attacking the Hanoi transformer site. The flight met about ten MIG-21's with Moore engaging three of them in turn.

Moore looked up at 9-10 o'clock and picked out one of the several MIG-21's orbiting to the left over Phuc Yen. He turned hard, nose high, to get at the MIG's at a 7 o'clock position. He got one in his sight reticle, and selected radar, while Sears went boresight until he obtained a full system lock-on.

"We've got him," called out Sears. "Fire!"

Moore depressed the trigger. The AIM-7 tracked smoothly toward the MIG's 6 o'clock position. The deadly missile gained on the MIG—2,000 feet, 1,000 feet, trailing steady. The MIG rolled out of the turn and disappeared from Moore's sight into the cumulus clouds at the southern end of Thud Ridge, but this maneuver wasn't sufficient to escape the explosion.

This air battle had taken place near Phuc Yen airfield, where the F-4's came under AAA fire in spite of the proximity of the MIG's. All flight members felt that the MIG's could have landed at the airfield at any time, but chose instead to lure the flight over the field, where the enemy appeared to be coordinating the attack between SAM's, MIG's, and AAA.

Two MIG-17's were bagged by pilots of a flight from the 355th TFW on 28 April, while on strike missions against the Han Phong causeway, 12 miles west of Hanoi. The first was downed by flight leader Maj. Harry E. Higgins and the second by another flight leader, Lt. Col. Arthur F. Dennis. Higgins preceded Dennis into the target area by 6 minutes. His flight had just pulled off the target when a number of MIG-17's attacked—there were about nine of them. Higgins later reported on the battle:

> After recovering from the bomb delivery, I observed a MIG-17 in my 2 o'clock position. I immediately turned into the MIG and engaged in a series of turning maneuvers, finally gaining the 6 o'clock position. While gaining this position, I completed my cockpit switch setting and, when reaching approximately 3,000 feet, fired the AIM-9 missile. The MIG immediately tightened his turn to the right and the missile missed by 1,000 feet behind and below the hostile aircraft.
>
> By this time my wingman, 1st Lt. Gordon Jenkins, had regained excellent position and we continued our turn to the west for egress from the area. Rolling out westerly, we immediately spotted two MIG-17's in our 1 o'clock position. As the MIG's approached in a head-on pass we could see they were firing cannon. As the closure distance decreased, we also fired bursts at the MIG aircraft without any visible damage. We turned to pursue the MIG's; however, they continued southeast and were well out of range as we fell into their 6 o'clock position.
>
> Again we turned to egress heading, and I spotted a single MIG-17 in a left turn, heading south. I immediately turned into the enemy and engaged afterburner for closure. I completed the switch settings for guns and began to close. The MIG tightened his turn, but was slow in doing so. This allowed me to gain a 30° cut-off angle and when I was approximately 1,500 feet I began to fire the 20-mm cannon. As I prolonged the firing I noticed the MIG began to smoke, and flames erupted from his left wing root section. He began a steep descending turn with the left wing down at approximately 1,000 feet.
>
> I continued to position myself for another firing pass, but we were forced to break hard right to offset two more MIG's who were firing at us from 1,000 feet in our 5–6 o'clock position. The MIG's chased us at a high rate of speed until we finally outdistanced them by applying negative-G forces and obtaining a great amount of airspeed. My last glance at the MIG which I had hit showed him burning and spiraling toward the ground at less than 500 feet.

The Dennis flight did not encounter a MIG until the F-105's were departing the target area. The MIG was on the tail of another F-105 and Dennis went to his assistance. In his own words, the engagement proved easy:

> I closed on the MIG-17, and when I obtained a missile tone in my headset I fired the AIM-9. The firing was normal; however, the missile did not guide. I continued closing until about 3,000 to 4,000 feet and began firing 20-mm, but realized I was still too far out for a good firing pass . . . . The MIG at this time was in a shallow right turn, level, and apparently did not see me because he did not attempt evasive action. I continued closing to approximately 1,500 feet, began firing, closing to about 700 feet, and the MIG burst into a large ball of flame. It continued to burn and trail smoke as it went into a steeper turn to the right and nosed over into a wide spiral toward the ground.
>
> I continued to watch it in its spiral near the ground, but I had to reverse my turn to move out of the target area because I was receiving SAM launch indications. When I rolled back to the left toward my egress route, the MIG impact with the ground should have been in my 7–8 o'clock position but I was unable to see it.

Two days later, on the morning of the 30th, another 355th TFW pilot, Capt. Thomas C. Lesan, downed a MIG-17 while he was leading the third and last flight of F-105's striking rail yards northeast of Bac Giang. Lesan describes his part in the air battle:

> Rattler* flight was attacked by three MIG-17's while ingressing, prior to pop and again at the top of the pop† prior to the bomb run. I continued my

---

*Radio call sign for the flight.
†This refers to a "pop-up maneuver," which tactical aircraft use in transitioning from the low-level approach phase of an attack mission to an altitude and point from which the target can be identified and attacked.

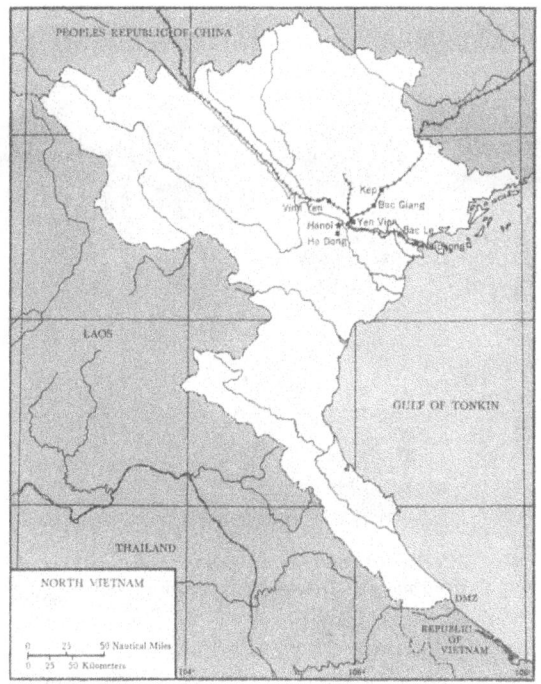

dive bomb run and jinked [constantly maneuvered] right after delivery at approximately 3,000 feet actual ground level and then back left and started a shallow climb. At this moment I sighted two MIG-17's at my 11 o'clock position, approximately 3,000 feet high and 3,000 feet out. I jettisoned my 450-gallon drop tanks and with my afterburner still engaged from the bomb run, began to pursue the two MIG's. I estimate that my overtake was in excess of 100 knots.

As I started to track the number two MIG they both started a rolling descending turn to the right and I followed, rolling to about 120° and descending at 30°. I tracked and opened fire at approximately 1,000 feet. I fired 100 rounds of 20-mm, noting hits impacting down the left side of the forward fuselage and on the left wing. With such a great rate of closure, I had to break left to avoid collision with the MIG. After clearing him and climbing to maintain an altitude advantage, I rolled right and observed the MIG slowly leveling out with his left wing in flames as his leader continued the right turn.

Trailing about 1 mile behind Lesan was Maj. James H. Middleton, Jr., who observed the flaming MIG start to spin out of control at about 4,000 ft. It then disappeared to the right out of his field of view.

But there were also repercussions. On the same day the USAF also lost three F-105's. Since the beginning of the year, F-4 aircraft had been employed more for strike missions than for MIGCAP, but if the bombing campaign was to be continued without unacceptable losses of strike aircraft, it would be necessary to divert a portion of them back to MIGCAP role. Accordingly, USAF leaders in Southeast Asia began to sandwich a flight of F-4's behind a lead flight of F-105's and to place another Phantom flight in trail behind strike forces. As a result, during May, 26 MIG's were destroyed with a loss of only 2 Phantoms in 72 USAF and USN MIG encounters. Most of the MIG victories were credited to USAF fighters. While many of them were the victims of the MIGCAP Phantom crews, several were downed by aggressive Thunderchief pilots.

The first victory in which F-4C's were providing MIGCAP barrier for F-105 flights came on 1 May 1967, while the F-105's were on a RESCAP mission. Maj. Robert G. Dilger was flight leader; 1st Lt. Mack Thies was his back-seater. Dilger detected two or three enemy aircraft approaching from his 12 o'clock position at 8,000 feet and descending, at which time he warned his flight of the MIG's, which then pulled up vertical and rolled to the right, enabling the F-4's to end up in a 6 o'clock positon to the first two MIG's. Dilger and his wingman engaged the enemy, and one of them fell. Dilger wrote:

> I acquired a boresight lock-on and fired an AIM-7. The MIG-17 dove for the deck and made a hard turn into the attack. The missile missed. I yo-yoed and again was at the MIG's 6 o'clock. I fired a Sidewinder which could not turn with the MIG-17, as he broke into the attack and went even lower. In exactly the same manner I yo-yoed and fired two more missiles from his 6 o'clock. On each attack he would violently break into the missile. On the fourth pass he broke hard right and struck the ground while trying to avoid the missile, which was tracking toward his 6 o'clock. He spread in flames across a large area.

On 4 May, the 8th TFW at Ubon provided two

flights of Phantoms for MIGCAP for five F–105 flights of the 355th TFW which were on a strike mission. Col. Robin Olds, 8th Wing commander, led the rear flight, flying with 1st Lt. William D. Lafever. The other F–4 flight was sandwiched midway in the strike force. MIG warnings crackled on Olds' radio just before his wingman sighted two MIG–21's at 11 o'clock, attacking the last of the Thunderchief flights. Colonel Olds' account picks up the encounter at this point:

> The MIG's were at my 10 o'clock position and closing on Drill [the F–105 flight] from their 7:30 position. I broke the rear flight into the MIG's, called the F–105's to break, and maneuvered to obtain a missile firing position on one of the MIG–21's. I obtained a boresight lock-on, interlocks in, went full system, kept the pipper on the MIG, and fired two AIM–7's in a ripple. One AIM–7 went ballistic. The other guided but passed behind the MIG and did not detonate. Knowing that I was then too close for further AIM–7 firing, I maneuvered to obtain AIM–9 firing parameters. The MIG–21 was maneuvering violently and firing position was difficult to achieve. I snapped two AIM–9's at the MIG and did not observe either missile. The MIG then reversed and presented the best parameter yet. I achieved a loud growl, tracked, and fired one AIM–9. From the moment of launch, it was obvious that the missile was locked on. It guided straight for the MIG and exploded about 5–10 feet beneath his tailpipe.
>
> The MIG then went into a series of frantic

Maj. Dilger (left) and Lt. Thies (right) explain to Lt. Col. Hoyt S. Vandenberg Jr. how they forced down a MIG–17 in a dogfight on 1 May 1967.

> turns, some of them so violent that the aircraft snap-rolled in the opposite direction. Fire was coming from the tailpipe, but I was not sure whether it was normal afterburner or damage-induced. I fired the remaining AIM–9 at one point, but the shot was down toward the ground and the missile did not discriminate. I followed the MIG as he turned southeast and headed for Phuc Yen. The aircraft ceased maneuvering and went in a straight slant for the airfield. I stayed 2,500 feet behind him and observed a brilliant white fire streaming from the left side of his fuselage. It looked like magnesium burning with particles flaking off. I had to break off to the right as I neared Phuc Yen runway at about 2,000 feet, due to heavy, accurate, 85–mm barrage. I lost sight of the MIG at that point. Our number 3 saw the MIG continue in a straight gentle dive and impact approximately 100 yards south of the runway.

Colonel Olds then took his flight to the target area and covered the last of the 355th TFW strike aircraft as they came off the target. Leading his flight to Hoa Lac airfield and dodging two SAM's on the way, he found five MIG–17's over that airfield.

"We went around with them at altitudes ranging from 1,500 to 6,000 feet, right over the airdrome,"

Olds reported. The F–4's ran low on fuel before any real engagements occurred, however, and were forced to break off this encounter.

Capt. Jacques A. Suzanne, leading a flight of four F–105's on a strike mission on 12 May, scored the next MIG kill. As the lead aircraft in a flak suppression flight of four F–105's approached the target area, five MIG–17's intercepted the strike group. Trying to engage the lead flight, the MIG pilots ended up as targets for Suzanne's flight. Suzanne recalls:

> At this time I turned into the MIG's and tracked the two that broke off to the right. Closing to 4,000 feet of range, I fired one burst of about 200 rounds. The MIG's then reversed to the left and at 800 to 1,000 feet I fired another burst until minimum range. Then I broke off as one MIG went under my left wing in a 70° dive, trailing white smoke. The MIG continued in this descent and disappeared under a shelf of clouds at approximately 1,000 feet of altitude. Crossbow 02* observed the MIG on the way down and saw a bright flash on the ground in the position that the MIG disappeared.

Seven Victories in One Day

On 13 May 1967, two Phantoms and five Thunderchiefs downed seven MIG–17's in aerial combat. The events of this day were reminiscent of Operation Bolo. Two flights of F–105's flew air strikes against the Yen Vien railroad yard, and a flight of F–4C's from the 8th TFW provided MIGCAP for them. Another flight of F–105's from the 388th TFW struck the Vinh Yen army barracks.

After bombing the first target, the F–105's detected three MIG–17's at an altitude of 1,000 feet and 10 miles away in a climbing right turn. The Thunderchiefs turned left to a position of 6 o'clock on the North Vietnamese, who commenced a head-on pass. Lt. Col. Philip C. Gast, flight leader, concentrated his attack on the lead MIG while Capt. Charles W. Couch in aircraft 3 focused his attack on

---

*Radio call sign for Suzanne's wingman, Capt. Lawrence D. Cobb.

the third MIG. When the MIG's closed the gap to between 5,000 and 6,000 feet, Gast fired a Sidewinder, which lost thrust and passed about 200 feet from the enemy aircraft. Couch received a tone from his Sidewinder, but since his aircraft was pointed in the general direction of the sun, he felt that most of the growl came from that celestial body and did not use his heat-seeking missile.

"As they approached head-on," Gast later stated, "I began firing my Vulcan gun at 3,000 feet and fired down to minimum range." The MIG–17 did not return fire. "I think we really caught them off guard."

Gast's wingman, Maj. Alonzo L. Ferguson, supported his flight leader's claim. "As I looked to the rear [after the MIG's passed below] I noted a gray cloud of smoke, tinged with pink, receding in the distance."

Couch's attack was also successful. He stated:

> I lined up on their number three man and fired a long burst from my 20-mm cannon. The MIG and I were closing head-on at this time, and at very close range he broke hard left and disappeared from my view. Another flight in trail with us observed a MIG pilot eject and another MIG in a spin. Major Ferguson saw pinkish smoke trailing from one MIG, presumably the one fired on by Col. Gast. The MIG–17 I was firing at took violent evasive action to avoid a head-on collision with me, and very likely could have entered a spin.

A second flight of F–105's, led by Maj. Robert G. Rilling, struck the Yen Vien railroad and encountered MIG's when leaving the target area. Rilling went after the first MIG:

> I called for afterburners and we closed on two of the MIG's, and when in range I fired my AIM–9. The missile detonated just to the right and under the tail of the MIG. The aircraft began burning immediately and pieces were observed falling off. I followed the aircraft through a 180° left turn in an attempt to use the Vulcan cannon. After completing a 180° left turn the MIG rolled hard right and down and impacted.

Maj. Carl D. Osborne, flying in aircraft position 3 in Rilling's flight, went after a second MIG. He had no trouble tracking the enemy aircraft. In his account he writes:

> I rolled into a slight right bank and the tone on the AIM-9 peaked up normally. Only a 10° left bank was required to hold the reticle on the MIG. The tone was holding good so I fired the missile and it began tracking and detonated at the MIG's 3-4 o'clock position. . . . He immediately turned left and began trailing smoke. My lead called [that] he had scored a hit also, on the other MIG, and to go after them. I made a hard left turn and observed the MIG that I had fired at still trailing smoke and descending, heading south-southeast. . . . My turn caused a great loss of airspeed and also allowed a third MIG-17 to turn inside of me by the time I had completed 180° of turn. This MIG was now at my 9 o'clock position and began firing. I didn't believe he was either in range of me or had any lead on me; however, my wingman was in a more vulnerable position, so I dropped the nose and unloaded the G's and began accelerating to 550-600 knots. As I began to dive I saw the MIG stop firing and break to his right and away from my element. He would have had a good pass on myself and aircraft 4, but I saw Captain Seymour, who had lagged in the left climbing turn and stayed low, in a good firing position on this MIG. Seymour was firing, but I was unable to assess any damage by Seymour except that my attacker broke off and stopped firing.

Capt. Paul A. Seymour, who had become separated from his flight and joined up with Rilling, not only observed the aerial victories of Rilling and Osborne but he himself may have damaged the MIG-17 which attacked Osborne. He claimed hits on the MIG's fuselage and right wing.

One of two F-4 flights providing MIGCAP for the Yen Vien air strike on 13 May was leaving the area when crews observed the air battle between F-105's and MIG-17's. Flight leader Maj. William L. Kirk and his pilot, 1st Lt. Stephen A. Wayne, and his wingman immediately broke off to go after the MIG's, while aircraft 3 and 4 remained high to provide air cover. Kirk accounted for his first MIG kill and reported:

> I observed two MIG-17's firing at an F-105 which was in a hard left turn. The F-105 reversed underneath and dove for the deck. The MIG's started to reverse, then pulled up and started a left turn again.
>
> In this reversal, I switched to heat-mode for Sidewinder missiles, obtained a good tone, and fired two Sidewinders. The first missile tracked well and exploded approximately 30 feet behind the MIG. The MIG started a very tight left diving spiral turn. The MIG was on fire from the trailing edge of his left wing to the tail section. I lost sight of the MIG in this spiral, as he went underneath my aircraft.

Kirk saw two more MIG-17's and fired a Sidewinder at them, but the missile did not have a tone and missed. He then attacked a third MIG with a Sparrow missile, but both the aircraft and the missile disappeared into a cloud with unknown results. Meanwhile, Lt. Col. Fred A. Haeffner* and 1st Lt. Michael R. Bever in aircraft 3 had observed Kirk's successful AIM-9 attack on the MIG just before Haeffner dove after two MIG's chasing Thunderchiefs. Haeffner attempted to fire only two AIM-7 missiles from an overhead position, but inadvertently fired three. Dropping below the nose and out of sight, the first missile failed to guide and missed the MIG by about 100 feet. The second fired from a slightly lower altitude, dropped out of sight, but reappeared. Haeffner and Bever saw it hit the MIG on the fuselage just behind the canopy. The MIG disintegrated. The third missile was last seen guiding to the vicinity of the destroyed MIG-17. Maj. Ronald E. Catton, flying in aircraft position 4, also saw the action. "The MIG seemed to blow up on the spot," he commented. "The second missile powdered the MIG; it broke up into many disorganized pieces."

The seventh MIG-17 of the day was destroyed by Maj. Maurice E. Seaver, Jr. of the 388th TFW. After pulling out from his bomb run, Seaver observed a camouflaged MIG-17 at his 10 o'clock position, about 1,000 feet away. He pulled in behind

---

*Haeffner was assigned to the 390th TFS, 366th TFW at the time of this aerial victory. However, he was serving a one-week exchange TDY with the 433d TFS, 8th TFW, and that squadron and wing earned the victory credit, rather than his parent squadron and wing.

A close-up of a MIG-17 in flight.

it and opened fire with his 20-mm cannon. The MIG pilot apparently did not see the Thunderchief, for he made no effort to evade. When the MIG was hit, it broke sharply to the right and its wing exploded. The entire encounter lasted less than 90 seconds.

Over the months of air-to-air combat, many MIG's escaped destruction by the F-4's simply because there was a deficiency in the Phantom's short-range kill capability. At medium range, they could use the infrared heat-seeking AIM-9 Sidewinder; at long range, they had the radar beam-riding AIM-7 Sparrow. But aircrews were unable to maneuver their F-4's to fire these missiles at short range, and many of the MIG's escaped. In May 1967, however, the F-4's began carrying the SUU-16 gun pods to complement the missiles, and immediately the short-range deficiency was corrected.

The first MIG's fell prey to this weapon on 14 May, when F-4C aircrews of the 366th TFW destroyed three MIG-17's; two of them were shot down by the SUU-16. An F-4 flight trailed an F-105 strike force attacking the Ha Dong army barracks and supply depot; another F-4 flight was spaced between the F-105 flights. Both of the Phantom flights were providing MIGCAP. The first flight encountered 16 MIG-17's, destroying two of them; the other flight encountered 10 MIG-17's and destroyed one.

The first flight, led by Maj. James A. Hargrove, Jr., and 1st Lt. Stephen H. DeMuth, heard MIG warnings after it departed its refueling point. The lead F-105 called bogies at 9 o'clock, and Hargrove spotted two F-105's leaving the target area. Four MIG-17's in two elements were in hot pursuit.

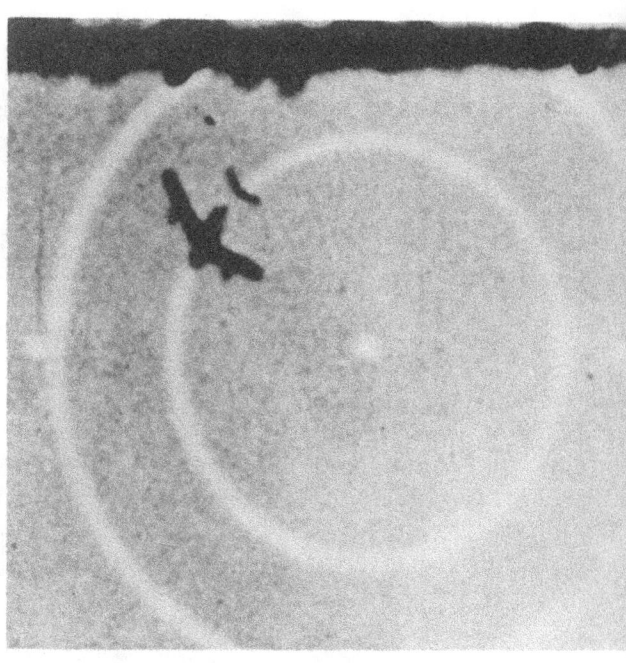

On the gun camera of his F-105 Thunderchief, Maj. Seaver recorded this view of the MIG-17 he shot down in the 90-second encounter on 13 May.

Dropping their fuel tanks, Hargrove and his wingman headed for one element while aircraft 3 and 4 attacked the second. For the next 20 minutes the scene was a beehive of activity as the F-4's took on in combat 7 of the 16 MIG's. At least one SAM was fired at the U.S. flight during the air battle.

Hargrove's victory came after 5 minutes of battle, during which he fired Sidewinders and Sparrows against three other MIG-17's. He missed all three. On his fourth engagement, he elected to use the SUU-16 gun pod. According to Hargrove:

> The MIG-17 was in a right-descending turn when we attacked from a 20° angle off its tail. I opened fire at approximately 2,000 feet from the MIG and continued firing until, at approximately 300 feet, flame erupted from the top of the MIG fuselage. Almost immediately thereafter the MIG exploded. . . . I broke left to avoid debris, then reversed to the right and saw the MIG, in two sections, falling vertically toward the ground. Due to other MIG's attacking our aircraft we were forced to exit the immediate area before the MIG struck the ground.

These two Phantom crews made history for the Air Force on 14 May 1967, when each crew shot down a MIG–17 with 20-mm Gatling guns mounted on their F-4's. Maj. Hargrove (l. to r.) and his pilot, Lt. DeMuth, Capt. Craig and his pilot, Lt. Talley.

An F-4C Refueling.

Five minutes later, Capt. James T. Craig, Jr., commander of aircraft 3, and his back-seater, 1st Lt. James T. Talley, also downed a MIG with a 20-mm gun after missing two other MIG–17's with Sparrow missiles. Craig describes his tactics:

Three MIG–17's were sighted at 9 o'clock low in a left turn. I barrel rolled to the right and rolled in behind the trailing MIG. He tightened up his left turn, then reversed hard to the right as I approached gun range. I followed the MIG through the turn reversal, pulled lead, and fired a 2½ second burst from my 20-mm cannon. Flames immediately erupted from his right wing root and extended past the tailpipe. As I yo-yoed high the MIG rolled out to wing level in a slight descent and I observed fire coming from the left fuselage area. I initiated a follow-up attack; however, before I could fire, the MIG burst into flames from the cockpit aft and immediately pitched over and dived vertically into the very low undercast. The tops of the clouds were approximately 4,000 feet MSL* with the higher mountains protruding slightly above them. The attitude of the aircraft and the proximity to the ground would have precluded a successful recovery. No ejection was observed.

"The kills with the gun mode could not have been made with a missile," Craig later commented. Both MIG's were picked off from incomplete Wagon Wheel formations.

MIG's encountered by the second flight also used the same circular tactics. Maj. Samuel O. Bakke and Capt. Robert W. Lambert, flying in the lead aircraft, got their victory at the same time that Craig and Talley made their kill. Unlike Hargrove's aircraft, Bakke's Phantom was not equipped with SUU-16 gun pods. All of the aircrews were in agreement that the 20-mm guns "would have been much more effective against the MIG-17's than any of the missiles."

The strike aircraft and Hargrove had alerted Bakke's flight about the MIG's. Bakke explains how he and his flight took the offensive:

> I observed several enemy aircraft at my 11 o'clock low position. The flight attacked these MIG's, diving from 17,000 feet MSL to the enemy's altitude of approximately 6,000 feet MSL. My first engagement . . . was unsuccessful due to the two Sidewinder missiles not guiding to the target. An attack was commenced on another MIG-17 in the area and discontinued because of the target outmaneuvering the attacker. After a high-speed yo-yo to an altitude of approximately 10,000 feet MSL I noticed two MIG's at my 10 o'clock low position.

Bakke and his wingman then attacked the enemy fighters by rolling outside in the direction of turn of the enemy. "As this roll commenced I saw a MIG-17 explode in flames and start spinning in a vertical nose-down attitude towards the ground," he recalled.

Continuing the attack on the two MIG-17's, Bakke chose one on the outside of his left turn and

———
*Mean sea level.

called the pilot to try for a radar lock-on. "My pilot called that he had a radar lock-on, and I squeezed the trigger with the MIG-17 inside my gunsight reticle. The AIM-7 would not fire," Bakke complained. His radar scope showed a "break-X" display, indicating that he was too close to the target for a successful Sparrow launch. Bakke then realized that with the interlock switch in the "in" position, the AIM-7 would not fire unless all missile firing parameters were satisfied. He continues in his account:

> I retarded my throttles to idle and gained proper range separation from the target. I again glanced at my radar scope and observed an attack display with the steering dot in the center of the allowable steering error (ASE) circle. The ASE circle was very small, indicating I was at minimum Sparrow missile range. I fired two Sparrow missiles while pursuing the target in a left turn. One missile did not guide and the other "homed in" on the target, causing an explosion and fire in the right aft wing root of the MIG-17.
>
> The MIG pitched up to a 30° nose-high attitude at approximately 5,000–6,000 feet altitude MSL and entered the clouds in a stalled condition. The average terrain in the battle area is from 1,000 to 3,000 feet with some mountain peaks of 4,500 feet present. I did not observe a parachute from the burning MIG.
>
> During this engagement I noticed another MIG-17, on fire from the under fuselage, pass below me and to my right. I was in a left turn and about to fire at the time. Another flight of F-4C's was in the area and engaged in aerial combat at the same time. The two MIG-17's seen in flames while I was engaged in my successful attack were probably destroyed by Craig's flight.

North Vietnam lost no MIG aircraft to USAF aircrews for the next 4 days, although air-to-air engagements continued daily. On the 20th, however, two MIG-21's were downed by aircrews of the 366th TFW and four MIG-17's were destroyed by 8th TFW aircrews. Both of the MIG-21's were defeated by a Phantom flight providing MIGCAP for a strike force attacking the Kinh No motor vehicle repair yards.

As the Phantom flight approached the target area, two MIG-21's were attacking the departing strike force. The F-4's immediately broke off to attack the enemy. Maj. Robert D. Janca, the flight leader, with 1st Lt. William E. Roberts, Jr. as his back-seater, reported the engagement:

> I spotted a MIG-21 at my 9-10 o'clock high position. The MIG started turning left into us. I lowered the nose and began a left turn into the MIG, at which time the MIG reversed to the right and started to climb. I continued in the left descending turn to close and then commenced a climbing turn. As the MIG continued to climb I put the pipper on him, received a good tone, and fired an AIM-9 missile with the MIG about 4,000 feet ahead, zero angle-off, and framed against the blue sky. The missile guided straight with very little flutter and detonated about ten to fifteen feet to the right of the MIG's tail. It appeared that a large piece of the MIG's tail came off along with other small pieces. The MIG pitched up and began a roll off to the right from about 8,000 feet, and then appeared to enter a spin. I continued my turn, watching the MIG as he disappeared from my line of sight at approximately 1,000 feet AGL (actual ground level). My pilot, Lt. Roberts, and Elgin 02 [Capt. Daniel S. Burr and 1st Lt. William A. Norton] saw the MIG strike the ground.

Meanwhile, Lt. Col. Robert F. Titus and 1st Lt. Milan Zimer (flying aircraft 3), who had initiated the attack, accompanied by aircraft 4, pursued the two MIG-21's they had seen as they entered the area. Before they could fire, someone called "break" and the flight broke off. The MIG's turned away, so the flight started to rejoin the strike force, when Titus spotted yet a third MIG. He attacked. Lieutenant Zimer, the back seat pilot, reported the engagement quite tersely:

> While en route to target and at the north end of Thud Ridge, the strike flight was attacked by several MIG type aircraft. Colonel Titus and I engaged three MIG's, of which we shot down a MIG-21C with a Sparrow missile. We were moving in for the kill on the first MIG we engaged with a full system lock-on, when aircraft 4 called MIG's at 6 o'clock. Colonel Titus immediately broke off the attack. We then rejoined the strike flight. We observed another MIG-21C and engaged him; with a full system lock-on, we fired three missiles. The first two did not guide, but the third missile destroyed the MIG-21C. [The] kill was observed by all members of the flight. We were returning to strike flight when we engaged a third MIG. This engagement we broke off because aircraft 4 was [at] minimum fuel.

Janca confirmed the Titus victory, observing how Titus fired "an AIM-7 missile which impacted on the right side of the MIG-21. The MIG exploded in flame and a short time later I observed the pilot, who had ejected, floating down in his chute."

An Old-Fashioned Dogfight

The other four MIG's destroyed during the afternoon of 20 May fell victims to two flights of the 8th TFW, Ubon, which were flying MIGCAP for an F-105 strike force attacking the Bac Le railroad yards. The first flight of Phantoms flew line abreast with the second Thunderchief flight. The other F-4 flight was high and to the right of the last F-105 flight. An EB-66 support and an Iron Hand SAM suppression flight were included in the strike force.

The force came in from the Gulf of Tonkin. As the aircraft crossed the coastal islands, the Phantoms jettisoned their centerline tanks. Shortly thereafter, about 20 miles east of Kep airfield, two SAM's streaked from the ground at the American aircraft, and the Iron Hand flight attacked the site with Shrike missiles. The SAM's immediately stopped guiding. But with the appearance of the SAM's, there simultaneously came a MIG warning. The mission called for the F-105 force to divide and strike two targets at the rail yards, with one Phantom flight accompanying the first division and the second remaining with the other division, so that each part of the strike force would receive protection. Fifteen miles short of the target, however, the first flight of F-4's sighted MIG's. The other flight sighted more MIG's several miles away. In the next 12 to 14 minutes there was a massive and aggressive dogfight with 8 F-4's battling 12-14 MIG-17's. Elements of each flight acted separately to provide support to other elements. While the F-4's engaged the MIG's, the F-105's proceeded to assigned targets.

Four MIG's were destroyed in a span of 5 to 6

minutes. The first fell to a Sidewinder of Maj. John R. Pardo, the aircraft commander, and 1st Lt. Stephen A. Wayne, the back seat pilot. Pardo reports:

> As our flight approached the area of the sighting, I observed four MIG-17's turning in behind the F-105's. Col. Olds fired one missile and told me to "go get him."
>
> I launched one Sparrow, which did not guide. I then launched one Sidewinder which guided and struck the number four MIG-17. I broke left to negate other MIG's at my 8 o'clock. I continued a 360° turn while positioning on another MIG-17 and observed an aircraft burning on the ground near where I observed my Sidewinder hit a MIG-17. This was at approximately 0830Z [Greenwich time].
>
> The remainder of the missiles I fired did not guide or were not observed due to evasive action necessitated by the tactical situation.

This was Lieutenant Wayne's second aerial victory; a week earlier he had flown with Major William L. Kirk, when the pair had downed a MIG-17.

Two other MIG-17's became the victims of Col. Robin Olds and his pilot, 1st Lt. Stephen B. Croker. These were aerial victories three and four for Olds, making him the leading MIG-killer at that time in Southeast Asia. An ace from World War II, the 8th TFW commander was battle-tested and experienced. Olds termed the events of 20 May "quite a remarkable air battle." According to his account:

> F-105's were bombing along the northeast railroad; we were in our escort position, coming in from the Gulf of Tonkin. We just cleared the last of the low hills lying north of Haiphong, in an east-west direction, when about 10 or 12 MIG-17's came in low from the left and, I believe, from the right. They tried to attack the F-105's before they got to the target.
>
> We engaged MIG-17's approximately 15 miles short of the target. The ensuing battle was an exact replica of the dogfights in World War II.
>
> Our flights of F-4's piled into the MIG's like a sledge hammer, and for about a minute and a half or two minutes that was the most confused, vicious dogfight I have ever been in. There were eight F-4C's, twelve MIG-17's, and one odd flight of F-105's on their way out from the target, who flashed through the battle area.
>
> Quite frankly, there was not only danger from the guns of the MIG's, but the ever-present danger of a collision to contend with. We went round and round that day with the battles lasting 12 to 14 minutes, which is a long time. This particular day we found that the MIG's went into a defensive battle down low, about 500 to 1,000 feet. In the middle of this circle, there were two or three MIG's circling about a hundred feet—sort of in figure-eight patterns. The MIG's were in small groups of two, three, and sometimes four in a very wide circle. Each time we went in to engage one of these groups, a group on the opposite side of the circle would go full power, pull across the circle, and be in firing position on our tails almost before we could get into firing position with our missiles. This is very distressing, to say the least.
>
> The first MIG I lined up was in a gentle left turn, range about 7,000 feet. My pilot achieved a boresight lock-on, went full system, narrow gate, interlocks in. One of the two Sparrows fired in ripple guided true and exploded near the MIG. My pilot saw the MIG erupt in flame and go down to the left.
>
> We attacked again and again, trying to break up that defensive wheel. Finally, once again, fuel considerations necessitated departure. As I left the area by myself, I saw that lone MIG still circling and so I ran out about ten miles and said that even if I ran out of fuel, he is going to know he was in a fight. I got down on the deck, about 50 feet, and headed right for him. I don't think he saw me for quite a while. But when he did, he went mad, twisting, turning, dodging and trying to get away. I kept my speed down so I wouldn't overrun him and I stayed behind him. He headed up a narrow little valley to a low ridge of hills. I knew he was either going to hit that ridge up ahead or pop over the ridge to save himself. The minute he popped over I was going to get him with a Sidewinder.
>
> I fired one AIM-9 which did not track and the MIG pulled up over a ridge, turned left, and gave me a dead astern shot. I obtained a good growl. I fired from about 25 to 50 feet off the grass and he was clear of the ridge by only another 50 to 100 feet when the Sidewinder caught him.

The missile tracked and exploded 5 to 10 feet to the right side of the aft fuselage. The MIG spewed pieces and broke hard left and down from about 200 feet. I overshot and lost sight of him.

I was quite out of fuel and all out of missiles and pretty deep in enemy territory all by myself, so it was high time to leave. We learned quite a bit from this fight. We learned you don't pile into these fellows with eight airplanes all at once. You are only a detriment to yourself.

The final MIG destroyed that day fell to the leader of the first flight, Maj. Philip P. Combies, with 1st. Lt. Daniel L. Lafferty flying rear seat. This was Combie's second MIG victory. Having engaged several MIG–17's without results, Combies climbed to reengage when he saw a MIG–17 in hot pursuit of Olds, about 1½ miles away. When Olds broke hard left, the MIG overshot and headed directly toward Kep airfield, about 8 miles away. Combies got behind and fired an AIM-9 with good tone:

> The missile impacted in the tailpipe area of the MIG and the MIG caught on fire. The MIG was at approximately 1,500 feet at the time of missile launch. The MIG went "belly up" and into an uncontrollable dive and eventually impacted into the ground.

Two days following this air battle, Lt. Col. Titus and his backseater, 1st Lt. Zimer, while leading a flight of four F–C's, repeated their earlier success. Titus' flight was one of two that was providing Phantom MIGCAP for a strike force directed against the Ha Dong army barracks and supply depot. Titus later related the afternoon's events:

Col. Olds, the first quadruple MIG-killer of the Vietnam War, prepares to nail four more red stars to the 8th TFW scoreboard. Other victors in the 20 May encounter (l. to r.) are: Maj. Combies, Lt. Lafferty, Maj. Pardo, and Lts. Croker and Wayne (front center).

> I was carrying a SUU–16 [20-mm gun pod] two days later [May 22] when I got two more MIG's, the second with a SUU–16. In that particular case we were escorting the Thuds [F–105's] inbound to the target, headed for the heart of Hanoi, and I had a feeling that we would get some kind of reaction. The MIG's had been flying that month and, of course, with the strike force headed for Hanoi it did seem to be a fruitful mission to get on, although I had just happened to chum up on the mission that day.
>
> I was leading the first flight that time, and we were south of formation, line abreast of the first two flights at about 16,000 feet, headed west to east, when suddenly out in front 11 miles I spotted a couple of MIG's. I happened to see the sun reflecting off them. I called my backseater and told him to go boresight, and immediately called that I was Padlocked [a code word meaning, essentially, "I'm attacking the MIG's"] and accelerating. I went into afterburner and started pushing forward. Because of numerous MIG calls in the area, I had already cleaned off my external tanks, so we were in a good fighting configuration.
>
> The MIG that we locked on to started a left turn and I lost sight of him and followed him on the radar. He made a turn around to the right, a hard climbing turn. I was unable to get lead on him. I

The 555th "Triple Nickel" Squadron was the first to receive improved Phantom models, F-4D's.

could merely keep him on the right hand of the scope. He stopped his climb and we leveled off. He was in a descent; he climbed again. Finally I told my back-seater that I thought there was something wrong with the radar. He agreed and we joined the Thud formation.

We were still in burner, came alongside the formation and came out of burner. I looked over my left shoulder and a MIG was making a pass on the formation. He fired a missile. I called him and turned into him just about the time he fired the missile. Having fired the missile, he started to climb—possibly after he saw me coming at him. In that particular area there was a scattered overcast condition, cirrus deck. It must have been around 20,000 feet. As I closed he went through the cirrus at a very high climb angle, at least 50°. It seemed a lot higher than that. I was in close pursuit, had a very strong Sidewinder tone, and I fired the missile. The missile was tracking as he disappeared into the cloud. The missile went through the same hole. I deviated slightly to the right, came out on top of the cloud deck, and noted some debris in the air and smoke off to the left. I don't know what it was, but there was some foreign matter in the air—very discernible. I mentioned it to my back-seater.

Then, almost instantaneously, I saw from my 1 o'clock position another MIG–21 . . . about a mile away. I turned toward him and put the pipper on him and got another Sidewinder tone and fired another missile. Almost immediately the MIG started a hard descending left turn and we went from, I would guess, 25,000 feet down to about 2,000 feet while he was doing all sorts of twisting, turning reversals, rolling all sorts of hard maneuvers. It was very impressive to see the rapid roll response and directional change ability of that airplane. I proceeded into the dive with him. We could not obtain a radar lock-on, presumably because of the ground return. We were right in the vicinity of the Hoa Lac airport. There was quite a bit of flak; SAM's were going off.

The MIG made a very high-G pull-out and leveled at approximately 1,500 to 2,000 feet above the ground. In his pull-out he was at wing level so I got the pipper on him and fired a long burst of the SUU–16 at him. I did not observe any impacts and thought I had missed him. However, he did slow down quite rapidly. I overshot, pulled up to the left, did a reversal, came back around and called for my number two to take him. About this time number two had overshot and came up to my right. I turned off watching the MIG and called for number three, and as I did so I observed the MIG was in a shallow, wing-rocking maneuver and continued on down in

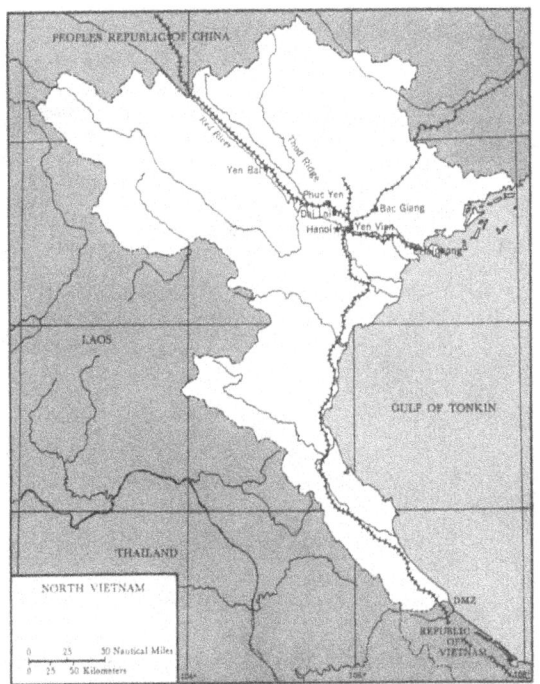

the shallow dive and impacted with the ground. Where he was hit I don't know, but apparently he was out of it after the first hits were taken.

After these two MIG–21 kills, USAF crews flying into North Vietnam encountered a lull of several days during which no enemy aircraft were downed. The air-to-air posture was improved somewhat on 28 May when the 555th "Triple Nickle" Tactical Fighter Squadron of the 8th TFW, Ubon, received F–4D aircraft. This improved Phantom model soon entered combat.

Colonel Olds on 2 June flew an F–4D in a flight otherwise composed of F–4C's. Providing MIGCAP for an F–105 strike force, the flight engaged 8 to 10 MIG's. Three "probable" MIG kills resulted, one of them claimed by Olds. Had his kill been confirmed, he would have become the first "ace" of the Southeast Asia war.

On the following day, F–105 pilots of the 388th TFW flying a strike mission against the Bac Giang railroad and highway bridge and adjacent railroad yards, did produce confirmed air-to-air victories by downing two MIG–17's. Capt. Larry D. Wiggins, flying aircraft 3, and Maj. Ralph L. Kuster, Jr. in position 2, each destroyed one of the enemy.

They were in the lead flight of a force of four strike and one Iron Hand flights launched from Korat RTAFB, Thailand. Inbound to the target in a standard "pod" formation, the four strike flights penetrated the SAM defenses. When the F–105's were about 15 miles short of the roll-in point, enemy 85-mm and 100-mm antiaircraft opened fire. During the dive-bomb run for flak suppression, Kuster fired a short burst in an effort to obtain photography of the active AAA gun emplacements adjacent to the target. He thus hoped to film the sites on the overrun of his gun camera. The flight recovered from the dive-bomb run with Kuster trailing 1,500 feet behind the lead, and Wiggins about a mile behind the flight leader.

Approximately 6 miles from the target the flight leader saw three MIG–17's at 10 o'clock low at a range of 2 miles. He called the MIGs' position and started a hard left turn. The second and third flight aircraft followed their leader, but aircraft 4 nearly collided with the second flight off the target and lost his flight in the turn. He elected to remain with the second flight during withdrawal.

Initial maneuvering did not permit a firing pass, and the three MIG's went into a tight left-hand orbit at about 500 feet altitude. The U.S. and enemy flights completed a circle and a half before Wiggins was able to fire his AIM–9B at the third MIG. The enemy plane attempted to evade the missile but was damaged. Wiggins' film showed that the missile went alongside the MIG's tailpipe and exploded. The aircraft began trailing a heavy white vapor. Continuing to close on the MIG as it rolled over and started down, Wiggins fired 376 rounds of 20-mm at a high angle-off. The MIG exploded in flame and crashed.

Meanwhile, the first MIG was at the flight leader's 11 o'clock position at a range of 1 mile, and a second MIG had crossed to the leader's 1:30 position at a range of 1/2 mile. Kuster reported these MIG's to his leader.

"If you can get one, go get him!" the leader told him. Being in a favorable position to attack the first MIG, Kuster tightened up his left turn, while the flight leader attacked the second MIG.

Kuster immediately obtained a 45° angle-off shot at MIG one at about 2,000 feet, while pulling

5 to 6 G's, he placed the pipper in front of MIG one and fired a short burst . . . . However, Kuster did not have enough lead and was unable to track the MIG through the turn. As he started a high-speed yo-yo to reduce his overshoot, MIG one reversed into a hard right turn, partially solving Kuster's tracking problem.

After a few maneuvers Kuster again fired a few bursts of 20-mm at a range of 1,200 feet, but observed no hits. The MIG rolled further left and banked into a 120° dive, with his nose about 20° below the horizon. Kuster closed rapidly at about 200 knots overtake speed, but the MIG pilot established a smooth, tight descending turn to the left, possibly reducing power to force an overshoot. Kuster, pulling maximum G's (just short of complete loss of vision) was able to align his Thunderchief fuselage with the MIG but was unable to pull lead. As a last resort, Kuster was able to rotate the F-105 fuselage by rapid aft stick movement, enough to put the sight well in front of the MIG. He opened fire at a little more than 200 feet range, forcing the MIG to fly through the stream of 20-mm cannon fire.

The underside of the MIG's left wing exploded two-thirds of the way between the fuselage and the external underslung fuel tank. Kuster relaxed back stick pressure as the fire and debris from the MIG engulfed the F-105. It passed about 25 feet below the MIG, as the MIG rolled inverted and crashed. Time from hit to impact was 4 to 5 seconds, during which no chute was observed, and the MIG did not roll from the inverted position . . .

USAF pilots scored three more victories on 5 June. One flight of four F-4's (of the 555th TFS) downed the first of the enemy trio while flying MIGCAP for an Iron Hand flight in the vicinity of Thud Ridge during the mid-afternoon. Several MIG-17's jumped aircraft 3 and 4. During the ensuing engagement the F-4's became separated and departed the area. Maj. Everett T. Raspberry, Jr., flight leader, was flying with Capt. Francis M. Gullick. He and his wingman attacked seven or eight other MIG's in a Wagon Wheel formation.

"Upon sighting the MIG-17's," recalled Raspberry, "I immediately engaged them to prevent the MIG's from attacking an Iron Hand flight patrol-

Maj. Kuster (left) watches Capt. Wiggins as he describes the tactics he used in downing a MIG-17 on 3 June 1967. Both Thunderchief pilots received credits for victories.

ling the area. After making several turns with the MIG's, I disengaged and flew southeast some 3-4 miles and then turned back into the MIG's." Approaching them for the second time, he spotted one at 12 o'clock high and attempted to hit him with an AIM-4. However, the missile did not guide. Again he left the fight to gain separation and once again came back—at low altitude. With a radar lock-on, he fired an AIM-7 at a MIG in his 11 o'clock position and missed.

"On my third approach to the MIG's," Raspberry continues his narrative, "I was between 500 and 1,000 feet actual ground level on a northwesterly heading. I could see three MIG-17's; one in my 12 o'clock, slightly high, and two more in my 11 o'clock position, slightly low." At last he connected, scoring his second victory of the war:

"My GIB locked on to a target which was obviously one of the MIG's I had seen in my 11 o'clock position as I turned slightly left and down to center the steering dot. I observed the rate of closure to be 900 knots. When the ASE circle was maximum diameter, I fired an AIM-7. The missile appeared to be headed straight for the oncoming MIG. I was unable to watch the impact because Col. Olds, [flying lead aircraft in the adjacent flight] called me to break right as a MIG was in my 4 o'clock and firing. My wingman

[Capt. Douglas B. Cairns] was able to see the AIM–7 as it approached the MIG and observed the MIG as it struck the ground. I would estimate the MIG's altitude at the time of [missile] impact at 100–300 feet."

The second aerial victory took place about 5 minutes later. Maj. Durwood K. Priester and his rear-seater, Capt. John E. Pankhurst, were leading a flight of four F–4C's on MIG combat air patrol when they downed their enemy aircraft. "Inbound to the target area," said Priester, "I observed three MIG–17's at my 3 o'clock low position." Priester's flight attacked the MIG's, diving from 17,000 to the enemy's altitude of approximately 8,000 feet. Priester observed:

> The number three MIG pulled up vertically as I started my dive. I pulled up and in trail with the number three MIG, as the MIG executed a hard right turn. I fired a short burst but saw no evidence of the 20-mm hitting the MIG.
>
> I did not have a gun sight and relaxed stick pressure while assuming I had overled the MIG due to the close proximity while firing. The MIG–17 started to reverse his turn and I fired another burst of 20-mm. Two large balls of flame exited the MIG's tailpipe, but the aircraft failed to burn. I rolled over and observed the shallow dive, wings level, and straight course of the damaged MIG as it impacted the ground and exploded. The MIG pilot did not eject and crashed with his aircraft.

The final MIG accounted for during the afternoon was downed a few minutes later when Capt. Richard M. Pascoe and his back-seater Capt. Norman E. Wells,* flying wingman for Colonel Olds, knocked a MIG–17 from the sky—the second aerial victory for both officers.

Olds' flight was on MIGCAP for a strike force and was covering the departure of F–105's. Monitoring the radio chatter of Priester's engagement with the MIG's, Olds' flight immediately reversed course to join in the fight. Proceeding south along Thud Ridge, Olds' wingman saw four MIG–17's battling Priester's flight and single MIG–17's high at 9 o'clock and 3 o'clock. Olds and Pascoe pursued the MIG at 9 o'clock; and aircraft 3 and 4 of his flight attacked the one at 3 o'clock. Olds expended all AIM–4 and AIM–7 missiles without effect, then passed the lead to Pascoe. "We picked up a single MIG–17 at approximately 5 nautical miles in front of us," reports Pascoe, and then:

> I fired two AIM–9's as the MIG started a slight climb and observed the first to impact at the extreme tail end and the second about three feet up the fuselage from the tail. The MIG continued in his left descending turn and struck the ground as the canopy was seen to leave the aircraft. The aircraft was totally destroyed.

Olds and his back-seater, 1st Lt. James L. Thibodeaux, saw the two AIM–9's of their wingman hit the MIG. The pilot ejected just before the MIG crashed "with a large fireball."

Another MIG Stand-Down

The heavy losses sustained by the NVN Air Force between April and June 1967 seriously undermined the effectiveness of the North Vietnamese fighter force. After 5 June the NVN Air Force stood down once more, obviously to take a fresh look at the situation. MIG's seldom ventured out during the remainder of June and July, but they did continue to train and to practice intercepts whenever U.S. forces were not in the northeastern corner of North Vietnam. In this period, American aircraft losses to MIG's were minimal, but SAM's and AAA began to take a heavy toll of them.

In the meantime, the U.S. air victory over the MIG force was believed to be so complete that Lt. Gen. William W. Momyer, commander of the Seventh Air Force, was prompted to report on 16 August to a Senate subcommittee that "we have driven the MIG's out of the sky for all practical purposes." While General Momyer's statement was momentarily true, the picture soon changed, and in late August the North Vietnamese pilots introduced new tactics. These called for the MIG's to approach American forces at low level, climb quickly to altitude, make a single firing pass, and then run for their home bases (including some in China).

---

*Pascoe and Wells were promoted following their aerial victory of January 6, 1967—Wells to Captain and Pascoe to Major. Pascoe however, had not yet donned his gold leaves.

Capts. Pascoe (left) and Wells add another star to an F-4C Phantom after claiming their second victory.

A contributing factor that aided MIG tactics after the June–July stand-down was the diversion of F–4's from MIGCAP to strike missions, leaving strike forces without adequate protection. Heavily-laden strike aircraft were unable to outrun the supersonic MIG–21's, and strike pilots were briefed to avoid confrontation whenever possible; and if MIG's were sighted, the former were to continue to the target at increased speed. When they could not outrun the MIG's and if the situation so dictated, the last strike flight could jettison its ordnance and attempt to short-stop the attack by engaging the enemy. Such a situation persisted through August and part of September.

On 23 August, five flights of F–105's from Korat—three flights in strike roles, one in a combined flak suppression and strike role, and one in an Iron Hand SAM suppression role—attacked the Yen Vien railroad yards. In addition, four flights of F–4's came from Ubon—three to strike and one for MIGCAP. All flights were composed of four aircraft each.

The five F–105 flights rendezvoused with the four F–4 flights in the refueling area, and then they crossed the Red River 6 miles southeast of Yen Bai, proceeding from there down Thud Ridge. The F–105 Iron Hand flight (two F–105D's and two F–105F's) led the force to the target area. The force then split into two "cells," the F–105 strike aircraft in a box formation and the F–4 strike aircraft following in a triangular formation. The single F–4 MIG-CAP flight flew to the left rear of the F–105 box.

"Bandits, northwest at 60 miles, heading 360°," someone warned on the radio, as one of the F–4 strike flights turned down Thud Ridge at 15,000 feet. Two MIG–21's then descended out of a 25,000-foot overcast and attacked from 6 o'clock. Each MIG fired an air-to-air missile, one at the lead F–4 and the other at number 4. Both missiles impacted and destroyed the American aircraft. The crew members ejected; there were only three good parachutes.

The number three aircrew in this F–4D flight observed the missile which downed his wingman. It had hit the aircraft's tailpipe and exploded. "He burst into a ball of flames," the number 3 aircraft commander later reported.

The number two F–4D aircrew also saw the missile which hit the lead aircraft; it passed their own left wing and impacted with the lead F–4D.

From this point on, the air battle turned into a confused dogfight. The sky over North Vietnam was filled with numerous engagements: F–4C's, F–4D's, and F–105D's battling numerous MIG–21's and MIG–17's. In the confusion, one F–4C aircrew fired two AIM–7 missiles at what they thought was a MIG but was actually an F–4D. Luckily, the aircraft commander identified the friendly aircraft in time.

"I told the guy in the backseat to break lock. It was no problem," he later commented. The missiles, one of which had been tracking well, went ballistic as soon as the radar lock-on was broken, and they did no damage. The aircrew fired upon was unaware of the incident, but continued down Thud Ridge.

The only USAF kill of the day was awarded to 1st Lt. David B. Waldrop, III, who in a flight of four F–105's of the 388th TFW downed a MIG–17. In the confusion of the air battle it is difficult to reconstruct the events, but apparently Waldrop attacked a MIG soon after dropping ordnance on the target. He describes the action:

> As I rolled to the right, I looked down and saw two MIG–17's. One was on the tail of an F–105 at the time. I picked up one and broke in on him. I plugged in my afterburner, picked up a little airspeed, closed in, and started hosing off my

cannon at him. Shortly afterwards, some fire shot out from his wingtips and about midway across the wing and he started a slow roll over to the right.

I backed off and fired again. He continued rolling right on in and blew up when he hit the ground.

"It was beautiful," reported Colonel Olds, flying the lead MIGCAP F-4D. "The MIG-17 was diving toward the ground with flames coming out of his tailpipe. It wasn't the afterburner; he was on fire. There was that great, great, huge Thud right behind him with fire coming out of his nose. It looked like a shark chasing a minnow." The MIG-17 was diving straight for the ground; Olds saw no parachute.

Maj. Billy R. Givens, Waldrop's flight leader, also engaged a MIG after his flight had left the target. He fired more than 900 rounds of 20-mm at the MIG, which had been chasing another F-105 and had in fact damaged that aircraft with gunfire. Givens initially was credited with a probable kill, but upon review by the Seventh Air Force's Enemy Aircraft Claims Evaluation Board, the claim was denied.

After Givens' engagement, Lieutenant Waldrop and his wingman pursued two more MIG's. Waldrop began a left roll and at 7,500 foot altitude began firing his 20-mm cannon at a range of 3,000 feet, 85° angle-off. He fired 300 rounds and observed hits on the MIG before ceasing fire at a range of 2,500 feet. Waldrop then rolled out and headed westerly in an inverted position, because he "wanted to see where he [the MIG] went." The MIG had disappeared into the clouds with Waldrop right behind him. Leaving the clouds and reacquiring visual contact, Waldrop found that his gun sight was inoperative. At 6,500 feet altitude and a range of 2,000 feet, Waldrop opened fire once more with a burst of 250 rounds. The burst struck the MIG's canopy area and Waldrop "worked the bullets back toward his tail." The MIG exploded, rolled into an inverted position, and impacted the ground. Flying at 3,500 feet, Waldrop pulled off and left the battle area, certain that he had two victories.

The 388th TFW's Enemy Aircraft Claims Board did in fact review and validate both of Waldrop's claims for 23 August using all available data—gun camera film, wingman testimony, testimony from other witnesses, and operations reports. But when the claims were processed by the Seventh Air Force Enemy Aircraft Claims Evaluation Board at a later date, the Board confirmed Waldrop's second claim but denied his first. Apparently, the evidence was insufficient to warrant an award for the first encounter.

The MIG tactics employed during the 23 August engagements came "as a complete surprise" to Olds. Had he been informed, the commander felt, he could have avoided the mass confusion. He found out later that higher headquarters knew that the MIG-21's had changed their tactics prior to this engagement, "but the word hadn't filtered down to our wing. That made me pretty mad because I lost two aircraft because of this new tactic."

If I had known about the new MIG tactic, I would have split my MIGCAP elements up; 3 and 4 would have accelerated below the strike force and ingressed 10–15 miles ahead of them. My wingman and I would have turned easterly toward the Ridge prior to the strike force . . . accelerated . . . gained 15–20 miles separation . . . and swooped over the force as they turned southeasterly down the Ridge. The GCI controller would already have picked us up on radar; he would have observed our turn. I'll bet you one hundred dollars that he'd called off the MIG's. He probably would have said, "Break, break, they're on to you." Then we would have turned in behind the strike force and continued ingress.

When the battle was over, the U.S. Air Force lost two F-4D's to MIG-21's, another F-4 to enemy AAA fire, and still another when an F-4 ran out of fuel before reaching the post-strike refueling tanker. One F-105 was badly damaged by MIG cannon fire.

From 23 August through 17 October 1967 there were no further MIG kills by USAF fighters. During this period the Air Force assigned a larger number F-4's to a purely MIGCAP role, but apparently the North Vietnamese elected to avoid confrontations. Strike forces, meanwhile, continued to pound enemy support and war-making installations.

Renewed Opposition

On 18 October, MIG pilots once again initiated a

This MIG-17, trailing flames and smoke, heads earthward on 18 October 1967—a victim of Maj. Russell's 20-mm cannon.

Capt. Joseph E. McGrath, a senior weapons controller assigned to the College Eye Task Force, listens to Maj. Kirk discuss the MIG kill which resulted from McGrath's initial spotting of the MIG on his radar and passing the information to Kirk, who downed the MIG in a dogfight.

campaign of dogged opposition against U.S. air forces. A strike force composed of four F-105 strike flights, one F-105F Iron Hand flight, and one F-4D MIGCAP flight struck the Dai Loi railroad bypass bridge on that afternoon. Three of the four strike flights encountered MIG-17's in the target area and one MIG was shot down. The F-4D MIGCAP flight trailed the Thunderchiefs into the target area and also encountered MIG-17's, but destroyed none. Maj. Donald M. Russell, flying an F-105 in number 4 position, provides an account of the victory:

After delivering my ordnance on the target, I broke hard right to join the remainder of the flight for egress. MIG's had been seen in the target area just prior to roll in. After about 180 degrees of turn, I saw a MIG-17 crossing from my left to right approximately 1,500–2,000 feet out. I came out of afterburner, extended the speed-brakes, and maneuvered to his 6 o'clock position. He rolled out of his right turn and started a slow left turn to position himself in an attack position on a preceding F-105. His left turn helped me to get into a good firing position, and I opened fire at an estimated 1,000 feet. I noticed flames from both sides of the MIG-17 aft of the cockpit area. I followed him for a few moments and saw the fire increase. The aircraft rolled right and headed straight down. I did not see the pilot eject and lost sight of him at about 2,000 feet going straight down in flames. There is no doubt that this MIG was destroyed in that, if the pilot were alive, he could not have recovered from the last observed altitude/attitude. Gun camera and KA-71 film show the MIG smoking profusely.

Renewed MIG opposition prompted Pentagon officials to authorize for the first time in the war a strike against Phuc Yen airfield, the largest of North Vietnam's air bases. Accordingly, 6 days after the Dai Loi strike, four strike forces of USAF F-105's and F-4's, working with U.S. Navy aircraft, struck the airfield. Pilots of the 8th, 355th, and 388th

Tactical Fighter Wings reported all bombs on target; the mission was highly successful in rendering the sprawling base unserviceable. Post-strike reconnaissance photos showed four MIG-21's, four MIG-17's, and one MIG-15 destroyed or badly damaged.

Seventh Air Force planners had anticipated a loss of 3 percent of the strike force to MIG's, flak, and SAM's during the Phuc Yen raid, but not one U.S. aircraft was lost. One MIG-21 was destroyed in air-to-air combat during the initial attack. It was downed by Maj. William L. Kirk and his backseater, 1st Lt. Theodore R. Bongartz, who were leading a MIGCAP flight in support of the first strike force.

"This kill wasn't quite the same one as my first one last May 13," Kirk commented. "That one was a MIG-17 and there was only one pass. I got him with my air-to-air missile. This time it was a good old-fashioned dogfight and we fought him for a long time."

We took position as fragged, and I positioned my flight line abreast, high and to the left of the trailing F-105 flight. MIG calls were heard as we entered NVN. They proved to be extremely accurate. When the MIG calls indicated that the MIG's were 6 o'clock at 8 miles I turned our flight back into the attack. As I rolled out of the 180° turn my pilot (Lieutenant Bongartz) acquired a radar lock-on to a target 30° right at 4 miles. I immediately looked to that position and visually identified a MIG-21.

At initial contact the MIG was slightly right and head-on. He appeared to go into a steep climb, initially, but as I started up with him he then rolled into me and put his nose back down. He appeared to be aggressive for the first 360° turn, then it appeared he was trying to disengage.

After several hard maneuvering turns and reversals, in which the MIG would run through a cloud at every opportunity, I acquired AIM-7 missile firing parameters and launched two missiles. The first guided well and exploded very close to the MIG. I did not observe the second missile. The first AIM-7 could possibly have damaged the MIG, even though I could see no visible damage, in fact I had the impression that the MIG started to decelerate immediately after missile detonation. I then switched to guns,

closed to about 500–700 feet, and started firing. The HEI* impacted on top of his fuselage between the wing roots . . . I could see large pieces coming off the fuselage, and the entire fuselage section was engulfed in flames.

The MIG pilot bailed out; the MIG-21 rolled to the right and crashed in approximately a 15° dive. I then turned and flew by the MIG pilot, hanging in his chute. I was not able to get a look at his face in that when he saw me approaching he turned his back.

MIG's continued their aggressive assaults, and on 26 October six MIG-17's jumped a flight of four F-4D's flying MIGCAP for a photographic mission 3 miles northwest of Phuc Yen airfield. As soon as the MIG's appeared the reconnaissance aircraft departed. In the ensuing battle, three of the MIG's were downed by air-to-air missiles. The aerial victories went to the flight leader: Capt. John D. Logeman, Jr., and 1st Lt. Frederick E. McCoy, II; aircraft number 3: Capt. William S. Gordon, III, and 1st Lt. James H. Monsees; and number 4: Capt. Larry D. Cobb and Capt. Alan A. Lavoy.

"Approximately 6 nautical miles before reaching Phuc Yen," recalled Logeman, "I observed four MIG-17's climbing up through a cloud layer at our 2 o'clock position."

I called the flight to turn into the MIG's, who were in a right climbing turn approaching our 4 o'clock position at approximately 5 miles range. I also called the reconnaissance flight to egress the area at this time.

As I completed my right turn, heading approximately 090° at 17,000 feet, I placed the pipper on the lead MIG-17 and fired two AIM-7E missiles in boresight mode. Range to the MIG was 2.5 to 3 miles. The first missile did not guide. The second missile came up into the reticle and appeared to be on a collision course with the MIG. We were head-on at this time and his cannons were firing. I pulled up to avoid the cannon fire and did not observe missile detonation. I immediately turned hard left to re-engage the MIG's on a west heading. During this left turn I observed a parachute in the area of intended missile impact and a MIG-17

---

*High explosive incendiary.

was descending inverted, trailing sparks from the fuselage. Aircraft 2 [Maj. John A. Hall and 1st Lt. Albert T. Hamilton] observed this parachute at the same time. Another MIG-17 was attacking at this time from my 10 o'clock position. He turned away at a range of about 2 miles. My rear seat pilot obtained a boresight, full system lock-on, and I attempted to fire two AIM-7E missiles. One did not leave the aircraft, but the second missile fired and appeared to be guiding. I broke off the attack at this point to maneuver away from a MIG-17's cannon attack from my 7 o'clock position. At this point I called the flight to egress for Bingo fuel.

Gordon's aerial victory came minutes after Logeman's. Watching the attack come in from 3 o'clock, Gordon turned his element to attack the eight MIG's, but he was too close to fire a missile. "I disengaged," he reported, " then gained lateral separation and reattacked." He observed:

Two MIG-17's were in the pipper head-on. My pilot obtained boresight, full system lock-on, and I attempted to fire two AIM-7E Sparrow missiles. . . . Only one fired. I was unable to see the missile detonate due to evasive maneuvering necessary to avoid the attacking MIG's.

I disengaged again and reversed back into the fight. At this time I observed a MIG pilot hanging in a white parachute in the same location that I had fired the missile. The MIG had been at approximately 16,000 feet in a slight climb and the parachute was at approximately 16,000 feet. Captain Cobb also saw the parachute. I disengaged and reengaged two more times without obtaining a good position to fire. On the next attempt I had a MIG-17 in my pipper for a tail shot. By the time I selected AIM-4D's, cooled the missile, listened for a tone, and fired the missile with self-track selected, the MIG had turned to a head-on firing attack. I fired the AIM-4 with a full system radar lock-on at a range of approximately 6,000 feet. Again I was unable to observe the missile impact due to evasive action necessary to avoid the attacking MIG; however, it appeared to guide straight for the MIG. At this time my pilot observed another chute at lower altitude, approximately 8,000 feet. At the same time he could still see the high parachute that we had observed first. After I had shot my second missile, my wingman observed two MIG-17's egressing the battle and pursued them, finally destroying one. Then Captain Logeman called the flight to egress due to low fuel.

The commander of aircraft 4, Captain Cobb, tells how he downed his MIG:

Gordon turned us into the MIG-17's and started to accelerate. On the first turn we were unable to fire, so he left the fight for separation. We then turned right and re-entered the fight. We were both able to fire a missile on this pass and we continued through the MIG's and out the other side of the fight. Gordon carried us out and up to the left. Again we turned to re-enter the fight. At this time, I observed an enemy chute in the middle of the battle. We again went through the battle but were unable to fire. We continued using these tactics during the attack.

On our last pass a MIG-17 obtained a 6 o'clock position on Gordon, but when I told him to break left, the MIG-17 broke off the attack. At this time I observed two MIG-17's at my 10 o'clock position. I cooled an AIM-4D, obtained a self-track lock-on, and fired the missile with 10-15° lead angle. I observed the AIM-4D impact on the tail of the MIG-17, and he exploded and started to roll right. At this time the MIG-17 pilot ejected and his plane spiraled earthward in flames.

On October 27 an F-105 pilot of the 355th TFW, Capt. Gene I. Basel, destroyed a MIG-17 in air-to-air combat. He was flying wing for the flight leader during large-scale attacks by USAF and USN fighters against railroad and highway bridges in the Hanoi area. His flight was one of three F-105 flights sent from Takhli to strike the Canal des Rapides bridge northeast of Hanoi. Their number 3 and 4 aircraft had aborted the mission over Thud Ridge when the fourth aircraft encountered wild pitch oscillations. The flight leader and Basel then joined a flak suppression flight in an attempt to maintain pod formation. About 2 minutes from the target the Takhli force encountered extremely heavy and accurate AAA fire and heavy SAM activity. Two F-105's were destroyed by surface-to-air missiles,

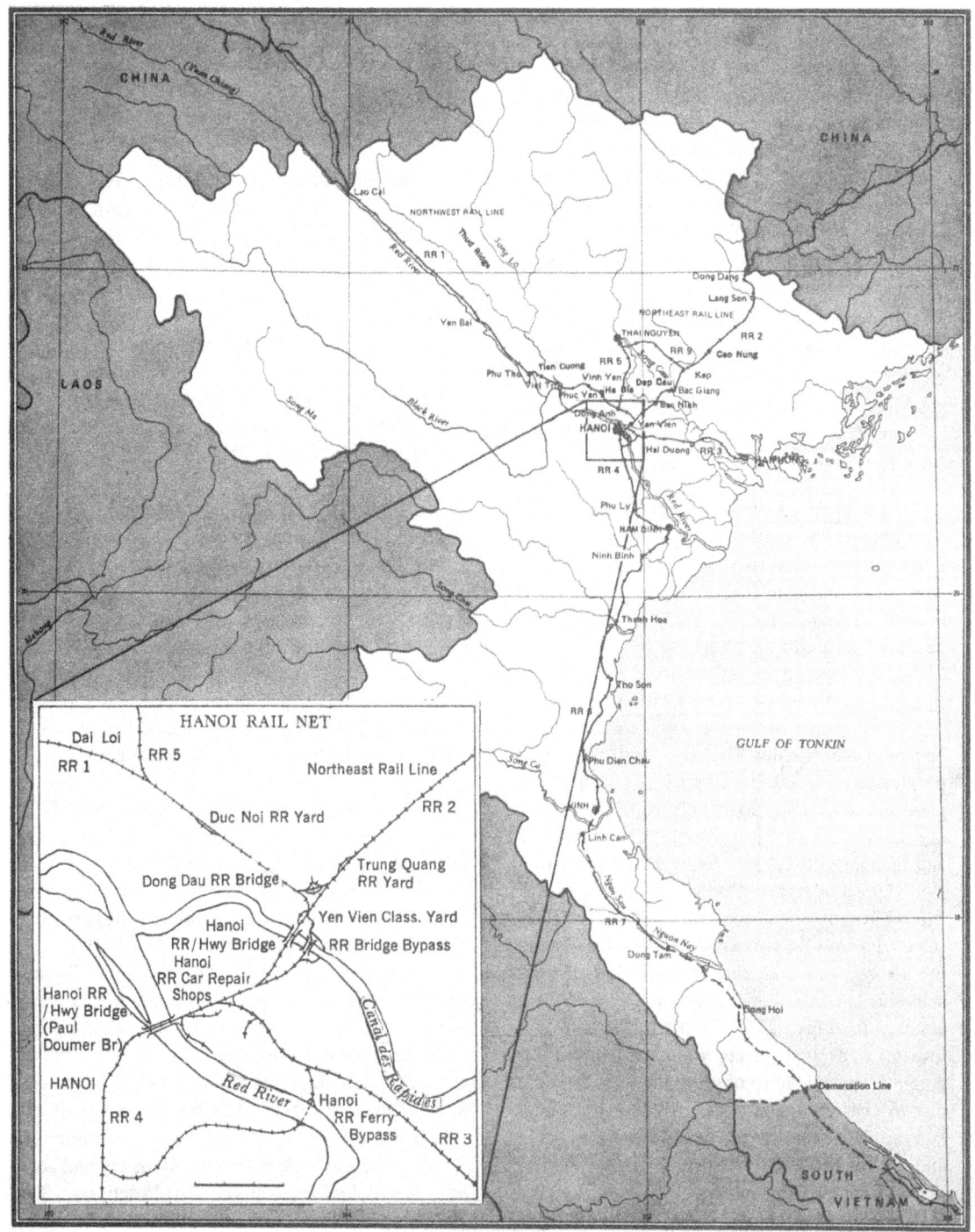

Capt. Basel points out on a map where he downed a MIG-17.

and one of the MIGCAP F-4D's was downed by AAA fire over Thud Ridge.

During target egress, Basel found himself in direct trail with his flight leader. As the leader pulled hard left to avoid flak and SAM's, Basel cut inside of him in a high-G turn, "belly up to him," in order to avoid a mid-air collision. Turning wide to assure separation, Basel rolled out at 3,000 feet on a southerly heading paralleling the Red River. His main thought at that moment was to join with anyone.

Looking about and flying straight and level, Basel sighted at his altitude two MIG-17's at 10 o'clock, heading due west at about 450 knots. "It was a perfect set-up for a high-speed pass," he recalled.

I switched to dive function on the mode selector and closed to within 2,000 feet pulling lead on him. He didn't see me, and was intent on positioning for an attack on the flight ahead of me until he felt the 20-mm impacts. At that time he reversed his direction abruptly, fire belching from his tailpipe. The MIG continued rolling left to a rear inverted position until lost from sight. At this time Lieutenant Tax [1st Lt. Cal W. Tax, flying the number four aircraft in the following flight] sighted the MIG jettisoning his tanks and torching* from the tailpipe. SAM's were launched at us at that time and we were forced to take evasive action, unable to further observe the crippled MIG's flight path. Lieutenant Tax and I then joined for mutual protection and egressed the area.

Although Captain Basel's claim for destroying a MIG-17 was initially denied because of a lack of information, it was confirmed after study of his gun camera film showed that the MIG-17 was on fire in its aft section and could not have recovered.

Heavy North Vietnamese MIG losses during October, both in the air and on the ground, were sufficient reason for another stand-down and more training, but the NVN Air Force did not resort to this action. Rather, in the next 2 months they gained a slight edge in the air-to-air war. As American aircraft losses mounted, USAF air strikes were conducted against every jet-capable airfield north of the 20th parallel except Hanoi's international airport: Gia Lam. Many NVN Air Force aircraft dispersed on a temporary basis to bases in China. Repairs in the meantime were made to North Vietnamese airfields and their MIG losses were replaced. By the end of 1967, the MIG inventory was thus still reasonably high. Yet, significantly during this 2-month period, USAF fighter crews succeeded in downing five MIG's in aerial combat.

On the afternoon of 6 November, two forces were sent out to strike Kep's airfield and railroad yard. The 8th TFW provided the MIGCAP F-4D's. Capt. Darrell D. Simmonds served as the MIGCAP flight leader, with 1st Lt. George H. McKinney, Jr., as his rear seat pilot. Since this flight was the only MIGCAP, it split into two elements to protect each side of the strike force should MIG's be sighted.

Approach to the target was uneventful; no SAM and no MIG warnings were issued. As the Iron Hand flight recovered from its Shrike release on Kep airfield, the first MIG warning came. The first F-105 strike flight was recovering from its bomb run when it was attacked by four MIG-17's. The F-4's at once turned south to engage the MIG's, but made no visual contact. The MIGCAP then turned back to the

---

*Because of a break or failure in the fuel system, raw fuel starts burning in the aftersection of the aircraft; and flame, rather than thrust, comes from the afterburner.

northeast to rejoin the departing strike force and now made MIG contact. In the next few minutes the two pilots in the lead aircraft destroyed two MIG-17's in short order. Captain Simmonds furnishes the account:

My initial contact with the MIG's came when my flight was on a 90° beam heading to the egressing force. A flight of four MIG-17's (not the same flight that we turned into) was closing in on the last egressing flight and started firing. I closed on the firing MIG and caused him to stop firing and take evasive action.

After several maneuvering tactics, I closed to within 1,500 feet of the MIG and fired my gun. At that time, the aft section of the MIG-17 burst into flames. We then pulled up and to the right and observed the canopy blow off, but no ejection occurred until just before impact with the ground. The chute of the MIG pilot streamered and disappeared into the trees just as the MIG impacted in a large orange fireball.

I turned the flight back toward the egress heading when my back seat pilot, 1st Lt. McKinney, spotted a lone MIG-17 at our 4 o'clock position, low and heading away from us. I called to the flight that we were going back in and turned to close on the MIG-17. He saw us coming and dropped to about 200 feet off the ground and started up a small valley. I dropped just below him and closed. When he saw me moving into lethal range, he broke hard left and climbed, giving me a tracking position. I moved to within 1,000 feet and opened fire. The MIG-17 disappeared in a large fireball and plummeted to the earth in many pieces.

Again I turned my flight toward the egress heading. MIG calls indicated that there were MIG's following us at six miles and closing. We did not have the fuel to engage and elected to accelerate and depart the area.

A U.S. Marine Corps aircraft commander flying with the 432d TRW teamed up with a USAF pilot for the next aerial victory. Eight F-105 and two F-4D flights were scheduled against three targets in Route Package 6A on 17 December. In support of the effort were two flights of F-105 Iron Hand aircraft, four flights of F-4D MIGCAP aircraft, and two flights of EB-66 ECM aircraft. The entire effort was divided into two forces, one striking the Lang Lau railroad bridge and the other hitting Phuc Yen airfield. MIG opposition proved extremely heavy, and one F-4D and one F-105D were destroyed. A single MIG-17 was destroyed by the MIGCAP flight in the strike against Phuc Yen.

Capt. Doyle D. Baker, the Marine Corps exchange pilot, commanded aircraft 3. His "guy-in-back" was 1st Lt. John D. Ryan, Jr. According to their preflight briefing, if their flight leader could obtain an immediate visual contact on any MIG which another flight member called out, he would give that aircraft permission to attack. As the strike force crossed the Red River and headed toward Thud Ridge, the F-4 flight trailed south of the main force by about 8 miles.

Suddenly came the warning: "Red bandit airborne out of Gia Lam." Shortly thereafter, aircraft 3 and 4 established a visual contact, and Baker requested and received permission to attack. According to his report, the Marine captain turned right from a heading of 30° to 270°, made a high-speed diving pass at the MIG-17, and fired his SUU-23. The MIG turned into him and attempted to evade the attack. Passing beneath the hostile aircraft, Baker performed a high-speed yo-yo, followed by a scissors maneuver as the MIG reversed his turn.

Keeping the MIG-17 in sight, Baker waited for separation, then performed a Split-S and made a second high-speed pass and fired his SUU-23. The MIG continued to turn into the attack, so Baker returned to 10,000 feet to allow separation. He made another high-speed pass, trying to fire the SUU-23, but discovered it was empty.

The MIG turned into the attack. Baker overshot and made a high-speed yo-yo to 10,000 feet to try to get more separation. The MIG then leveled his wings at 2,000 feet and headed 120° at approximately 0.6 Mach. Baker maneuvered his Phantom into a 2-nautical mile stern attack and launched one AIM-4D while in a 10° dive, passing through 3,000 feet. The missile hit the tailpipe of the MIG, and Baker observed persistent fire and black smoke trailing from the hostile aircraft. The left wing of the MIG dropped sharply, and it began an uncontrollable downward roll from 2,000 feet. Baker executed a climbing right turn and lost sight of his kill.

New MIG Tactics

By mid-December 1967, MIG-21's were coordinating their attacks with those of MIG-17's. each from different quandrants, in multiple passes. These tactics were observed on the 19th, when two large strike forces were sent into North Vietnam to hit Viet Tri and Tien Cuong railroad yards.

The first force, which never reached its target, consisted of four F-105 and two F-4D MIGCAP flights. It was attacked by six MIG-21's and four to eight MIG-17's. The USAF aircraft jettisoned their ordnance and jumped into the numerous engagements. None of the aircraft was damaged, and one of the MIGCAP aircraft—number 01—crewed by Maj. Joseph D. Moore and 1st Lt. George H. McKinney, Jr., poured enough gunfire into a MIG-17 to receive credit for a one-half MIG kill; the other half was awarded to Majors William M. Dalton, pilot, and James L. Graham, EWO, in an F-105 Iron Hand aircraft in the second force.

Major Moore relates the engagement:

As the force crossed the Black River . . . another flight (also MIGCAP) called bogies closing at 6 o'clock. I turned my flight back into the bogies which were identified as F-4's after approximately 135° of turn. I completed 360° of turn and rolled out behind the force. At this time the F-105's called MIG's and jettisoned ordnance. I acquired four MIG-17's milling through the strike force. I selected one at 12 o'clock, approximately 2½ miles in range, and we obtained radar lockon.

As I was about to fire an AIM-7E, another MIG-17 popped up at 12 o'clock. I switched to guns and began tracking the second MIG-17, who was in a gentle left turn. I began firing at approximately 1,500 feet, but rate of fire was very slow as the gun was not up to speed. The MIG increased his rate of turn, then abruptly relaxed G's. At this time I observed smoke coming from the MIG's fuselage. I passed within 100 feet of the MIG and yo-yoed high. As I looked back to see the MIG go in, I observed another MIG closing on me from 5 o'clock high and was forced to unload and accelerate away. When I was confident of

A North Vietnamese MIG-17 makes a firing pass at an F-105 in the air battle north of Hanoi on 19 Dec. 1967. This action was filmed by the gunsight of another F-105.

sufficient separation I turned back to re-engage. I observed no MIG's, so continued northeast. The area of probable impact was the same area where the F-105's had jettisoned ordnance, so an exact impact point could not be determined.

The second force, consisting of four F-105 strike flights, one F-105F Iron Hand flight, and two F-4D MIGCAP flights, was more successful in accomplishing the day's mission. The four strike flights reached the Dai Loi railroad bridge, while the Iron Hand and MIGCAP flights engaged the same MIG's.

Maj. Robert R. Huntley, flying the lead aircraft in an F-105F Iron Hand flight, engaged and damaged one MIG-17. He thought he and his EWO, Capt. Ralph W. Stearman, had downed the enemy aircraft, but his claim was turned down by Seventh Air Force's Enemy Aircraft Claims Evaluation Board after careful study of all factors and sources of information.

Majors Dalton and Graham, flying aircraft 2 in Huntley's flight, attacked the MIG-17 earlier damaged by Moore and McKinney and were subsequently credited with one-half of an aerial victory. Finally Capt. Philip M. Drew, pilot, and Maj. William H. Wheeler, EWO flying in aircraft 3, downed a MIG–17 for themselves.

Major Dalton tells how he completed the destruction of the MIG damaged by Moore and McKinney:

The mission progressed as normal until approximately 35 miles southwest of the target. At that time bomb smoke was noted to the right of course, indicating that the strike planes had jettisoned their bombs. Shortly thereafter, a MIG warning was broadcast. I saw a MIG pull up in a steep climb approximately five or six miles at 12 o'clock and called it out. As we continued on course of 068°, several aircraft came into view: F–4's, F–105's, and four to six MIG's.

As we slacked off G's I was inside and approximately 1,500–2,000 feet to the rear of lead, and at this time I saw a MIG–17 low and right, apparently going after Huntley. I called him and started slowing down and turning right to get behind him. I closed as much as I could and started tracking and fired. I fired a short burst but was not tracking him, so I let up on the trigger, repositioned the pipper ahead of the MIG, let him fly up to it, and tracked him. Again I opened fire. As verified by my gun camera film, I observed impacts on the left wing and left side of the fuselage under the cockpit, at which time the MIG broke up and left. I turned to follow him but he rolled and started down inverted off to my left. At this time my EWO, Major Graham, called another MIG at our 7 o'clock coming down. I broke left into him and noted that two F–4's were in pursuit. The MIG rolled inverted and headed for the deck; the F–4's followed and fired a missile. I did not see the missile impact the MIG. At this time we contacted lead again but were unable to rejoin, and started to leave the area to rejoin aircraft 3 and 4. During egress, I observed two impact points...which I assumed were downed MIG's.

About this time Drew and Wheeler destroyed their MIG–17 "We were warned that there were two MIG's closing at our 7 o'clock position," said Wheeler. Drew describes the kill:

I turned hard into them, dived down into a valley, picked up my airspeed, and did a hard 180° turn back to the south. I picked up a MIG at my 1 o'clock high position going about the same direction that I was going. He appeared to be by himself. I was low on him and I don't believe he ever saw me. As he started a gentle right turn (about 40° of bank), I started my attack.

I had no problem tracking him, so I continued my attack, firing 756 rounds of 20-mm, until I could see the end of the MIG's wing tips on each side of the canopy bow which put him about 100 feet away. Prior to breaking off my attack, I saw numerous 20-mm rounds impacting in his fuselage and his right wing root area. As I crossed over the top of him, I clearly saw the aircraft markings on the top of his left wing. Major Wheeler, my EWO, called that we had another MIG attacking us from our left and that he was shooting. I looked to my left and picked up the new attacker about 1,000 feet out at 9 o'clock with his guns ablaze. I looked back at my target one last time and saw him rolling further right into a 120° bank turn and a 30° dive from about 7,000 feet altitude. Due to my position, I could not see beyond the tail of the MIG that I had fired on to observe the intensity of the smoke and fire. I was still close to him, though, since I could now clearly see the red star on his fuselage and the same insignia on the under side of his left wing as was on the top. I then pushed over, obtained 2 negative G's, and continued rolling to the left until I reached 50 feet above the ground and lost my attacker.

I made a slow 360° turn back to the area, looking for more MIG's and to pick up my wingman. My wingman joined up as I completed my turn . . . I looked back at my 4 o'clock position and saw black and gray smoke mushrooming up from where an aircraft had impacted the ground. This is a point that coincided exactly with the direction and attitude of flight from my MIG. By this time we were all well below Bingo fuel and there were no other aircraft, friendly or enemy, in the area other than aircraft 2, 3, and 4, so we initiated emergency refueling as soon as possible and returned to base.

Beginning in January 1968, MIG pilots were less prone to flee toward China. Instead, they became more aggressive and frequently returned for a second pass against American strike aircraft. The number of their kills increased and the MIG threat became more significant. U.S. forces therefore scheduled more MIGCAP missions and, at the same time, reduced the size of strike forces to provide better force protection.

The first confrontation of the new year took place on the morning of 3 January. The strike force was involved in a major effort and consisted of two separate forces. Alpha Force aimed at the Dong Dau railroad bridge in the Hanoi area and was made up of four F-105 strike flights, two F-105 Iron Hand flights, and two F-4D MIGCAP flights. This force was attacked by MIG-21's on its approach to the target. Bravo Force, consisting of three F-4D strike flights, one F-4D flak suppression flight, and two F-4D MIGCAP flights, was directed against the Trung Quang railroad yard. It was attacked by MIG-17's during withdrawal. The two forces approached from different directions and at different times, thus effectively splitting the NVN MIG forces.

No USAF aircraft was damaged. Bravo force engagements resulted in the destruction of two MIG-17's, one by a strike F-4D and the other by a MIGCAP aircrew. The strike aircraft was crewed by Lt. Col. Clayton K. Squier and 1st Lt. Michael D. Muldoon of the 435th TFS, 8th TFW. Squier's report describes his success:

> I engaged four MIG-17 aircraft in a head-on pass during egress from the strike target approximately 6 miles south of Bac Giang. The MIG's passed within 200-300 feet of my aircraft, going the opposite direction. I chandelled in afterburner to the left, cooling an AIM-4 missile for the reengagement. After approximately 360° of turn I visually acquired two MIG-17's 3 miles ahead, in trail and in a gentle left turn. I selected the trailing aircraft, tracked, closed to positively identify the type aircraft, and launched the AIM-4.
>
> The missile tracked directly to the aft section of the MIG-17, impacted in a ball of fire and smoke. The MIG immediately started a solid trail of gray/white smoke and continued in a gentle left turn with no maneuvering observed. As I passed to the right rear of the MIG-17 and slid to the outside of the turn, other aircraft in the immediate area diverted my attention and I lost sight of the smoking aircraft. I gathered my flight together and continued the egress.

Other pilots witnessed the impact and saw the smoke trailing the falling aircraft.

While Squier was firing his AIM-4, he was attacked by another MIG-17 which aimed cannon fire at him from a range of 1,000 feet, but missed. His wingman in aircraft 2 was also fired upon by a flight of two MIG-17's, but again with no damage resulting. Meanwhile, the F-4 MIGCAP flight observed the engagements and descended to get a closer look at what was going on. Maj. Bernard J. Bogoslofski and Capt. Richard L. Huskey, flying lead aircraft, observed a MIG-17 firing on Squier's wingman and decided to get it. Bogoslofski reports the encounter:

> The MIG-17 was tracking one F-4 in a tight left turn and gunfire was observed coming from the MIG-17. I was high and 5 o'clock to the MIG-17 and rolled in on him from 11,000 feet at an estimated 80° dive angle. I tracked the MIG-17 and began firing 20-mm. The MIG-17 tightened his left turn and I performed a vertical pirouette left in order to continue tracking him, using high-G and at least 80° of dive angle, high angle-off. A burst of fire appeared on the MIG's left wing and fragmentation of the aircraft's left wing was observed as I initiated a recovery.

Maj. Albert S. Borchik, Jr., in aircraft 4 of Bogoslofski's flight, and Maj. Ronald L. Markey, commanding aircraft 3, saw the pilot eject and the MIG hit the ground.

Approximately 2 weeks later, on the 18th, three large strike forces hit targets in North Vietnam. Alpha Force, scheduled against the Bac Giang thermal power plant, was made up of one F-105 Iron Hand flight, one F-4D flak-suppression flight, one F-4D strike flight, and one element of an F-4D MIGCAP flight; the other element aborted before entering North Vietnam due to ECM malfunctions. Alpha Force met coordinated attacks from SAM's, AAA, and MIG-17's, and in the air-to-air engagements the F-4D strike flight lost aircraft 1 and 2 but not before the flight leader had engaged and destroyed a MIG-17. Bravo Force consisted of four F-105 strike flights, one F-105 Iron Hand flight, and one F-4D MIGCAP flight. Bravo Force's target was the Ha Gia railroad siding, but strong resistance from two MIG-17's and two MIG-21's, in coordinated attacks, forced the Thunderchiefs to jettison ordnance 2 minutes short of the target. Charlie Force, composed of one F-105 Iron Hand flight, four F-105 strike flights, and two F-4D MIGCAP flights was assigned to deliver its ordnance on the Dap Cau railroad by pass. There were no incidents involving this force.

As Alpha force approached the target, Capt. Robert L. Rutherford, flying an F-4D in the fourth slot, observed two MIG-17's at 1 and 2 o'clock, in a climbing left turn. The flight was then at 12,000-foot altitude, above the MIG's, and beginning a descent to the target. Rutherford released his Walleye air-to-ground missile early and started a hard right climbing turn together with aircraft 3. The flight leader and his wingman, meanwhile, continued their normal descent toward the target, released their ordnance, and then began a right climbing turn. By this time Rutherford saw two more MIG-17's in trail with the first two.

Aircraft 2, the target of the second MIG element, called out: "They're shooting," and seconds later his aircraft was on fire. Other members of his flight saw him crash about 1 to 2 miles from the target. No parachutes.

In the meantime, the lead aircraft, crewed by Maj. Kenneth A. Simonet and 1st Lt. Wayne O. Smith, continued in a right climbing turn and observed a third MIG in the 10 o'clock position. Simonet immediately reversed left, cooled an AIM-4D, and fired the missile. It went up the tailpipe of the MIG and exploded. The MIG caught on fire, went out of control, and crashed. No parachute was observed. During this encounter a fourth MIG-17 pulled in behind Simonet, firing his cannon. Simonet's F-4 took hits and began trailing smoke. The MIG broke off the attack and Simonet turned to the east, attempting to withdraw. His F-4 soon showed open flame and he and his back-seater ejected. Their parachutes were observed descending to the ground.

Although Major Simonet and Lieutenant Smith did not return from this mission, their commanding officer submitted in their behalf a claim for the destruction of enemy aircraft. "Post flight analysis and review of the mission tapes of the air battle that took place," he commented, "indicate that their aircraft fired a missile and destroyed a MIG-17 on this mission."

The next victory came on 5 February when a small strike force attacked a target in the Thai Nguyen area. The U.S. Air Force lost a Thunderchief but downed a MIG-21. The force consisted of one F-105 Iron Hand flight, one F-105 strike flight, and two F-4D MIGCAP flights. A MIG-21 downed one of the F-105's while the MIG pilot's wingman was destroyed by a MIGCAP Phantom crewed by Capt. Robert G. Hill and 1st Lt. Bruce V. Huneke.

Inbound to the target, the strike force had received MIG warnings: "Two blue bandits airborne, Phuc Yen." The warnings continued, indicating two MIG-21's headed northwest out of Phuc Yen, apparently intent upon intercepting the approaching strike aircraft. Hill was the first to see a MIG. His flight leader instructed him to take the lead and go after it. While the flight turned left to attack, the flight members lost sight of the MIG-21, and an F-105 was destroyed by his air-to-air missile. The American pilot safely ejected moments before his aircraft rolled over and disappeared into the undercast. Hill and his wingman were rolling out of their 360° turn at 23,000 feet when the F-105 was hit.

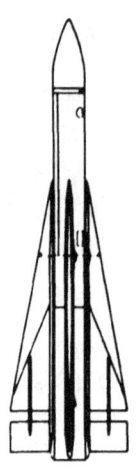
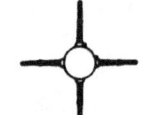

AIM-4E Falcon missile

Suddenly they saw a second MIG-21 climbing toward them. Hill picks up the story:

> I sighted a MIG-21 at my 10 o'clock position, low, as he was breaking off from an attack on an F-105. I immediately attacked and positioned myself in his 6 o'clock. The initial engagement was with the SUU-23 and 100 rounds were expended with no visible effects. I then cooled an AIM-4D. It never got a high tone. But I fired it, thinking "it may track." The missile did not appear to guide. The second AIM-4D worked exactly as advertised, and was observed to detonate on the MIG-21's aft section. I then selected radar and fired two AIM-7E's and attempted to fire a third. The first missile was launched with a boresight lock-on and did not appear to guide. The second AIM-7E was fired with a full system lock-on and appeared to guide. The third missile did not fire. At this time, aircraft 4 called a break as we were passing through 40,000 feet with a second MIG-21 on our tail, firing a missile.

Hill's second Falcon hit the MIG in the tailpipe, resulting in a 40-foot diameter, gray-white explosion. The MIG then exploded in a large red fireball of flame, blowing off the tail section. It fell straight down and impacted. No parachute was observed.

American forces were often successful against such multiple MIG passes because of improved MIG warnings and vectoring by the warning platforms. At times, too, MIG pilots became careless and screamed down on U.S. aircraft without benefit of their ground control. One such attack occurred on 6 February. A flight of four F-4D's providing MIGCAP for a strike mission were egressing the target area when a MIG-21 suddenly appeared, making a pass from the rear quarter, high. The flight broke up and went after the MIG. Three F-4 aircrews missed with their missiles, but the fourth, crewed by Capt. Robert H. Boles and 1st Lt. Robert B. Battista, found the MIG-21 directly in front of their aircraft. "Upon ingress, our flight was to the rear and the right side of the force," reports Boles.

After several MIG calls, we turned into the threat and engaged two MIG-21's. I visually acquired the MIG's at approximately three miles. One MIG made a climbing turn away from the flight, while the lead MIG turned left and down.

The flight leader and his wingman went down after the MIG while Captain [Joel S.] Aronoff [in aircraft 3] and I stayed high, initially. During the ensuing engagement aircraft 1, 2, and 3 each fired several missiles at the MIG. Although I had a radar lock-on and was within delivery parameters, I did not fire because Captain Aronoff did not immediately answer my radio transmissions when I asked if I were cleared to fire.

During the engagement, the MIG tried evasive maneuvers which consisted mainly of climbing and descending turns. When Captain Aronoff cleared me to fire, I was line abreast, 1,500–2,000 feet out from his plane. I attempted to fire two AIM-7's. The first missile did not come off. The second missile fired as advertised and guided toward the MIG. At firing, I held the MIG at 12 o'clock.... The interlocks were in, and we had a full system lock. The aim dot was centered. We were in a slight climb at the time. I watched the missile guide and just prior to impact the MIG either initiated a left turn or rocked his wings to the left in order to look back at our flight. The missile detonated at the left aft wing root section, and the MIG exploded. I then exclaimed over the radio that I got the MIG and asked Captain Aronoff to confirm it. He acknowledged the MIG's destruction. At that time the flight leader called for the egress.

Kep airfield was the target for a mission on 12 February, but enroute the primary mission was aborted because of adverse weather. The strike aircraft, accompanied by two MIGCAP flights from Ubon's 8th TFW, proceeded then to the alternate target: Cao Nung railroad yard. The two MIGCAP flights escorted the withdrawing strike flight to the coast and returned to sweep the target area. While withdrawing for the second time, each flight tracked two MIG-21's. Only one flight met with any success; the lead aircraft, crewed by Lt. Col. Alfred E. Lang, Jr., and 1st Lt. Randy P. Moss, downed one MIG-21. "I sighted two bogies at my 9 o'clock position approximately 4,000 feet high in a shallow left turn about 75 miles east of Hanoi," said Lang.

> I advised Col. Spencer that I had a lock-on at 22 miles and was maneuvering to accomplish an identification. I directed that his element fall into trail.

As I closed on the bogey, Lieutenant Moss (GIB) continually advised me of the bogey's azimuth, altitude, range and our overtake speed. He also had me recheck my armament switches and fuel status. At 8 miles Lieutenant Moss reaffirmed that the aim dot was centered, that we were in range, and then called out ranges at one mile intervals until I fired. At 6 miles I identified the second bogey as a MIG-21 and fired two AIM-7E's at 4½ miles, approximately 60° off his tail, with a full system lock-on, 600 knots overtake and the steering dot centered. Altitude was approximately 34,000 feet and airspeed 1.3 Mach. At this time I also cleared Col. Spencer to fire.

Lieutenant Moss and I both tracked our missiles visually and observed the first missile to explode in the MIG's 7-8 o'clock position and the second missile explode in the MIG's 10 o'clock position. As the MIG flew through the explosion he rolled inverted, yawed 30-40 degrees right to the direction of the flight, and then entered a tumbling spin. The pilot did not eject and the aircraft continued in an uncontrollable spin. I then sighted the other MIG, which had been approximately 3 miles in front of the destroyed MIG. We acquired lock-on from dead astern and closed to 9-10 miles, but had to break off the attack because aircraft 4 was minimum fuel. We recovered at our home base.

Colonel Robert V. Spencer, flying in aircraft 3 with 1st Lt. Richard W. Cahill as the rear-seater, had in the meantime fired two AIM-7 missiles at the lead MIG. The first, according to his account, guided and tracked toward the target, detonating short of the enemy aircraft. Spencer reported that the second missile guided, tracked, and exploded very near the MIG's 6 to 9 o'clock position. The MIG then "pitched violently upward and fell into an uncontrolled, tumbling spin."

Maj. Stuart W. Levy and 1st Lt. Gerald J. Crosson, Jr., observed the engagement from aircraft 4. Levy reported seeing Spencer's second missile "detonate on the MIG or within close proximity" and then observed the MIG "in an uncontrollable spin or tumble."

Lieutenant Crosson's report differed slightly; he said that Spencer's first AIM-7 exploded "four ship lengths behind the MIG" and that the second Sparrow appeared "to have been further to the MIG's rear." He also saw the MIG roll and then go into a flat, nose-high spin which developed into a nose-down spin. The aircrews of numbers 4 and 2 (Capt. Alexander D. Kelly and 1st Lt. Allan R. Sweeny) also observed the "destruction" of the MIG-21 by their flight leader. The Seventh Air Force later confirmed the kill by Lang and Moss, but denied the claim submitted by Spencer and Cahill.

The next aerial victories for the U.S. Air Force were the last before a 4-year hiatus set in. Two MIG-17's were destroyed during a strike against Phuc Yen airfield on 14 February 1968. In the strike force were two flights of Iron Hand F-105's, one F-4D strike flight, and two F-4D MIGCAP flights (one fragged as "fast" CAP and the other charged with "slow" CAP). All of the MIGCAP aircrews were briefed to expect the standard coordinated MIG-17/MIG-21 effort, with the MIG-17's flying a low Wagon-Wheel orbit and the MIG-21's flying high altitudes, and both under GCI control. One F-4 flight was armed with AIM-7 and AIM-9 air-to-air missiles; the other with AIM-4 and AIM-7 missiles and SUU-23 gun pods.

MIG warnings proved to be excellent, and the second F-4 flight turned to approach two MIG-21's as the strike force was inbound to the target. The F-4's obtained a radar lock-on, but the MIG's withdrew without contact and the flight rejoined the strike force near Thud Ridge. These two MIG-21's avoided the F-4's, but then attacked one of the trailing F-105 Iron Hand flights. After a brief engagement, one element of the F-105's returned to Korat while the other continued on to the target area. As the strike force continued, the F-4 flight sighted four MIG-17's at 11 o'clock, range of 3 miles, headed toward it.

The MIG-17's were performing a left-hand Wagon Wheel maneuver at 8,000 feet over the flats northeast of Phuc Yen as the F-4 flight commenced a climbing spiral to the right to gain separation and to set up for a pass. The flight leader, Lt. Col. Wesley D. Kimball, and his wingman, Maj. Ray M. Burgess, went through the wheel with Kimball attempting to get a MIG with an AIM-4. The missile did not get a high tone, so he did not fire. Kimball

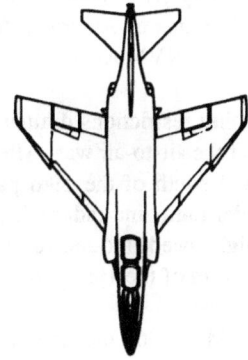 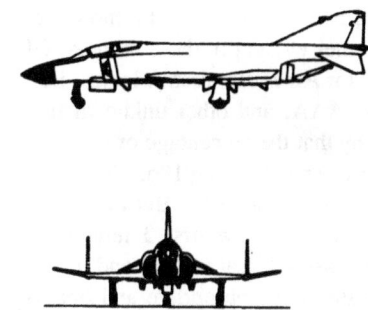

F-4D Fighter

and Burgess dived through the MIG orbit pattern, pulled up at 7,000 feet, and started to climb. It was at this moment that Maj. Rex D. Howerton and 1st Lt. Ted L. Voigt II, in aircraft position 3, entered the fray. One of the MIG's attempted to fall in behind the number one element. "Observing this," said the major,

> I began my attack and rolled in approximately 2,500 feet behind the MIG and fired an AIM-4D missile. The missile appeared to guide, but thinking that I might be inside minimum parameters I selected guns and began firing the SUU-23 cannon. Cannon hits were noted on the MIG and shortly thereafter the MIG exploded and began to break up. The missile was not seen to impact or destruct. The MIG went down in flames with one wing and the tail section separated.

Kimball and Burgess then made another pass at another MIG. Kimball fired 350 rounds of 20-mm from a range of 2,000 feet, but saw no hits. Very low on fuel at this point, his flight left the area.

Within 2 or 3 minutes after this engagement began, the other MIGCAP flight attacked these same MIG-17's. The lead aircraft, crewed by Col. David O. Williams, Jr., and 1st Lt. James P. Feighny, Jr., soon downed one of them. Williams reports:

> On February 14, following vectors given to the flight by surveillance agencies, we sighted four MIG-17's in a left-hand orbit pattern approximately 10 miles northwest of Phuc Yen, at approximately 15,000 feet. I observed Kimball's flight execute an attack on the MIG's and then rolled in behind his 3 and 4 on a trailing MIG. I observed the MIG start a right hand turn and dove down from approximately 24,000 feet to his 5:30 to 6 o'clock position at approximately 1.2 Mach.
>
> I asked my rear seat pilot if he was locked on and he replied he was, but wasn't sure it was the right target, so he asked me to put the pipper on him and he selected gyro out and relocked, at which time he verified that we were now locked on to the MIG. I fired one AIM-7E Sparrow missile in full system lock-on, interlocks in, in-range light on at approximately ¾ mile. The missile tracked perfectly and detonated near the left side of the MIG's fuselage. The MIG immediately shed its empennage and burst into a bright orange fire in a flat spin. I immediately yo-yoed high and then rolled over to clear my tail.
>
> As I looked back, I observed the MIG to be in a flat spin, burning profusely. At about the same time I observed a parachute with a man hanging from it. The chute was bright orange and white and was of a square pattern. I then turned back left and observed another MIG-17 in a nose-down snapping spin with no left wing. The left wing was 1,000 to 1,500 feet above the MIG and tumbling downward. I also observed what appeared to be pieces of the tail fluttering downward behind the MIG. This MIG impacted in rice paddy terrain northeast of a large river. When I rolled back to the right, I observed the first MIG impact in a rice paddy close to the foot of Thud Ridge, exploding in a large orange fireball.

In sum, USAF fighter crews, all flying F-4D

Phantoms, destroyed eight MIG's in aerial combat during January and February 1968. Yet a more significant factor becomes evident in these months. Of the possible causes for American aircraft losses, i.e., to MIG's, SAM's, AAA, and other unknown factors, it is noteworthy that the percentage of losses to MIG's was a mere 1 percent during 1965, 3 percent in 1966, and 8 percent during 1967. But this figure leaped to 22 percent during the first 3 months of 1968. With this increasing threat and the end of bad weather, the time appeared appropriate and opportune for another major American effort against North Vietnam's MIG force. But then, on 31 March, President Lyndon B. Johnson announced the first of a series of bombing restrictions. Effective 1 April, all bombing north of 20° North latitude would cease. Two days later, the bomb line was further moved southward to 19°, permitting air strikes only in Route Packages 1, 2, and the southern third of 3. Thus, nearly all of North Vietnam became a MIG sanctuary; the only jet-capable airfields within the limited operating area of American forces were not being used by the NVN Air Force for MIG operations.

These bombing restrictions dramatically changed the character of the air-to-air war. After 3 April 1968 MIG's ventured south of the 19th parallel, for the most part, under radio and radar silence. They continued their high-speed, hit-and-run tactics but usually retreated north of the 19th parallel after making single firing passes.

Only on 23 May 1968 did any sizeable force of MIG's venture south of the bomb line. One MIG–21 was downed by a U.S. Navy Talos missile. Some MIG's were lost to the Navy later in that year, but the U.S. Air Force scored no additional aerial victories. After 28 September 1968, North Vietnamese MIG activity virtually ceased, and on 1 November 1968 all bombing in North Vietnam was halted by Presidential proclamation.

North Vietnamese prepare to launch a surface-to-air missile.

(Top) North Vietnamese pilots rush for their MIG-17's in response to alarm that USAF planes are in the area.

(Left) A single MIG with markings, in flight.

LAUNCH POSITION
CENTRAL GUIDANCE AREA

III

Combat Narratives 1972–1973

(Far left) A USAF RF–101 reconnaisance pilot photographed one of the North Vietnamese surface-to-air missiles in flight.

(Left) North Vietnamese surface-to-air missiles were launched from sites such as this one near Haiphong.

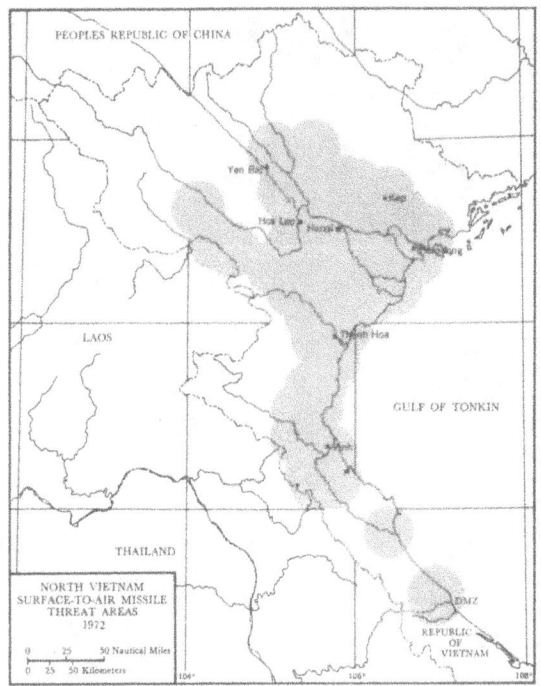

Following the USAF victories on 14 February 1968, there was an interruption in shootdowns that lasted more than 4 years.* The next USAF aerial victory over a MIG did not come until 21 February 1972. Numerous changes took place during this period, e.g., the election of President Richard M. Nixon, the withdrawal of the bulk of American forces from South Vietnam, and a renewed emphasis on turning over responsibility for conduct of the war to the South Vietnamese armed forces.

North Vietnam used this breathing spell to improve and strengthen its air defenses with the material assistance of the Soviet Union and Communist China. Additional AAA and SAM sites appeared at strategic points, particularly in Quang Binh Province. New airfields were also constructed, and coverage of North Vietnam ground control intercept radars was extended southward. American commanders noted that MIG aircraft airborne below 20° North latitude increased from a daily average of five flights in late 1971 to an average of 10 per day early in 1972. By March 1972 the North Vietnamese fighter inventory included 93 MIG–21's, 33 MIG–19's, and 120 MIG–15's and –17's—although prob-

---

*The hiatus, as noted in the previous chapter, followed President Johnson's 31 March 1968 decision to halt the bombing of North Vietnam above the 20th parallel and to invite North Vietnam to begin peace negotiations. Seven months later the President ordered an end of all bombing north of the DMZ in hopes of bringing about an end to all hostilities.

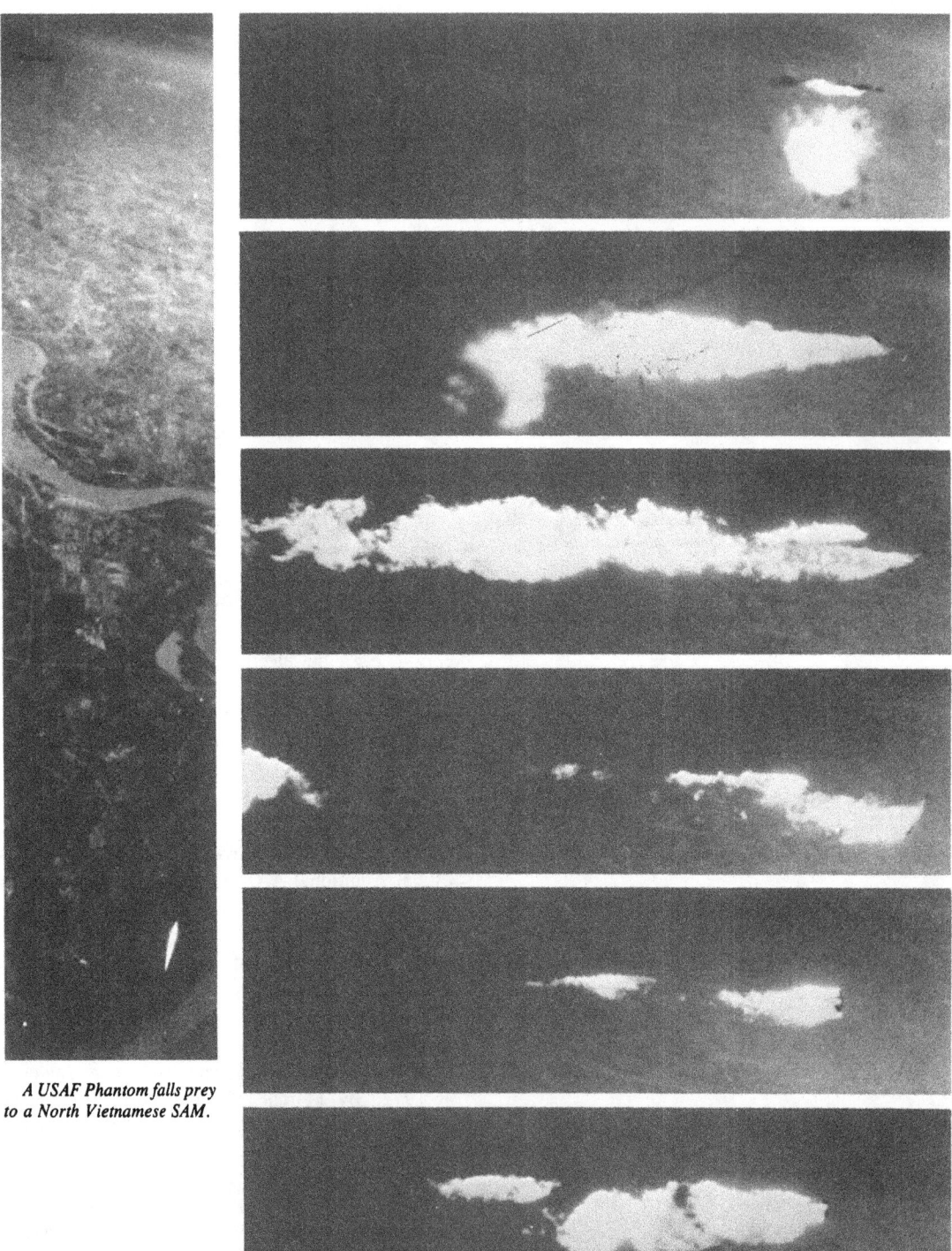

A USAF Phantom falls prey to a North Vietnamese SAM.

ably no more than 190 of these aircraft were combat ready.

By early 1972 North Vietnam had what was generally recognized as one of the best, if not the best, air defense system in the world. Its strongest features were excellent radar integration, the Soviet-built SA-2 surface-to-air missile, and the MIG-21 aircraft. And an intangible advantage was the fact that this defense system operated over its own homeland. The enemy air defense system, therefore, had an impressive array of firepower from ground level to 19 miles in the air. Further, its MIG-21's could be vectored by radar with split-second timing against U.S. strike and support forces. It was no secret that the North Vietnamese could determine the structure of American strike forces soon after the U.S. aircraft left the ground.

American forces had the advantage of special chaff-dispensing flights which helped to degrade the enemy's SAM and AAA gunlaying radars. This degradation was further supplemented by EB-66 electronic jamming, U.S. Navy jamming, and jamming pods installed on all strike aircraft. In the Gulf of Tonkin the U.S. Navy operated an early warning radar ship nicknamed Red Crown (officially designated: Positive Identification Radar Advisory Zone Ship), while the U.S. Air Force had an airborne counterpart, coded Disco, to provide forces with MIG warnings. Red Crown was more effective along coastal and Disco in inland areas.

Notwithstanding the standdown in North Vietnam, B-52 strikes continued in Laos, and USAF fighters flew combat air patrols and escort flights. Early in 1972, MIG's began increasingly to penetrate Laos to try to check these strikes, but USAF F-4's were on hand to greet them. So for a brief period of time during the inactivity over North Vietnam, the F-4's engaged MIG's in air-to-air combat over Laos.

Victories over Laos

The first U.S. Air Force aerial victory in 4 years and, more significantly, the first at night took place on 21 February 1972 over northeast Laos, about 90 miles southwest of Hanoi. Maj. Robert A. Lodge was aircraft commander and 1st Lt. Roger C. Locher was his weapon systems officer in an F-4D flying MIGCAP. They were from the 555th TFS, which formerly had been a part of the 8th TFW but was now a part of the 432d Tactical Reconnaissance Wing.

"Red Crown called out bandits (MIG's) at our 060° position and proceeded to vector us on an intercept," recalls Maj. Lodge. He adds further:

> I descended to minimum en route altitude, and at approximately 1323Z [2123 local] my WSO detected and locked on a target at the position Red Crown was calling Bandit.
>
> The target was level at zero azimuth and closing, with the combined velocity of both aircraft in excess of 900 knots. I fired three AIM-7E's, the first at approximately 11 nautical miles, the second at 8 nautical miles and the third at 6 nautical miles. The first missile appeared to guide and track level, and detonated in a small explosion. The second missile guided in a similar manner and detonated with another small explosion, followed immediately by a large explosion in the same area. This secondary explosion was of a different nature than the two missile detonations and appeared like a large POL [petroleum, oil and lubricants] explosion with a fireball. The third missile started guiding in a corkscrew manner and then straightened out. No detonation was observed for the third missile. We had no more AIM-7's left, and broke off and egressed at low altitude.
>
> Two other MIG-21's then attempted to pursue us. We were low, over 500 knots computed airspeed, and the MIG's broke off after about a 30-nautical mile chase and continued to drop back. Another F-4 was flying radar trail during the entire flight and was about 5,000 feet higher than us on the final attack.

This MIG engagement ushered in the final phase of aerial warfare that continued to the end of Southeast Asia hostilities in 1973.

A week later, the 555th Tactical Fighter Squadron added another MIG-21 to its expanding list of aerial victories. Lt. Col. Joseph W. Kittinger, Jr., flying F-4D MIGCAP with 1st Lt. Leigh A. Hodgdon in the rear seat, emerged victors in an air battle. Their

F–4D was accompanied by another crewed by Maj. R. Carroll and Capt. David L. Harris.

Before taking off for their MIGCAP in northern Laos, they had been briefed to anticipate enemy diversionary flights which sought to lure unsuspecting F–4's into a hazardous environment. American fighter pilots were well aware that the North Vietnamese monitored all radio conversations between U.S. air defense agencies and airborne fighters and used such information to their advantage. About 2000 hours on the night of 1 March Kittinger's flight took up a MIGCAP position in northeastern Laos. Disco soon advised the flight that MIG's were airborne in the area and vectored the Phantoms to make contact. Kittinger's report of the engagement follows:

Col. Kittinger survived his captivity as a prisoner of war. He is shown greeting the home-coming crowd upon his return on 28 March 1973.

At approximately 18 miles the system broke lock but it was quickly reacquired. A slow left turn ensued to keep the dot centered. Altitudes were slowly increased from 8,200 feet to 11,500 feet. The Vc on the scope was extremely difficult to interpret; however, it appeared that we were not really overtaking the target, so the outboard tanks were dropped. Heading of the aircraft changed to approximately 360° at time of firing. At approximately 6 miles the "in-range" light illuminated, followed by an increase in the ASE circle. Trigger was squeezed and crew felt a thump as the missile was ejected; however, missile motor did not ignite. The trigger was squeezed again and held for approximately 3 seconds; however, missile did not fire. Trigger was squeezed again and missile #3 fired. The missile made a small correction to the left then back to the right and guided straight away. The pilot maintained the dot centered.

Approximately 5 to 6 seconds after launch, detonation was observed. Almost simultaneously, two enemy missiles were observed coming from the vicinity of the detonation. Evasive action prevented more thorough observations of detonation. The flight turned to a heading of 210°, maintained 9,000 feet, airspeed 500 knots, and egressed the area.

Colonel Kittinger was serving on his third tour of duty in Southeast Asia, which began in May 1971. A few days after his victory, his Phantom was shot down in another aerial battle, only 17 days before he was due to return home. Kittinger thus became a prisoner of war. Earlier in his Air Force career, he had gained recognition as "the first man in space" when he ascended in a small gondola under a huge balloon to 96,000 feet on 2 June 1957. He eclipsed his own record on 16 August 1960 by rising to 102,800 feet and then returning to earth by parachute.

A new aspect was added to the air war in Southeast Asia on 30 March 1972, when the North Vietnamese formally invaded the south. They quickly moved through the demilitarized zone into Quang Tri Province. In response to the NVN offensive, American air resources were ordered to active interdiction of MIG's in North Vietnam. That same day there was one aerial victory.

Captains Frederick S. Olmsted, Jr., aircraft commander, and Gerald R. Volloy, weapon systems officer, were pulling F–4D alert duty at Udorn late in the day when they were scrambled to take up an orbit near the Laotian border. About 20 minutes after reaching their orbit point, Red Crown called a bandit and vectored the flight to intercept. According to Volloy:

Red Crown provided vectors until approximately 20 nautical miles, and at 15 nautical miles I established radar contact with the bandit. A full system lock-on was acquired at 12 nautical miles, and all missile-firing parameters were satisfactory. We fired one AIM–7 at approximately 8 nautical miles with no visible results. Another AIM–7 was fired at approximately 6 nautical miles; the missile appeared to fire properly and guided well, straight off the aircraft. When no visible results were seen a third AIM–7 was fired at approximately 4 nautical miles. This missile appeared to guide well, appeared to track straight off the aircraft and then disappeared from view.

A few seconds later, both I and my aircraft commander, Captain Olmsted, observed at 1 o'clock, almost level, approximately 1–2 nautical miles ahead, a large reddish-yellow fireball that sustained itself for a few seconds. The fireball first appeared, and then trailed what seemed to be sparks behind it. The fiery sparks paralleled our flight path, toward us, and the entire fire pattern was estimated to be 150–200 feet in length. Visual contact was lost with the fireball due to our egress breakaway. A subsequent query to Red Crown confirmed that the bandit had disappeared from their scopes as well. It was at this time that we egressed from the area.

As the North Vietnamese offensive continued, it became apparent to American forces that the enemy had to be hit at his supply points. On 16 April strike forces were sent to bomb fuel depots, warehouses, and truck parks in the vicinity of Haiphong and on the outskirts of Hanoi. These were the first American raids into the Hanoi-Haiphong area since President Johnson's partial bombing halt had been announced on 31 March 1968. As anticipated, the enemy resisted ferociously, firing thousands of rounds of antiaircraft artillery and about 200 surface-to-air missiles. In the air war, MIG–21's met and engaged American strike aircraft. Two MIG's were destroyed by a MIGCAP F–4D flight assigned to protect the strike aircraft.

Capt. Frederick S. Olmsted, Jr., who had downed a MIG–21 two weeks earlier, and his WSO, Capt. Stuart W. Maas, destroyed the first of two MIG's. Captain Olmsted describes the action in detail:

On the morning of 16 April 1972 Capt. Stuart W. Maas and I were assigned to lead a four-ship MIGCAP that was to render cover for strike forces ingressing and egressing the target area as well as providing the first line of defense for SAR [Search and Rescue] forces orbiting close to the North Vietnam border in northern Laos.

We took off from Udorn RTAFB at 0830 and proceeded northward to a pre-strike holding orbit where we were to await the strike force. At the appointed time we turned eastward and proceeded to take our flight to the assigned orbit. . . As we approached the southern point of the orbit, I made an initial check-in with Red Crown. As our flight drew closer to the border, SAM launch warnings and calls to other flights also on the same frequency increased. A large number of these calls were to warn them of nearby enemy aircraft, but not once was the flight specifically warned.

We crossed the orbit's southern point and began a descending left turn to head toward the northern point, pick up maneuvering airspeed, and place us in clearer airspace. There were numerous layered decks of clouds above, and below were scattered cumulus and rain showers.

As we rolled out on a heading of 340°, Captain Maas picked up two hostile aircraft indications on the radar scope and at 20 nautical miles Captain Maas made a radio call to my flight, warning them of the danger. At 11 nautical miles, Captain Maas again made another radio call to prepare the flight for engagement. At this time I instructed the flight to jettison tanks, and within seconds Captain Maas locked on and tracked the bogies down the scope and off the left side.

As they passed just overhead, I visually identified them as hostile and pulled up into a right, climbing turn. As we broke through the cloud deck, we reacquired the MIG–21's. At this point the flight split, with aircraft 3 and 4 taking one MIG, ourselves and our wing man the other. After a series of turns with the bandit a new, full-system radar lock-on was acquired and, with firing parameters met, the first AIM–7 was fired. It guided to the MIG and sheared off a portion of the right wing. The MIG appeared to tighten up the left turn, so a second missile was fired. Apparently it never guided, so a third missile was triggered. This one flew true and the MIG was seen to explode by Captain Maas, myself, and the two crewmen of aircraft 2 who were in a fighting wing position. At this time we broke down and left, picking up speed to exit the area.

The second MIG–21 was destroyed by aircraft 3, crewed by Maj. Edward D. Cherry and Capt. Jeffrey S. Feinstein. Cherry's account of his MIG engagement picks up at the point the MIG's were spotted by radar:

> Olmsted had made contact with at least two MIG's on his radar and was leading the flight to the MIG's. He obtained visual contact with two MIG–21's and called them to us. The MIG–21's passed overhead and Olmsted started a right turn to engage them.
>
> While in the right turn, our wingman obtained a visual contact with a third MIG–21 and called for us to roll out and turn left. The MIG flew into a cloud layer but we were in hot pursuit. Shortly after breaking through the cloud layer I obtained visual contact with the MIG–21 at 12 o'clock high, in a right, climbing turn. I maneuvered my aircraft into firing position and attempted to fire an AIM–9 heat missile but did not observe the missile launch. (From an analysis afterward, it appears that the missile launched but did not guide.)
>
> We were now in an 80° climb and an 80° right bank. Captain Feinstein obtained a full system radar lock-on and I made two more attempts to fire a missile at the MIG but observed no launch. We went over the top with the MIG in a descending right turn. Our wingman took the lead with us assuming fighting wing formation. Our wing man fired all four of his radar missiles at the MIG and missed. During this time he lost his radio and did not hear our repeated radio calls to break out of the way so we could shoot. While he was shooting, Captain Feinstein obtained a full system lock-on on the MIG.
>
> We regained radio contact with our wingman, passed him on the right, and reassumed lead position in the element. Most of this time our planes were in an 80° right descending turn. I fired one AIM–7 radar missile which impacted the MIG–21 just aft of the right wing post. The MIG's right wing immediately separated and the aircraft went into a wild, gyrating spin to the left, trailing smoke and aircraft fragments. Captains Crane and Lachman in aircraft 4 also observed the missile impact and explosion. The MIG pilot ejected immediately and I, along with Captain Feinstein and aircraft 4, observed the parachute and the pilot. I estimate that we passed within 500 feet of the MIG pilot's chute.

A third MIG–21 was also destroyed on the same day in a separate engagement. Capt. James C. Null and his WSO, Capt. Michael D. Vahue, flying an F–4D, had been scrambled from Udorn and vectored into northern Laos to investigate a possible hostile track. The target was declared hostile shortly after the flight reached the orbit, and Null was authorized to initiate the attack. He reports:

> The flight jettisoned all external tanks. Aircraft 4 acquired a radar lock-on when the target was 19 miles out. He was given the lead and attempted to fire, but all AIM–7's malfunctioned. A flight of two MIG–21's passed overhead, and we started a hard right turn.
>
> A vector of 275° for 12 miles was received and visual and radar contact was made at that point. We closed on the target, confirmed it was a flight of two MIG–21's, and maneuvered to their 12 o'clock position. Radar lock-on was acquired and when in range three AIM–7's were fired, the second of which proximity fused* on the left side of the wingman's tail section, tearing it from the fuselage. We then passed overhead and observed the MIG to be on fire in the aft section of the fuselage and out of control at approximately 2,000 feet altitude. No chutes were observed. We then egressed and heard from a controlling agency that a single hostile aircraft was orbiting in the vicinity of the engagement.

Linebacker Operations

The month of May 1972 was significant in the Vietnamese war. On the 8th, President Richard M. Nixon announced the resumption of bombing of North Vietnam and the mining of entrances to its ports. The mines were set to activate on the 11th.

---

*A proximity fuze is designed to detonate a bomb, mine, or charge when activated by an external influence in close vicinity of a target.

The Presidential announcement was in effect the "execute" order for Operation Linebacker, the nickname given renewed and generally unrestricted air strikes against military targets in North Vietnam. Throughout April and the first week of May, additional U.S. Navy attack carriers joined the line in the Gulf of Tonkin, large numbers of B–52 heavy bombers were deployed to points from which they could reach Southeast Asia, and more tactical fighter aircraft were placed in Thailand to supplement air power there. The stage had been set for implementation of the new policy.

During an air strike in the Hanoi area on 8 May, two MIG's fell to USAF F–4D aircrews. Two different MIGCAP flights, both from the 432d TRW, supported this strike and each encountered MIG's in the target area. Maj. Barton P. Crews and his WSO, Capt. Keith W. Jones, Jr., downed a MIG–19—the first enemy aircraft of this type destroyed by an Air Force crew. Major Crews describes his skirmish:

> On 8 May 1972, a flight of four F–4D's was fragged to provide MIGCAP for strike flights hitting the Hanoi area. I was scheduled as number three, with Capt. Keith W. Jones as my weapon systems officer. After the flight arrived at the preplanned orbit point the flight proceeded north of Yen Bai airfield and then made a 180° right turn heading south.
>
> After crossing the Red River, the lead aircraft called, "Bogies, 12 o'clock." I immediately acquired them visually and identified them as four MIG–19's.
>
> I called over the radio, "They're not friendly."
>
> The lead aircraft commander confirmed that, and directed the engagement. I set up my attack on the northernmost element of MIG–19's and started a closure on what appeared to be the number two man. My WSO stated that he couldn't get a lock-on so I pulled the pipper up to the MIG and fired one AIM–7. I estimated the range was under 3,000 feet. I did not see the missile impact as I directed my attention to the lead MIG. Captain Jones stated he saw a yellowish chute go by.
>
> As I was trying to get my pipper on the lead MIG he did a hard break and ruined my tracking solution.
>
> At that time my number four aircraft said over the radio, "That's a kill."
>
> Shortly after that my number four WSO, Lieutenant Holland, called, "Bandits at 6 o'clock."
>
> I then broke off my engagement and went into the clouds and lost the MIG's. Later, on the ground, 1st Lt. William S. Magill and 1st Lt. Michael T. Holland, the aircraft commander and weapon systems officer on my wing, confirmed seeing a chute and observing the MIG do a slow roll to inverted position and start down.

The other MIGCAP flight was trailing the strike force over Hoa Binh and heard the radio chatter as Crews' flight engaged its MIG's. Red Crown requested assistance for a flight of F–4 strike aircraft, which was also engaging MIG's near Yen Bai. Before they could reach the battle area, the flight disengaged, but Red Crown advised that another group of bandits were approaching from the east. Maj. Robert A. Lodge, flight leader, with Capt. Roger C. Locher as his WSO, turned his flight eastward and crossed the Red River. Locher soon acquired two targets on his radar, and the flight turned to engage

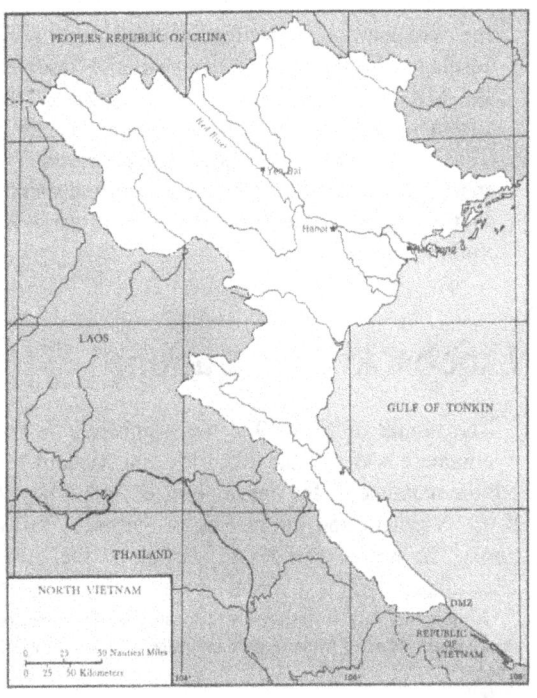

them. As Lodge closed on a MIG, he saw another at 1 o'clock. "I continued to close on our radar target while watching the second, closer one," he said.

At about one mile I saw that the other aircraft was a silver MIG-21.

We broke radar contact with the leading MIG and locked on to the wingman. We were about Mach 1.4, with the MIG about as fast as us in afterburner. I was low on the MIG, and I do not believe he was aware he was under attack. He was in a right turn, initially, then reversed to the left. I fired two AIM-7 missiles in ripple fire at a distance of 4,500 feet, using a pure pursuit attack at about 20° angle-off.

Both missiles guided directly to the target. The first hit the MIG's right wing, which was breaking up when the second missile hit the center of the fuselage. I observed no bailout. I last saw the MIG disintegrating and out of control. The lead MIG broke up hard and I lost visual contact with him. My wingman then engaged the MIG unsuccessfully.

We disengaged at Bingo fuel and egressed the area. Passing the initial area outbound while descending, I observed a parachute to the left of my aircraft at an estimated 300 feet away. I almost hit the chute. There was a yellow canopy and a body in the chute but I did not notice if the pilot was alive. Egress was then uneventful with a normal recovery.

Operation Linebacker commenced on 9 May, and American forces did well in air-to-air engagements. During May and June the ratio of kills was better than one to one in favor of the American forces. Fighter aircrews of the 432d Tactical Reconnaissance Wing, based at Udorn, scored the majority of kills. The wing was the primary counter-air unit in Southeast Asia during 1972. The addition of this role to its mission made it the only composite—strike-interdiction, counter-air, and reconnaissance—wing in the conflict and, more notable, its role made possible the majority of MIG kills. The 432d Wing's counter-air mission was diversified, including ingress MIGCAP, egress CAP, and barrier CAP (different types of combat air patrol).

The entire USAF effort, however, was directed toward strikes against enemy military targets. Combat air patrols were employed toward this end and not to destroy MIG's. Counter-MIG tactics, when employed, generally used the fluid-four formation for all daytime MIGCAP and escort missions, while at night the MIGCAP aircraft flew separate two-plane elements, with the second element in maneuvering radar trail formation.

Ingress CAP's were primarily flown for protection of chaff and chaff escort flights from MIG attack. This required two or three flights of four F-4's each, which preceded the chaff mission aircraft into a target area and remained until the mission aircraft left the hostile zone. MIGCAP flights often arrived at the target scene before strike aircraft and remained until the latter departed.

"On all missions," Maj. Gen. Alton D. Slay* commented, "we mounted at least two target area MIGCAP's, and one or two egress CAP's. The egress CAP was launched so as to arrive on station near the projected North Vietnam exit point of the strike force at about 10 minutes prior to expected earliest egress time."

All egress CAP F-4's were freshly refueled aircraft and able to take over the protection of strike planes from the MIGCAP F-4's, since the latter would be low on fuel upon egressing. Combat air patrol missions, composed of a flight of four aircraft, were responsible for the protection of all types of allied air forces: fighter-bombers, heavy bombers, reconnaissance aircraft, gunships, electronic communications aircraft, and search and rescue aircraft. Egress CAP also was responsible for covering the post-strike reconnaissance flight.

Finally, barrier CAP provided a buffer zone between threat areas and specialized friendly aircraft, including refueling tankers, SAR forces, and EC-121 and EB-66 electronic communications and surveillance aircraft. The barrier CAP flight was usually made up of flights of two F-4's.

All strike formations were escorted by at least one, and sometimes two, flights of F-4's. These aircraft were not limited to the immediate vicinity of the strike force, but were allowed to turn into approaching MIG's—provided advance warning was available.

---

*Deputy Chief of Staff, Operations, Seventh Air Force, December 1971–August 1972.

The most troublesome MIG tactic was the low approach and zoom attack. Although the MIG's relied almost without exception on hit-and-run tactics—single passes at high speeds—the F-4's, nevertheless, enjoyed a high success rate because of crew aggressiveness.

"Triple-Nickel" Hits Jackpot

USAF pilots scored more victories on MIGCAP flights than on any other type of mission. While on MIGCAP, aircrews flying F-4D's of the "Triple-Nickel" Squadron—the 555th TFS of the 432d TRW—scored the next five USAF victories of the air war to make it six straight for the squadron. Three of these victories came on 10 May, and all of the MIG killers were of the same flight.

Maj. Robert A. Lodge, serving as the flight leader with Capt. Roger C. Locher as his weapon systems officer, was involved in the initial engagement. The account of the victory is told for Major Lodge by Lt. Col. Wayne T. Frye:

> Fifty miles south of Yen Bai Captain Locher held two separate hostile contacts on the nose at 40 miles. I then positioned my flight into modified fluid-four formation and set up for the impending engagement. The MIG's continued down the center of the scope and I accelerated to 1.4 Mach. Twenty nautical miles from the radar contact I began a 5° wing-level climb and armed my missiles. At 13 nautical miles the "in-range" light came on. I waited until the ASE circle began to contract and fired one AIM-7 at a range of 8 nautical miles at the leading MIG element. The missile came off the aircraft and began climbing at a 15–20° angle, tracking straight away. When the missile motor burned out, the missile detonated. I immediately fired the second AIM-7 at 6 nautical miles. It also came off and began climbing at a 20° angle, tracking straight away. The missile contrailed for about 5–8 seconds, and then I observed the missile detonation, followed immediately by a huge reddish-orange fireball. I could not see the MIG visually at this time. I continued my climb and 5 seconds later saw a MIG-21 with the left wing missing, trailing fire with pieces falling off, the aircraft out of control, pass 1,000 feet to the left side of my aircraft. The pilot had already ejected. The flight then engaged the remainder of the flight of bandits.

Colonel Frye signed Lodge's claim statement, because Lodge was shot down by a heat-seeking missile from one of the MIG's shortly after his successful engagement. Captain Locher, who was rescued 23 days later, described the loss of the F-4 after the enemy missile hit:

MIG-21's in flight.

The "Triple-Nickel" Squadron displayed its motto on this sign.

We immediately went out of control, flopping from side to side. Then fire started coming in the back of the cockpit. It seared my canopy with bubbles and I couldn't see out any more. The airplane slowed down and we went into a flat spin.

Locher ejected and came down in "a kind of deep-dished valley." For the next 23 days he subsisted on fruit, nuts, berries, and water from banana trees. After his rescue he and other flight members reconstructed details of the 10 May engagement so that Lodge could also claim the destruction of an enemy aircraft.

The second MIG–21 downed by Lodge's flight came minutes after. Lodge's wingman, 1st Lt. John D. Markle, and his WSO, Capt. Stephen D. Eaves, scored the aerial victory. Lieutenant Markle reports:

> Lodge initiated the attack. We engaged a MIG–21 that was a threat to the flight. The MIG was engaged with a full system radar lock-on. Two AIM–7 missiles were launched by us. I observed the second missile to climb slightly and turn right approximately 15°. Soon after missile launch, I visually identified a MIG–21 passing from my left to my right. The AIM–7 continued on a collision course with the MIG–21. Upon impact the missile detonated and a large yellow fireball resulted. The right wing of the MIG departed the aircraft and the airframe immediately began to descend out of control. The kill was witnessed by aircraft 4, 1st Lt. Tommy L. Feezel, aircraft commander, and Capt. Lawrence H. Pettit, weapon systems officer.

The flight's third aerial victory followed immediately. Capt. Richard S. "Steve" Ritchie, aircraft commander, and Capt. Charles B. DeBellevue, weapon systems officer in aircraft 3 secured the first of a string of MIG kills which would bring the coveted distinction of "Ace" and would subsequently make DeBellevue the ranking ace of the Vietnam conflict. Ritchie accounts for his and DeBellevue's initial aerial victory:

> Upon reaching our patrol area west of Phu Tho and south of Yen Bai, Red Crown advised us of bandits approaching from the northeast. Shortly thereafter, both Lodge and I obtained a radar

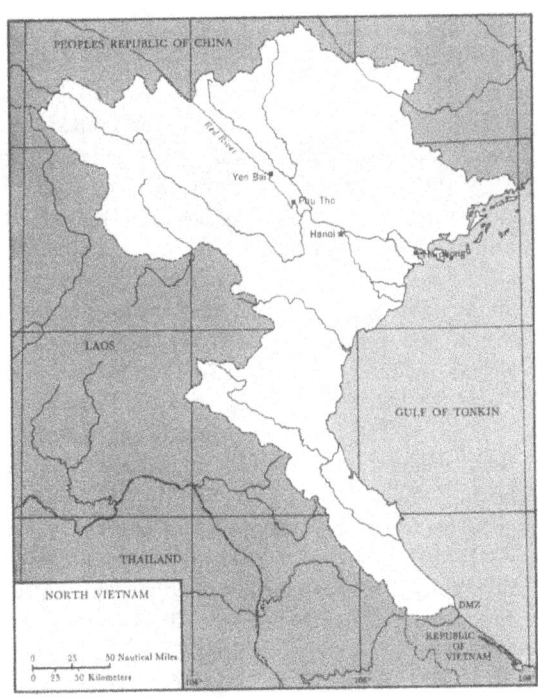

> contact. The bandits were declared hostile and our flight engaged the flight of four MIG–21's.
>
> Lodge fired two missiles at the attacking MIG's from a front-quarter aspect, utilizing a full system radar lock-on. A detonation and fireball were seen as one of the missiles impacted the number two MIG. Meanwhile, Markle achieved a radar lock-on on the number three MIG–21 and fired two AIM–7 missiles. Another yellow fireball was observed and the number three MIG began to disintegrate.
>
> At this time, we switched the attack to the number four MIG, which was now a threat to Lodge and Markle, while Lodge pursued the number one MIG. As we converted to the rear, I achieved a radar lock-on and fired two AIM–7's at a range of approximately 6,000 feet. The first missile guided to the target and appeared to pass just under the MIG–21. The second missile guided perfectly and impacted the target, causing another yellow fireball.
>
> As we flew past the falling debris, my weapon systems officer observed a dirty yellow parachute and what is believed to be the MIG–21 pilot.

A MIG–21 downed the following day was not

officially credited to an aircrew until 2 years later. Credit for this victory was retained by the Seventh Air Force, since the circumstances for the kill made it difficult to identify the aircrews involved. It was known that two wings, the 432d TRW and the 388th TFW, had fighter aircraft involved in an intensive engagement on 11 May, and that an F-4D aircrew, using an AIM-7 radar-guided missile, had made the kill. Reexamining operational reports and summaries of air operations, and interviewing the participants, post-battle analysts finally resolved the dilemma, and on 15 July 1974, PACAF awarded credit for the aerial victory to Capt. Stephen E. Nichols, aircraft commander, and 1st Lt. James R. Bell, weapon systems officer, of the "Triple-Nickel" squadron.

Nichols and Bell were flying in a group of four F-4D's, providing MIGCAP support for a Linebacker mission against bridge and airfield targets near Hanoi, when the flight encountered MIG-21's, apparently operating under GCI control. A MIG-21, possibly one of two encountered by the flight, had just downed an Iron Hand F-105. A MIG also destroyed the F-4 of the flight leader. Nichols and Bell knocked down one of the MIG's with an AIM-7E missile, but they had to make a hurried exit because of fuel shortage and therefore did not see the Sparrow hit the MIG. Post-kill analysis, however, confirmed that the MIG-21 was destroyed by a Sparrow, and Nichols' was the only U.S. aircraft that shot a Sparrow during the engagement.

On 12 May two senior lieutenant colonels bagged the first MIG-19 for the "Triple Nickel." The aircraft commander, Wayne T. Frye, commander of the squadron, and his weapon systems officer, James P. Cooney, who headed the 432d TRW's operations tactics division, were flying MIGCAP northwest of Yen Bai airfield in a flight of four F-4D's. Maj. Sidney B. Hudson, the flight leader, verified their victory:

> I observed four MIG-19's taking off with a left turn out. I proceeded to attack the lead MIG-19 and in the ensuing fight my wingman had the second, third and fourth MIG-19's flushed out in front of him. I fired inside range with my missiles and saw none impact. As I reversed and egressed the area, I observed a large yellow fireball in the area of the missile detonations of aircraft 2.

Colonel Frye's own account provides more details of the skirmish:

> The engagement occurred at low level (500–1,000 feet) approximately 2 miles southwest of Yen Bai airfield. Three AIM-7's were fired at the fourth MIG-19 in a flight of four in trail at an approximate range of 2,000 feet. After firing these missiles, I momentarily diverted my attention inside the cockpit to check switchology for my two remaining missiles. When I looked back out, a cloud of debris located where the target had previously been, passed under my aircraft almost immediately. Rate of closure at the time of firing was 250 knots.

Frye later noted that he and Cooney had "probably set a world's record for the total age of an aircrew in an F-4 Phantom for a MIG kill." He was 41 years old and his WSO was 44. Frye also speculated that they were "probably the first two lieutenant colonels in the same airplane to get a MIG." He was correct on both counts.

A flight of F-4E's on 23 May flew to the vicinity of Kep airfield as a chaff flight escort. Once the chaff aircraft had completed their activity, the F-4's switched to MIGCAP. Lt. Col. Lyle L. Beckers and Capt. John Huwe engaged and destroyed a MIG with an AIM-7 missile, while another Phantom, crewed by Capt. James M. Beatty and 1st Lt. James M. Sumner, destroyed a MIG-21 with 20-mm gunfire in the same engagement. These victories occurred during an engagement with eight MIG's.

After the chaff flight departed the area, the F-4's passed a few miles north of Kep airfield and spotted four MIG-21's preparing to take off and two MIG-17's airborne, at 8 o'clock low. Beatty feinted toward the MIG-17's, and they turned tail. Meanwhile, Beckers spotted two MIG-19's south of the field and went after them. He describes his victory:

> The MIG's were down around 3,000–4,000 feet, silver in color and very easy to see. They were in an easy left turn heading east, and I was about 7 miles away heading south. I probably had 500 knots and was still accelerating. As I came straight down into them, the clouds hindered my attack, but I also don't think they saw me. The MIG's went behind one of the clouds, and we lost sight momentarily. When I picked them up again,

I was about 2,000 feet away with approximately 75° angle-off. Too much angle-off to fire anything.

I continued my yo-yo, came around to the outside, and then back down at them trying to work for an AIM–7 shot. I pulled in deep at 6 o'clock and descended to 1,500–2,000 feet to get a good look-up angle for the radar. I placed the pipper on the trailing MIG at 2 nautical miles, 10° angle-off, 550 knots, 2–G, and used auto-acquisition to get a full-system radar lock-on. They pulled into a climbing left turn, again trying to get away.

I paused for settling time, then fired two AIM–7's in ripple. The first missile guided to a direct hit with the second missile guiding within 20 feet but failing to detonate. From the time that I spotted the MIG's heading east, turned south, made my first pass, overshot, rolled back and got a kill, the total elapsed time was about 45 seconds.

As the MIG went out of control, Beckers saw five other MIG–19's in a Wagon Wheel over the airfield. He made several passes at them but was unable to down another. Meanwhile, Beatty and Sumner set up cover for their flight leader and observed Beckers' MIG kill. Soon thereafter, while Beckers was trying to get another MIG, Beatty spotted two MIG–21's on their tail. Beatty immediately started after these North Vietnamese and was soon in a position to use his 20-mm cannon. In his account he writes:

> I had enough time to let the gunsight settle, and when the pipper got about one airplane length in front of him, I fired. The tracers helped me a great deal. I thought I had missed him until I closed to inside a thousand feet, where I could see my 20-mm was right on. I estimate that I put 50–100 rounds in him, and his plane began to come apart and roll to the left.

On 31 May Phantoms destroyed two more MIG–21's in two separate engagements about 15 minutes apart. Both F–4 flights came from the 432d TRW. The MIG–21's were intercepted in pairs while the two Phantom flights were flying MIGCAP in conjunction with strikes. While one flight continued to provide cover for strike flights attacking targets near Kep airfield, the other engaged the first set of MIG's. The second-flight Phantoms quickly decided to enter the fray and turned left to join up. During the turn, the element leader, Capt. Bruce G. Leonard, Jr. and Capt. Jeffrey S. Feinstein, his weapon systems officer, observed a MIG–21 at 10 o'clock heading toward his flight.

When Leonard initiated intercept, he relates: "We started a level left turn and observed the MIG–21 pass between the elements. The MIG turned away and disengaged. When clear of the MIG, our flight turned southwest toward our assigned orbit point."

Leonard's flight leader obtained a radar contact and turned 25°; contact was at 25 nautical miles and 20° left. He acquired a visual contact on two MIG–21's, turned left to engage, and fired two AIM–7's, front-quartering head-on and missed.

Captain Feinstein got a radar contact on two aircraft at 6 nautical miles and 20° left. He attempted to lock on but the radar malfunctioned. Captain Feinstein then saw one of the two MIG's that he had on radar come head-on, shooting two air-to-air missiles at our element. We were on the left of the leader and in a left turn. A MIG–21 came from right to left in front of us at about 4,000 feet range. The angle-off was 90°, and I fired one AIM–9 at the MIG with no results. The MIG then went out of view.

The flight turned another 90° and aircraft 3 and 4 were positioned over 1 and 2. We did not observe the leader fire two AIM–7's at another MIG–21. A MIG–21 then came in front of us and was at 12 o'clock, 3,000 feet in range, turning left. We performed a hard left turn through 40° of heading when the MIG–21 rolled out and started to descend. Our aircraft was then at the MIG's 6 o'clock, about 1 nautical mile. We obtained a high tone from the AIM–9 and fired at the MIG–21. The time was 1531 local, 0831 Zulu.

At this time the flight leader called a right turn to 090° and Captain Feinstein called out that there were two MIG–21's at 9 o'clock, 1 nautical mile, turning with us. To maintain flight integrity and cover the flight leader, we had to turn away from the present engagement and could not press the attack further. Because we turned immediately away from the attack, we could not see the missile impact. During the time of the engagement the flight had continuous SAM radar and missile launch indications. Our wingman observed the flight taking 85-mm antiaircraft fire at the time we were firing.

Meanwhile, the other flight of F–4 Phantoms was engaging MIG–21's and Captains Steve Ritchie and Lawrence H. Pettit destroyed one. Ritchie later stated:

On 31 May 1972 I was the flight leader of a flight of four F–4's assigned to MIGCAP northeast of Thai Nguyen. Shortly after crossing the coast northeast of Haiphong, heading generally northwest, Red Crown advised us of blue bandits 40 nautical miles west-southwest of our position, at a heading of 080°. Red Crown continued to give excellent information on the position of the bandits.

With the bandits at 7 to 8 o'clock, 14 miles range, I began a descending left turn. Shortly thereafter I spotted a flight of two MIG–21's at 10 o'clock high. I continued the left turn and maneuvered to a 7 o'clock position on the number two MIG. The lead MIG broke up and away.

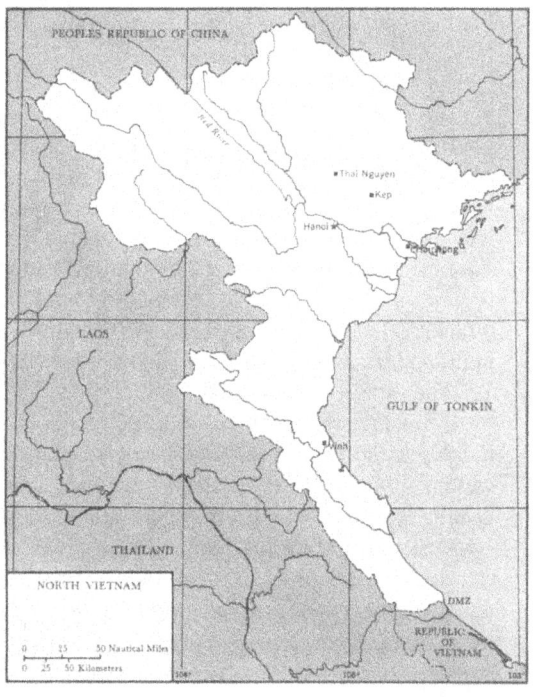

At this time my weapon systems officer, Captain Larry Pettit, achieved a full-system lock-on and I fired four AIM–7 missiles. The first missile corkscrewed off and to the right. The next two missiles detonated early. The fourth missile guided perfectly and impacted the MIG in the forward fuselage area. The fuselage from the wings forward broke off and the remainder of the MIG entered a flat left spin until impacting the ground.

These aerial victories earned for both Ritchie and Feinstein their second kills. Both later gained three more.

MIG's Intensify Threat

Operation Linebacker grew in intensity and enemy resistance remained high. Scores of American fighter-bombers ranged from Hanoi southward to the coastal city of Vinh on 2 June, threatening North Vietnam's supply and transportation system. More than 250 aircraft of all services were involved in these strikes, damaging or destroying bridges, trucks, surface craft, supply warehouses, and storage areas.

During these heavy attacks, a MIG–19 was downed by an F–4E escorting strike aircraft about 40 miles northeast of Hanoi. The Phantom flight from the 58th TFS, 432d TRW, encountered two MIG–19's, one of which the flight leader, Maj. Philip W. Handley and his WSO, 1st Lt. John J. Smallwood, destroyed with 20-mm gunfire. "After approximately 15 minutes on station," said Handley, "aircraft 3 and 4 became separated from the first element during a particularly violent SAM break. At the same time, they hit Bingo fuel and began egress."

Shortly thereafter, while my wingman and I were egressing, we were attacked from 6 o'clock low by a flight of two MIG–19's. After a brief engagement, I shot down the number two MIG–19 with 20-mm cannon fire at a slant range of about 300 feet. The MIG–19 was observed to roll slowly off on his right wing and begin to trail smoke from his left wing root. His nose continued to drop, and he crashed almost vertically into a green meadow 8 seconds after I fired a 300–round

(Top) An AA unit in Hanoi.
(Bottom) A North Vietnamese surface-to-air missile unit.

burst. The kill was witnessed by Capt. Stanley C. Green, aircraft commander, and Capt. Douglas W. Eden, weapon systems officer in number 2.

Linebacker continued unabated except for the period between 14 and 18 June, when bombing of Hanoi was suspended for the duration of a visit to that city by the President of the USSR. Then in late June and continuing into the next month the ratio of kills was reversed in favor of North Vietnam's MIG's.

The problem of losses to enemy air defenses was serious. Even though SAM defenses were extensive and well disciplined, their effectiveness was seriously degraded by friendly chaff, support jamming, ECM pods on U.S. aircraft, and special SAM suppression missions. MIG's, on the other hand, became increasingly effective, instead of becoming less of a threat as anticipated. The North Vietnamese constantly refined MIG tactics, employed excellent GCI radars, and further improved their warning and identification system of American forces. Nevertheless, USAF fighter aircrews succeeded in destroying seven MIG-21's between 21 June and 29 July.

The first of this series of kills took place on the 21st of June, when a flight of four F-4E's from the 469th TFS at Korat escorted two flights of chaff-dispensing aircraft over Route Package 6 in North Vietnam. Two MIG-21's engaged the U.S. aircraft, one attacking the chaff force and the other pursuing the lead Phantom, flown by Col. Mele Vojvodich, Jr., and Maj. Robert M. Maltbie. "I saw three different MIG's and got off a shot at one of them. I didn't see the missile impact because I was distracted by a MIG-21 on my right," Vojvodich commented. The aircraft in position 3, crewed by Lt. Col. Von R. Christiansen and Maj. Kaye M. Harden, probably saved Vojvodich from destruction. "We were flying escort for two flights of chaff-dispensing aircraft on 21 June 1972," reported Christiansen, "when at least two MIG-21 aircraft attacked the chaff force." He continues:

At about 0649Z, two MIG-21 aircraft were initially sighted at 12 o'clock high to the chaff force, crossing our egress course from left to right. At this time the MIG-21's were two to three thousand feet above the chaff force, partially obscured by a 500-foot-thick broken overcast cloud layer. The chaff force was positioned less than 100 feet below the base of the overcast. As the MIG's came abreast of the chaff force, they executed a hard nose low turn to the left, quickly positioning at 6 o'clock on the chaff force and the lead MIG-21 commenced an attack.

While following his leader through the turn, the number two MIG appeared to sight Vojvodich and his wingman below him. He then pulled high momentarily to gain a favorable position and initiated an attack on the two F-4's. Possibly because our element was positioned high on the left in fluid-four formation, it appeared that the number two MIG did not see me and my wingman.

Upon observing him rapidly closing at 6 o'clock on Vojvodich and his wingman, we called them to break left. The MIG's rate of closure was such that he continued nearly straight ahead after firing two Atoll missiles at aircraft 2, who managed to evade both of them with his hard turn to the left. By going to maximum power and performing an acceleration maneuver, we were able to stabilize our position at 5 to 6,000 feet behind the number two MIG in a slight descending turn. He was in afterburner power.

After acquiring a full system radar lock-on, we attempted to fire two AIM-7 missiles, but neither AIM-7 missile launched. We then switched to heat and picked up a strong IR [infrared] tone from our second AIM-9 missile when the number two MIG was positioned in the gunsight reticle. Three AIM-9 missiles were ripple-fired at the MIG, who was in a level, gentle bank to the left. The first missile appeared to guide normally, but detonated about 50 feet right of the MIG's tail. Major Harden observed the second missile guide directly into the MIG's tail, causing the aircraft to explode and burn fiercely from the canopy aft. The pilot ejected immediately and was observed to have a yellow parachute. I did not observe the second AIM-9 impact on the MIG, because I immediately transferred my attention to the number one MIG, which was pulling off high after attacking an F-4 of another flight.

We initiated a maximum power pull-up toward the number one MIG and thereafter maneuvered with him at very high speed until achieving a position at his 6 o'clock. During this time, number one MIG executed numerous evasive maneuvers while descending from 20,000 feet to 1,000 feet as we closed for a gun attack. Radar lock-on was obtained and although tracking was by no means perfect, firing was initiated from about 3,000 feet with a short burst. Thereafter, we fired several short bursts while slowly closing range and attempting to refine the tracking solution. Suspecting a gunsight lead prediction problem, we began to aim slightly in front of the MIG and observed strikes on the left wing just as the gun fired out. The engagement was terminated due to Bingo fuel state at that time.

"Colonel Christiansen saved the men in our lead aircraft by telling them to break just at the right time," Major Harden reported. "Two missiles from a MIG exploded close behind them. We turned into the low MIG and fired two Sidewinders. One of them knocked the tail section off of the MIG and the pilot ejected. The aircraft spun to the ground in flames." In addition, there was another MIG damaged in the engagement. This marked the first confirmed victory by a 388th TFW aircraft since 23 August 1967.

Three MIG-21's became the prey of U.S. Air Force aircrews on 8 July during two separate engagements involving two different squadrons. A flight of four F-4's from the 4th TFS gave that squadron its first MIG victory of the war. The flight was, on that morning, providing escort to a chaff flight in the Hanoi area and had just escorted the aircraft from the threat area. Returning for a sweep, the flight again departed when Red Crown warned that bandits were attacking. Captains Richard F. Hardy and Paul T. Lewinski, in aircraft 3, then engaged and destroyed a MIG-21:

The flight turned into the MIG threat and then turned outbound again. While egressing, aircraft 2 called a break to our element; a MIG-21 was attacking. We broke, and the flight leader and his wingman attacked the first MIG. When aircraft 3 and 4 reversed, a second MIG-21 had just overshot and we fired an AIM-9 which did not guide due to his entry into a cloud. We attempted to fire three more AIM-9's which did not come off the rails. We locked-on in boresight and fired two AIM-7's. The first AIM-7 guided to a direct hit and the second guided into the wreckage. The MIG's right wing was blown off and the fuselage tumbled end over end. No chute was observed.

The other two MIG-21's destroyed on the same day were downed by the same aircrew: Captains Steve Ritchie and Charles DeBellevue, who were flying the lead F-4E in a flight of four from the 555th TFS. The flight was on MIGCAP in support of a Linebacker strike, flying at medium to low altitude west of Phu Tho and south of Yen Bai. Captain Ritchie provides details of this team's double MIG victory:

Disco and Red Crown advised our flight of bandits southeast of our position, approximately 35–40 nautical miles. The flight headed toward the threat in patrol formation and crossed the Black River on a southerly course. Red Crown

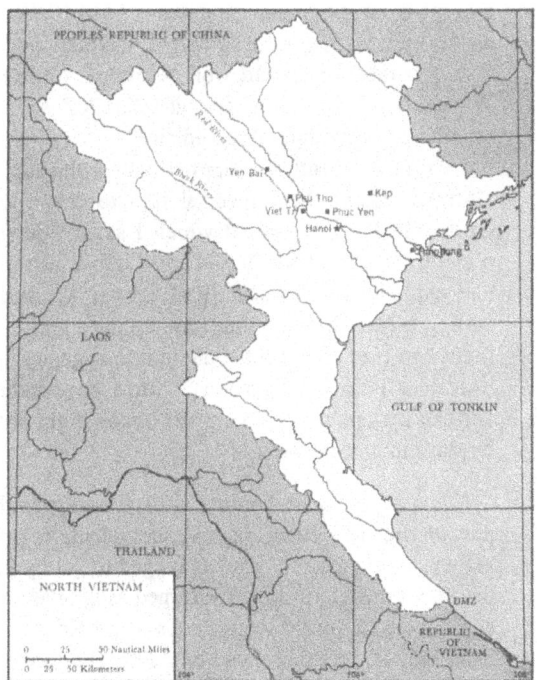

and Disco shortly thereafter advised that the bandits and our flight had merged.

The flight then turned to the north, met two MIG-21's at 10 o'clock, made a slight left turn, and passed the MIG's head-on. I then unloaded and executed a hard left turn as the MIG's turned right. I maneuvered to a 5 o'clock position on the number two MIG, obtained an auto-acquisition boresight radar lock-on, and fired two AIM-7 missiles. The first missile impacted the number two MIG, causing a large yellow fireball as the MIG broke into parts. It continued to disintegrate until impacting the ground.

I then unloaded again for energy and turned hard right in pursuit of the lead MIG-21, who was now in a rear-quarter threatening position on aircraft 4. I maneuvered into a similar position on the lead MIG as was achieved on his wingman previously. Another radar auto-acquisition lock-on was obtained and one AIM-7 missile fired. The missile impacted the MIG, resulting in a large yellow fireball. This MIG also broke into parts and began to disintegrate. The front of the aircraft was observed impacting the ground in a large fireball.

The flight remained in tactical support formation throughout the flight and egressed as a flight of four. For Ritchie these two aerial victories increased his score to four. DeBellevue now had three MIG kills, all earned while flying with Ritchie.

Ten days later, on 18 July, another MIG-21 was destroyed. This one fell victim to Lt. Col. Carl G. Baily and his WSO, Capt. Jeffrey S. Feinstein, of the 13th TFS, 432d TRW. This F-4D team was one of four MIGCAP aircraft protecting strike flights hitting targets near Phuc Yen airfield. Colonel Baily later said of the air battle:

At 0224Z, as our flight was ingressing west of Hanoi, aircraft 4 called out, "Bandits," and broke hard right. This caused the elements to be separated, but I elected to continue inbound as the other flight was requesting our assistance. They were low on fuel and were being pursued by MIG's.

At 0227Z, Captain Feinstein got a radar contact and vectored me and our wingman toward it. At a range of 3 miles I got a visual contact with a single silver MIG.

The WSO locked on the MIG, and Col. Baily fired four AIM-7 missiles as the MIG dived, attempting to separate. They missed their mark, but he quickly followed with an AIM-9, which did not miss. It blew off the MIG's right wing and caused the enemy aircraft to snap-roll to the right. During the second snap it hit the ground and disintegrated.

Baily and Feinstein repeated their performance on 29 July with another MIG-21. They were flying lead in a four-ship F-4 MIGCAP formation which was sent into North Vietnam during the early morning hours to protect forces attacking targets on the Northeast Railway near Kep airfield. Feinstein describes his fourth aerial victory:

At 0211Z, while proceeding to our assigned orbit point near Kep airfield, Red Crown gave the code words for "MIG activity." A minute-and-half later I picked up radar contacts in the vicinity of Phuc Yen airfield.

Red Crown began vectoring our flight toward the southwest on two bandits and I had radar contacts at that position. At 0217Z I obtained a radar lock-on, and the flight began a hard left turn, attempting to close within firing range. Lt.

MIG-killers head for a pre-mission briefing at Udorn. Capts. DeBellevue and Ritchie (front row), and Col. Baily and Capt. Feinstein (back row).

Col. Baily was able to close to 5 miles but could not get in range due to the bandit's high rate of speed. We lost the radar lock-on at 6 miles. After completing the turn, we reacquired another contact which was probably the same bandit.

We called the position of the contact (on the nose for 8 miles) to Red Crown, and Red Crown confirmed that it was a bandit and stated that he had three bandits in front of us. We closed in on an attack as Red Crown continued to call the bandit's position.

At about 4 miles, Lieutenant Kirchner and Captain Rogers had visual contact with a silver MIG and called his position in front of the flight as the MIG went into a descending turn. At 0219Z, Colonel Baily began firing AIM-7 missiles. The first missile did not ignite. The second and third missiles ripple-fired at 0219:10Z at 2¼ miles range, guided down and to the left, bursting into a large fireball at 0219:15Z. This was observed by other members of the companion flight. Lieutenant Kirchner stated that after visually acquiring the MIG, he observed the two missiles guide to the MIG and explode. He observed the MIG to emerge from the fireball in flames. At 0219:47Z, as we were turning right to egress, Colonel Baily also observed an aircraft well below us, on fire. We continued our turn, and at 0220:20Z seven members of our flight observed an F-4 in a spin at our 9 o'clock position at approximately the same altitude. After a hard reversal turn to check an unidentified single aircraft which I saw at our 6 o'clock, we observed the F-4 crash into a hillside and explode at 0220:45Z. Red Crown was still calling a MIG in our immediate vicinity and the flight egressed after a futile attempt to engage this bandit. All times, ranges, and turns have been verified by tape recorders carried on the flight and by the radar scope film.

"The MIG's were coming at us at a very high rate of speed," Baily later described the aerial victory to newsmen. "They managed to get by us before we engaged them. We turned as hard as we could, started toward them, and got them right in front of us, coming head-on. Jeff [Feinstein] locked-on the MIG and I fired two missiles. They both guided right in and splashed him good."

"The credit all goes to Jeff," he said. "When you get them head-on, the guy with the radar does all the work. I just sat up front and squeezed the trigger."

The same morning Lt. Col. Gene E. Taft and his WSO, Capt. Stanley M. Imaye of the 4th TFS, 366th TFW, also destroyed a MIG-21. Flying an F-4E, they were escorting a chaff force deep into North Vietnam when surface-to-air missiles and MIG-21's threatened the strike force. The two chaff flights withdrew from the strike area while the two F-4 escort flights engaged the MIG's. One got in firing position behind two of the F-4's, and Taft and Imaye maneuvered their aircraft behind the MIG before he could fire. Taft further narrates:

As the MIG approached 11 o'clock, the auto-acquisition switch was activated with no lock-on noted. The GIB went out of boresight to radar in an attempt to lock on. The MIG was called level at that instant. The switch was returned to boresight and auto-acquisition attempted with successful lock-on. The range bar indicated the MIG at approximately 4 o'clock position, 9,000 feet. Four seconds were counted and the trigger squeezed once. One AIM-7 left the aircraft and tracked smoothly to the MIG. Missile detonation was observed and simultaneously the MIG's wing appeared to separate, fire was observed out of the wing, and the MIG rolled uncontrollably. No chute was observed. No impact was observed. After detonation occurred, our flight rolled off in a fairly tight descending turn. After approximately 150° of turn, an F-4 was observed, out of control, on fire, in an inverted flat spin on the inside of our aircraft. Approximately 5 seconds later two good chutes were noted, and the aircraft impacted on a mountainside. Our flight began an orbit of the area, but aircraft 4 was Bingo fuel and the flight egressed with no other encounters or sightings.

Late in July the U.S. put a more sophisticated MIG warning system into operation, and the kill ratio again turned in favor of the Americans. For the remainder of Linebacker operations, U.S. pilots destroyed four MIG's for every lost Phantom or Thunderchief.

The next aerial victory was unique in that the USAF Phantom was piloted by a Marine, Capt. Lawrence G. Richard, and his weapon systems officer was a naval aviator, Lt. Cdr. Michael J. Ettel. Both were exchange officers attached for duty with the 58th TFS, 432d TRW. They were flying the lead F-4E in a flight of four aircraft on a weather reconnaissance mission in North Vietnam on 12 August. Captain Richard describes the flight's encounter:

As I crossed the Red River, I was informed by Red Crown that bandits were airborne, out of Bullseye heading 180°. At this time I was 35 nautical miles northwest of them heading 020°, proceeding on my fragged route. The bandits then turned to a heading of 360° and commenced an attack. At this time, with the bandits at my 6 o'clock at 30 nautical miles, I turned the flight to a heading of 180° and accelerated the flight. Red Crown continued giving bandit information and I visually acquired two aircraft at my 9:30 about 4 nautical miles, starting a turn to my 6 o'clock.

At this time I did a slice turn to the left, sending my supporting element high. I acquired a boresight lock-on on the lead aircraft, which was

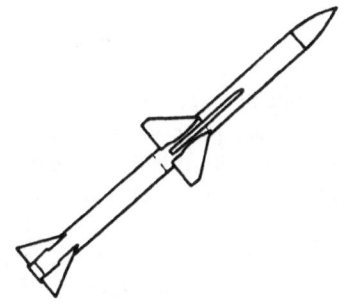

U.S. Sparrow (AIM-7) air-to-air missile

a silver MIG-21. I closed to 1¼ nautical miles with 30° angle-off and fired one AIM-7, which appeared to guide, but missed as the MIG-21 broke hard into the AIM-7 and met me head-on. At this time I unloaded and went after his wingman, who was in about a 2- to 3-G turn. I acquired a boresight lock-on to this MIG-21, which was light green camouflage in color, closed to 1 nautical mile with 20° angle-off and fired another AIM-7 which impacted just forward of the vertical fin. The aircraft pitched up and some pieces of the aircraft broke away. At this time I turned the flight to a heading of 210° and egressed the area. The kill was witnessed by Lt. Col. Lee Williams, aircraft commander, and Maj. Thomas Leach, weapon systems officer on aircraft 3.

The 8th Tactical Fighter Wing, which had figured so prominently in the Rolling Thunder* phase of the war in Southeast Asia, again temporarily entered the MIG-killer business on 15 August. On that day, a chaff-dispensing F-4E from the 336th TFS, crewed by Capts. Fred W. Sheffler and Mark A. Massen, engaged a MIG-21. Temporarily attached to the 8th Wing for combat, the flight of F-4E's was supporting routine Linebacker strikes in Route Package 6. The MIG-21 apparently hesitated, believing that the chaff aircraft carried no air-to-air missiles. Sheffler provides the following account:

Our mission was to provide support for two strike flights targeted with laser-guided bombs

---

*Nickname assigned to air strikes conducted against targets and lines of communications in NVN. Commencing on 2 March 1965, the program was intended to weaken the enemy's logistics system by striking targets on a continuing basis. Rolling Thunder was suspended on 31 October 1968.

against a thermal power plant and a railroad bridge along the Northwest Railroad at Viet Tri and Phu Tho, respectively. We were the right outside aircraft in a formation of two flights of four. One minute prior to our first target our escort, the other flight, called a single bandit coming down from high 6 o'clock and attacking us on the right.

Our flight began a hard turn to the right in an attempt to negate the enemy's attack. Escort told us that there were now two MIG's in the attack. We continued our turn, trying to visually pick up the MIG's. A camouflaged MIG-21 overshot at this time on my right, no further than one or two thousand feet away. Captain Massen, my weapon systems operator, called for me to auto-acquire.*

I placed my pipper on the MIG and toggled the proper switch on my throttles. We achieved an immediate radar lock-on. I continued our turn to the right, striving to pick up the second MIG. Unable to achieve firing parameters, aircraft 3 gave me the lead, and at the same time Captain Massen cleared me to fire. I made a quick check to see if the MIG-21 was still at my 12 o'clock and then squeezed off an AIM-7 missile. By this time the MIG-21 was about four to five thousand feet in front of me. For the next 10 seconds, until missile impact, I divided my attention between monitoring the AIM-7's flight and checking our 4 to 6 o'clock for his partner.

The missile made two minor corrections in flight; one just prior to impact on the left side, just forward of the tail section. He did not appear to take any evasive action up until the last second, when he hardened up his turn to the left. After impact and explosion, the MIG-21 entered a 45° dive, trailing smoke and flames from his aft section. I estimate his altitude when hit at between 9,000 and 10,000 feet MSL. At this time the second MIG-21 came by on our right in a hard left turn and went between our two flights head-on. We continued our turn and egressed the area at low altitude. Because of the ensuing engagement with the second MIG-21, I was unable to observe a chute or impact of the MIG-21 with the ground. However, the back-seater of an aircraft of the follow-on strike flight observed a large fire on the side of a hill near the area of the engagement during ingress, and it was still burning during his egress some 15 minutes later.

Four days later, on 19 August, another MIG was destroyed. Capt. Sammy C. White, flying his final Linebacker mission, and his WSO, 1st Lt. Frank J. Bettine, crewed an F-4E in a flight of four chaff-dispensing aircraft. Their joint statement describes how a MIG-21 attacked the escort flight and was promptly dispatched:

Not long after entering North Vietnam, the WSO in aircraft 2, Capt. Forrest Penney, saw a MIG-21 in the flight leader's 6 o'clock position and called for a break. As the F-4E's broke, the MIG-21 faltered momentarily, then elected to disengage. We rolled off into the MIG's 6 o'clock and, following some maneuvering, fired an AIM-7 which tracked on the MIG and detonated. After the missile impacted, the MIG began to smoke and burn, followed by the ejection of the aircraft's pilot. Having reached minimum fuel, we egressed the area.

The First USAF Aces

After 7 years of air-to-air combat in Southeast Asia, the U.S. Air Force finally produced its first ace of the war when Steve Ritchie had his fifth MIG victory confirmed for 28 August 1972. He thereby joined the ranks of fighter aces of past wars. There was a competition being waged between Ritchie and Feinstein, and the latter had tallied his fourth MIG victory on 29 July. Ritchie's fourth had been scored on 8 July. The question was whether Ritchie, a pilot, or Feinstein, a navigator, would become the Air Force's first ace in Southeast Asia. Each had had a potential fifth claim disallowed. Feinstein, flying with Maj. John L. Mesenbourg, had claimed an aerial victory in an engagement on 9 June, but approval was denied by the Seventh Air Force's Enemy Aircraft Claims Evaluation Board because of a lack of sufficient evidence. Ritchie's claim of a MIG-21 on 13 June was also rejected because of insufficient evidence.

---

*Refers to detecting, identifying and locating the target (MIG) in enough detail so that the pilot can fire the missile. Unable to track the MIG visually, the pilot wants this acquisition to be automatically picked up on radar.

The 28 August skirmish resolved the issue. Ritchie flew the lead aircraft of a MIGCAP flight, with Capt. Charles B. DeBellevue as his WSO, during a Linebacker strike mission. "We acquired a radar lock-on on a MIG-21 that was head-on to us," Ritchie said.

We converted to the stern and fired two AIM-7 missiles during the conversion. These missiles were out of parameters and were fired in an attempt to get the MIG to start a turn. As we rolled out behind the MIG, we fired the two remaining AIM-7's. The third missile missed, but the fourth impacted the MIG. The MIG was seen to explode and start tumbling toward the earth. The kill was witnessed by Captain John Madden, aircraft commander in number 3.

"It was an entirely different situation," Ritchie noted to newsmen. The MIG flew at "a much higher altitude than any of my other MIG kills and at a much greater range. I don't think the MIG pilot ever really saw us. All he saw were those missiles coming at him and that's what helped us finally get him."

The new ace complimented the ground crews who kept the F-4's combat-ready: "There's no way we could have done it without them," he said. "In fact, I got my first and fifth MIG in the same plane. Crew Chief Sergeant Reggie Taylor was the first one up the ladder when the plane landed and you just couldn't believe how happy he was. I think he was more excited than I."

DeBellevue, whose total victories rose to four with this day's kill, commented on teamwork: "The most important thing is for the crew to work well together," he said. "They have to know each other. I know what Steve is thinking on a mission and can almost accomplish whatever he wants before he asks. I was telling him everything he had to know when he wanted it, and did not waste time giving him useless data."

An F-4E of the 388th TFW, one of two F-4's and two F-105G's flying a hunter-killer mission, made the next MIG kill. They were flying SAM suppression in the vicinity of Phuc Yen airfield on 2 September, when a MIG-19 attacked aircraft 2, an F-105. His Atoll air-to-air missile narrowly missed the Thunderchief's left wing by approximately 20 feet. Its aircraft commander, Maj. Thomas J. Coady, flying with Maj. Harold E. Kurz, made a hard right turn, and escaped destruction. The MIG pilot then pressed a cannon attack against the lead aircraft, also an F-105 and crewed by Maj. Edward Y. Cleveland and Capt. Michael B. O'Brien. A hard right turn also saved them. As the MIG broke off, it passed over aircraft 3, an F-4E flown by Maj. Jon I. Lucas and 1st Lt. Douglas G. Malloy. In an inverted position the MIG headed east, probably trying for Phuc Yen.

"He came in from our 4 o'clock position," said Major Lucas, "and I started a left turn to maneuver into firing position." Lucas adds:

The MIG then started a left-descending turn at which time I called for an auto-acquisition. The weapon systems officer, Lieutenant Malloy, went to boresight and confirmed the switch settings. I hit the auto-acquisition switch with the MIG-19 framed in the reticle. Lieutenant Malloy confirmed a good lock-on. I counted 4 seconds and squeezed the trigger. The left aft missile light went out, indicating expenditure of an AIM-7. I started to select Master Arm and Guns to follow up with a gun attack. At that time, approximately 0440Z, a SAM was observed tracking our aircraft, and a turn was initiated into the SAM to negate its track. We then turned back towards the MIG and observed a pastel orange parachute with a man hanging in the harness. Missile impact was not observed due to the turn into the SAM, but Cleveland and his wingman called the MIG-19 burning and spiraling towards the ground and also observed the parachute.

During Linebacker strikes on 9 September, a

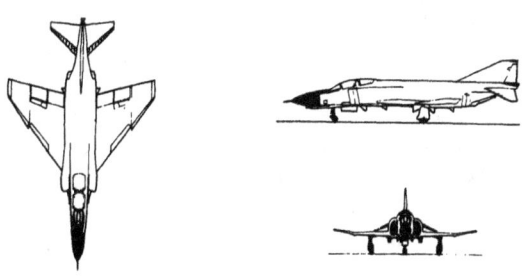

Phantom II—F-4E Fighter

Admiring Capt. Ritchie's fifth star are: (l. to r.) Capt. DeBellevue, Sgt. Reggie Taylor, the aircraft's crew chief; Capt. Ritchie; and Sgt. Ronald W. Buttrey, the aircraft's night crew chief.

MIG-21's at Phuc Yen.

flight of four F-4D's on MIGCAP west of Hanoi shot down three MIG's. Two were MIG-19's downed by flight leader Capt. John A. Madden, Jr., and his WSO, Capt. Charles DeBellevue. For Madden, the victories constituted his first and second MIG kills, but for DeBellevue they were numbers five and six, moving him up as the leading MIG destroyer of the war. Before their MIG victories, however, Capt. Calvin B. Tibbett and 1st Lt. William S. Hargrove in aircraft 3 destroyed a MIG-21.

The flight was alerted to the presence of MIG's some 50 miles away. "We knew the MIG's would be returning soon to land at Phuc Yen airfield," Captain Madden later reported. "We just kind of sat back and waited for them." When DeBellevue acquired the MIG's on radar, the flight maneuvered to attack. Madden made the first move:

> We got a visual on a MIG about 5 miles out on final approach with his gear and flaps down. Getting a lock on him, I fired my missiles but they missed. We were coming in from the side-rear and slipped up next to that MIG no more than 500 feet apart. He got a visual on us, snatched up his flaps and hit afterburners, accelerating out. It became obvious that I wasn't going to get another shot at the MIG. That's when Captain Tibbett closed in on the MIG.

Captain Tibbett had been watching the engagement carefully and saw that the two AIM-7 missiles fired by Madden did not guide.

Madden then cleared us to fire, since we were in a good position for an AIM-9 attack. We fired two AIM-9 missiles which appeared not to guide, closed to gun range, and fired the 20-mm cannon. The MIG-21 sustained numerous hits along the fuselage and left wing. The MIG pilot ejected, and the aircraft started a gentle roll and nose-down attitude toward the ground. The altitude was approximately 1,000 feet.

As the flight made a turn to withdraw, two MIG-19's swarmed in for an attack. DeBellevue describes the next two engagements:

> We acquired the MIG's on radar and positioned as we picked them up visually. We used a slicing low-speed yo-yo to position behind the MIG-19's and started turning hard with them. We fired one AIM-9 missile, which detonated 25 feet from one of the MIG-19's. We then switched the attack to the other MIG-19 and one turn later we fired an AIM-9 at him.
>
> I observed the missile impact the tail of the MIG. The MIG continued normally for the next few seconds, then began a slow roll and spiraled downward, impacting the ground with a large

fireball. Our altitude was approximately 1,500 feet at the moment of the MIG's impact.

Madden and DeBellevue returned to their base, thinking they had destroyed only the second MIG-19. Only later did investigation reveal that they were the only aircrew to shoot at a MIG-19 which crashed and burned on the runway at Phuc Yen that day. Captains Daleky and Murphy, in number 4 position, were hit by antiaircraft fire as the flight left the battle area and headed back for Udorn. They were soon rescued from northern Laos, over which they were forced to bail out. Their report of the MIG-19 engagements, along with photo analysis and debriefing interviews of other flight aircrews helped confirm the destruction of the first as well as the second MIG engaged by Madden and DeBellevue.

Even without the extra kill, Captain DeBellevue was the Air Force's second ace of the war. As events would later demonstrate, he emerged as the leading MIG-killer of the conflict, for no one later matched his score. When asked how he felt about becoming an ace, the navigator commented: "I feel pretty good about it. It's the high point of my career. There's no other job that you have to put out as much for. It's frustrating, and yet when you do shoot down a MIG, it's so rewarding."

The events of the 9th were reenacted 3 days later when aircrews of the 388th TFW downed three MIG-21's. Two were destroyed by aircrews in a flight of four F-4E's escorting chaff flights northeast of Hanoi, in the vicinity of Kep airfield. Three or four MIG's came in from 4 to 6 o'clock and attacked one of the chaff flights as it approached the target area. The lead F-4, crewed by Lt. Col. Lyle L. Beckers and 1st Lt. Thomas M. Griffin, observed a MIG aligning itself to the rear of the chaff flight from which point he could launch a missile. According to Becker's account:

> I obtained an auto-acquisition lock-on and attempted to fire two AIM-7 missiles. The MIG-21 fired an Atoll missile at the chaff flight and broke straight down. I pursued and fired two AIM-9 missiles, one of which impacted the MIG's left wing. Flames and smoke were observed coming from the left wing. I then selected guns and proceeded to fire 520 rounds of HEI/tracer. Projectile impacts and additional fire were observed on the

Capt. DeBellevue, USAF's second ace, sits in the cockpit of his F-4D.

fuselage of the MIG. The MIG-21 was last observed in a steep descent, burning.

An Atoll missile from the MIG, however, found its mark and destroyed one of the chaff aircraft before Beckers and his WSO could drive him off. Meanwhile, Maj. Gary L. Retterbush with 1st Lt. Daniel L. Autrey in the back seat of aircraft 2 attacked another MIG-21. "We turned into the MIG's and accomplished a radar lock-on," Retterbush reported. "Two AIM-7's were fired but did not guide. Three AIM-9's were fired, but missed by a matter of feet. We then closed on and downed a MIG-21 with 20-mm cannon, firing approximately 350 rounds. The 20-mm with tracer was observed impacting the fuselage, wing, and canopy, causing fire and smoke."

The MIG went into an uncontrolled climb with its nose 65 degrees up, slowed to 150 knots, then dropped. Major Retterbush reported that as the MIG dropped past him he saw the pilot slumped forward in the cockpit. The cannon had found its mark. As the F-4E's left the battle area, they observed a smoke trail and a large fireball.

Later in the day another F-4* flight from the 388th TFW escorted a strike flight in an attack against the Tuan Quan railroad bridge when two MIG-21's attacked. The first MIG appeared in an 8

---

*Aircraft 1, 3 and 4 were F-4E's; aircraft 2 was an F-4D.

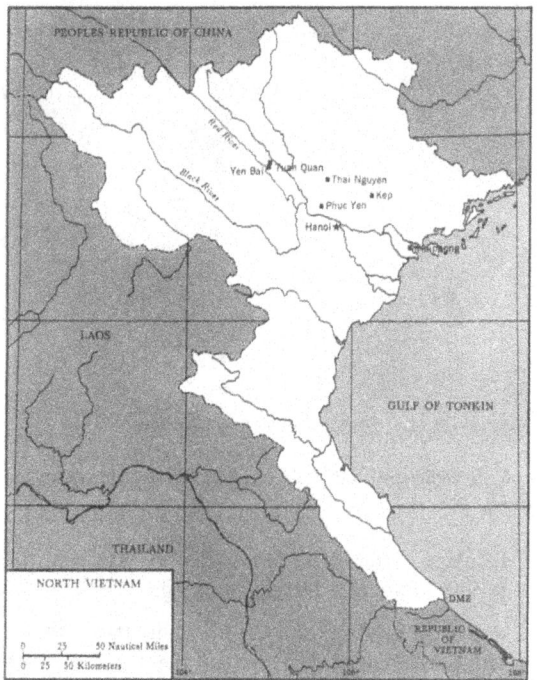

o'clock position and lined up on the strike flight. The lead aircraft fired one AIM-7 missile ballistically to distract the MIG, then turned in pursuit as the MIG broke away. This "shot across the bow" detonated about 1,000 feet in front of the Phantom. In hot pursuit, the flight leader then fired another AIM-7, followed by three AIM-9 missiles. They all missed. The second AIM-7 detonated 500 feet from the target, and the nearest AIM-9 detonated about 200 feet from the MIG.

The number 2 aircraft, piloted by Capt. Michael J. Mahaffey, with 1st Lt. George I. Shields in the rear seat, had better luck with its ordnance during the engagement. As the flight leader was chasing the first MIG, a second MIG-21 dropped between the two F-4's. "It went right across in front of us," Mahaffey latter commented, "and it looked a lot bigger than I thought a MIG was supposed to look."

We rolled right, tracked, and fired one AIM-9 which guided and impacted the MIG in the tail section, blowing off parts of the aircraft. The MIG went into a spin from 16,000 feet and more pieces fell off the aircraft. It was last seen in a spin below 8,000 feet, about 20 nautical miles southwest of Yen Bai airfield.

Another MIG-21 was destroyed during Linebacker operations on 16 September. The victors were Capt. Calvin B. Tibbett and his WSO, 1st Lt. William S. Hargrove, flying in position 3 in a flight of four F-4E's from the 555th TFS on escort for U.S. strike forces. It was their second aerial victory within a week. Tibbett gives the following account of the engagement:

A MIG-21 was spotted going southeast down the Red River. A low-level chase started and the lead flight, Capt. John A. Madden and Capt. Michael A. Hilliard, fired two radar and four heat-seeking missiles, none of which detonated or appeared to guide.

The flight leader cleared us to fire, and we fired four heat missiles, the last of which guided and detonated near the aft portion of the fuselage. The MIG started a turn, then pitched down. The MIG pilot ejected just before the aircraft struck the ground.

Air Force fighter crews scored no additional aerial victories until the first week of October, although Linebacker operations continued uninterrupted. In the meantime, MIG's were destroyed on the ground. On 1 October, for example, the U.S. made some of its heaviest attacks against Phuc Yen, Yen Bai, Vinh, and Quang Lang airfields. At least five MIG's were destroyed and nine others damaged.

The first aerial victory for the month came on 5 October when MIG's from Kep airfield opposed a strike force. An Air Force escort flight of F-4E's dispatched from the 388th TFW engaged the enemy in a heated battle. A MIG-21 was downed by Capt. Richard E. Coe and 1st Lt. Omri K. Webb, III in the lead aircraft. Coe reports:

We received vectors from Disco for two MIG's off Bullseye on ingress to initial point. They seemed to be heading in our direction. Disco gave continuous vectors until the flight we were escorting called MIG's at 8 o'clock high.

The formation began a hard left turn. After two turns I observed two MIG-21's in route formation at 10 o'clock high, at about 3 miles and heading 280°. We began a lazy one-G descending turn to get to 6 o'clock. The auto-acquisition switch was activated with the MIG's still in the pipper. I then

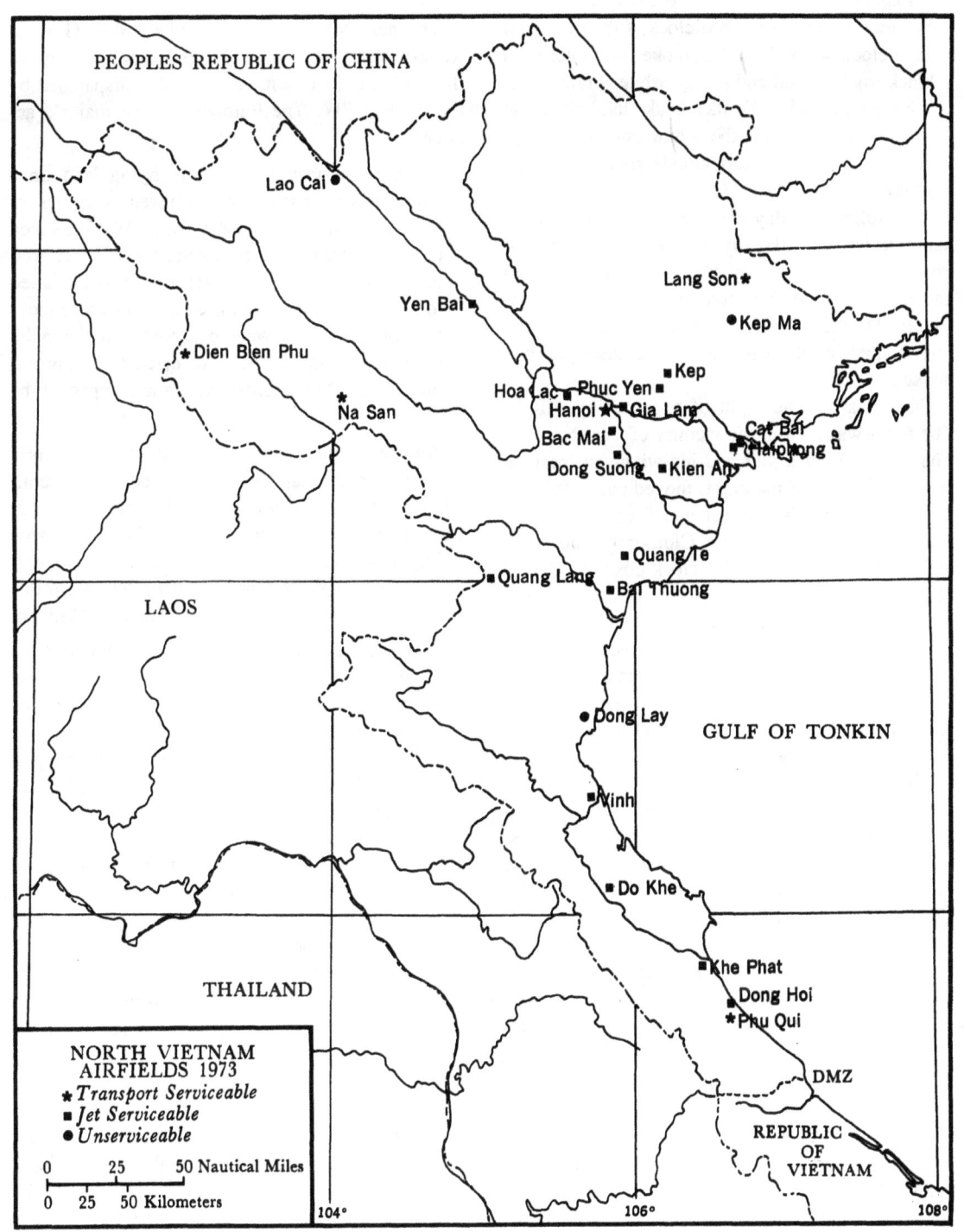

fired one AIM-7. At this time someone called, "Someone has a MIG at 6 o'clock, tracking." We rolled up to check 6 o'clock. I then checked 12 o'clock where I saw a smoke trail entering a black smoke cloud and a large white column exiting the other side. We then broke hard right and on roll-out observed the white column leading down to two large dirt clouds rising from the ground.

The following day two F-4E aircrews of a hunter-killer team destroyed a MIG-19. The first Phantom was manned by Maj. Gordon L. Clouser and 1st Lt. Cecil H. Brunson, and the other by Capt. Charles D. Barton and 1st Lt. George D. Watson. The manner in which this MIG was destroyed was unusual.

Disco warned the flight of approaching MIG's. The flight was then in the vicinity of Thai Nguyen. The F-105 flight leader and his wingman, making up the other half of the flight, moved out of the area as prebriefed while Clouser and Barton turned to make contact with the enemy. Clouser then observed a MIG-21 sliding into a 7 o'clock position; Barton observed a MIG-19 attempting to achieve a 6 o'clock position on the element. Clouser called a hard left break to provide self-protection for the Phantoms and to divert the MIG's from the F-105's. Because of the ordnance on board, the maneuverability of the F-4's was limited, and therefore they jettisoned the ordnance and fuel tanks.

The MIG's were dangerously close to a firing position and the two back-seaters, Brunson and Watson, warned their pilots of the danger. To disrupt enemy tracking, Barton went into a vertical dive in afterburner with a weaving pattern. Meanwhile, Clouser was able to maneuver out of the MIG's range without resorting to a dive. The MIG-19 pilot followed Barton's aircraft, its guns blazing, and Clouser rolled in behind the MIG to create a sandwich. The MIG-21 sandwiched Clouser, creating an F-4/MIG-19/F-4/MIG-21 chain. Barton continued the dive and bottomed out at 300 feet above a valley floor between two mountain peaks. The MIG-19 pilot was apparently so engrossed with the chase that he failed to notice the vertical dive angle until it was too late. His aircraft impacted with the ground. Both F-4E's recovered and the MIG-21 hastily withdrew from the battle. Each F-4E crew member was subsequently credited with one-half of a MIG kill.

The next MIG fell on 8 October. Maj. Gary L. Retterbush and Capt. Robert H. Jasperson crewed the lead aircraft in a flight of F-4E's dispatched by the 388th TFW. The following is the major's account:

On 8 October 1972, while flying lead on a strike escort mission, we received warnings of MIG's coming in from the north. We jettisoned our tanks and maneuvered behind a MIG-21 who began evasive action. Our infrared missiles failed to fire, so we closed and fired the 20-mm cannon. Several good hits were observed and the MIG burst into flames. The pilot ejected at approximately 1,500 feet before the aircraft impacted the ground.

Another maneuvering action resulted in a third aerial victory for Capt. John A. Madden, Jr., aircraft commander, and a second MIG kill for his WSO, Capt. Lawrence H. Pettit, on 12 October. They were flying MIGCAP in support of Linebacker operations. "We ingressed North Vietnam over Cam Pha on a westerly heading," reported Captain Madden.

At 0311Z, two bandits were airborne from Phuc Yen and heading northeast. We vectored now on a more northerly heading to position ourselves between the MIG's and strike forces.

Red Crown stated that the MIG's were in a port turn, and we then engaged a silver MIG-21 head-on. As the MIG passed abeam, we sliced around in a right turn to get behind and beneath him. Coming out of the right sliding turn, we sighted the MIG-21 in a port turn. We were 90° angle-off and passed within 1,000 feet behind him as we slid to the outside of his turn. We turned back to the left to get behind the MIG. He pulled up, rolled over and Split-S'd into the clouds.

At this time we were 20,000 feet and the cloud layer was solid undercast between 16,000 feet and 18,000 feet. We rolled over and dove after the MIG through the cloud deck. We picked him up underneath and pressed after him. He was last observed in an 80° dive at 9,000 feet, entering a 7/8's cloud deck with unknown base. We broke off our attack just at the top of these clouds and egressed on a heading of 120°.

The MIG crashed. Because the aggressive attack and hot pursuit caused the MIG to execute and prolong a maneuver from which he could not recover, Captains Madden and Pettit submitted a claim for the MIG's destruction.

Aircraft 2, crewed by Capt. George Norwood and 1st Lt. David F. Bland, served as Madden's wingman during these maneuvers, but this aircrew apparently did not submit a claim for a portion of the MIG-21's destruction. The Enemy Aircraft Claims Evaluation Board at Seventh Air Force considered this claim on 16 November but deferred it pending further information. On the 20th the board confirmed the MIG-21's destruction and gave credit for the aerial victory to Madden and Pettit.

USAF's Third Ace

The third and final USAF ace of the war in Southeast Asia obtained his fifth aerial victory on 13 October. More significantly, Capt. Jeffrey S. Feinstein was the second navigator ace. Flying a backseater for his squadron commander, Lt. Col. Curtis D. Westphal, during a MIGCAP near Kep airfield, Feinstein later recalls, "We received a call that bandits were in the area and heading our way. There were two of them and I got a visual on them when they were about 2 miles off." Colonel Westphal describes the engagement:

U.S. Air Force Ace Capt. Feinstein poses on top of his F-4D aircraft.

> At 1321 hours we received initial word that two bandits were airborne from the vicinity of Hanoi, heading north. At 1324 hours our flight, under Red Crown control, turned to engage the MIG's. Shortly thereafter Captain Feinstein obtained radar contact at 17 nautical miles. Red Crown confirmed the contact as being the bandits, and our flight closed on a front quarter attack.
>
> Due to the presence of friendlies in the area, we decided not to fire at that point. After closing to 1 mile, Captain Feinstein obtained a visual contact on one of the two MIG-21's. We turned left to engage. At 1328 we fired three AIM-7 missiles. All eight members of the flight observed the second AIM-7 hit the MIG-21 in the aft section, at which time it burst into flames.
>
> We saw the MIG pilot eject at approximately 5 seconds after missile impact. The entire flight then observed the MIG-21 going down in flames until it disappeared through the undercast.

Air combat on 15 October led to the destruction of three additional MIG-21's by Air Force fighter crews, one from the 388th TFW and the other two from the 432d TRW. The first kill was credited to Maj. Robert L. Holtz and his WSO, 1st Lt. William C. Diehl. The flight had been dispatched by the 388th Wing to escort three flights of F-4 strike aircraft to the vicinity of Viet Tri. Numerous MIG's were engaged by this flight before Holtz finally downed one of them. His claim statement provides a record of their activities:

> I and my GIB engaged a number of MIG-21's in the vicinity of Viet Tri and succeeded in destroying one MIG-21.
>
> While escorting a strike package of three flights of F-4's from Ubon we were vectored by Red Crown to two MIG's in my 12 o'clock position. These bandits were picked up visually at about 2 miles and a hard left turn was made to engage as they passed overhead and away at a rapid rate. Seeing that these two were no longer a threat, we started to return to escort duties when my wingman saw and engaged another MIG-21 with

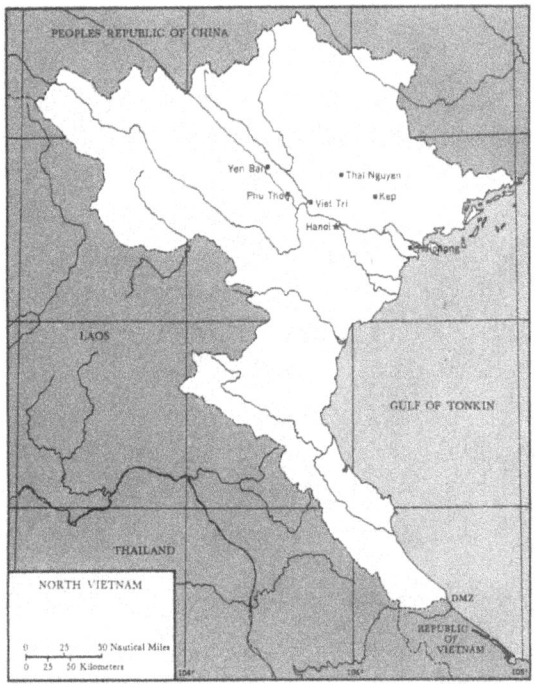

myself flying fighting wing. This MIG headed for the clouds and disappeared.

At this time the strike flights were too far ahead of us to catch, so I called for an orbit in the vicinity of Viet Tri to cover the strike flights on egress. While in this orbit my wingman and I reengaged one more time each, with negative results, until we got separated by numerous F-4's going through our flight after another MIG. While in a right hand turn to rejoin my wingman I circled a cloud and noted a white parachute about 3,000 to 4,000 feet AGL.* At this time I told Lieutenant Diehl to mark the time and position in case it was one of our pilots.

I then noted a silver MIG-21 orbiting the descending parachute about the same altitude (3,000 to 4,000 feet) and within a 30° cone of my nose to the right. The MIG was not maneuvering but instead was in a lazy right bank of about 20° and about 3,000 feet ahead. I fired an AIM-9 which came off the rail, did a slow roll and then went straight up the MIG's tail and exploded, blowing pieces of tail section and almost one complete

---

*Above ground level.

elevator off the aircraft. The MIG rolled violently to the right and started towards the ground, nose down at about 20° to 30° and on fire. At this time I disengaged and egressed the area.

The second aerial victory of the day was achieved by Captains Gary M. Rubus and his WSO, James L. Hendrickson, of the 432d TRW. The flight was providing inbound MIGCAP in support of a Linebacker mission at the time. Captain Rubus tells of the kill:

Northwest of Bullseye, while under Red Crown control, our flight vectored south against a pair of MIG-21's. A radar contact was established at a distance of 16 nautical miles, followed by a visual contact shortly thereafter. I fired an AIM-7 at a range of 4 nautical miles which detonated prematurely in front of my aircraft. A second AIM-7 was fired at a range of 4,500 feet which did not guide. I closed to cannon range and fired a burst from approximately 1,100 feet, followed by a second burst from approximately 800 feet. Both bursts impacted the MIG-21, and shortly thereafter I observed the pilot eject. The MIG-21 was trailing gray smoke, rolled left, and impacted the ground about 2 nautical miles beyond the point where the pilot ejected.

The flight lead, flown by Lt. Col. Carl Funk and Maj. James Malaney, had attempted to attack the MIG first, but had cleared Rubus to fire when Funk's radar lock broke twice in succession. Rubus attributed his kill to overall teamwork in the engagement. After he downed the MIG-21, Red Crown advised the flight that four more MIG's were airborne and coming their way, but Funk's flight had reached Bingo fuel level and had to retreat for home.

Meanwhile, the strike flights which Funk's aircraft had been assigned to protect were unable to reach their primary target: a fuel storage area in the Thai Nguyen area. The strike aircraft, therefore, hit the alternate target: Yen Bai airfield. At least one MIG was destroyed and two were damaged on the ground during this attack.

Another F-4 flight was also dispatched by the 432d TRW for MIGCAP in support of this Linebacker mission. Two members of this flight, Majors Ivy J. McCoy and Frederick W. Brown,

WSO, made the third MIG–21 kill of the day. McCoy records the action:

> Red Crown informed us that the other MIG-CAP was engaged with MIG's and for us to remain with the strike flight. Red Crown called new bandits airborne from Phuc Yen and vectored us 096° towards them. Red Crown estimated their altitude at 12,000. We continued the vectors until we merged. Having no visual contact, we made a 180° left turn and continued towards bandits.
>
> On a heading of 040° contrails were observed by myself at 1 o'clock. Red Crown informed me that they were probably my bandits. My wingman called bandits visual at 2 o'clock. I turned and visually acquired a MIG–21 in a right descending turn. I spiraled down with the MIG–21, calling for Major Brown to lock on. I then fired three AIM–7's during an elapsed time of 23 seconds.
>
> The first two missiles I did not observe. The third fell away to the left. The MIG was continuing down in a right 20° bank turn. I then selected heat and fired three AIM–9's. The third missile was visually acquired by myself at 200–300 feet aft of the MIG–21 and was observed to fly up the tailpipe of the MIG–21. The entire aft section of the MIG–21 was a fireball and was disintegrating. This occurred at 1425:40 hours. The timing is precise. Col. Robert E. Wayne, my wingman in aircraft 2, observed the missile impacting the MIG–21 and verified that the entire aft section of the MIG–21 was one large fireball. Capt. Glenn A. Profitt in aircraft 3 observed the missile impacting and the entire aft section of the MIG coming apart. Immediately after missile impact he observed the MIG pilot eject and also observed chute deployment. Our flight then egressed as a flight of four.

Operation Linebacker came to an end on 22 October 1972, and many of the fighter squadrons which had been temporarily deployed to Southeast Asia were returned to their home bases or sent elsewhere in the Far East. Linebacker's demise was premature, however, for it soon became apparent that the North Vietnamese had no intention of stopping wholesale infiltration into South Vietnam so long as American aircraft remained south of the 20th parallel.

President Nixon, on 18 December, gave the order to attack the enemy in his home territory once again, this time with a concentrated force unprecedented in the Vietnam conflict. The new operation—actually a resumption of the previous campaign—was coded Linebacker II.

Primary targets for Linebacker II consisted of rail complexes, storage facilities and supply areas, power plants, radio broadcasting stations, air bases, and SAM sites in the area around Hanoi and Haiphong. Beginning with 18 December, except for a standdown on Christmas Day when no missions were flown, targets were attacked day and night. Enemy air defenses posed a formidable obstacle to the attacking forces. But during this phase, SAM's posed the major threat. All of the B–52 bombers lost during this phase of the war were downed by surface-to-air missiles.

Score Two for B–52 Gunners

With the resumption of Linebacker operations, USAF fighter aircrews and—for the first time in the air war—gunners aboard B–52 bombers, accounted for five MIG–21 kills.*

The first victory credited to a gunner came on the night of 18 December. S/Sgt. Samuel O. Turner, normally stationed at March AFB, California, but on temporary duty with the 307th Strategic Wing based at U-Tapao airfield, Thailand, was the tail gunner aboard a B–52D, part of the heavy bomber force hitting targets in the Hanoi area. Turner describes the engagement:

> We were a few ships back from the lead aircraft. As we approached our target area, numerous surface-to-air missiles began coming up and exploding around us. We did not divert or turn back. We had our target and planned to hit it, regardless.
>
> As we drew nearer to the target the intensity of the SAM's picked up. They were lighting up the sky. They seemed to be everywhere. We released our bombs over the target and had just proceeded outbound from the target when we learned that

---

*During the Korean War, there were 27 victories recorded by B–29 gunners.

A North Vietnamese SAM fired at USAF strike aircraft northwest of Hanoi.

A SAM burst recorded on camera.

there were MIG aircraft airborne near a particular reference point.

Our navigator told us the reference point was in our area and before long we learned the enemy fighter had us on its radar. As he closed on us I also picked him up on my radar when he was a few miles from our aircraft.

A few seconds later, the fighter locked on to us. As the MIG closed in, I also locked on him. He came in low in a rapid climb. While tracking the first MIG, I picked up a second enemy aircraft at 8 o'clock at a range of about 7½ miles. He appeared stabilized—not attacking us, obviously allowing the other fighter room to maneuver and conduct his run first.

As the attacking MIG came into firing range, I fired a burst. There was a gigantic explosion to the rear of the aircraft. I looked out the window but was unable to see directly where the MIG would have been. I looked back at my radar scope. Except for the one airplane out at 8 o'clock, there was nothing. And within 15 seconds, even he broke away and we lost contact with him.

Turner's MIG kill was witnessed by another gunner, M/Sgt. Lewis E. LeBlanc, who confirmed the kill. LeBlanc saw a fireball at the MIG-21's approximate range and azimuth.

The mission of protecting the heavy bomber fleet was generally assigned to F–4 MIGCAP flights which accompanied every bomber wave over North Vietnam. One MIGCAP aircrew demonstrated unusual aggressiveness and persistence and scored a victory without even hitting the MIG. This rare feat was achieved by Capt. Gary L. Sholders and his WSO, 1st Lt. Eldon D. Binkley, who were the lead aircraft on 21/22 December. Sholders explains their accomplishment:

Our flight dropped off the tanker at 1948Z and proceeded north toward the assigned orbit point. Upon contact with Red Crown, the flight was

Gen. John C. Meyer, commander-in-chief, SAC, awards the Silver Star to S/Sgt. Samuel O. Turner, the first B–52 gunner to shoot down an enemy aircraft.

advised of enemy aircraft activity west of Hanoi. Red Crown began vectoring at 2003Z.

We elected not to pursue the bandit immediately because his altitude was below an overcast which covered virtually all of the Hanoi area. Our flight established a left orbit at approximately 60 miles from Hanoi. We remained in this orbit until approximately 2018Z, when Red Crown advised that the bandit had climbed to 16,000 feet.

We made a hard left turn to 100°, established immediate radar contact with a single enemy aircraft crossing right to left, range 18 miles. Clearance to fire was obtained from Red Crown, and we rolled into a 5-mile trail position on the bandit. The bandit then engaged his after-burner and began a steep climb. We obtained a lock-on using boresight mode, and closed to approximately 3 miles when the radar broke lock at approximately 2022Z.

Red Crown advised our flight shortly thereafter that the bandit was south at 10 miles. We then turned to reengage. The flight remained within 8 miles of the bandit in a maneuvering engagement, using intermittent radar returns and vectors from Red Crown, until approximately 2033Z.

We were unable to obtain a radar lock-on during this period of time. Red Crown advised the flight at 2033Z that the bandit was south at 7 miles, heading home. We then turned southeast, attempting to reacquire the bandit heading toward Hanoi; no contact was made on this heading. We then made a right turn to the northwest and immediately acquired radar contact with an enemy aircraft at 25 miles on the nose, apparently heading for Yen Bai airfield.

We pursued the bandit, closing to approximately 20 miles as the bandit appeared to be orbiting Yen Bai. The bandit then turned northeast. Using radar we were able to close to approximately 7 miles. We pursued the bandit until approximately 2046Z, when the engagement was terminated for fuel considerations. At the termination of the engagement, the bandit was on the nose at 7 miles. Our position at that time was approximately 010°, 60 miles from Hanoi. Shortly after termination of the engagement, one of the controlling agencies called a bandit north of Hanoi.

Intelligence sources confirmed (on 24 December) that an enemy aircraft went down in the early morning hours of 22 December 1972. Ours was the only flight in the area that engaged an enemy aircraft for any length of time on 21/22 December; in addition, the only flight that pursued an enemy aircraft after he had apparently attempted a landing at Yen Bai airfield. On the strength of the aforementioned evidence, we claim one enemy aircraft destroyed due to continued pursuit which resulted in fuel starvation for the enemy aircraft.

Lt. Col. James E. Brunson and Maj. Ralph S. Pickett, destroyed a MIG–21 on 22 December. Their flight was escorting strike aircraft in Route Package 6. According to Brunson (the flight leader), two MIG's were encountered:

After pre-strike refueling, the flight—the ingress MIGCAP in this Linebacker II mission—proceeded north toward Phu Tho en route to their assigned CAP area near Kep airfield . . . Two bandits started climbing out to the northwest of Hanoi. Red Crown was controlling the flight as they crossed into North Vietnam. Red Crown reported the MIG's as heading 290° and climbing through 26,000 feet. Red Crown gave our flight a vector of 020° and called the MIG's 30° right, 46 miles, at 29,000 feet, with friendlies between our flight and the MIG's.

The MIG's turned south toward us and the friendlies. Red Crown vectored us for a head-on intercept. Red Crown called the MIG's at 020° and 16 miles from us when the flight leader got a radar lock-on in that position and asked for clearance to fire. Red Crown cleared him to fire if a visual identification was made, as friendly aircraft were still in the area.

Our flight jettisoned the centerline fuel tanks and accelerated. The MIG was about 10,000 feet higher than the flight, and as aircraft 1 started his pull-up to center the radar steering dot, he saw a silver MIG–21 above him.

The flight leader put the MIG in his gunsight pipper and fired four AIM–7 missiles in rapid succession with full radar lock-on, maintaining a steep climb toward the MIG. Both the aircraft commander and weapon systems officer observed

B-52 in flight.

one of the AIM-7 missiles detonate in the tail section of the MIG-21, causing the tail section and large pieces . . . to separate. The MIG went into an uncontrollable spin. No bail-out . . . was observed.

The flight was still in good formation and turned to engage the second MIG in the flight, which was observed by aircraft 3. This MIG escaped and the flight returned to base due to fuel.

Airman First Class Albert E. Moore, a B-52 gunner, won credit for the next MIG. A tail gunner during a bombing raid on the Thai Nguyen railroad yards on 24 December, he acquired a fast-moving bogey on his radar scope. He notified his crew to dispense chaff and flares, got target lock-on at 4,000 yards, and as the bandit closed to 2,000 yards, opened fire. He continued firing until the blip blossomed on his scope, then disappeared. His feat was witnessed by T/Sgt. Clarence W. Chute, also a gunner, who saw the MIG-21 "on fire and falling away."

U.S. strikes resumed once again on the 26th. Two days later, a MIG-21 fell prey to Maj. Harry L. McKee and his WSO, Capt. John E. Dubler, who were on MIGCAP duty. They met a MIG-21 west of Hanoi and promptly downed it. "Red Crown called the position of a bandit heading west," said Maj. McKee:

Captain Dubler made radar contact with the bandit at 90 nautical miles range at approximately 2150 hours. Red Crown called our position as being 270° and 92 nautical miles from Bullseye at 2156.30. . . .we were in trail with the MIG and had radar contact 30° left at 11 nautical miles.

We were cleared to close by Red Crown and a full system lock-on was made at 10 nautical miles. My wingman [Capt. Kimzey W. Rhine] called 'locked on' shortly thereafter.

Both aircraft fired on my verbal command with the radar dot centered. I fired two AIM-7 missiles at 2157:20; Rhine fired one AIM-7 at the same time. Order of firing was aircraft 1, one AIM-7; then aircraft 2, one AIM-7; then aircraft 1, second AIM-7. We all observed a large fireball approximately 4 nautical miles distant at 12 o'clock at 2157:30. Missile firing was at maximum ASE circle expansion. . . . It appeared that all three AIM-7's guided. Further, it appeared that the first missile impacted the MIG, followed immediately by impact of the missile fired by Rhine.

At missile firing our airspeed was Mach 1.05, altitude 30,500 feet, and heading 010°. Moments later I observed a fireball on the ground in the vicinity of the shoot-down. We continued to operate as a flight of two, in a MIGCAP capacity, until 2235 hours, whereupon we egressed . . .

Major McKee may have intended to have his wingmen, Captains Rhine and James W. Ogilvie in aircraft 2, share in the aerial victory. Seventh Air Force's claims evaluation board—though initially viewing this MIG kill as a joint effort—decided to credit only McKee and Dubler.

Linebacker II achieved the desired political results, and on 29 December 1972 President Nixon ended massive raids above the 20th parallel. Fighting continued south of the bomb line, and American pilots were permitted to cross the parallel in pursuit of North Vietnamese aircraft attacking B–52's and other U.S. aircraft. Such an incident took place at 0230 hours on 8 January 1973 and resulted in the destruction of a MIG–21 by Capt. Paul D. Howman and his WSO, 1st Lt. Lawrence W. Kullman, of the 432d TRW. This victory was the only USAF MIG kill in 1973 and the last of the war. "We were flying a MIGCAP in Route Package 3, 80 miles southwest of Hanoi,'' relates Howman:

. . .when we received a MIG warning from Red Crown at 1930Z [0230 hours, 8 January local time]. The bandit call put the MIG 240° and 14 nautical miles from Bullseye, which was approximately 65 nautical miles north-northeast of our position.

After the second bandit call at 1932Z, Red Crown vectored us 330° and called the MIG at 020° and 60 nautical miles from our position.

We continued the intercept until we were 020° and 26 nautical miles from the MIG. At this time, Red Crown gave us clearance to fire as well as a vector of 026°. During this entire time we had radar contacts on the bandit. We descended and obtained a visual contact with the MIG's afterburner at 10 nautical miles, and a full system radar lock-on at 6 nautical miles.

Crew boards B–52.

They fired two missiles. The first detonated approximately 50 to 100 feet from the MIG, but the second hit its target. The MIG burst into flames and broke into three distinct pieces.

A few days later, a Presidential order halted all bombing of North Vietnam, and on 29 January 1973, the Vietnam cease-fire went into effect.

IV

The Men: Their Units, Tools, and Tactics

Only two enemy aircraft, both MIG–17's, fell to USAF fighter aircrews during 1965, for North Vietnam had yet to commit its full MIG force in its active air defense system. With intensified MIG opposition to USAF air strikes during 1966, the number of engagements increased and the score of aerial victories rose: there were 17 confirmed enemy losses (12 MIG–17's and 5 MIG–21's) to Air Force aircrews that year. The first significant year in the air-to-air war was 1967, during which 59 enemy aircraft (42 MIG–17's and 17 MIG–21's) fell to USAF aerial combatants. Air Force aircrews began 1968 with 8 kills (5 MIG–17's and 3 MIG–21's) in the first two months, but these were the last aerial victories of the year. President Johnson restricted all aerial strikes and protective operations to regions below the 19th parallel. The North Vietnamese seldom ventured south of the bomb line.

There were no USAF aerial victories between 1968 and 1972. But the air war then moved northward again, as American strike forces raided in reprisal for increased enemy activity, and the North Vietnamese Air Force employed its aerial power to counteract the increasing threat. During this phase, which continued into the beginning of the next year when the last Air Force aerial victory was recorded,

the enemy lost 51 aircraft (8 MIG–19's and 43 MIG–21's) to USAF fighter and bomber crews.

The MIG-Killers

Of the confirmed total of 137 kills by USAF fliers, official credit was awarded to 207 individuals. Pilots of single-place F–105D aircraft earned 25 victories; two-man aircrews of F–4C, F–4D, F–4E, and F–105F aircraft earned 108. One victory credit was shared by F–105F and F–4D aircrews, and one by two F–4E's. Gunners aboard B–52D heavy bombers earned two aerial victories in the last stages of the war.

The 137 victories have been compiled and are presented here in two lists (Tables 1 and 2). The numerous claims for the destruction of enemy aircraft which were never confirmed are not included in the lists. The first presents all USAF aerial victories in chronological order; the second lists alphabetically the USAF or attached fliers who earned aerial victories. There is some duplication of information between the lists, as there is between the lists and the combat narratives presented in earlier chapters. Information has been reduced to tabular form primarily as a convenience to those who desire a quick reference or an overall picture, without wading through the discussions of each engagement.

(Left) F–105 refuels in flight.

TABLE 1.—CHRONOLOGICAL ORDER

Date	Type Enemy Acft.	Type USAF Acft.	Primary Weapon Used	USAF Squadron	Parent Unit	Aircrew Personnel	Crew Position	Official Credit
1965								
10 Jul	MIG-17	F-4C	AIM-9	45 TFS	2 AD	Cpt Thomas S Roberts Cpt Ronald C Anderson	AC P	1.0 1.0
10 Jul	MIG-17	F-4C	AIM-9	45 TFS	2 AD	Cpt Kenneth E Holcombe Cpt Arthur C Clark	AC P	1.0 1.0
1966								
23 Apr	MIG-17	F-4C	AIM-9	555 TFS	8 TFW	Cpt Max F Cameron 1Lt Robert E Evans	AC P	1.0 1.0
23 Apr	MIG-17	F-4C	AIM-7	555 TFS	8 TFW	Cpt Robert E Blake 1Lt S W George	AC P	1.0 1.0
26 Apr	MIG-21	F-4C	AIM-9	480 TFS	35 TFW	Maj Paul J Gilmore 1Lt William T Smith	AC P	1.0 1.0
29 Apr	MIG-17	F-4C	AIM-9	555 TFS	8 TFW	Cpt William B D Dowell 1Lt Halbert E Gossard	AC P	1.0 1.0
29 Apr	MIG-17	F-4C	maneuvering	555 TFS	8 TFW	Cpt Larry R Keith 1Lt Robert A Bleakley	AC P	1.0 1.0
30 Apr	MIG-17	F-4C	AIM-9	555 TFS	8 TFW	Cpt Lawrence H Golberg 1Lt Gerald D Hardgrave	AC P	1.0 1.0
12 May	MIG-17	F-4C	AIM-9	390 TFS	35 TFW	Maj Wilbur R Dudley 1Lt Imants Kringelis	AC P	1.0 1.0
29 Jun	MIG-17	F-105D	20mm		388 TFW	Maj Fred L Tracy	P	1.0
14 Jul	MIG-21	F-4C	AIM-9	480 TFS	35 TFW	Cpt William J Swendner 1Lt Duane A Buttell Jr	AC P	1.0 1.0
14 Jul	MIG-21	F-4C	AIM-9	480 TFS	35 TFW	1Lt Ronald G Martin 1Lt Richard N Krieps	AC P	1.0 1.0
18 Aug	MIG-17	F-105D	20mm	34 TFS	388 TFW	Maj Kenneth T Blank	P	1.0
16 Sep	MIG-17	F-4C	AIM-9	555 TFS	8 TFW	1Lt Jerry W Jameson 1Lt Douglas B Rose	AC P	1.0 1.0
21 Sep	MIG-17	F-105D	20mm	421 TFS	388 TFW	1Lt Karl W Richter	P	1.0
21 Sep	MIG-17	F-105D	20mm	333 TFS	355 TFW	1Lt Fred A Wilson Jr	P	1.0

118

Date	MIG	Aircraft	Weapon	TFS	TFW	Crew	Role	Score
05 Nov	MIG-21	F-4C	AIM-7	480 TFS	366 TFW	Maj James E Tuck / 1Lt John J Rabeni Jr	AC / P	1.0 / 1.0
05 Nov	MIG-21	F-4C	AIM-9	480 TFS	366 TFW	1Lt Wilbur J Latham Jr / 1Lt Klaus J Klause	AC / P	1.0 / 1.0
04 Dec	MIG-17	F-105D	20mm	469 TFS	388 TFW	Maj Roy S Dickey	P	1.0
1967								
02 Jan	MIG-21	F-4C	AIM-7	555 TFS	8 TFW	1Lt Ralph F Wetterhahn / 1Lt Jerry K Sharp	AC / P	1.0 / 1.0
02 Jan	MIG-21	F-4C	AIM-9	555 TFS	8 TFW	Cpt Walter S Radeker III / 1Lt James E Murray III	AC / P	1.0 / 1.0
02 Jan	MIG-21	F-4C	AIM-9	555 TFS	8 TFW	Col Robin Olds / 1Lt Charles C Clifton	AC / P	1.0 / 1.0
02 Jan	MIG-21	F-4C	AIM-9	433 TFS	8 TFW	Cpt Everett T Raspberry Jr / 1Lt Robert W Western	AC / P	1.0 / 1.0
02 Jan	MIG-21	F-4C	AIM-7	433 TFS	8 TFW	Maj Philip P Combies / 1Lt Lee R Dutton	AC / P	1.0 / 1.0
02 Jan	MIG-21	F-4C	AIM-7	433 TFS	8 TFW	Cpt John B Stone / 1Lt Clifton P Dunnegan Jr	AC / P	1.0 / 1.0
02 Jan	MIG-21	F-4C	AIM-7	555 TFS	8 TFW	1Lt Lawrence J Glynn Jr / 1Lt Lawrence E Cary	AC / P	1.0 / 1.0
06 Jan	MIG-21	F-4C	AIM-7	555 TFS	8 TFW	Cpt Richard M Pascoe / 1Lt Norman E Wells	AC / P	1.0 / 1.0
06 Jan	MIG-21	F-4C	AIM-7	555 TFS	8 TFW	Maj Thomas M Hirsch / 1Lt Roger J Strasswimmer	AC / P	1.0 / 1.0
10 Mar	MIG-17	F-105D	20mm	354 TFS	355 TFW	Cpt Max C Brestel	P	1.0
10 Mar	MIG-17	F-105D	20mm	354 TFS	355 TFW	Cpt Max C Brestel	P	1.0
26 Mar	MIG-17	F-105D	20mm	333 TFS	355 TFW	Col Robert R Scott	P	1.0
19 Apr	MIG-17	F-105F	20mm	357 TFS	355 TFW	Maj Leo K Thorsness / Cpt Harold E Johnson	P / EWO	1.0 / 1.0
19 Apr	MIG-17	F-105D	20mm	354 TFS	355 TFW	Maj Frederick G Tolman	P	1.0
19 Apr	MIG-17	F-105D	20mm	354 TFS	355 TFW	Maj Jack W Hunt	P	1.0
19 Apr	MIG-17	F-105D	20mm	354 TFS	355 TFW	Cpt William E Eskew	P	1.0
23 Apr	MIG-21	F-4C	AIM-7	389 TFS	366 TFW	Maj Robert D Anderson / Cpt Fred D Kjer	AC / P	1.0 / 1.0
26 Apr	MIG-21	F-4C	AIM-7	389 TFS	366 TFW	Maj Rolland W Moore Jr / 1Lt James F Sears	AC / P	1.0 / 1.0

119

TABLE 1.—CHRONOLOGICAL ORDER—Continued

Date	Type Enemy Acft.	Type USAF Acft.	Primary USAF Weapon Used	USAF Squadron	Parent Unit	Aircrew Personnel	Crew Position	Official Credit
28 Apr	MIG-17	F-105D	20mm	357 TFS	355 TFW	Maj Harry E Higgins	P	1.0
28 Apr	MIG-17	F-105D	20mm	357 TFS	355 TFW	LtC Arthur F Dennis	P	1.0
30 Apr	MIG-17	F-105D	20mm	333 TFS	355 TFW	Cpt Thomas C Lesan	P	1.0
01 May	MIG-17	F-4C	maneuvering	390 TFS	366 TFW	Maj Robert G Dilger 1Lt Mack Thies	AC P	1.0 1.0
04 May	MIG-21	F-4C	AIM-9	555 TFS	8 TFW	Col Robin Olds 1Lt William D Lafever	AC P	1.0 1.0
12 May	MIG-17	F-105D	20mm	333 TFS	355 TFW	Cpt Jacques A Suzanne	P	1.0
13 May	MIG-17	F-105D	20mm	354 TFS	355 TFW	LtC Philip C Gast	P	1.0
13 May	MIG-17	F-105D	20mm	354 TFS	355 TFW	Cpt Charles W Couch	P	1.0
13 May	MIG-17	F-105D	AIM-9	333 TFS	355 TFW	Maj Robert G Rilling	P	1.0
13 May	MIG-17	F-105D	AIM-9	333 TFS	355 TFW	Maj Carl D Osborne	P	1.0
13 May	MIG-17	F-4C	AIM-9	433 TFS	8 TFW	Maj William L Kirk 1Lt Stephen A Wayne	AC P	1.0 1.0
13 May	MIG-17	F-4C	AIM-7	433 TFS	8 TFW	LtC Fred A Haeffner 1Lt Michael R Bever	AC P	1.0 1.0
13 May	MIG-17	F-105D	20mm	44 TFS	388 TFW	Maj Maurice E Seaver Jr	P	1.0
14 May	MIG-17	F-4C	20mm	480 TFS	366 TFW	Maj James A Hargrove Jr 1Lt Stephen H DeMuth	AC P	1.0 1.0
14 May	MIG-17	F-4C	20mm	480 TFS	366 TFW	Cpt James T Craig Jr 1Lt James T Talley	AC P	1.0 1.0
14 May	MIG-17	F-4C	AIM-7	480 TFS	366 TFW	Maj Samuel O Bakke Cpt Robert W Lambert	AC P	1.0 1.0
20 May	MIG-21	F-4C	AIM-7	389 TFS	366 TFW	LtC Robert F Titus 1Lt Milan Zimer	AC P	1.0 1.0
20 May	MIG-21	F-4C	AIM-9	389 TFS	366 TFW	Maj Robert D Janca 1Lt William E Roberts Jr	AC P	1.0 1.0
20 May	MIG-17	F-4C	AIM-9	433 TFS	8 TFW	Maj John R Pardo 1Lt Stephen A Wayne	AC P	1.0 1.0

Date	MiG	Aircraft	Weapon	Squadron	Wing	Crew	Role	Score
20 May	MIG-17	F-4C	AIM-7	433 TFS	8 TFW	Col Robin Olds	AC	1.0
						1Lt Stephen B Croker	P	1.0
20 May	MIG-17	F-4C	AIM-9	433 TFS	8 TFW	Maj Philip P Combies	AC	1.0
						1Lt Daniel L Lafferty	P	1.0
20 May	MIG-17	F-4C	AIM-9	433 TFS	8 TFW	Col Robin Olds	AC	1.0
						1Lt Stephen B Croker	P	1.0
22 May	MIG-21	F-4C	AIM-9	389 TFS	366 TFW	LtC Robert F Titus	AC	1.0
						1Lt Milan Zimer	P	1.0
22 May	MIG-21	F-4C	20mm	389 TFS	366 TFW	LtC Robert F Titus	AC	1.0
						1Lt Milan Zimer	P	1.0
03 Jun	MIG-17	F-105D	AIM-9/20mm	469 TFS	388 TFW	Cpt Larry D Wiggins	P	1.0
03 Jun	MIG-17	F-105D	20mm	13 TFS	388 TFW	Maj Ralph L Kuster Jr	P	1.0
05 Jun	MIG-17	F-4D	AIM-7	555 TFS	8 TFW	Maj Everett T Raspberry Jr	AC	1.0
						Cpt Francis M Gullick	P	1.0
05 Jun	MIG-17	F-4C	20mm	480 TFS	366 TFW	Maj Durwood K Priester	AC	1.0
						Cpt John E Pankhurst	P	1.0
05 Jun	MIG-17	F-4C	AIM-9	555 TFS	8 TFW	Cpt Richard M Pascoe	AC	1.0
						Cpt Norman E Wells	P	1.0
23 Aug	MIG-17	F-105D	20mm	34 TFS	388 TFW	1Lt David B Waldrop III	P	1.0
18 Oct	MIG-17	F-105D	20mm	333 TFS	355 TFW	Maj Donald M Russell	P	1.0
24 Oct	MIG-21	F-4D	20mm	433 TFS	8 TFW	Maj William L Kirk	AC	1.0
						1Lt Theodore R Bongartz	P	1.0
26 Oct	MIG-17	F-4D	AIM-7	555 TFS	8 TFW	Cpt John D Logeman Jr	AC	1.0
						1Lt Frederick E McCoy II	P	1.0
26 Oct	MIG-17	F-4D	AIM-7	555 TFS	8 TFW	Cpt William S Gordon III	AC	1.0
						1Lt James H Monsees	P	1.0
26 Oct	MIG-17	F-4D	AIM-4	555 TFS	8 TFW	Cpt Larry D Cobb	AC	1.0
						Cpt Alan A Lavoy	P	1.0
27 Oct	MIG-17	F-105D	20mm	354 TFS	355 TFW	Cpt Gene I Basel	P	1.0
06 Nov	MIG-17	F-4D	20mm	435 TFS	8 TFW	Cpt Darrell D Simmonds	AC	1.0
						1Lt George H McKinney Jr	P	1.0
06 Nov	MIG-17	F-4D	20mm	435 TFS	8 TFW	Cpt Darrell D Simmonds	AC	1.0
						1Lt George H McKinney Jr	P	1.0
17 Dec	MIG-17	F-4D	AIM-4	13 TFS	432 TRW	Cpt Doyle D Baker (USMC)	AC	1.0
						1Lt John D Ryan Jr	P	1.0

TABLE 1.—CHRONOLOGICAL ORDER—Continued

Date	Type Enemy Acft.	Type USAF Acft.	Primary USAF Weapon Used	USAF Squadron	Parent Unit	Aircrew Personnel	Crew Position	Official Credit
19 Dec	MIG-17	F-4D	20mm	435 TFS	8 TFW	Maj Joseph D Moore 1Lt George H McKinney Jr	AC P	0.5 0.5
		F-105F	20mm	333 TFS	355 TFW	Maj William M Dalton Maj James L Graham	P EWO	0.5 0.5
19 Dec	MIG-17	F-105F	20mm	357 TFS	355 TFW	Cpt Philip M Drew Maj William H Wheeler	P EWO	1.0 1.0
1968								
03 Jan	MIG-17	F-4D	AIM-4	435 TFS	8 TFW	LtC Clayton K Squier 1Lt Michael D Muldoon	AC P	1.0 1.0
03 Jan	MIG-17	F-4D	20mm	433 TFS	8 TFW	Maj Bernard J Bogoslofski Cpt Richard L Huskey	AC P	1.0 1.0
18 Jan	MIG-17	F-4D	AIM-4	435 TFS	8 TFW	Maj Kenneth A Simonet 1Lt Wayne O Smith	AC P	1.0 1.0
05 Feb	MIG-21	F-4D	AIM-4	13 TFS	432 TRW	Cpt Robert G Hill 1Lt Bruce V Huneke	AC P	1.0 1.0
06 Feb	MIG-21	F-4D	AIM-7	433 TFS	8 TFW	Cpt Robert H Boles 1Lt Robert B Battista	AC P	1.0 1.0
12 Feb	MIG-21	F-4D	AIM-7	435 TFS	8 TFW	LtC Alfred E Lang Jr 1Lt Randy P Moss	AC P	1.0 1.0
14 Feb	MIG-17	F-4D	20mm	555 TFS	8 TFW	Maj Rex D Howerton 1Lt Ted L Voigt II	AC P	1.0 1.0
14 Feb	MIG-17	F-4D	AIM-7	435 TFS	8 TFW	Col David O Williams Jr 1Lt James P Feighny Jr	AC P	1.0 1.0
1972								
21 Feb	MIG-21	F-4D	AIM-7	555 TFS	432 TRW	Maj Robert A Lodge 1Lt Roger C Locher	AC WSO	1.0 1.0
01 Mar	MIG-21	F-4D	AIM-7	555 TFS	432 TRW	LtC Joseph W Kittinger Jr 1Lt Leigh A Hodgdon	AC WSO	1.0 1.0
30 Mar	MIG-21	F-4D	AIM-7	13 TFS	432 TRW	Cpt Frederick S Olmsted Jr Cpt Gerald R Volloy	AC WSO	1.0 1.0
16 Apr	MIG-21	F-4D	AIM-7	13 TFS	432 TRW	Cpt Frederick S Olmsted Jr Cpt Stuart W Maas	AC WSO	1.0 1.0

Date	MiG	A/C	Weapon	Sqn	Wing	Crew		Role	Credit
16 Apr	MIG-21	F-4D	AIM-7	13 TFS	432 TRW	Maj Edward D Cherry	Cpt Jeffrey S Feinstein	AC / WSO	1.0 / 1.0
16 Apr	MIG-21	F-4D	AIM-7	523 TFS	432 TRW	Cpt James C Null	Cpt Michael D Vahue	AC / WSO	1.0 / 1.0
08 May	MIG-19	F-4D	AIM-7	13 TFS	432 TRW	Maj Barton P Crews	Cpt Keith W Jones Jr	AC / WSO	1.0 / 1.0
08 May	MIG-21	F-4D	AIM-7	555 TFS	432 TRW	Maj Robert A Lodge	Cpt Roger C Locher	AC / WSO	1.0 / 1.0
10 May	MIG-21	F-4D	AIM-7	555 TFS	432 TRW	Maj Robert A Lodge	Cpt Roger C Locher	AC / WSO	1.0 / 1.0
10 May	MIG-21	F-4D	AIM-7	555 TFS	432 TRW	1Lt John D Markle	Cpt Stephen D Eaves	AC / WSO	1.0 / 1.0
10 May	MIG-21	F-4D	AIM-7	555 TFS	432 TRW	Cpt Richard S Ritchie	Cpt Charles B DeBellevue	AC / WSO	1.0 / 1.0
11 May	MIG-21	F-4D	AIM-7	555 TFS	432 TRW	Cpt Stephen E Nichols	1Lt James R Bell	AC / WSO	1.0 / 1.0
12 May	MIG-19	F-4D	AIM-7	555 TFS	432 TRW	LtC Wayne T Frye	LtC James P Cooney	AC / WSO	1.0 / 1.0
23 May	MIG-19	F-4E	AIM-7	35 TFS	366 TFW	LtC Lyle L Beckers	Cpt John F Huwe	AC / WSO	1.0 / 1.0
23 May	MIG-19	F-4E	20mm	35 TFS	366 TFW	Cpt James M Beatty Jr	1Lt James M Sumner	AC / WSO	1.0 / 1.0
31 May	MIG-21	F-4E	AIM-9	13 TFS	432 TRW	Cpt Bruce G Leonard Jr	Cpt Jeffrey S Feinstein	AC / WSO	1.0 / 1.0
31 May	MIG-21	F-4D	AIM-7	555 TFS	432 TRW	Cpt Richard S Ritchie	Cpt Lawrence H Pettit	AC / WSO	1.0 / 1.0
02 Jun	MIG-19	F-4E	20mm	58 TFS	432 TRW	Maj Philip W Handley	1Lt John J Smallwood	AC / WSO	1.0 / 1.0
21 Jun	MIG-21	F-4E	AIM-9	469 TFS	388 TFW	LtC Von R Christiansen	Maj Kaye M Harden	AC / WSO	1.0 / 1.0
08 Jul	MIG-21	F-4E	AIM-7	4 TFS	366 TFW	Cpt Richard F Hardy	Cpt Paul T Lewinski	AC / WSO	1.0 / 1.0
08 Jul	MIG-21	F-4E	AIM-7	555 TFS	432 TRW	Cpt Richard S Ritchie	Cpt Charles B DeBellevue	AC / WSO	1.0 / 1.0
08 Jul	MIG-21	F-4E	AIM-7	555 TFS	432 TRW	Cpt Richard S Ritchie	Cpt Charles B DeBellevue	AC / WSO	1.0 / 1.0

TABLE 1.—CHRONOLOGICAL ORDER—Continued

Date	Type Enemy Acft.	Type USAF Acft.	Primary USAF Weapon Used	USAF Squadron	Parent Unit	Aircrew Personnel	Crew Position	Official Credit
18 Jul	MIG-21	F-4D	AIM-9	13 TFS	432 TRW	LtC Carl G Baily Cpt Jeffrey S Feinstein	AC WSO	1.0 1.0
29 Jul	MIG-21	F-4D	AIM-7	13 TFS	432 TRW	LtC Carl G Baily Cpt Jeffrey S Feinstein	AC WSO	1.0 1.0
29 Jul	MIG-21	F-4E	AIM-7	4 TFS	366 TFW	LtC Gene E Taft Cpt Stanley M Imaye	AC WSO	1.0 1.0
12 Aug	MIG-21	F-4E	AIM-7	58 TFS	432 TRW	Cpt Lawrence G Richard (USMC) LtCdr Michael J Ettel (USN)	AC WSO	1.0 1.0
15 Aug	MIG-21	F-4E	AIM-7	336 TFS	8 TFW	Cpt Fred W Sheffler Cpt Mark A Massen	AC WSO	1.0 1.0
19 Aug	MIG-21	F-4E	AIM-7	4 TFS	366 TFW	Cpt Sammy C White 1Lt Frank J Bettine	AC WSO	1.0 1.0
28 Aug	MIG-21	F-4D	AIM-7	555 TFS	432 TRW	Cpt Richard S Ritchie Cpt Charles B DeBellevue	AC WSO	1.0 1.0
02 Sep	MIG-19	F-4E	AIM-7	34 TFS 35 TFS	388 TFW 388 TFW	Maj Jon I Lucas 1Lt Douglas G Malloy	AC WSO	1.0 1.0
09 Sep	MIG-21	F-4D	20mm	555 TFS	432 TRW	Cpt Calvin B Tibbett 1Lt William S Hargrove	AC WSO	1.0 1.0
09 Sep	MIG-19	F-4D	AIM-9	555 TFS	432 TRW	Cpt John A Madden Jr Cpt Charles B DeBellevue	AC WSO	1.0 1.0
09 Sep	MIG-19	F-4D	AIM-9	555 TFS	432 TRW	Cpt John A Madden Jr Cpt Charles B DeBellevue	AC WSO	1.0 1.0
12 Sep	MIG-21	F-4E	AIM-9/20mm	35 TFS	388 TFW	LtC Lyle L Beckers 1Lt Thomas M Griffin	AC WSO	1.0 1.0
12 Sep	MIG-21	F-4E	20mm	35 TFS	388 TFW	Maj Gary L Retterbush 1Lt Daniel L Autrey	AC WSO	1.0 1.0
12 Sep	MIG-21	F-4D	AIM-9	469 TFS	388 TFW	Cpt Michael J Mahaffey 1Lt George I Shields	AC WSO	1.0 1.0
16 Sep	MIG-21	F-4E	AIM-9	555 TFS	432 TRW	Cpt Calvin B Tibbett 1Lt William S Hargrove	AC WSO	1.0 1.0
05 Oct	MIG-21	F-4E	AIM-7	34 TFS	388 TFW	Cpt Richard E Coe 1Lt Omri K Webb III	AC WSO	1.0 1.0

Date	MiG	Aircraft	Weapon	Sqn	Wing	Crew	Role	Credit
06 Oct	MIG-19	F-4E	maneuvering	34 TFS	388 TFW	Maj Gordon L Clouser	AC	0.5
						1Lt Cecil H Brunson	WSO	0.5
	MIG-19	F-4E	maneuvering	34 TFS	388 TFW	Cpt Charles D Barton	AC	0.5
						1Lt George D Watson	WSO	0.5
08 Oct	MIG-21	F-4E	20mm	35 TFS	388 TFW	Maj Gary L Retterbush	AC	1.0
						Cpt Robert H Jasperson	WSO	1.0
12 Oct	MIG-21	F-4D	maneuvering	555 TFS	432 TRW	Cpt John A Madden Jr	AC	1.0
						Cpt Lawrence H Pettit	WSO	1.0
13 Oct	MIG-21	F-4D	AIM-7	13 TFS	432 TRW	LtC Curtis D Westphal	AC	1.0
						Cpt Jeffrey S Feinstein	WSO	1.0
15 Oct	MIG-21	F-4E	AIM-9	34 TFS	388 TFW	Maj Robert L Holtz	AC	1.0
						1Lt William C Diehl	WSO	1.0
15 Oct	MIG-21	F-4E	20mm	307 TFS	432 TRW	Cpt Gary M Rubus	AC	1.0
						Cpt James L Hendrickson	WSO	1.0
15 Oct	MIG-21	F-4D	AIM-9	523 TFS	432 TRW	Maj Ivy J McCoy Jr	AC	1.0
						Maj Frederick W Brown	WSO	1.0
18 Dec	MIG-21	B-52D	.50 cal		307 SW	SSgt Samuel O Turner	G	1.0
22 Dec	MIG-21	F-4D	maneuvering	555 TFS	432 TRW	Cpt Gary L Sholders	AC	1.0
						1Lt Eldon D Binkley	WSO	1.0
22 Dec	MIG-21	F-4D	AIM-7	555 TFS	432 TRW	LtC James E Brunson	AC	1.0
						Maj Ralph S Pickett	WSO	1.0
24 Dec	MIG-21	B-52D	.50 cal		307 SW	A1C Albert E Moore	G	1.0
28 Dec	MIG-21	F-4D	AIM-7	555 TFS	432 TRW	Maj Harry L McKee Jr	AC	1.0
						Cpt John E Dubler	WSO	1.0
1973								
08 Jan	MIG-21	F-4D	AIM-7	4 TFS	432 TRW	Cpt Paul D Howman	AC	1.0
						1Lt Lawrence W Kullman	WSO	1.0

Last Thuds in Vietnam, a photo taken by Maj. Don Kutyna of his "Polish Glider."

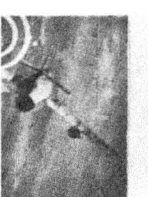

A MIG kill recorded on camera.

TABLE 2.—ALPHABETICAL ORDER

Individual/Rank Crew Position/Home Town	USAF Sqdn.	Parent Unit	Date	Cr.	Type Enemy Acft.	Type USAF Acft.	Radio Call Sign	Primary USAF Weapon Used
Anderson, Robert D, Maj AC, Tulsa, Oklahoma	389 TFS	366 TFW	23 Apr 67	1.0	MIG-21	F-4C	Chicago 03	AIM-7
Anderson, Ronald C, Cpt P, Fairbanks, Alaska	45 TFS	2 AD	10 Jul 65	1.0	MIG-17	F-4C	Unknown 04	AIM-9
Autrey, Daniel L, 1Lt WSO, Hialeah, Florida	35 TFS	388 TFW	12 Sep 72	1.0	MIG-21	F-4E	Finch 03	20mm
Baily, Carl G, LtC AC, Denver, Colorado	13 TFS	432 TRW	18 Jul 72 29 Jul 72	1.0 1.0	MIG-21 MIG-21	F-4D F-4D	Snug 01 Cadillac 01	AIM-9 AIM-7
Baker, Doyle D, Cpt (USMC) AC	13 TFS	432 TRW	17 Dec 67	1.0	MIG-17	F-4D	Gambit 03	AIM-4
Bakke, Samuel O, Maj AC, Fort Morgan, Colorado	480 TFS	366 TFW	14 May 67	1.0	MIG-17	F-4C	Elgin 01	AIM-7
Barton, Charles D, Cpt AC, Greenville, SC	34 TFS	388 TFW	06 Oct 72	0.5	MIG-19	F-4E	Eagle 04	Maneuvering
Basel, Gene I, Cpt P, Lakeside, California	354 TFS	355 TFW	27 Oct 67	1.0	MIG-17	F-105D	Bison 02	20mm
Battista, Robert B, 1Lt P, Montgomery, Alabama	433 TFS	8 TFW	06 Feb 68	1.0	MIG-21	F-4D	Buick 04	AIM-7
Beatty, James M Jr, Cpt AC, Eau Claire, Pa.	35 TFS	366 TFW	23 May 72	1.0	MIG-21	F-4E	Balter 03	20mm
Beckers, Lyle L, LtC AC, Gregory, SD	35 TFS 35 TFS	366 TFW 388 TFW	23 May 72 12 Sep 72	1.0 1.0	MIG-19 MIG-21	F-4E F-4E	Balter 01 Finch 01	AIM-7 AIM-9/20mm
Bell, James R, 1Lt WSO, Springfield, Ohio	555 TFS	432 TRW	11 May 72	1.0	MIG-21	F-4D	Gopher 02	AIM-7
Bettine, Frank J, 1Lt WSO, Hartshorne, Oklahoma	4 TFS	366 TFW	19 Aug 72	1.0	MIG-21	F-4E	Pistol 03	AIM-7
Bever, Michael R, 1Lt P, Kansas City, Missouri	433 TFS	8 TFW	13 May 67	1.0	MIG-17	F-4C	Harpoon 03	AIM-7
Binkley, Eldon D, 1Lt WSO, Winston-Salem, NC	555 TFS	432 TRW	22 Dec 72	1.0	MIG-21	F-4D	Bucket 01	Maneuvering
Blake, Robert E, Cpt AC, Presque Isle, Maine	555 TFS	8 TFW	23 Apr 66	1.0	MIG-17	F-4C	Unknown 04	AIM-7

TABLE 2.—ALPHABETICAL ORDER (cont'd)

Individual/Rank Crew Position/Home Town	USAF Sqdn.	Parent Unit	Date	Cr.	Type Enemy Acft.	Type USAF Acft.	Radio Call Sign	Primary USAF Weapon Used
Blank, Kenneth T, Maj P, Franklin, Nebraska	34 TFS	388 TFW	18 Aug 66	1.0	MIG-17	F-105D	Honda 02	20mm
Bleakley, Robert A, 1Lt P, Cedar Rapids, Iowa	555 TFS	8 TFW	29 Apr 66	1.0	MIG-17	F-4C	Unknown 01	Maneuvering
Bogoslofski, Bernard J, Maj AC, Granby, Connecticut	433 TFS	8 TFW	03 Jan 68	1.0	MIG-17	F-4D	Tampa 01	20mm
Boles, Robert H, Cpt AC, Lexington, SC	433 TFS	8 TFW	06 Feb 68	1.0	MIG-21	F-4D	Buick 04	AIM-7
Bongartz, Theodore R, 1Lt P, Catonsville, Maryland	433 TFS	8 TFW	24 Oct 67	1.0	MIG-21	F-4D	Buick 01	20mm
Brestel, Max C, Cpt P, Chappell, Nebraska	354 TFS	355 TFW	10 Mar 67 10 Mar 67	1.0 1.0	MIG-17 MIG-17	F-105D F-105D	Kangaroo 03 Kangaroo 03	20mm 20mm
Brown, Frederick W, Maj WSO, Grand View, Wash.	523 TFS	432 TRW	15 Oct 72	1.0	MIG-21	F-4D	Chevy 01	AIM-9
Brunson, Cecil H, 1Lt WSO, Memphis, Tennessee	34 TFS	388 TFW	06 Oct 72	0.5	MIG-19	F-4E	Eagle 03	Maneuvering
Brunson, James E, LtC AC, Eddyville, Kentucky	555 TFS	432 TRW	22 Dec 72	1.0	MIG-21	F-4D	Buick 01	AIM-7
Buttell, Duane A Jr, 1Lt P, Chillicothe, Illinois	480 TFS	35 TFW	14 Jul 66	1.0	MIG-21	F-4C	Unknown 01	AIM-9
Cameron, Max F, Cpt AC, Stanford, NC	555 TFS	8 TFW	23 Apr 66	1.0	MIG-17	F-4C	Unknown 04	AIM-9
Cary, Lawrence E, 1Lt P, Pawnee City, Nebraska	433 TFS	8 TFW	02 Jan 67	1.0	MIG-21	F-4D	Rambler 02	AIM-7
Cherry, Edward D, Maj AC, Marietta, Georgia	13 TFS	432 TRW	16 Apr 72	1.0	MIG-21	F-4D	Basco 03	AIM-7
Christiansen, Von R, LtC AC, Seattle, Washington	469 TFS	388 TFW	21 Jun 72	1.0	MIG-21	F-4E	Iceman 03	AIM-9
Clark, Arthur C, Cpt P, McAllen, Texas	45 TFS	2 AD	10 Jul 65	1.0	MIG-17	F-4C	Unknown 03	AIM-9
Clifton, Charles C, 1Lt P, Fort Wayne, Indiana	555 TFS	8 TFW	02 Jan 67	1.0	MIG-21	F-4C	Olds 01	AIM-9

Name	Squadron	Wing	Date	Credit	MIG	Aircraft	Call sign	Weapon
Clouser, Gordon L, Maj AC, Norman, Oklahoma	34 TFS	388 TFW	06 Oct 72	0.5	MIG-19	F-4E	Eagle 03	Maneuvering
Cobb, Larry D, Cpt AC, Lambert, Missouri	555 TFS	8 TFW	26 Oct 67	1.0	MIG-17	F-4D	Ford 04	AIM-4
Coe, Richard E, Cpt AC, East Orange, NJ	34 TFS	388 TFW	05 Oct 72	1.0	MIG-21	F-4E	Robin 01	AIM-7
Combies, Philip P, Maj AC, Norwich, Connecticut	433 TFS	8 TFW	02 Jan 67 20 May 67	1.0 1.0	MIG-21 MIG-17	F-4C F-4C	Rambler 04 Ballot 01	AIM-7 AIM-9
Cooney, James P, LtC WSO, Newburgh, New York	555 TFS	432 TRW	12 May 72	1.0	MIG-19	F-4D	Harlow 02	AIM-7
Couch, Charles W, Cpt P, Caseyville, Illinois	354 TFS	355 TFW	13 May 67	1.0	MIG-17	F-105D	Chevrolet 03	20mm
Craig, James T Jr, Cpt AC, Abilene, Texas	480 TFS	366 TFW	14 May 67	1.0	MIG-17	F-4C	Speedo 03	20mm
Crews, Barton P, Maj AC, Fort Lauderdale, Fla.	13 TFS	432 TRW	08 May 72	1.0	MIG-19	F-4D	Galore 03	AIM-7
Croker, Stephen B, 1Lt P, Middletown, Delaware	433 TFS	8 TFW	20 May 67 20 May 67	1.0 1.0	MIG-17 MIG-17	F-4C F-4C	Tampa 01 Tampa 01	AIM-7 AIM-9
Dalton, William M, Maj P, Stephens City, Virginia	333 TFS	355 TFW	19 Dec 67	0.5	MIG-17	F-105F	Otter 02	20mm
DeBellevue, Charles B, Cpt WSO, Lafayette, Louisiana	555 TFS	432 TRW	10 May 72 08 Jul 72 08 Jul 72 28 Aug 72 09 Sep 72 09 Sep 72	1.0 1.0 1.0 1.0 1.0 1.0	MIG-21 MIG-21 MIG-21 MIG-21 MIG-19 MIG-19	F-4D F-4E F-4E F-4D F-4D F-4D	Oyster 03 Paula 01 Paula 01 Buick 01 Olds 01 Olds 01	AIM-7 AIM-7 AIM-7 AIM-7 AIM-9 AIM-9
DeMuth, Stephen H, 1Lt P, Medina, Ohio	480 TFS	366 TFW	14 May 67	1.0	MIG-17	F-4C	Speedo 01	20mm
Dennis, Arthur F, LtC P, Sherman, Texas	357 TFS	355 TFW	28 Apr 67	1.0	MIG-17	F-105D	Atlanta 01	20mm
Dickey, Roy S, Maj P, Ashland, Kansas	469 TFS	388 TFW	04 Dec 66	1.0	MIG-17	F-105D	Eglin 04	20mm
Diehl, William C, 1Lt WSO, Tampa, Florida	34 TFS	388 TFW	15 Oct 72	1.0	MIG-21	F-4E	Parrot 03	AIM-9
Dilger, Robert G, Maj AC, Tampa, Florida	390 TFS	366 TFW	01 May 67	1.0	MIG-17	F-4C	Stinger 01	Maneuvering
Dowell, William B D, Cpt AC, Tampa, Florida	555 TFS	8 TFW	29 Apr 66	1.0	MIG-17	F-4C	Unknown 03	AIM-9

TABLE 2.—ALPHABETICAL ORDER (cont'd)

Individual/Rank Crew Position/Home Town	USAF Sqdn.	Parent Unit	Date	Cr.	Type Enemy Acft.	Type USAF Acft.	Radio Call Sign	Primary USAF Weapon Used
Drew, Philip M, Cpt P, Alexandria, Louisiana	357 TFS	355 TFW	19 Dec 67	1.0	MIG-17	F-105F	Otter 03	20mm
Dublei, John E, Cpt WSO, Omaha, Nebraska	555 TFS	432 TRW	28 Dec 72	1.0	MIG-21	F-4D	List 01	AIM-7
Dudley, Wilbur R, Maj AC, Alamogordo, NM	390 TFS	35 TFW	12 May 66	1.0	MIG-17	F-4C	Unknown 03	AIM-9
Dunnegan, Clifton P Jr, 1Lt P, Winston-Salem, NC	433 TFS	8 TFW	02 Jan 67	1.0	MIG-21	F-4C	Rambler 01	AIM-7
Dutton, Lee R, 1Lt P, Wyoming, Illinois	433 TFS	8 TFW	02 Jan 67	1.0	MIG-21	F-4C	Rambler 04	AIM-7
Eaves, Stephen D, Cpt WSO, Honolulu, Hawaii	555 TFS	432 TRW	10 May 72	1.0	MIG-21	F-4D	Oyster 02	AIM-7
Eskew, William E, Cpt P, Boonville, Indiana	354 TFS	355 TFW	19 Apr 67	1.0	MIG-17	F-105D	Panda 01	20mm
Eittel, Michael J, LtCdr (USN) WSO, St Paul, Minn.	58 TFS	432 TRW	12 Aug 72	1.0	MIG-21	F-4E	Dodge 01	AIM-7
Evans, Robert E, 1Lt P, Haina, Hawaii	555 TFS	8 TFW	23 Apr 66	1.0	MIG-17	F-4C	Unknown 03	AIM-9
Feighny, James P Jr, 1Lt P, Laramie, Wyoming	435 TFS	8 TFW	14 Feb 68	1.0	MIG-17	F-4D	Killer 01	AIM-7
Feinstein, Jeffrey S, Cpt WSO, East Troy, Wisconsin	13 TFS	432 TRW	16 Apr 72 31 May 72 18 Jul 72 29 Jul 72 13 Oct 72	1.0 1.0 1.0 1.0 1.0	MIG-21 MIG-21 MIG-21 MIG-21 MIG-21	F-4D F-4E F-4D F-4D F-4D	Basco 03 Gopher 03 Snug 01 Cadillac 01 Olds 01	AIM-7 AIM-9 AIM-9 AIM-7 AIM-7
Frye, Wayne T, LtC AC, Maysville, Kentucky	555 TFS	432 TRW	12 May 72	1.0	MIG-19	F-4D	Harlow 02	AIM-7
Gast, Philip C, LtC P, Ewing, Missouri	354 TFS	355 TFW	13 May 67	1.0	MIG-17	F-105D	Chevrolet 01	20mm
George, S W, 1Lt P, Canadian, Oklahoma	555 TFS	8 TFW	23 Apr 66	1.0	MIG-17	F-4C	Unknown 04	AIM-7
Gilmore, Paul J, Maj AC, Alamogordo, NM	480 TFS	35 TFW	26 Apr 66	1.0	MIG-21	F-4C	Unknown 01	AIM-9

Name	Squadron	Wing	Date	Credit	Enemy	Aircraft	Call Sign	Weapon
Glynn, Lawrence J Jr, 1Lt AC, Arlington, Massachusetts	433 TFS	8 TFW	02 Jan 67	1.0	MIG-21	F-4C	Rambler 02	AIM-7
Golberg, Lawrence H, Cpt AC, Duluth, Minnesota	555 TFS	8 TFW	30 Apr 66	1.0	MIG-17	F-4C	Unknown 04	AIM-9
Gordon, William S III, Cpt AC, Wethersfield, Conn.	555 TFS	8 TFW	26 Oct 67	1.0	MIG-17	F-4D	Ford 03	AIM-7
Gossard, Halbert E, 1Lt P, Oklahoma City, Oklahoma	555 TFS	8 TFW	29 Apr 66	1.0	MIG-17	F-4C	Unknown 03	AIM-9
Graham, James L, Maj EWO, Lancaster, Pennsylvania	333 TFS	355 TFW	19 Dec 67	0.5	MIG-17	F-105F	Otter 02	20mm
Griffin, Thomas M, 1Lt WSO, New Orleans, Louisiana	35 TFS	388 TFW	12 Sep 72	1.0	MIG-21	F-4E	Finch 01	AIM-9/20mm
Gullick, Francis M, Cpt P, Albuquerque, New Mexico	555 TFS	8 TFW	05 Jun 67	1.0	MIG-17	F-4D	Drill 01	AIM-7
Haeffner, Fred A, LtC AC, Fargo, North Dakota	433 TFS	8 TFW	13 May 67	1.0	MIG-17	F-4C	Harpoon 03	AIM-7
Handley, Philip W, Maj AC, Wellington, Texas	58 TFS	432 TRW	02 Jun 72	1.0	MIG-19	F-4E	Brenda 01	20mm
Harden, Kaye M, Maj WSO, Jacksonville, Florida	469 TFS	388 TFW	21 Jun 72	1.0	MIG-21	F-4E	Iceman 03	AIM-9
Hardgrave, Gerald D, 1Lt P, Jackson, Tennessee	555 TFS	8 TFW	30 Apr 66	1.0	MIG-17	F-4C	Unknown 04	AIM-9
Hardy, Richard F, Cpt AC, Chicago, Illinois	4 TFS	366 TFW	08 Jul 72	1.0	MIG-21	F-4E	Brenda 03	AIM-7
Hargrove, James A Jr, Maj AC, Garden City Beach, SC	480 TFS	366 TFW	14 May 67	1.0	MIG-17	F-4C	Speedo 01	20mm
Hargrove, William S, 1Lt WSO, Harlingen, Texas	555 TFS	432 TRW	09 Sep 72 16 Sep 72	1.0 1.0	MIG-21 MIG-21	F-4D F-4E	Olds 03 Chevy 03	20mm AIM-9
Hendrickson, James L, Cpt WSO, Columbus, Ohio	307 TFS	432 TRW	15 Oct 72	1.0	MIG-21	F-4E	Buick 03	20mm
Higgins, Harry E, Maj P, Alexandria, Indiana	357 TFS	355 TFW	28 Apr 67	1.0	MIG-17	F-105D	Spitfire 01	20mm
Hill, Robert G, Cpt AC, Tucson, Arizona	13 TFS	432 TRW	05 Feb 68	1.0	MIG-21	F-4D	Gambit 03	AIM-4
Hirsch, Thomas M, Maj AC, Rockford, Illinois	555 TFS	8 TFW	06 Jan 67	1.0	MIG-21	F-4C	Crab 02	AIM-7

TABLE 2.—ALPHABETICAL ORDER (cont'd)

Individual/Rank Crew Position/Home Town	USAF Sqdn.	Parent Unit	Date	Cr.	Type Enemy Acft.	Type USAF Acft.	Radio Call Sign	Primary USAF Weapon Used
Hodgdon, Leigh A, 1Lt WSO, Kingsport, Pennsylvania	555 TFS	432 TRW	01 Mar 72	1.0	MIG-21	F-4D	Falcon 54	AIM-7
Holcombe, Kenneth E, Cpt AC, Detroit, Michigan	45 TFS	2 AD	10 Jul 65	1.0	MIG-17	F-4C	Unknown 03	AIM-9
Holtz, Robert L, Maj AC, Milwaukee, Wisconsin	34 TFS	388 TFW	15 Oct 72	1.0	MIG-21	F-4E	Parrot 03	AIM-9
Howerton, Rex D, Maj AC, Oklahoma City, Oklahoma	555 TFS	8 TFW	14 Feb 68	1.0	MIG-17	F-4D	Nash 03	20mm
Howman, Paul D, Cpt AC, Wooster, Ohio	4 TFS	432 TRW	08 Jan 73	1.0	MIG-21	F-4D	Crafty 01	AIM-7
Huncke, Bruce V, 1Lt P, Hanford, California	13 TFS	432 TRW	05 Feb 68	1.0	MIG-21	F-4D	Gambit 03	AIM-4
Hunt, Jack W, Maj P, Freeport, Texas	354 TFS	355 TFW	19 Apr 67	1.0	MIG-17	F-105D	Nitro 01	20mm
Huskey, Richard L, Cpt P, Cleveland, Tennessee	433 TFS	8 TFW	03 Jan 68	1.0	MIG-17	F-4D	Tampa 01	20mm
Huwe, John F, Cpt WSO, Dell Rapids, SD	35 TFS	366 TFW	23 May 72	1.0	MIG-19	F-4E	Balter 01	AIM-7
Imaye, Stanley M, Cpt WSO, Honolulu, Hawaii	4 TFS	366 TFW	29 Jul 72	1.0	MIG-21	F-4E	Pistol 01	AIM-7
Jameson, Jerry W, 1Lt AC, Middletown, Indiana	555 TFS	8 TFW	16 Sep 66	1.0	MIG-17	F-4C	Unknown 04	AIM-9
Janca, Robert D, Maj AC, Hampton, Virginia	389 TFS	366 TFW	20 May 67	1.0	MIG-21	F-4C	Elgin 01	AIM-9
Jasperson, Robert H, Cpt WSO, Minneapolis, Minn.	35 TFS	388 TFW	08 Oct 72	1.0	MIG-21	F-4E	Lark 01	20mm
Johnson, Harold E, Cpt EWO, Blakeburg, Iowa	357 TFS	355 TFW	19 Apr 67	1.0	MIG-17	F-105F	Kingfish 01	20mm
Jones, Keith W Jr, Cpt WSO, Glen Ellyn, Illinois	13 TFS	432 TRW	08 May 72	1.0	MIG-19	F-4D	Galore 03	AIM-7
Keith, Larry R, Cpt AC, Peoria, Illinois	555 TFS	8 TFW	29 Apr 66	1.0	MIG-17	F-4C	Unknown 01	Maneuvering

Name / Location	Sqn	Wing	Date	Score	MiG	A/C	Callsign	Weapon
Kirk, William L, Maj AC, Rayville, Louisiana	433 TFS	8 TFW	13 May 67 24 Oct 67	1.0 1.0	MIG-17 MIG-21	F-4C F-4D	Harpoon 01 Buick 01	AIM-9 20mm
Kittinger, Joseph W Jr, LtC AC, Orlando, Florida	555 TFS	432 TRW	01 Mar 72	1.0	MIG-21	F-4D	Falcon 54	AIM-7
Kjer, Fred D, Cpt P, Allen, Nebraska	389 TFS	366 TFW	23 Apr 67	1.0	MIG-21	F-4C	Chicago 03	AIM-7
Klause, Klaus J, 1Lt P, Franklin, Pennsylvania	480 TFS	366 TFW	05 Nov 66	1.0	MIG-21	F-4C	Opal 02	AIM-9
Krieps, Richard N, 1Lt P, Chesterton, Indiana	480 TFS	35 TFW	14 Jul 66	1.0	MIG-21	F-4C	Unknown 02	AIM-9
Kringelis, Imants, 1Lt P, Lake Zurich, Illinois	390 TFS	35 TFW	12 May 66	1.0	MIG-17	F-4C	Unknown 03	AIM-9
Kullman, Lawrence W, 1Lt WSO, Hartley, Delaware	4 TFS	432 TRW	08 Jan 73	1.0	MIG-21	F-4D	Crafty 01	AIM-7
Kuster, Ralph L Jr, Maj P, St. Louis, Missouri	13 TFS	388 TFW	03 Jun 67	1.0	MIG-17	F-105D	Hambone 02	20mm
Lafever, William D, 1Lt P, Losantville, Indiana	555 TFS	8 TFW	04 May 67	1.0	MIG-21	F-4C	Flamingo 01	AIM-9
Lafferty, Daniel L, 1Lt P, Eddyville, Illinois	433 TFS	8 TFW	20 May 67	1.0	MIG-17	F-4C	Ballot 01	AIM-9
Lambert, Robert W, Cpt P, Virginia Beach, Virginia	480 TFS	366 TFW	14 May 67	1.0	MIG-17	F-4C	Elgin 01	AIM-7
Lang, Alfred E Jr, LtC AC, East Orange, NJ	435 TFS	8 TFW	12 Feb 68	1.0	MIG-21	F-4D	Buick 01	AIM-7
Latham, Wilbur J Jr, 1Lt AC, Eagle Grove, Iowa	480 TFS	366 TFW	05 Nov 66	1.0	MIG-21	F-4C	Opal 02	AIM-9
Lavoy, Alan A, Cpt P, Norwalk, Connecticut	555 TFS	8 TFW	26 Oct 67	1.0	MIG-17	F-4D	Ford 04	AIM-4
Leonard, Bruce G Jr, Cpt AC, Greensboro, NC	13 TFS	432 TRW	31 May 72	1.0	MIG-21	F-4E	Gopher 03	AIM-9
Lesan, Thomas C, Cpt P, Lebanon, Ohio	333 TFS	355 TFW	30 Apr 67	1.0	MIG-17	F-105D	Rattler 01	20mm
Lewinski, Paul T, Cpt WSO, Schenectady, New York	4 TFS	366 TFW	08 Jul 72	1.0	MIG-21	F-4E	Brenda 03	AIM-7
Locher, Roger C, 1Lt/Cpt WSO, Sabetha, Kansas	555 TFS	432 TRW	21 Feb 72 08 May 72 10 May 72	1.0 1.0 1.0	MIG-21 MIG-21 MIG-21	F-4D F-4D F-4D	Falcon 62 Oyster 01 Oyster 01	AIM-7 AIM-7 AIM-7

TABLE 2.—ALPHABETICAL ORDER (cont'd)

Individual/Rank Crew Position/Home Town	USAF Sqdn.	Parent Unit	Date	Cr.	Type Enemy Acft.	Type USAF Acft.	Radio Call Sign	Primary USAF Weapon Used
Lodge, Robert A, Maj AC, Columbus, Ohio	555 TFS	432 TRW	21 Feb 72 08 May 72 10 May 72	1.0 1.0 1.0	MIG-21 MIG-21 MIG-21	F-4D F-4D F-4D	Falcon 62 Oyster 01 Oyster 01	AIM-7 AIM-7 AIM-7
Logeman, John D Jr, Cpt AC, Fond Du Lac, Wisconsin	555 TFS	8 TFW	26 Oct 67	1.0	MIG-17	F-4D	Ford 01	AIM-7
Lucas, Jon I, Maj AC, Steubenville, Ohio	34 TFS	388 TFW	02 Sep 72	1.0	MIG-19	F-4E	Eagle 03	AIM-7
Maas, Stuart W, Cpt WSO, Williamsburg, Ohio	13 TFS	432 TRW	16 Apr 72	1.0	MIG-21	F-4D	Basco 01	AIM-7
Madden, John A, Jr, Cpt AC, Jackson, Mississippi	555 TFS	432 TRW	09 Sep 72 09 Sep 72 12 Oct 72	1.0 1.0 1.0	MIG-19 MIG-19 MIG-21	F-4D F-4D F-4D	Olds 01 Olds 01 Vega 01	AIM-9 AIM-9 Maneuvering
Mahaffey, Michael J, Cpt AC, Patterson, California	469 TFS	388 TFW	12 Sep 72	1.0	MIG-21	F-4D	Robin 02	AIM-9
Malloy, Douglas G, 1Lt WSO, Dayton, Ohio	35 TFS	388 TFW	02 Sep 72	1.0	MIG-19	F-4E	Eagle 03	AIM-7
Markle, John D, 1Lt AC, Hutchinson, Kansas	555 TFS	432 TRW	10 May 72	1.0	MIG-21	F-4D	Oyster 02	AIM-7
Martin, Ronald G, 1Lt AC, Lake Villa, Illinois	480 TFS	35 TFW	14 Jul 66	1.0	MIG-21	F-4C	Unknown 02	AIM-9
Massen, Mark A, Cpt WSO, Downey, California	336 TFS	8 TFW	15 Aug 72	1.0	MIG-21	F-4E	Date 04	AIM-7
McCoy, Frederick E II, 1Lt P, Sheboygen, Wisconsin	555 TFS	8 TFW	26 Oct 67	1.0	MIG-17	F-4D	Ford 01	AIM-7
McCoy, Ivy J Jr, Maj AC, Baton Rouge, Louisiana	523 TFS	432 TRW	15 Oct 72	1.0	MIG-21	F-4D	Chevy 01	AIM-9
McKee, Harry L Jr, Maj AC, Austin, Texas	555 TFS	432 TRW	28 Dec 72	1.0	MIG-21	F-4D	List 01	AIM-7
McKinney, George H Jr, 1Lt P, Bessemer, Alabama	435 TFS	8 TFW	06 Nov 67 06 Nov 67 19 Dec 67	1.0 1.0 0.5	MIG-17 MIG-17 MIG-17	F-4D F-4D F-4D	Sapphire 01 Sapphire 01 Nash 01	20mm 20mm 20mm
Monsees, James H, 1Lt P, Santa Clara, California	555 TFS	8 TFW	26 Oct 67	1.0	MIG-17	F-4D	Ford 03	AIM-7

Name	Squadron	Wing	Date	Credit	MiG	Aircraft	Callsign	Weapon
Moore, Albert E, A1C, G, San Bernadino, California		307 SW	24 Dec 72	1.0	MIG-21	B-52D	Ruby III	.50 caliber
Moore, Joseph D, Maj, AC, Spartanburg, SC	435 TFS	8 TFW	19 Dec 67	0.5	MIG-17	F-4D	Nash 01	20mm
Moore, Rolland W Jr, Maj, AC, Barberton, Ohio	389 TFS	366 TFW	26 Apr 67	1.0	MIG-21	F-4C	Cactus 01	AIM-7
Moss, Randy P, 1Lt, P, Great Falls, SC	435 TFS	8 TFW	12 Feb 68	1.0	MIG-21	F-4D	Buick 01	AIM-7
Muldoon, Michael D, 1Lt, P, Perry, New York	435 TFS	8 TFW	03 Jan 68	1.0	MIG-17	F-4D	Olds 01	AIM-4
Murray, James E III, 1Lt, P, McKeesport, Pennsylvania	555 TFS	8 TFW	02 Jan 67	1.0	MIG-21	F-4C	Olds 04	AIM-9
Nichols, Stephen E, Cpt, AC, Durham, NC	555 TRS	432 TRW	11 May 72	1.0	MIG-21	F-4D	Gopher 02	AIM-7
Null, James C, Cpt, AC, Oklahoma City, Oklahoma	523 TFS	432 TRW	16 Apr 72	1.0	MIG-21	F-4D	Papa 03	AIM-7
Olds, Robin, Col, AC, Washington, DC	555 TFS	8 TFW	02 Jan 67	1.0	MIG-21	F-4C	Olds 01	AIM-9
	433 TFS	8 TFW	04 May 67	1.0	MIG-21	F-4C	Flamingo 01	AIM-9
			20 May 67	1.0	MIG-17	F-4C	Tampa 01	AIM-7
			20 May 67	1.0	MIG-17	F-4C	Tampa 01	AIM-9
Olmsted, Frederick S Jr, Cpt, AC, San Diego, CA	13 TFS	432 TRW	30 Mar 72	1.0	MIG-21	F-4D	Papa 01	AIM-7
			16 Apr 72	1.0	MIG-21	F-4D	Basco 01	AIM-7
Osborne, Carl D, Maj, P, Potlatch, Idaho	333 TFS	355 TFW	13 May 67	1.0	MIG-17	F-105D	Random 03	AIM-9
Pankhurst, John E, Cpt, P, Midland, Michigan	480 TFS	366 TFW	05 Jun 67	1.0	MIG-17	F-4C	Oakland 01	20mm
Pardo, John R, Maj, AC, Hearne, Texas	433 TFS	8 TFW	20 May 67	1.0	MIG-17	F-4C	Tampa 03	AIM-9
Pascoe, Richard M, Cpt, AC, Lakeside, California	555 TFS	8 TFW	06 Jan 67	1.0	MIG-21	F-4C	Crab 01	AIM-7
			05 Jun 67	1.0	MIG-17	F-4C	Chicago 02	AIM-9
Pettit, Lawrence H, Cpt, WSO, Jackson Heights, NY	555 TFS	432 TRW	31 May 72	1.0	MIG-21	F-4D	Icebag 01	AIM-7
			12 Oct 72	1.0	MIG-21	F-4D	Vega 01	AIM-7 Maneuvering
Pickett, Ralph S, Maj, WSO, Beaulaville, NC	555 TFS	432 TRW	22 Dec 72	1.0	MIG-21	F-4D	Buick 01	AIM-7
Priester, Durwood K, Maj, AC, Hampton, SC	480 TFS	366 TFW	05 Jun 67	1.0	MIG-17	F-4C	Oakland 01	20mm

TABLE 2.—ALPHABETICAL ORDER (cont'd)

Individual/Rank Crew Position/Home Town	USAF Sqdn.	Parent Unit	Date	Cr.	Type Enemy Acft.	Type USAF Acft.	Radio Call Sign	Primary USAF Weapon Used
Rabeni, John J Jr, 1Lt P, Southboro, Massachusetts	480 TFS	366 TFW	05 Nov 66	1.0	MIG-21	F-4C	Opal 01	AIM-7
Radeker, Walter S III, Cpt AC, Asheville, NC	555 TFS	8 TFW	02 Jan 67	1.0	MIG-21	F-4C	Olds 04	AIM-9
Raspberry, Everett T Jr, Cpt AC, Fort Walton Beach, Fla.	555 TFS	8 TFW	02 Jan 67 05 Jun 67	1.0 1.0	MIG-21 MIG-17	F-4C F-4D	Ford 02 Drill 01	AIM-9 AIM-7
Retterbush, Gary L, Maj AC, Lebanon, Indiana	35 TFS	388 TFW	12 Sep 72 08 Oct 72	1.0 1.0	MIG-21 MIG-21	F-4E F-4E	Finch 03 Lark 01	20mm 20mm
Richard, Lawrence G, Cpt, (USMC) AC, Lansdale, Pa.	58 TFS	432 TRW	12 Aug 72	1.0	MIG-21	F-4E	Dodge 01	AIM-7
Richter, Karl W, 1Lt P, Holly, Michigan	421 TFS	388 TFW	21 Sep 66	1.0	MIG-17	F-105D	Ford 03	20mm
Rilling, Robert G, Maj P, South Berwick, Maine	333 TFS	355 TFW	13 May 67	1.0	MIG-17	F-105D	Random 01	AIM-9
Ritchie, Richard S, Cpt AC, Reidsville, NC	555 TFS	432 TRW	10 May 72 31 May 72 08 Jul 72 08 Jul 72 28 Aug 72	1.0 1.0 1.0 1.0 1.0	MIG-21 MIG-21 MIG-21 MIG-21 MIG-21	F-4D F-4D F-4E F-4E F-4D	Oyster 03 Icebag 01 Paula 01 Paula 01 Buick 01	AIM-7 AIM-7 AIM-7 AIM-7 AIM-7
Roberts, Thomas S, Cpt AC, LaGrange, Georgia	45 TFS	2 AD	10 Jul 65	1.0	MIG-17	F-4C	Unknown 04	AIM-9
Roberts, William E Jr, 1Lt P, Quitman, Oklahoma	389 TFS	366 TFW	20 May 67	1.0	MIG-21	F-4C	Elgin 01	AIM-9
Rose, Douglas B, 1Lt P, Chicago, Ill.	555 TFS	8 TFW	16 Sep 66	1.0	MIG-17	F-4C	Unknown 04	AIM-9
Rubus, Gary M, Cpt AC, Banning, California	307 TFS	432 TRW	15 Oct 72	1.0	MIG-21	F-4E	Buick 03	20mm
Russell, Donald M, Maj P, Westbrook, Maine	333 TFS	355 TFW	18 Oct 67	1.0	MIG-17	F-105D	Wildcat 04	20mm
Ryan, John D Jr, 1Lt P, Pasadena, TX	13 TFS	432 TRW	17 Dec 67	1.0	MIG-17	F-4D	Gambit 03	AIM-4
Scott, Robert R, Col P, Des Moines, Iowa	333 TFS	355 TFW	26 Mar 67	1.0	MIG-17	F-105D	Leech 01	20mm

Name	Squadron	Wing	Date	Credit	Enemy	Aircraft	Call Sign	Weapon
Sears, James F, 1Lt P, Milan, Missouri	389 TFS	366 TFW	26 Apr 67	1.0	MIG-21	F-4C	Cactus 01	AIM-7
Seaver, Maurice E Jr, Maj P, Highland, California	44 TFS	388 TFW	13 May 67	1.0	MIG-17	F-105D	Kimona 02	20mm
Sharp, Jerry K, 1Lt P, Corpus Christi, Texas	555 TFS	8 TFW	02 Jan 67	1.0	MIG-21	F-4C	Olds 02	AIM-7
Sheffler, Fred W, Cpt AC, Akron, Ohio	336 TFS	8 TFW	15 Aug 72	1.0	MIG-21	F-4E	Date 04	AIM-7
Shields, George I, 1Lt WSO, Georgetown, Conn.	469 TFS	388 TFW	12 Sep 72	1.0	MIG-21	F-4D	Robin 02	AIM-9
Sholders, Gary L, Cpt AC, Lebanon, Oregon	555 TFS	432 TRW	22 Dec 72	1.0	MIG-21	F-4D	Bucket 01	Maneuvering
Simmonds, Darrell D, Cpt AC, Vernon, Texas	435 TFS	8 TFW	06 Nov 67 06 Nov 67	1.0 1.0	MIG-17 MIG-17	F-4D F-4D	Sapphire 01 Sapphire 01	20mm 20mm
Simonet, Kenneth A, Maj AC, Chicago, Illinois	435 TFS	8 TFW	18 Jan 68	1.0	MIG-17	F-4D	Otter 01	AIM-4
Smallwood, John J, 1Lt WSO, Atlanta, Georgia	58 TFS	432 TRW	02 Jun 72	1.0	MIG-19	F-4E	Brenda 01	20mm
Smith, Wayne O, 1Lt P, Clearwater, Florida	435 TFS	8 TFW	18 Jan 68	1.0	MIG-17	F-4D	Otter 01	AIM-4
Smith, William T, 1Lt P, Wayne, Pennsylvania	480 TFS	35 TFW	26 Apr 66	1.0	MIG-21	F-4C	Unknown 01	AIM-9
Squier, Clayton K, LtC AC, Oakland, California	435 TFS	8 TFW	03 Jan 68	1.0	MIG-17	F-4D	Olds 01	AIM-4
Stone, John B, Cpt AC, Coffeeville, Miss.	433 TFS	8 TFW	02 Jan 67	1.0	MIG-21	F-4C	Rambler 01	AIM-7
Strasswimmer, Roger J, 1Lt P, Bronx, New York	555 TFS	8 TFW	06 Jan 67	1.0	MIG-21	F-4C	Crab 02	AIM-7
Sumner, James M, 1Lt WSO, Manchester, Missouri	35 TFS	366 TFW	23 May 72	1.0	MIG-21	F-4E	Balter 03	20mm
Suzanne, Jacques A, Cpt P, Lake Placid, New York	333 TFS	355 TFW	12 May 67	1.0	MIG-17	F-105D	Crossbow 01	20mm
Swendner, William J, Cpt AC, Alamogordo, NM	480 TFS	35 TFW	14 Jul 66	1.0	MIG-21	F-4C	Unknown 01	AIM-9
Taft, Gene E, LtC AC, Ventura, California	4 TFS	366 TFW	29 Jul 72	1.0	MIG-21	F-4E	Pistol 01	AIM-7

TABLE 2.—ALPHABETICAL ORDER (cont'd)

Individual/Rank Crew Position/Home Town	USAF Sqdn.	Parent Unit	Date	Cr.	Type Enemy Acft.	Type USAF Acft.	Radio Call Sign	Primary USAF Weapon Used
Talley, James T, 1Lt P, Nixon, Texas	480 TFS	366 TFW	14 May 67	1.0	MIG-17	F-4C	Speedo 03	20mm
Thies, Mack, 1Lt P, Houston, Texas	390 TFS	366 TFW	01 May 67	1.0	MIG-17	F-4C	Stinger 01	Maneuvering
Thorsness, Leo K, Maj P, Las Vegas, Nevada	357 TFS	355 TFW	19 Apr 67	1.0	MIG-17	F-105F	Kingfish 01	20mm
Tibbett, Calvin B, Cpt AC, Waynesville, Missouri	555 TFS	432 TRW	09 Sep 72 16 Sep 72	1.0 1.0	MIG-21 MIG-21	F-4D F-4E	Olds 03 Chevy 03	20mm AIM-9
Titus, Robert F, LtC AC, Hampton, Virginia	389 TFS	366 TFW	20 May 67 22 May 67 22 May 67	1.0 1.0 1.0	MIG-21 MIG-21 MIG-21	F-4C F-4C F-4C	Elgin 03 Wander 01 Wander 01	AIM-7 AIM-9 20mm
Tolman, Frederick G, Maj P, Portland, Maine	354 TFS	355 TFW	19 Apr 67	1.0	MIG-17	F-105D	Nitro 03	20mm
Tracy, Fred L, Maj P, Goldsboro, NC		388 TFW	29 Jun 66	1.0	MIG-17	F-105D	Unknown 02	20mm
Tuck, James E, Maj AC, Virgilina, Virginia	480 TFS	366 TFW	05 Nov 66	1.0	MIG-21	F-4C	Opal 01	AIM-7
Turner, Samuel O, SSgt G, Atlanta, Georgia		307 SW	18 Dec 72	1.0	MIG-21	B-52D	Brown III	.50 caliber
Vahue, Michael D, Cpt WSO, Battle Creek, Michigan	523 TFS	432 TRW	16 Apr 72	1.0	MIG-21	F-4D	Papa 03	AIM-7
Voigt, Ted L II, 1Lt P, Nelsonville Ohio	555 TFS	8 TFW	14 Feb 68	1.0	MIG-17	F-4D	Nash 03	20mm
Volloy, Gerald R, Cpt WSO, Cincinnati, Ohio	13 TFS	432 TRW	30 Mar 72	1.0	MIG-21	F-4D	Papa 01	AIM-7
Waldrop, David B III, 1Lt P, Nashville, Tennessee	34 TFS	388 TFW	23 Aug 67	1.0	MIG-17	F-105D	Crossbow 03	20mm
Watson, George D, 1Lt WSO, Trenton, Missouri	34 TFS	388 TFW	06 Oct 72	0.5	MIG-19	F-4E	Eagle 04	Maneuvering
Wayne, Stephen A, 1Lt P, Fairmount, Indiana	433 TFS	8 TFW	13 May 67 20 May 67	1.0 1.0	MIG-17 MIG-17	F-4C F-4C	Harpoon 01 Tampa 03	AIM-9 AIM-9

Name	Unit	Wing	Date	Score	Enemy	Aircraft	Callsign	Weapon
Webb, Omri K III, 1Lt WSO, Leesville, SC	34 TFS	388 TFW	05 Oct 72	1.0	MIG-21	F-4E	Robin 01	AIM-7
Wells, Norman E, 1Lt/Cpt P, Redwood City, California	555 TFS	8 TFW	06 Jan 67 05 Jun 67	1.0 1.0	MIG-21 MIG-17	F-4C F-4C	Crab 01 Chicago 02	AIM-7 AIM-9
Western, Robert W, 1Lt P, Carrollton, Alabama	555 TFS	8 TFW	02 Jan 67	1.0	MIG-21	F-4C	Ford 02	AIM-9
Westphal, Curtis D, LtC AC, Bonduel, Wisconsin	13 TFS	432 TRW	13 Oct 72	1.0	MIG-21	F-4D	Olds 01	AIM-7
Wetterhahn, Ralph F, 1Lt AC, New York City, NY	555 TFS	8 TFW	02 Jan 67	1.0	MIG-21	F-4C	Olds 02	AIM-7
Wheeler, William H, Maj EWO, Fort Walton Beach, Fla.	357 TFS	355 TFW	19 Dec 67	1.0	MIG-17	F-105F	Otter 03	20mm
White, Sammy C, Cpt AC, Hot Springs, Arkansas	4 TFS	366 TFW	19 Aug 72	1.0	MIG-21	F-4E	Pistol 03	AIM-7
Wiggins, Larry D, Cpt P, Houston, Texas	469 TFS	388 TFW	03 Jun 67	1.0	MIG-17	F-105D	Hambone 03	AIM-9/20mm
Williams, David O Jr, Col AC, Rockport, Texas	435 TFS	8 TFW	14 Feb 68	1.0	MIG-17	F-4D	Killer 01	AIM-7
Wilson, Fred A Jr, 1Lt P, Mobile, Alabama	333 TFS	355 TFW	21 Sep 66	1.0	MIG-17	F-105D	Vegas 02	20mm
Zimer, Milan, 1Lt P, Canton, Ohio	389 TFS	366 TFW	20 May 67 22 May 67 22 May 67	1.0 1.0 1.0	MIG-21 MIG-21 MIG-21	F-4C F-4C F-4C	Elgin 03 Wander 01 Wander 01	AIM-7 AIM-9 20mm

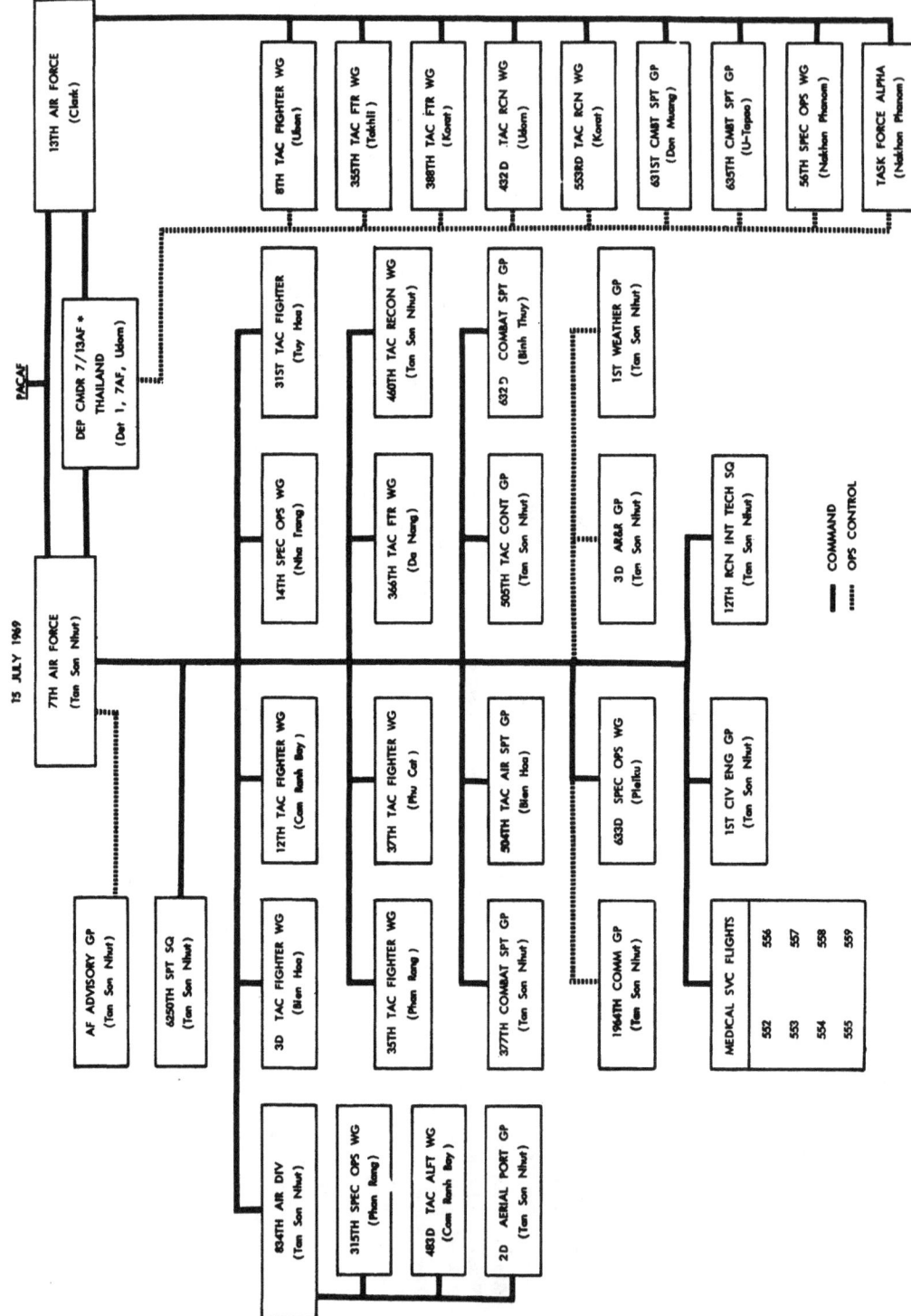

ORGANIZATION, 7TH AIR FORCE AND 7/13 AIR FORCE

*The Deputy Commander, 7/13AF, represented the Commander, 7AF, and served as CINCPACAF's representative in Thailand

Their Units

The pilots, electronic warfare and weapon systems officers, gunners, and others involved directly or indirectly in the aerial conflict in Southeast Asia were organized into hundreds of USAF units, ranging in structure from flights upward through squadrons, groups, wings, divisions, and numbered air forces under PACAF. The mission of these units was to support the strike forces, which were primarily the tactical squadrons directly engaged in air-to-ground combat operations. Only those tactical units with a combat mission in Southeast Asia were directly involved in and credited with the destruction of 137 MIG's. These credits were awarded to 21 USAF tactical fighter squadrons flying F-4C/D/E's and F-105D/F's, the 307th Strategic Wing flying B-52D's, and the 388th Tactical Fighter Wing flying F-105D's. Most of the combat men credited with victories belonged then to the squadrons, although a few were assigned directly to the wings.

The composition, organization, and command of these combat elements are based on principles set down by the War Department in the 1920's. These principles reflect both peacetime and wartime contingencies, and they have been adapted over the years to keep abreast of the great strides in aviation technology. Accordingly, many of the squadrons participating in the Southeast Asia war boast of records as well in the Korean War and World War II, and some even trace their origins to World War I.

The official lineage and data on assignments, stations, aircraft and missiles, operations, service streamers, campaigns, and emblems prior to the operations in Southeast Asia can be found in *Air Force Combat Units of World War II* or in *Combat Squadrons of the Air Force, World War II* (USGPO, 1961 and 1969), edited by Maurer Maurer. Information in the following table contains only data covering the units just prior to and during their assignments in Southeast Asia.

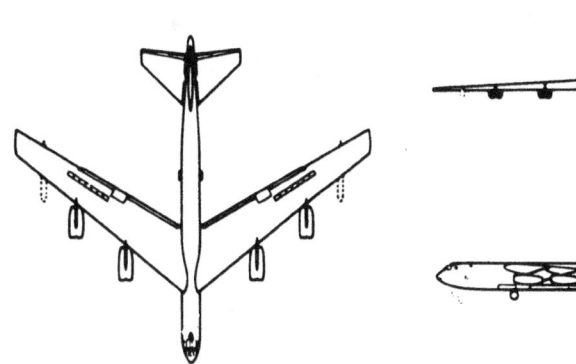
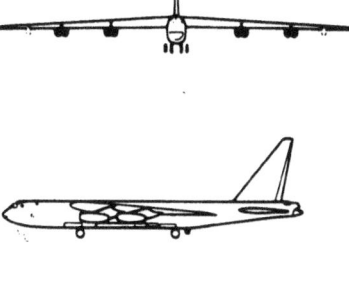

B-52C/D Bomber

TABLE 3—UNITS CREDITED WITH THE DESTRUCTION OF MIG'S IN AIR-TO-AIR COMBAT

Organizational Action	Date	Assignment	Location	Operations
Seventh Air Force				
Activated	Mar 66	Pacific Air Forces		Took over conduct of air operations in SEA from the inactivated 2d Air Division. 135 of the 137 USAF aerial victories were made by Seventh Air Force components.
Organized	Apr 66		Tan Son Nhut AB, RVN	
Moved	Mar 73		Nakhon Phanom AB, Thailand	
2d Air Division				
	Mar 54	US Air Forces in Europe	Saudi Arabia	No combat components assigned. Supervised US facilities.
Reassigned; moved	Sep 62	Pacific Air Forces	Tan Son Nhut AB, RVN	Directed USAF operations in SEA, Sep 62–Apr 66. Replaced by Seventh Air Force. 2 of the USAF aerial victories were by a component of 2d AD.
Reassigned	Oct 62	Thirteenth Air Force		
Discontinued	Apr 66			
8th Tactical Fighter Wing				
	Jul 64	831st Air Division	George AFB, Calif.	Tactical operations in the U.S.
Reassigned; moved	Dec 65	Thirteenth Air Force	Ubon AB, Thailand	Air combat in SEA, Dec 65–Jan 73. Earned 38.5 aerial victories, 23 Apr 65–15 Aug 72.
Attached	Dec 65	2d Air Division		
Attached	Apr 66	Seventh Air Force		
35th Tactical Fighter Wing				
Activated	Mar 66	Pacific Air Forces		
Organized	Apr 66	Seventh Air Force	Da Nang AB, RVN	Air combat in SEA, Apr 66–Jul 71. Earned 4 aerial victories, 26 Apr–14 Jul 66.
Moved	Oct 66		Phan Rang AB, RVN	
Inactivated	Jul 71			
307th Strategic Wing				
Activated	Apr 70	Eighth Air Force	U-Tapao AB, Thailand	Air combat in SEA, Apr 70–Dec 72. Earned 2 aerial victories, Dec 72.
355th Tactical Fighter Wing				
Constituted and activated	Apr 62	Tactical Air Command		TAC operations and exercises to Nov 65. Combat in SEA, Nov 65–Oct 70. Earned 19.5 aerial victories, 21 Sep 66–19 Dec 67.
Organized	Jul 62	831st Air Division	George AFB, Calif.	
Reassigned; moved	Jul 64	835th Air Division	McConnell AFB, Kans.	
Reassigned; moved	Nov 65	Thirteenth Air Force	Takhli AB, Thailand	
Attached	Nov 65	2d Air Division		
Attached	Apr 66	Seventh Air Force		
Inactivated	Dec 70			

355th Tactical Fighter Wing

8th Tactical Fighter Wing

307th Strategic Wing

2d Air Division

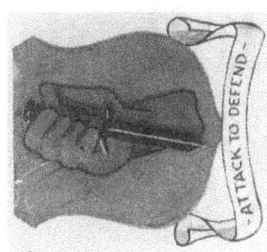
35th Tactical Fighter Wing

Seventh Air Force

TABLE 3—UNITS CREDITED WITH THE DESTRUCTION OF MIG'S IN AIR-TO-AIR COMBAT—Continued

Organizational Action	Date	Assignment	Location	Operations
366th Tactical Fighter Wing				
Reassigned; moved	Oct 64	832d Air Division	Holloman AFB, NM	TAC operations and exercises, to Mar 66.
Reassigned	Mar 66	2d Air Division	Phan Rang AB, RVN	Combat in SEA, Mar 66–Oct 72. Earned 18 aerial victories, 5 Nov 66–19 Aug 72.
Moved	Apr 66	Seventh Air Force	Da Nang AB, RVN	
Reassigned; moved	Jun 72	Thirteenth Air Force	Takhli AB, Thailand	
Reassigned; moved	Oct 72	832d Air Division	Mountain Home AFB, Idaho	
388th Tactical Fighter Wing				
Activated	Mar 66	Pacific Air Forces		
Organized	Apr 66	Thirteenth Air Force	Korat AB, Thailand	Combat in SEA, Apr 66–Jan 73. Earned 17 aerial victories, 29 Jul 66–15 Oct 72.
432d Tactical Reconnaissance Wing				
Activated	Aug 66	Pacific Air Forces		
Organized	Sep 66	Thirteenth Air Force	Udorn AB, Thailand	Combat in SEA, Sep 66–Jan 73. Earned 36 aerial victories, 17 Dec 67–8 Jan 73.
Redesignated 432d Tactical Fighter Wing	Nov 74			
4th Tactical Fighter Squadron				
Reassigned; moved	Jun 65	33d Tactical Fighter Wing	Eglin AFB, Fla.	
Reassigned; moved	Apr 69	366th Tactical Fighter Wing	Da Nang AB, RVN	Combat operations in SEA, Apr 69–Jan 73.
Moved	Jun 72		Takhli AB, Thailand	Earned 4 aerial victories, 8 Jul 72–8 Jan 73.
Reassigned; moved	Oct 72	432d Tactical Reconnaissance Wing	Udorn AB, Thailand	
13th Tactical Fighter Squadron				
Constituted and activated	May 66	Pacific Air Forces		
Organized	May 66	18th Tactical Fighter Wing		Combat operations in SEA, May 66–Jan 73.
Attached	May 66	388th Tactical Fighter Wing	Korat AB, Thailand	Earned 11 aerial victories, 3 Jun 67–13 Oct 72.
Reassigned; moved (attachment ends)	Oct 67	432d Tactical Reconnaissance Wing	Udorn AB, Thailand	
34th Tactical Fighter Squadron				
Activated	May 66	Pacific Air Forces		
Organized	May 66	41st Air Division		Combat operations in SEA, May 66–Jan 73.
Attached	May 66	388th Tactical Fighter Wing	Korat AB, Thailand	Earned 5.5 aerial victories, 18 Aug 66–15 Oct 72.
Reassigned (no change in attachment)	Jan 68	347th Tactical Fighter Wing		
Reassigned (attachment ends)	Mar 71	388th Tactical Fighter Wing		

432d Tactical Reconnaissance Wing

388th Tactical Fighter Wing

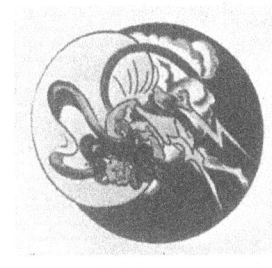
4th Tactical Fighter Squadron

366th Tactical Fighter Wing

TABLE 3—UNITS CREDITED WITH THE DESTRUCTION OF MIG'S IN AIR-TO-AIR COMBAT—Continued

Organizational Action	Date	Assignment	Location	Operations
35th Tactical Fighter Squadron				
Deployed; attached	Jun 64	41st Air Division	Yokota AB, Japan	Tactical air operations and air defense in Japan and Korea, 1953-71. Flew combat operations in SEA, Sep–Nov 64, from mid-Oct to mid-Nov 65 as a unit and by augmenting other squadrons in 1966 and 1967, and as a unit again from Apr to Oct 1972. Earned 5.5 aerial victories, 23 May–8 Oct 72.
Returned (attachment ends)	Sep 64	2d Air Division	Korat AB, Thailand	
Reassigned	Nov 64		Yokota AB, Japan	
Deployed; attached	Apr 65	6441st Tactical Fighter Wing	Takhli AB, Thailand	
Returned (attachment ends)	May 65	2d Air Division	Yokota AB, Japan	
Deployed; attached	Jun 65		Takhli AB, Thailand	
Returned (attachment ends)	Oct 65	2d Air Division	Yokota AB, Japan	
Reassigned	Nov 65	41st Air Division		
Reassigned	Nov 66	347th Tactical Fighter Wing		
Deployed for 11 short periods	Jun 68–Jan 71			
Reassigned; moved	Mar 71	3d Tactical Fighter Wing	Osan AB, Korea	
Deployed; attached	Apr 72	366th Tactical Fighter Wing	Yokota AB, Japan	
Deployed; attached	Jun 72	388th Tactical Fighter Wing	Kunsan AB, Korea	
Returned (attachment ends)	Oct 72		Da Nang AB, RVN	
			Korat AB, Thailand	
			Kunsan AB, Korea	
44th Tactical Fighter Squadron				
Reassigned; moved	Apr 67	18th Tactical Fighter Wing	Kadena AB, Okinawa	Carried out FEAF (later, PACAF) operations, Sep 47–Apr 67. Combat operations in SEA, Apr 67–Mar 71. Earned 1 aerial victory, 13 May 67.
Reassigned; moved	Oct 69	388th Tactical Fighter Wing	Korat AB, Thailand	
Reassigned	Dec 70	355th Tactical Fighter Wing	Takhli AB, Thailand	
Reassigned; moved	Mar 71	Thirteenth Air Force		
		18th Tactical Fighter Wing	Kadena AB, Okinawa	
45th Tactical Fighter Squadron				
Activated	Apr 62	Tactical Air Command	MacDill AFB, Fla.	TAC operations, Oct 62–Jun 71. Combat operations in SEA, Apr–Aug 65. Earned first 2 aerial victories of the conflict, Jul 65.
Organized	May 62	15th Tactical Fighter Wing		
Attached	May 62	12th Tactical Fighter Wing		
Attachment ends	Jul 62	15th Tactical Fighter Wing		
Deployed; attached	Apr 65	2d Air Division	Ubon AB, Thailand	
Returned (attachment ends)	Aug 65		MacDill AFB, Fla.	
58th Tactical Fighter Squadron				
Activated	Sep 70	33d Tactical Fighter Wing	Eglin AFB, Fla.	TAC operations, Sep 70–. Combat operations in SEA, Apr–Oct 72. Earned 2 aerial victories, 2 Jun–12 Aug 72.
Deployed; attached	Apr 72	432d Tactical Reconnaissance Wing	Udorn AB, Thailand	
Returned (attachment ends)	Oct 72		Eglin AFB, Fla.	

45th Tactical Fighter Squadron

44th Tactical Fighter Squadron

58th Tactical Fighter Squadron

35th Tactical Fighter Squadron

TABLE 3—UNITS CREDITED WITH THE DESTRUCTION OF MIG'S IN AIR-TO-AIR COMBAT—Continued

Organizational Action	Date	Assignment	Location	Operations
307th Tactical Fighter Squadron				
Deployed; attached	Jun 62	Tactical Air Command	Homestead AFB, Fla.	TAC operations, 1962–65. Combat operations in SEA, Jun–Dec 65. TAC operations, 1966. USAFE operations, 1966–71. TAC operations, 1971–. Combat in SEA, Jul–Oct 72. Earned 1 aerial victory, 15 Oct 72.
Attached	Jun 65	2d Air Division	Bien Hoa AB, RVN	
Attached	Jul 65	6251st Tactical Fighter Wing		
Returned (attachment ends)	Nov 65	3d Tactical Fighter Wing		
Reassigned; moved	Dec 65		Homestead AFB, Fla.	
Reassigned; moved	Apr 66	401st Tactical Fighter Wing	Torrejon AB, Spain	
Reassigned; moved	Jul 71	31st Tactical Fighter Wing	Homestead AFB, Fla.	
Deployed; attached	Jul 72	432d Tactical Reconnaissance Wing	Udorn AB, Thailand	
Returned (attachment ends)	Oct 72		Homestead AFB, Fla.	
333d Tactical Fighter Squadron				
Reassigned; moved	Jul 58	4th Tactical Fighter Wing	Seymour Johnson AFB, NC	Combat operations in SEA, Dec 65–Oct 70. Earned 7.5 aerial victories, 21 Sep 66–19 Dec 67.
Reassigned; moved	Dec 65	355th Tactical Fighter Wing	Takhli AB, Thailand	
Reassigned; moved	Oct 70	23d Tactical Fighter Wing	McConnell AFB, Kans.	
336th Tactical Fighter Squadron				
Deployed; attached	Dec 57	4th Tactical Fighter Wing	Seymour Johnson AFB, NC	Combat operations in SEA, Apr–Sep 72. Earned 1 aerial victory, 15 Aug 72.
	Apr 72		Ubon AB, Thailand	
Returned (attachment ends)	Sep 72	8th Tactical Fighter Wing	Seymour Johnson AFB, NC	
354th Tactical Fighter Squadron				
	Oct 64	355th Tactical Fighter Wing	McConnell AFB, Kans.	Combat operations in SEA, Mar–Jun 65 and Dec 65–Oct 70. Earned 8 aerial victories, 10 Mar–27 Oct 67.
Deployed; attached	Mar 65	18th TFW; 2d Air Division	Kadena AB, Okinawa and Korat AB, Thailand	
Returned (attachment ends)	Jun 65		McConnell AFB, Kans.	
Reassigned	Nov 65	835th Air Division		
Reassigned; moved	Nov 65	355th Tactical Fighter Wing	Takhli AB, Thailand	
Reassigned	Dec 70	Thirteenth Air Force		
Reassigned; moved	Apr 71	4453d Combat Crew Training Wing	Davis-Monthan AFB, Ariz.	
357th Tactical Fighter Squadron				
Activated	Apr 62	Tactical Air Command	George AFB, Calif.	Combat operations in SEA, Jun–Nov 65 and Feb 66–Sep 70. Earned 4 aerial victories, 19 Apr–19 Dec 67.
Organized	Jul 62	355th Tactical Fighter Wing	McConnell AFB, Kans.	
Moved	Jul 64		McConnell AFB, Kans.	
Deployed; attached	Jun 65	2d Air Division	Korat AB, Thailand	
Returned (attachment ends)	Nov 65	835th Air Division	McConnell AFB, Kans.	
Reassigned; moved	Jan 66	355th Tactical Fighter Wing	Takhli AB, Thailand	
Inactivated	Dec 70			

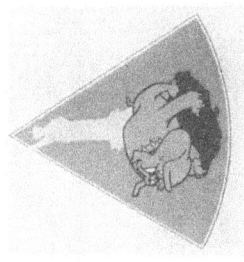
354th Tactical Fighter Squadron

336th Tactical Fighter Squadron

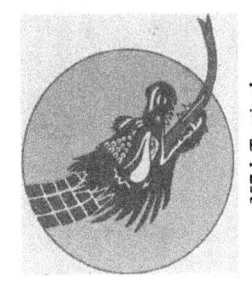
357th Tactical Fighter Squadron

307th Tactical Fighter Squadron

TABLE 3—UNITS CREDITED WITH THE DESTRUCTION OF MIG'S IN AIR-TO-AIR COMBAT—Continued

Organizational Action	Date	Assignment	Location	Operations
		389th Tactical Fighter Squadron		
Moved	Jul 63	366th Tactical Fighter Wing	Holloman AFB, NM	
Moved	Mar 66		Phan Rang AB, RVN	Combat operations in SEA, Mar 66–Oct 71. Earned 6 aerial victories, 23 Apr 67–22 May 67.
Reassigned; moved	Oct 66	37th Tactical Fighter Wing	Da Nang AB, RVN	
Reassigned	Jun 69	12th Tactical Fighter Wing	Phu Cat AB, RVN	
Reassigned; moved	Mar 70	347th Tactical Fighter Wing	Mountain Home AFB, Idaho	
	Oct 71			
		390th Tactical Fighter Squadron		
Moved	Jul 63	366th Tactical Fighter Wing	Holloman AFB, NM	
Reassigned; moved	Oct 65	6252d Tactical Fighter Wing	Clark AB, Philippines	Combat operations in SEA, Nov 65–Jun 72. Earned 2 aerial victories, 12 May 66–1 May 67.
Reassigned	Apr 66	35th Tactical Fighter Wing	Da Nang AB, RVN	
Reassigned	Oct 66	366th Tactical Fighter Wing		
Reassigned; moved	Jun 72	347th Tactical Fighter Wing	Mountain Home AFB, Idaho	
		421st Tactical Fighter Squadron		
Reassigned; moved	Nov 65	835th Air Division	McConnell AFB, Kans.	Combat operations in SEA, Nov 65–Apr 67. Earned 1 aerial victory, 21 Sep 66. TAC operations, Apr 67–Apr 69. Deployed in Korea, Apr–Jun 69. Combat operations in SEA, Jun 69–Jan 73.
Reassigned	Nov 65	6234th Tactical Fighter Wing	Korat AB, Thailand	
Reassigned; moved	Apr 66	388th Tactical Fighter Wing	MacDill AFB, Fla.	
Reassigned; moved	Apr 67	15th Tactical Fighter Wing	Homestead AFB, Fla.	
Reassigned; moved	Jul 67	4531st Tactical Fighter Wing	McConnell AFB, Kans.	
Reassigned; moved	Dec 67	23d Tactical Fighter Wing	Da Nang AB, RVN	
Reassigned; moved	Apr 69	366th Tactical Fighter Wing	Kunsan AB, Korea	
Attached (en route to SEA)	Apr 69	457th Tactical Fighter Wing	Da Nang AB, RVN	
Arrived (attachment ends)	Jun 69	366th Tactical Fighter Wing	Takhli AB, Thailand	
Moved	Jun 72		Udorn AB, Thailand	
Reassigned; moved	Oct 72	432d Tactical Reconnaissance Wing		
		433d Tactical Fighter Squadron		
Activated	·Jul 64	Tactical Air Command	George AFB, Calif.	Combat operations in SEA, Dec 65–Jan 73. Earned 12 aerial victories, 2 Jan 67–6 Feb 68.
Organized	Jul 64	8th Tactical Fighter Wing	Ubon AB, Thailand	
Moved	Dec 65			
		435th Tactical Fighter Squadron		
	Jul 58	8th Tactical Fighter Wing	George AFB, Calif.	Combat operations in SEA, Jul 66–Jan 73. Earned 6.5 aerial victories, 6 Nov 67–14 Feb 68.
Moved	Jul 66		Udorn AB, Thailand	
Moved	Jul 67		Ubon AB, Thailand	

421st Tactical Fighter Squadron

435th Tactical Fighter Squadron

390th Tactical Fighter Squadron

433d Tactical Fighter Squadron

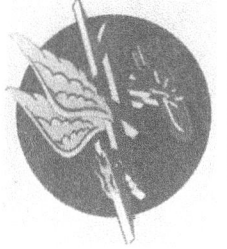

389th Tactical Fighter Squadron

TABLE 3—UNITS CREDITED WITH THE DESTRUCTION OF MIG'S IN AIR-TO-AIR COMBAT—Continued

Organizational Action	Date	Assignment	Location	Operations
469th Tactical Fighter Squadron				
	Jul 64	355th Tactical Fighter Wing	McConnell AFB, Kans.	
Deployed	Nov 64		Yokota AB, Japan	
Deployed	Dec 64		Kadena AB, Okinawa	
Deployed; attached	Jan 65	2d Air Division	Korat AB, Thailand	Combat operations in SEA, Nov 65–Oct 72.
Returned (attachment ends)	Mar 65		McConnell AFB, Kans.	Earned 4 aerial victories, 4 Dec 66–12 Sep 72.
Reassigned; moved	Nov 65	6234th Tactical Fighter Wing	Korat AB, Thailand	
Reassigned	Apr 66	388th Tactical Fighter Wing		
Inactivated	Oct 72			
480th Tactical Fighter Squadron				
Reassigned; moved	Jul 63	366th Tactical Fighter Wing	Holloman AFB, NM	Combat operations in SEA, Feb 66–Nov 71.
Attached	Feb 66	2d Air Division	Da Nang AB, RVN	Earned 9 aerial victories, 26 Apr 66–5 Jun 67.
Reassigned	Feb 66	6252d Tactical Fighter Wing		
Attached	Apr 66	Seventh Air force		
Attached	Apr 66	6252d Tactical Fighter Wing		
Reassigned (attachment ends)	Jun 66	35th Tactical Fighter Wing		
Reassigned	Oct 66	35th Tactical Fighter Wing		
Reassigned	Apr 69	366th Tactical Fighter Wing		
Reassigned; moved	Mar 70	37th Tactical Fighter Wing	Phu Cat AB, RVN	
Reassigned	Nov 71	12th Tactical Fighter Wing		
Inactivated				
523d Tactical Fighter Squadron				
	Jun 65	27th Tactical Fighter Wing	Cannon AFB, NM	
Reassigned; moved	Nov 65	405th Fighter Wing	Clark AB, Philippines	Combat operations in SEA, Apr–Oct 72.
Air echelon attached	Apr 72	432d Tactical Reconnaissance Wing	Udorn AB, Thailand	Earned 2 aerial victories, 16 Apr–15 Oct 72.
Air echelon returned (atchmt ends)	Oct 72		Clark AB, Philippines	
Reassigned; moved	Aug 73	27th Tactical Fighter Wing	Cannon AFB, NM	

523d Tactical Fighter Squadron

469th Tactical Fighter Squadron

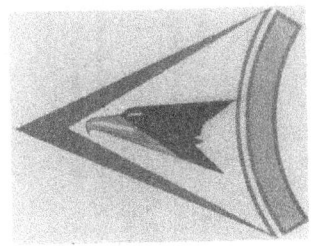

480th Tactical Fighter Squadron

TABLE 3—UNITS CREDITED WITH THE DESTRUCTION OF MIG'S IN AIR-TO-AIR COMBAT—Continued

Organizational Action	Date	Assignment	Location	Operations
555th Tactical Fighter Squadron				
Activated and organized	Jan 64	12th Tactical Fighter Wing	MacDill AFB, Fla.	
Deployed; attached	Dec 64	51st Fighter-Interceptor Wing	Naha AB, Okinawa	
Returned (attachment ends)	Mar 65		MacDill AFB, Fla.	
Deployed; attached	Dec 65	51st Fighter-Interceptor Wing	Naha AB, Okinawa	
Attached	Feb 66	8th Tactical Fighter Wing	Udorn AB, Thailand	Combat operations in SEA, Feb 66–Jan 73. Earned 39 aerial victories, 23 Apr 66–28 Dec 72.
Reassigned (attachment continues)	Mar 66	Thirteenth Air Force		
Reassigned	Mar 66	8th Tactical Fighter Wing		
Moved	Jul 66		Ubon AB, Thailand	
Moved	May 68		Udorn AB, Thailand	
Reassigned	Jun 68	432d Tactical Reconnaissance Wing		
Reassigned; moved	Jul 74	58th Tactical Fighter Training Wing	Luke AFB, Ariz.	

555th Tactical Fighter Squadron

Aircraft and Armament

Numerous aircraft types and missile systems were employed by the U.S. Air Force in Vietnam. However, three basic aircraft coupled with three basic missiles and 20-millimeter or .50-caliber guns were responsible for the MIG's destroyed by the Air Force.

Aircraft employed were the F-4 Phantom in the C, D, and E series; the D and F series of the F-105 Thunderchief; and the B-52D Stratofortress.

The Thunderchiefs accounted for 27½ MIG-17's. The F-105 was basically a single purpose aircraft—one of the few in the Air Force inventory—intended primarily for low-level, air-to-ground operations. Its air-to-air capability was only secondary. An all-weather fighter-bomber, the F-105 was capable of delivering conventional as well as nuclear and thermonuclear weapons.

Two Thunderchief series were introduced into Vietnam: the single-seat F-105D and the two-seat F-105F. Speed, maneuverability, and aerial firepower qualified them for use in counter-air, close-support, and interdiction roles in either limited or general war situations.

Both series of this aircraft were capable of low- and high-level bomber missions, in any weather, day or night, and over any type of terrain. The pilot was able to fly a complete mission on instruments, while never observing the ground, except for takeoff and landing maneuvers.

Standard installed armament was a 20-millimeter (20-mm) automatic multi-barrel gun, the Vulcan, capable of firing 6,000 rounds a minute. Additionally, the F-105 could carry sixteen 750-pound bombs and clusters of rockets, or guided and unguided missiles.

The main elements of the aircraft's weapon delivery system were its toss-bomb computer, a monopulse search and ranging radar, and a display to feed information to the pilot. When releasing bombs, this system automatically computed release times, automatically released, and even maneuvered the aircraft during the delivery if the pilot desired. This system, called the Thunderstick fire control system, also handled the problems of air-to-air and air-to-ground attacks with missiles or guns.

F-105F's were used in a mission support role on bombing raids. Called Wild Weasel, they protected bomber aircraft by detecting and attacking enemy surface-to-air (SAM) missile sites with their specialized electronic-countermeasure (ECM) systems and radar tracking air-to-ground missiles.

The Thunderchiefs had a wing span of 34 feet 11 inches. They were capable of speeds from Mach 1.11 at sea level to Mach 2.1 above 36,000 feet. Each model could carry a bomb load of 12,000 pounds and had an unrefueled range of 2,000 miles.

Phantom aircraft downed a total of 107½ MIGs: 33½ MIG-17's, 8 MIG-19's, and 66 MIG-21's.

The F-4 Phantom began its career as a single-place, all-weather fighter with the U.S. Navy. It quickly evolved into a sophisticated multi-mission fighter-bomber. In 1962 the Tactical Air Command selected the C model for operational use.

Brought in large numbers into the Air Force inventory, the basic aircraft underwent very few modifications. One major change was the installation of a full set of flight controls in the rear cockpit, since the Air Force desired to man the aircraft with two pilots, unlike the Navy which had a crew composed of a pilot and radar operator. Another alteration was the addition of an inertial-guidance system which told the pilot his latitude and longitude at any given time. These and other minor modifications increased the aircraft's air-to-ground capability.

The D-model of the Phantom was further improved with the installation of a lead computing sight and a central air data computer to handle bombing and navigation. These systems allowed the computation problem and weapon release to be handled automatically in all bombing modes—dive, level, and night, or all-weather—and thus further improved the air-to-ground capability of the aircraft.

The F-4E, as the earlier models, could perform air superiority, close-air, and interdiction missions using either conventional or nuclear munitions. Changes made in this version included the addition of an internally mounted 20-millimeter gun in the nose, an improved fire control system, and engines with increased thrust. A miniature radar installed in the nose enabled retention of the radar-guided Sparrow (AIM-7) missile system in addition to the multi-barrel cannon, which was based on the Gatling concept and was similar to that used in the Thunderchief. The C and D models used 20-millimeter guns housed in SUU–16 and SUU–23 gun pods, respectively.

The F–4 had some unusual features as well. It was able to fly at speeds as low as 150 to 165 miles per hour, which permitted loitering over a ground combat area or short landings. It also had a "dash" speed in excess of 1,600 miles per hour. This aircraft was capable of carrying twice the weapons payload of a World War II B–17.

The F–4 of Vietnam fame had a 38-foot 5-inch wing span; it was 58 feet 3 inches long. It had a range of over 1,000 miles without refueling and could carry a bomb load of 14,000 pounds.

The B–52D's downed two MIG–21's. This aircraft was a strategic heavy bomber powered by eight jet engines. It was used for conventional bombing. It had four .50-caliber machine guns mounted in the tail section. The B–52 was a large aircraft with a wing span of 195 feet and a length of 156 feet. It was capable of speeds of 650 miles per hour, had an unrefueled range of 6,000 miles, and could carry up to 85 of the 500-lb. or 42 of the 750-lb. bombs in the weapons bay plus 12 of the 750-lb. bombs on each of two under-wing pylons.

Three basic air-to-air missiles were responsible for MIG kills: the AIM–4, AIM–7, and AIM–9. The AIM–4 Falcon, used on F–4D aircraft, downed five MIG's—four MIG–17's and one MIG–21. Amongst the smallest missiles in service, the Falcon family consisted of several different series of missiles guided either by radar or by a heat-seeking (infrared) homing device. Series changes improved the capabilities of the Falcon. Performance against high-speed maneuvering targets was increased; an all-aspect attack capability was achieved, enabling the missile to attack from all angles, and accuracy and resistance to electronic-countermeasures (ECM) were improved. A new solid fuel, two-level thrust rocket motor provided a lighter launching thrust followed by a lower-level thrust to sustain missile velocity; and more powerful high-explosive warheads were fitted. Falcons ranged in size from 6 feet 6 inches to 7 feet 2 inches and were capable of speeds from Mach 2 to Mach 4. All models had an effective range of more than 5 miles.

The AIM–7 Sparrow, used by F–4's, accounted for 50 MIG kills—more than any other missile. Eight were MIG–17's, four were MIG–19's, and 38 were MIG–21's.

Sparrow was a solid fuel, radar-homing, air-to-air guided missile with a high-explosive warhead. It could be used against high-performance aircraft under all-weather conditions and from all angles, including head-on. The AIM–7 used in Southeast Asia had a supersonic capability, and aircraft flying either subsonic or supersonic speeds could launch the missile. First used by the U.S. Navy in 1958, the Sparrow later became part of the primary armament on USAF and USMC fighters.

Later models of the Sparrow had significantly greater performance capabilities than the earlier model because of a series of engineering and design changes. These included an advanced fire control system consisting essentially of a radar in the nose of the aircraft which carried it, a fire control computer, and cockpit displays and controls. The radar searched for, acquired, and tracked the target; the information was then fed to the computer which generated signals enabling the pilot to attack targets with great success. The Sparrows, about 12 feet long, could fly farther than 10 miles.

AIM–9 Sidewinders downed 33 MIG's: 14 MIG–17's, 2 MIG–19's, and 17 MIG–21's.

Sidewinder was one of the simplest and least costly guided weapons produced in quantity. It had few electronic components and less than 2 dozen moving parts. It required little training to handle and assemble. Powered by a single-stage, solid-propellant rocket, this supersonic air-to-air missile was developed by the U.S. Navy for fleet defense and was later adopted by the U.S. Air Force for Century series and F–4 aircraft. Series B, D, and E of this missile used a passive guidance system which homed in on the engine exhaust of a target aircraft. Series C utilized a semiactive radar guidance system. Sidewinders were approximately 9 feet 4 inches long, capable of speeds up to Mach 2.5. They had an effective range of more than 2 miles.

Table 4 outlines the MIG kills made by the combined use of these weapons and weapon systems.

North Vietnam received its primary weapon systems in large part from the Soviet Union. These weapons included the MIG–17, MIG–19, and MIG–21 aircraft which employed the Atoll and Al-

TABLE 4.—AIRCRAFT & WEAPONS COMBINATIONS USED IN MIG VICTORIES

USAF Aircraft	Weapons/Tactics	MIG-17	MIG-19	MIG-21	Total
F-4C	AIM-7 Sparrow	4	0	10	14
	AIM-9 Sidewinder	12	0	10	22
	20-mm gunfire	3	0	1	4
	Maneuvering tactics	2	0	0	2
		21	0	21	42
F-4D	AIM-4 Falcon	4	0	1	5
	AIM-7 Sparrow	4	2	20	26
	AIM-9 Sidewinder	0	2	3	5
	20-mm gunfire	4	0	2	6
	Maneuvering tactics	0	0	2	2
		12	4	28	44
F-4E	AIM-7 Sparrow	0	2	8	10
	AIM-9 Sidewinder	0	0	4	4
	AIM-9/20-mm gunfire (combined)	0	0	1	1
	20-mm gunfire	0	1	4	5
	Maneuvering tactics (2 F-4E's)	0	1	0	1
		0	4	17	21
F-4D/F-105F	20-mm gunfire	1	0	0	1
		1	0	0	1
F-105D	20-mm gunfire	22	0	0	22
	AIM-9 Sidewinder	2	0	0	2
	AIM-9/20-mm gunfire (combined)	1	0	0	1
		25	0	0	25
F-105F	20-mm gunfire	2	0	0	2
		2	0	0	2
B-52D	50-caliber gunfire	0	0	2	2
		0	0	2	2
GRAND TOTAL		61	8	68	137

kali missiles, and an internal cannon.

The MIG-17 Fresco was an advanced version of the MIG-15. The newer model had a short afterburner, a redesigned wing with a mean-sweep angle of 42°, an extended inboard leading edge sections, large trailing-edge root fairings, modified flaps, and rounded tips. A single-seat aircraft with one power plant, it was used as a day-interceptor in the A and B series, a fighter-bomber in the C series, and a limited all-weather and night-fighter in the D and E series.

The C series, the most widely used variant of the day-fighter, carried a 37-mm cannon under the lower starboard nose and two 23-mm cannons under the lower port nose. A supplementary 23-mm gun package could be installed at the wing-tank position. Four underwing packs of eight 55-mm air-to-air rockets, or a total of 100 lbs. of bombs could also be carried. Normally, two external fuel tanks were also fitted.

The standard all-weather version of this aircraft was in the D series. Armament was revised to three 23-mm cannons and thirty-two 55-mm rockets in external pods below the wings.

The E model was equipped with a scan-intercept radar carried in an extended lip over the intake; a small fixed scanner was mounted in a conical housing on the intake dividing wall. The cockpit windshield extended farther forward than on the other models. A typical intercept load would consist

(Clockwise, starting with Top Left) Sgt. Donald F. Clements (left) an A1C Greg E. Sniegowski load an SUU-23 gun pod at Phu Cat Air Base, South Vietnam.

Sgt. John F. Host and A1C William B. Bokshar guide an SUU-23 20-mm Vulcan cannon into the gun services shop for overhauling.

A1C Gary P. Mincer (l. to r.), Sgt. Vernon E. Kisinger, A1C Lonnie J. Hartfield, and Sgt. Phineas T. Barry prepare to load a Sparrow missile on an F-4 at Cam Ranh Bay Air Base.

F-105 Thunderchiefs of the 388th TFW stand ready for night maintenance at Korat Air Base, Thailand.

Two Sidewinder missiles mounted under the wing of an F-105

Sgt. James E. Faison carefully unpacks a Sidewinder air-to-air missile at Da Nang Air Base, South Vietnam.

(Top Left) North Vietnamese Air Force pilots discuss mission.

(Top Right) A North Vietnamese SA-2 Guideline missile unit hastens to respond to an alert.

(Center) A North Vietnamese crew unloads a 37-mm AA Gun used against USAF fighters.

(Bottom) MIG-17's parked on the runway of Kien An Airfield, North Vietnam.

of two or four Alkali radar-guided missiles or four pods each containing eight 55-mm missiles. It could be armed with two 23-mm and one 37-mm cannons. Four 210-mm missiles could also be carried for ground attacks.

The MIG–19 Farmer was a single-seat, mid-wing, twin-jet fighter. Its wings and slab-shaped tail surfaces were swept back more than 40°, and it had a short fuselage, flat on both top and bottom. This aircraft was a logical development from previous MIG series, but the engines differed. It has two axial flow jet engines, while earlier MIG's had centrifugal jets.

Guns were installed in the wings of the Farmer and armament used by various series of this aircraft consisted of a 37-mm cannon mounted below the starboard side of the nose; a 23-mm cannon mounted at the wing root; a 30-mm cannon mounted at the wing root; 55-mm unguided air-to-air rockets carried in pods below the wings; and pylon-mounted beam-riding missiles.

MIG–19's were used as day fighters, night fighters, interceptors, and all-weather fighters. They were about 38 ft. long, had a maximum speed of Mach 1.3, and a range of 750 miles without refueling.

The original MIG–21 was known as the Faceplate but later models were designated the Fishbed. Faceplate differed substantially in design from the Fishbed model. Its wings were swept extremely; the Fishbed model had a mid-set delta wing.

Armament used by the MIG–21 included a 37-mm cannon, 50-mm air-to-air rockets which were pod-mounted, 55-mm rockets mounted on the wings, Atoll missiles attached by underwing pylons, and 30-mm cannon in long fairings on the fuselage.

This aircraft was a fairly simple interceptor and proved to be an all-around good performer, fully capable of challenging all but the very latest U.S. fighters. Even the most sophisticated American fighters did not dismiss the MIG–21 lightly. In its various model series, it played such roles as all-weather interceptor, day point-defense interceptor, and clear-weather fighter. Within the various series, Faceplate and Fishbed ranged in length from 49 feet to 54.4 feet, in wingspan from 25 to 38.8 feet. They carried loads from 20,500 to 31,240 pounds, unrefueled range was from 700 to 1,000 miles, and speed was about Mach 2.3.

The North Vietnamese Air Force used the Atoll air-to-air missile, which was similar to the U.S. AIM–9 Sidewinder in dimensions and weight. It was widely employed on MIG–21's. Propelled by a solid-propellant rocket motor, it carried a conventional high explosive warhead. Structurally, the Atoll had diametrically opposed pairs of forward control surfaces, linked, and working in unison for missile steering. The rear surfaces incorporated small tabs with inserted gyroscopic wheels driven by airstream. These apparently stayed locked until after launch, when they came into play to provide either more stability or a measure of control augmentation for steering. This missile was about 2.8 meters long; the forward control surfaces were 45 centimeters long, and the tail plane 53 centimeters long.

Their Tactics

The MIG-killers in Southeast Asia needed more than excellent aircraft and armament to score the 137 confirmed victories. To gain a tactical advantage from which to fire their weapons in air-to-air encounters they needed to know how to maneuver their aircraft. Because an aircraft can fly freely in space, it would seem that there are an infinite number of maneuvering situations and solutions to a given tactical encounter. Such however is not the case. Because of the pull of gravity and aircraft performance, the number and types of maneuvers are circumscribed within a "field of maneuver"—shaped like an elongated sphere. The size and shape of this sphere are determined by the turn and speed characteristics of the aircraft and the pull of gravity.

While the ability to perform basic fighter maneuvers is important, it is secondary to judgment. And the only true way to develop the quality of judgment necessary to excell in air-to-air combat is by training against aircraft of varied performance capability. This means that a pilot must know the enemy's capability as well as his own in order to decide when and how to perform each maneuver.

If a comparison of kills to losses in air combat could be used to illustrate superior performance, the ratio of more than two MIG kills for each loss would

FIELD OF MANEUVER

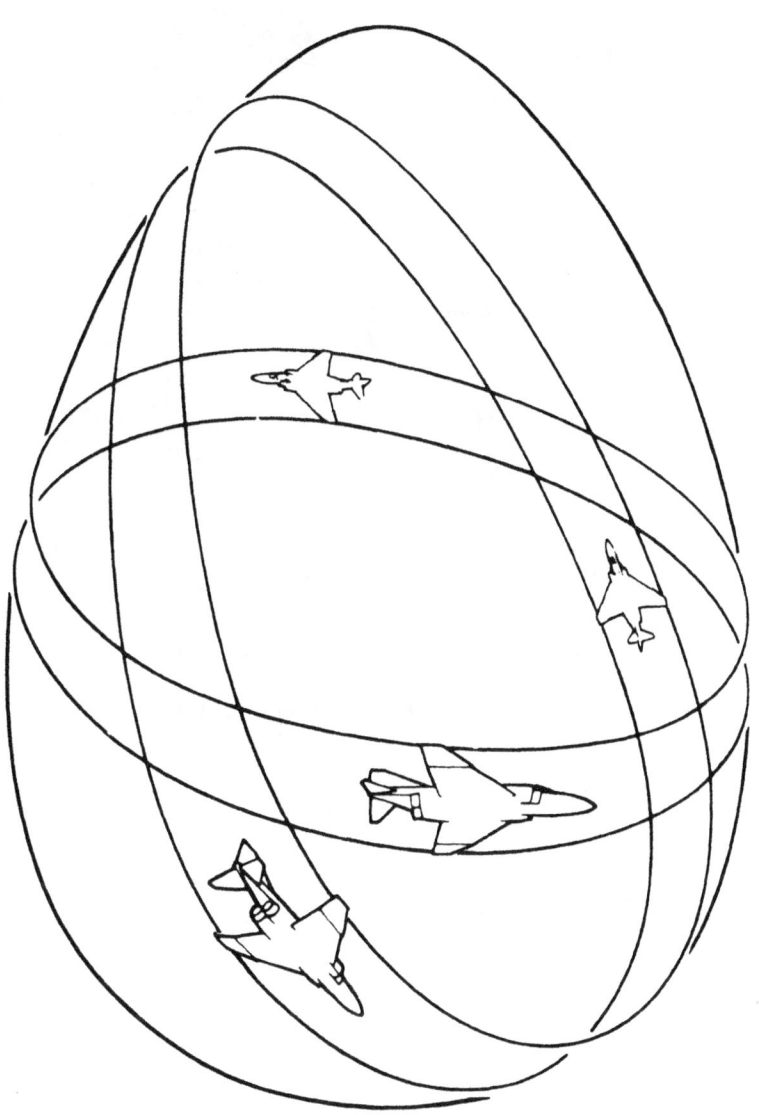

show sounder judgment or better U.S. aircraft, possibly both, in favor of the MIG-killers.

Some of the maneuvers and tactics which the USAF pilots used in Southeast Asia are described and illustrated in this section.

Escort Formations

The purpose of escort tactics was to provide protection for escorted aircraft as well as for the escorts. The tactics employed in Southeast Asia depended on

BASIC ESCORT FORMATION

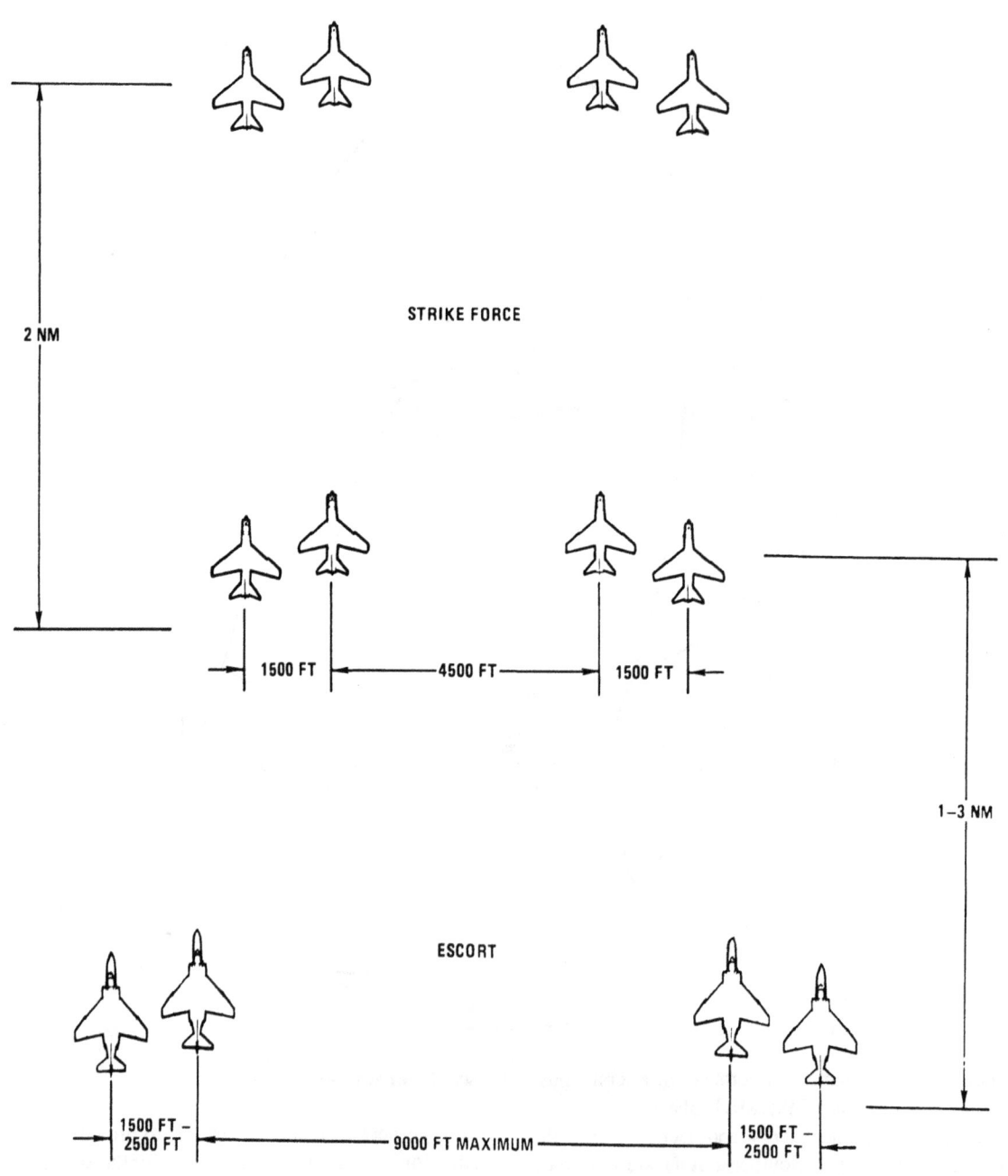

FLUID FOUR

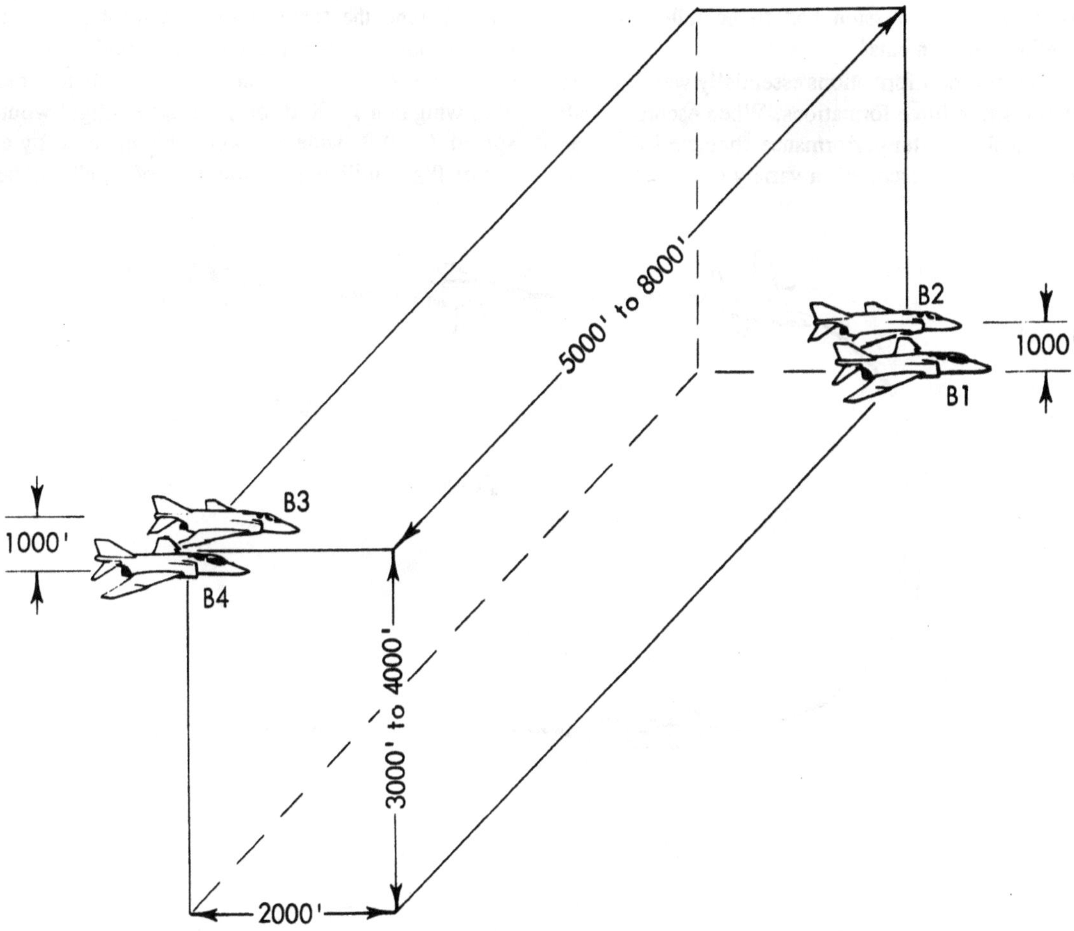

FINGERTIP OR FINGER FOUR
(All at Same Elevation)

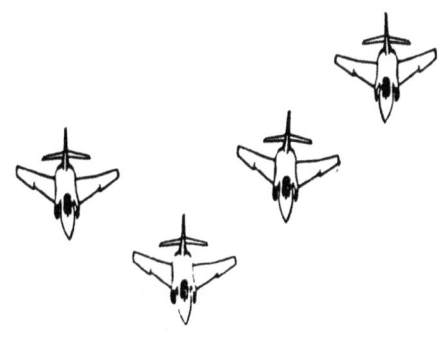

the size and speed of the escorted force and on the anticipated tactics of the enemy. Obviously, tactics for each escort mission had to be tailored to fit specific requirements.

Fighter escort formations essentially were dictated by the strike force formations. When escort aircraft had equal or better performance characteristics than the force being escorted, a variety of escort formations could be developed. Generally, the escort would prefer to fly a fluid formation approximately 2 miles behind the force. To obtain most protection from a four-ship escort, the force formations would spread the elements no more than 4,500 ft. apart with wingmen 1,500 ft. out. The strike flight would spread 7,500 ft. wide and would be managed by an escort flight utilizing a maximum of 9,000 ft. be-

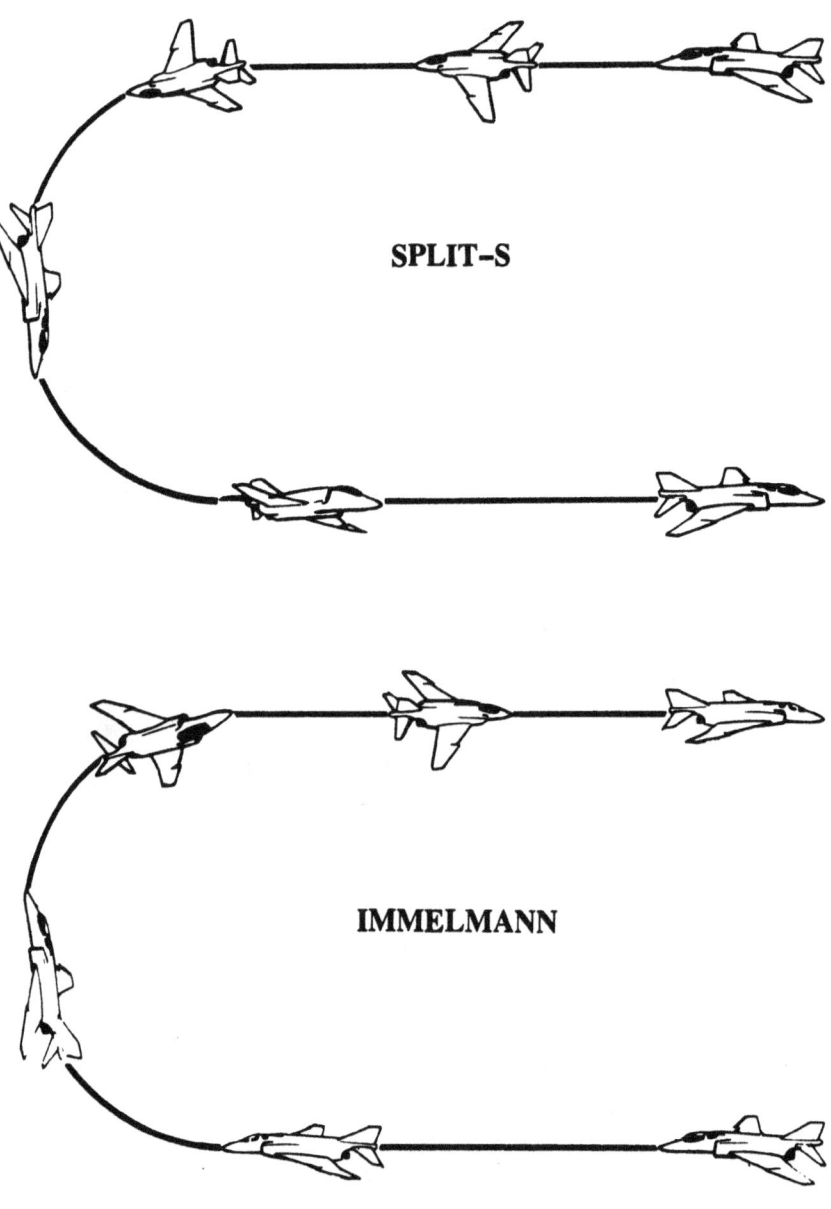

SPLIT-S

IMMELMANN

tween elements, maintaining line abreast with wingmen 1,500 to 2,500 ft. out and 0-30° back.

In case of chaff flights, escorts placed themselves high or outside during chaff bomb delivery to avoid falling canisters. Weather conditions too dictated a different position for better visual coverage.

Fluid-Four Formation

The fluid-four formation consists of a four-ship formation, an optimum for air-to-air combat. It is offensive, maneuverable, and has good mutual support. It was employed during daylight hours only and any time counter-air activity was anticipated. The lookout capability with four aircraft allows sizing the formation to cope with any threat expected. This means that even in some surface-to-air missile environments the formation can be sized to provide ECM coverage and yet retain air-to-air capability. The fluid-four formation consists of two elements. The second element maneuvers off the flight leader's element so as to provide mutual support both from positioning and lookout. The wingmen fly off the flight and element leaders, and they position themselves to provide the best coverage for the entire formation. The fulfillment of each individual's responsibility allows the flight to conduct offensive operations with security from a lethal 6 o'clock attack.

Split-S

This maneuver produces a 180° rotation about the aircraft's longitudinal axis followed by a 180° change of heading in the vertical plane.

Immelmann

Maneuver in which the aircraft completes the first half of a loop and then rolls over to an upright position, thus changing direction 180° with a simultaneous gain in altitude.

Scissors Maneuver

This maneuver is a series of turn reversals performed in an effort to achieve an offensive position after an attacker has been forced into a flight path overshoot. Once the attacker has overshot, he is outside the defender's turn radius and will not be able to get back inside unless the defender continues his turn. By reversing his turn, the defender presents a high angle-off to the attacker and will force another flight path overshoot if the attacker continues the attack. As the scissors progresses, the attacker should be forced to the 12 o'clock position.

An advantage should be achieved as soon as possible, since the rapid loss of energy associated with this maneuver may preclude a true firing position and place the defender in a vulnerable position for

SCISSORS

VERTICAL ROLLING SCISSORS

another attacker. In aircraft with equal performance capabilities, if the attacker overshoots and presses the attack, the defender would reverse his turn to continue the engagement. By maintaining his original defensive turn, the defender eventually solves the attacker's positioning problem. The most critical factor in using the scissors maneuver is judging when to perform the initial reversal. A reversal too soon may solve the attacker's overshoot problem. A reversal too late will allow the attacker to stem his lateral separation and retain an offensive position.

Vertical Rolling Scissors

The vertical rolling scissors is a defensive, descending, rolling maneuver in the vertical plane. The purpose of the maneuver is to gain an offensive advantage if the enemy overshoots a flight path in a vertical plane. The maneuver is used when the enemy cuts off in the vertical plane during the defender's zoom maneuver. When it is observed that the enemy is cutting off, the USAF aircraft would turn down into him to increase the angle of overshoot. Once the overshoot has been achieved, the nose of the USAF aircraft will be low and the enemy's nose high, so to press the attack, the enemy must pull his nose down also. At this point, when the enemy has been committed nose-low, the USAF attacker would roll 180° toward the defender's flight path and pull into him. If the timing is right the enemy will not be able to match his attacker's attitude, and he will overshoot in front of the attacker's flight path. The rolling maneuver is then continued around to the enemy's 6 o'clock position.

High- and Low-Speed Yo-Yo

The high-speed yo-yo is a maneuver in the vertical and horizontal planes designed to reduce angle-off or maintain nose-tail separation and thus prevent an overshoot of the defender's defensive turn. To employ this maneuver effectively, correct timing is essential. As soon as the attacker realizes that he will be unable to stay inside the defender's turn radius, he should plan to employ the high-speed yo-yo. This is accomplished by maintaining back stick pressure and slightly decreasing bank, relative to the defender, and allowing the nose to arc up through the vertical (assuming the enemy's turn is in the horizontal plane). The effect of gravity on turn and velocity, combined with a turn in a new plane, will enable the attacker to reduce angle-off and maintain nose-tail separation (assuming equal aircraft). The attacker now must pull his nose down toward the enemy's 6 o'clock position. If too little nose-tail separation is evident at the apex of his yo-yo, the attacker should perform a roll-away from the turn to an in-trail or lag-pursuit position.

While the high-speed yo-yo is designed to convert airspeed to altitude, the low-speed yo-yo converts altitude into airspeed in order to increase the rate of closure and at the same time allow an attacker to slide inside the opponent's turn radius.

Barrel Roll Attack

The offensive barrel roll is a three-dimensional maneuver used to reduce a high angle-off while maintaining nose-tail separation. Its purpose is much the same as the high speed yo-yo. It is used instead of the high speed yo-yo at a large angle-off in order to lower the apex of the attack. The range at which the maneuver is begun varies greatly and depends primarily on overtake and angle-off. Generally, it is initiated at a range of 1 to 3 miles, but the attacker must be flying at a relatively high calibrated airspeed.

The maneuver is initiated by rolling to match the defender's angle of bank, then loading the aircraft. As soon as the aircraft is loaded, the pilot rolls it in the opposite direction (over the top).

Pop-up Maneuvers

Pop-up tactics are used in attacking a high priority target in a SAM environment. The attacking aircraft approaches the target area in low-level penetration to enhance survivability, achieve deception, and surprise the defenses. In preplanning for such an attack, a significant initial point and a pop-up point are selected. After passing the initial point the aircraft is maneuvered until the target falls within a desirable angle extending from the nose of the aircraft to the target. Airspeed is increased, and at pop-up point the aircraft initiates a wing-level pullup, climbs to an apex altitude above the target suitable for strafing or dive-bombing. Withdrawal following weapons release depends on target environment and subsequent intentions.

HIGH-SPEED YO-YO

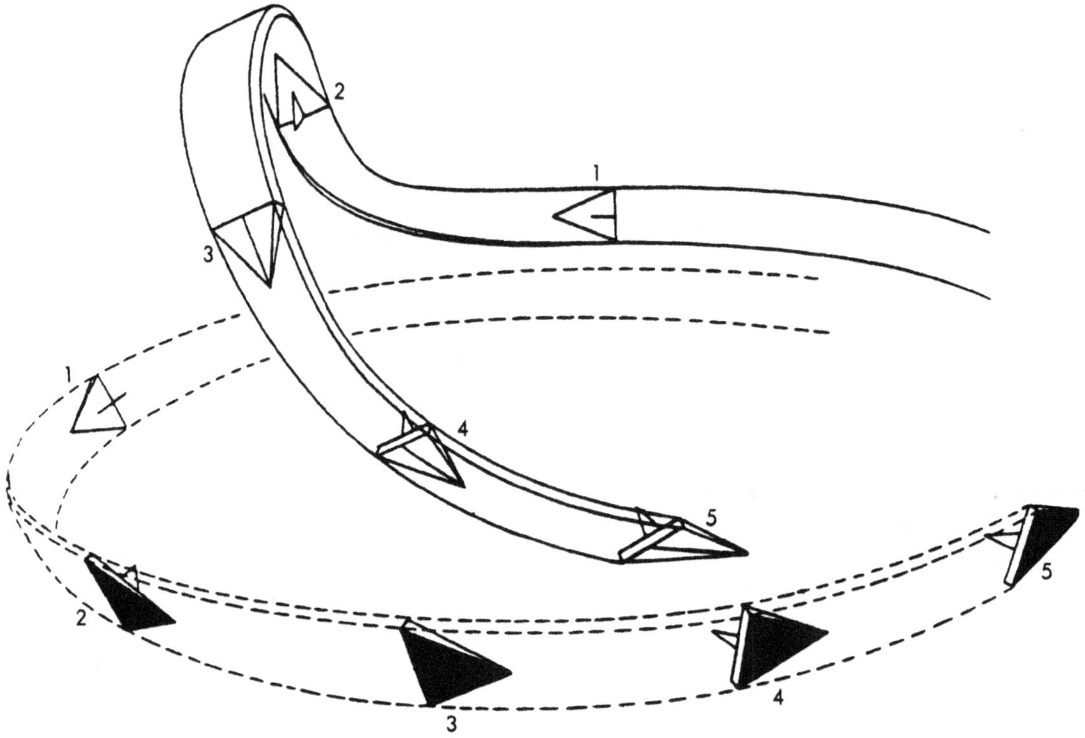

LOW-SPEED YO-YO

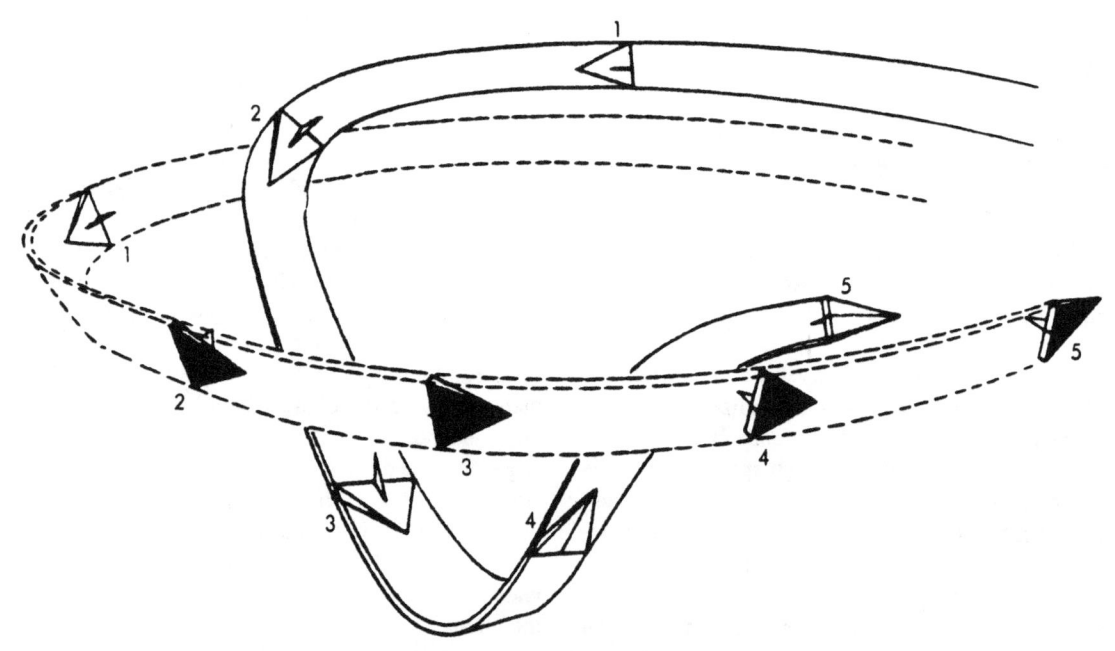

BARREL ROLL ATTACK

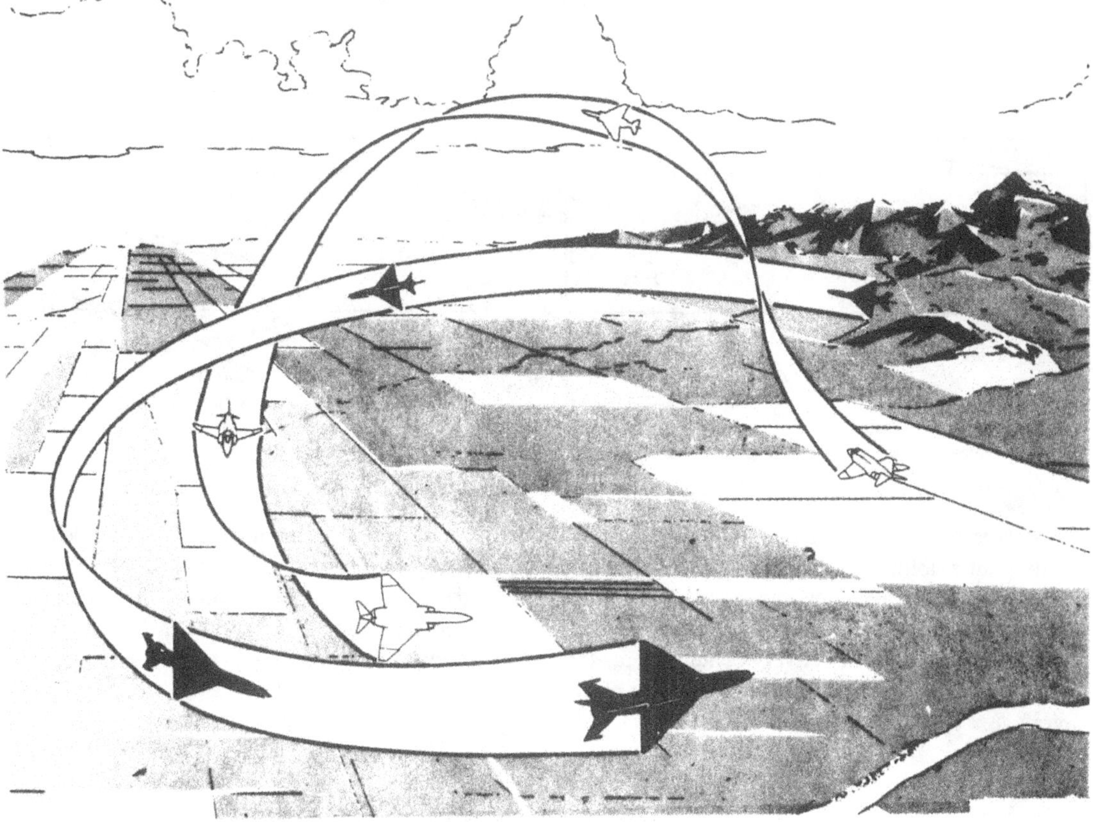

AS PORTRAYED IN PERSPECTIVE SKETCH

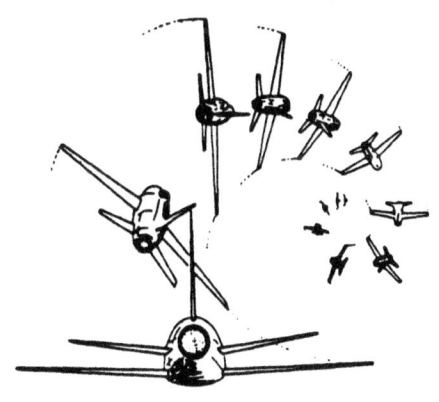

POP-UP TACTIC

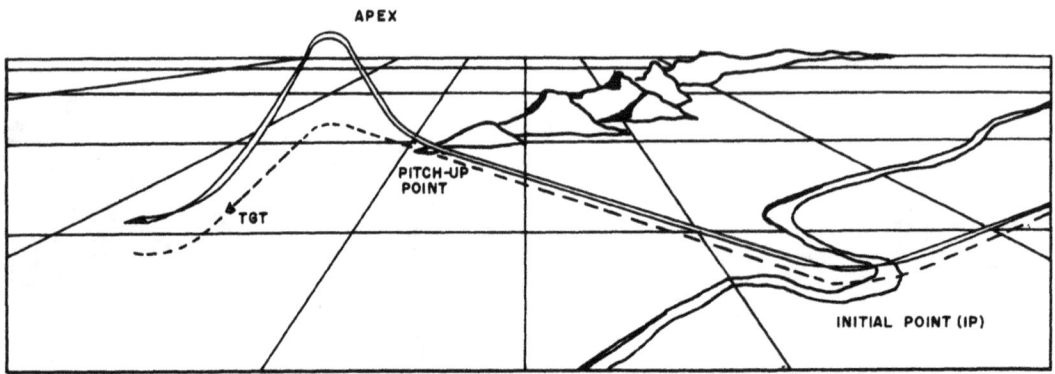

A successful attack using pop-up tactics depends on the pilot's ability to maneuver his aircraft to a precise position in space relative to the target. This position in space is determined by the type ordnance carried, the precomputed delivery conditions for the ordnance, and the maneuvering characteristics of the aircraft.

Wagon Wheel

The Wagon Wheel was a very significant tactic devised by the North Vietnamese Air Force in mid-1967 for MIG-17 defense. This tactic was in fact a modification of the Lufberry Circle. The Wagon Wheel was composed of a group of MIG-17's operating from a static orbit. Whenever they came under attack, they would enter an orbiting wheel formation to provide 6 o'clock coverage for each other, thereby enhancing their mutual defense. Through the use of the Wagon Wheel, the MIG-17's could effectively utilize their superior turning capability to force an overshoot by USAF aircraft while still providing 6 o'clock coverage for the preceding MIG in the orbit.

The wheel formation was used in one of two ways: (1) the circle could tighten to prevent the faster moving, heavier U.S. aircraft from getting into the turn, or (2) each time a USAF aircraft engaged an orbiting MIG, another MIG would cross the circle at full power to gain a firing position on the attacker.

Among the methods introduced for attacking MIG-17's in a Wagon Wheel formation was one in which U.S. aircrews initiated a tangential attack from outside the periphery of the Wagon Wheel to gain position for an AIM-7 shot. When lock-on and positive identification were secured outside of minimum missile range, this attack was effective and presented little threat to the attacking aircraft. However, the low altitudes of the Wheel created excessive noise problems on the attacking aircraft's scope, and radar lock-ons were the exception rather than the rule. It was extremely difficult to burn through ground clutter or to attain a full system lock-on. When this tangential attack was initiated for an AIM-9 or gun attack, the high angle-off of the attacking aircraft made it relatively easy for the MIG to force an overshoot before a tracking solution was achieved.

WAGON WHEEL FORMATION

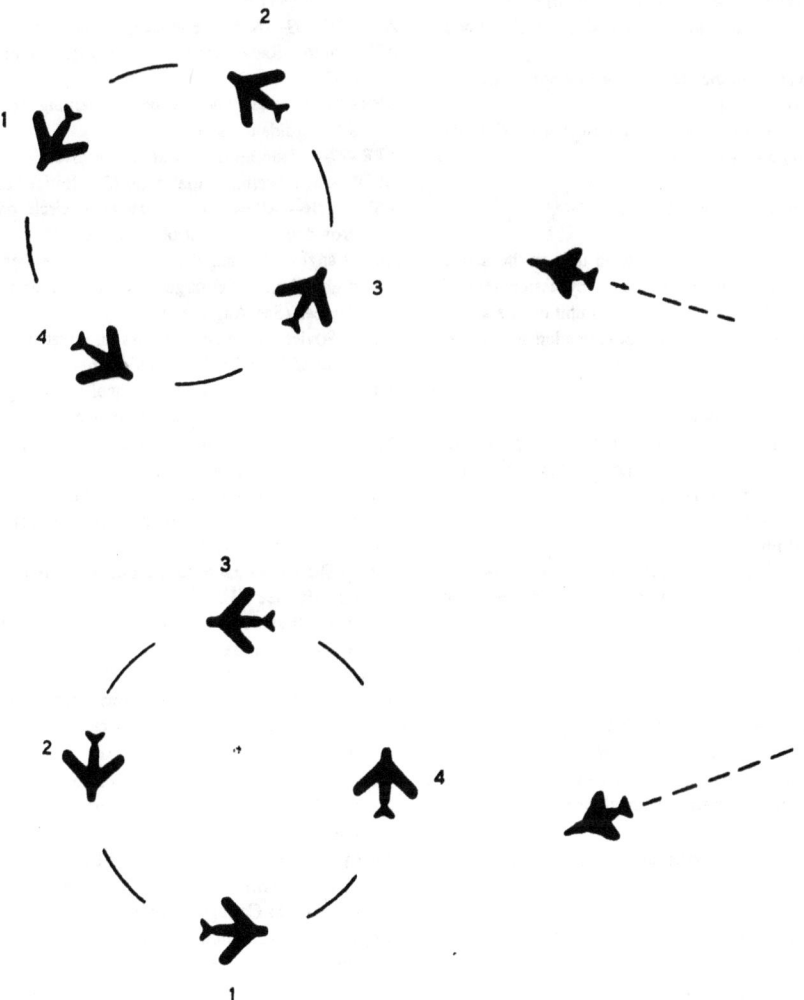

GLOSSARY OF TERMS AND ABBREVIATIONS

AA—Air-to-air (weapon)

AAA—Antiaircraft artillery

AAM—Air-to-air missile

AB—Afterburner (with respect to jet aircraft, see definition below); Air Base (with respect to an installation)

AC—Aircraft commander; the pilot designated in command of a given aircraft

Acceleration maneuver—Another term for a low-speed Yo-Yo. (See Yo-Yo, Low-Speed)

Ace—Unofficial term for a person with five or more aerial victories over enemy aircraft

Acft—Aircraft

ACM—Air combat maneuvering

ACT—Air combat tactics

Activate—1922–1959: To place a constituted unit on the active list and bring it into physical existence by assignment of personnel. 1960–: To place a constituted unit on the active list and thus make it available for organization by assignment of personnel

AD—Air Division

ADF—Automatic direction finder

Afterburner—An auxiliary burner attached to the tail pipe of a jet engine for injecting fuel into the hot exhaust gases and burning it to provide extra thrust

AGL—Above ground level

AGM—Air-to-ground missile

AGM-45—Shrike air-to-ground missile, anti-radiation type

AGM-78—Standard Arm air-to-ground missile, anti-radiation type

AI—Airborne intercept

AIM—Air-intercept missile

Aim-dot—(See Dot)

AIM-4D—Falcon air-to-air missile, passive IR type

AIM-9—Sidewinder air-to-air missile, passive IR type (B, D, E, G, and J models) and radar-guided (C model)

AIM-7—Sparrow air-to-air missile, semiactive radar type (D and E models)

Aiming error—Deviation of the actual aim point from the desired aim point.

Air abort—Cancellation of an aircraft mission for any reason other than enemy action, at any time from take-off to mission completion

AI radar—Airborne intercept radar

Aircrew—The full complement of air officers and airmen who man, or are designated to man, an aircraft in the air; also applied in certain contexts to the pilot of a single-place aircraft; often shortened to "crew"

ALQ-51—Broadband deception ECM system

ALQ-71—Noise jamming ECM pod (production model of the QRC-160-1)

Angle-off—Angular position off the tail of the reference aircraft (See Aspect angle)

APQ 100/109—Airborne intercept radar in F-4C/D aircraft

APR-25/26—Radar scanner aboard B-52 and certain fighter aircraft

APR-26—Crystal video airborne warning receiver to detect SA-2 guidance signals

APR-27—Airborne radar warning receiver

ARIP—Air refueling initial point (See Initial Point)

ASE Circle—Allowable steering error circle on radar display, provided by fire control computer

Aspect angle—The angular measurement between the line of the flight of an aerial target and the attacker's line of sight, in degrees (See Angle-off)

Atoll—Soviet-built air-to-air missile, infrared seeker type, similar to U.S. AIM-9 IR-homing missile

Attach—To place units or personnel in an organization where such placement is relatively temporary

Auto-acquisition—Automatic radar lock-on capability in the front cockpit of an F-4 aircraft

Auto-track—Automatic tracking in which a servo-mechanism keeps the radar beam trained on the target

AW—Automatic weapons

Back—The individual occupying the back, or rear, seat of an F-4 aircraft (See GIB)

Ballistic—Unguided, i.e. follows a ballistic trajectory when thrust is terminated

Bandit—Term for an enemy aircraft

BARCAP—Barrier combat air patrol; fighter cover between the strike force and an area of expected threat; a MIG Screen for one or more missions (See CAP)

Barrel roll—A 360° rolling maneuver in which the flight path of the aircraft describes a helix about the intended direction of the flight (See p. 167)

Big Eye—Term for USAF airborne EC-121 early warning radar aircraft; term used from Apr 1965 to Mar 1967, then changed to College Eye (See College Eye; Disco)

Bingo (fuel)—Minimum fuel quantity reserve established for a given geographical point to permit aircraft to return safely to its home base, an alternate base, or an aerial refueling point

Blip (radar)—A spot of light on a radar scope, representing the relative position of a reflecting object such as an aircraft; sometimes called "pip"

Bogey—Unidentified aircraft

Bogies—Two or more unidentified aircraft

Boresight mode—Radar operation mode in which the antenna is aligned and locked 2° below the fuselage reference line of the F-4 aircraft

Break—An emergency turn in which maximum performance is desired instantly to destroy an attacker's tracking solution

Break X—Minimum range indication for missile launch; X appears on the radar scope at minimum range

Brown Cradle—Nickname for EB-66C aircraft equipped with ECM equipment used in jamming enemy fire control radars

Bullseye—A reference point in North Vietnam

"Burner"—Afterburner

CAP—Combat air patrol; an aircraft patrol provided over an objective area, over the force protected, over the critical area of a combat zone, or over an air defense area, for the purpose of intercepting and destroying hostile aircraft before they reach their target (See BARCAP, CAP/Strike, Fast CAP, FORCAP, MIGCAP, RESCAP, SARCAP, Slow CAP and Strike/CAP)

CAP/Strike—Aircraft fragged (q.v.) with a primary CAP role and a secondary strike role; such aircraft are permitted to jettison strike ordnance and actively pursue any enemy aircraft sighted. They are not restricted to defensive encounters.

Cartwheel—(See Wheel)

CAS—Calibrated air speed (in knots); also, close air support

Cell(s)—Cellular unit(s); unit(s) of airborne military aircraft, usually bombers and/or tankers, made up of a number of individually organized cells or teams which may operate independently of one another to provide flexibility

Centerline tank—A fuel tank carried externally on the centerline of the aircraft

Chaff—A type of confusion reflector, which consists of thin, narrow metallic strips of various lengths to provide different responses, used to create false signals on radar scopes

Chandelle—A maximum performance climbing turn in which speed is converted to altitude while reversing direction

Chatter (radio)—Multiple communications on the same radio frequency, usually applied to communications which are of little interest to the individual using the term

Christmas truce—Period from 25 Dec 1965 to 30 Jan 1966, when bombing of North Vietnam was halted

Close—To decrease separation between aircraft

Closure—Relative closing velocity

Cloud Nine—Slang term referring to a feeling of elation or haziness

Col—Colonel

College Eye—Term for USAF EC-121 airborne early warning, intercept control, MIG warning, and vectoring aircraft from Mar 1967 to Dec 1968 (See Big Eye; Disco)

Combat-spread—A loose formation which affords each flight member the opportunity for maximum visual look-out

Constitute—To designate a unit (by name, or number and name) and place it on the inactive list, thus making it available for activation

Cool (ed)(ing)—Employment of a gas for cooling the heat-seeker head of the AIM-4D air-to-air missile in preparation for firing

Cover—The protection given to a surface area or force, or to a force of aircraft in the air, by maintaining fighter aircraft in the air to repel or divert attack, especially air attack; also, the aircraft providing, or designated to provide, the protection

Cpt—Captain

CR—Credit, or aerial victory credit

Cross-turn—A rapid, simultaneous 180° change of heading by the members of an element or flight, in which half of the unit turns toward the other half

Cut-off (tactic)—Employing the shortest route to intercept an enemy airborne target

Deck—A flight altitude just above the surface, as used in such phrases as "to hit the deck," "to fly on the deck," and "to dive toward the deck"

Defensive spiral—A descending, accelerating dive using high-G and continuous roll to negate an attack and to gain lateral separation

Defensive split—A controlled separation of a target element into different planes, used in an attempt to force the interceptors to commit themselves to one of the members of the target element

Defensive turn—A basic defensive maneuver designed to prevent a attacker from achieving a launch or firing position; the intensity of the turn is determined by the angle-off, range and closure of the attacking aircraft

Demobilize—To withdraw all personnel from an organized unit and withdraw the unit's designation, thereby terminating the unit's existence

Deploy—To relocate forces to desired areas of operation

DF—Direction finding

Disband—To withdraw the designation of an inactive unit, or withdraw all personnel and the designation of an active or organized unit, thereby terminating the unit's existence

Disco—Radio call sign for College Eye, the EC-121 aircraft which provided airborne navigational assistance, border warnings, and MIG warnings

Discontinue—To withdraw all personnel of an organized unit

Disengage—To break off combat with the enemy

DME—Distance measuring equipment

DMZ—Demilitarized zone

Dogfight—An aerial battle, especially between opposing fighters, involving considerable maneuvering and violent aerobatics on both sides

Dot—Electronic dot appearing on the radar scope when radar is locked on, providing computed steering vectoring information (See Aim-dot; Steering-dot.)

EB-66—A light reconnaissance bomber which has several configurations for gathering electronic intelligence data or for radiating jamming to provide protection for strike forces

Echelon—A formation in which flight members are positioned sequentially on one side of the lead aircraft

ECM—Electronic countermeasures: the prevention or reduction of effectiveness in enemy equipment and tactics used by electromagnetic radiations; some activities exploit the enemy's emissions of these radiations

ECM pod—Pylon or fuselage-mounted container which houses multiple transmitters and associated electronic devices; a self-protection device for aircraft penetrating an electronically-controlled ground-to-air defense system

Element—USAF term for the basic fighting unit (two aircraft)

Encounter—A series of time-continuous actions between specific US and enemy (or bogey) aircraft

Engagement—An encounter which involves hostile, or aggressive action by one or more of the participants

Envelope—A volume of airspace within which a particular weapon or weapon system must operate, be expended, or be employed in order to achieve maximum effectiveness; also field of maneuver (See p. 160)

EWO—Electronic warfare officer

FAC—Forward air controller

Faceplate—North Atlantic Treaty Organization designator for early models of the MIG–21

Falcon—Nickname for the AIM–4 air-to-air missile, passive IR type

Farmer—North Atlantic Treaty Organization designator for the MIG–19

Fast CAP—Combat air patrol for strike aircraft, particularly fighters, as opposed to slow CAP

Fast-FAC—A forward air controller in an F–4 or other fighter aircraft

FCS—Fire control system

Fighting Wing—A formation by which the wingman can provide optimum coverage and maintain maneuverability during maximum performance maneuvers

Finger-four—(See Fingertip)

Fingertip—A four-aircraft formation in which the aircraft occupy positions suggested by the four fingertips of either hand, the fingers being held together in a horizontal plane

1st Lt (or 1Lt)—First Lieutenant

Fishbed—North Atlantic Treaty Organization designator for later models of the MIG–21

Flak—Antiaircraft shrapnel

Flak envelope—A varying vertical unit of airspace in which a particular type of AAA is effective (See Envelope)

Flame(d) out—The extinguishment of the flame in a reaction engine, especially a jet engine

Flight—USAF term for a tactical fighter unit, usually consisting of two elements, each element of two aircraft

Flight integrity—Aircraft maneuvering in relation to, and in support of, one another

Fluid element—The second or supporting element in a fluid-four formation, flying in a high or low element position

Fluid-four—A tactical formation having the second element spread in both the vertical and horizontal planes to enhance maneuverability, mutual support and look-out ability (See p.165)

FORCAP—Force combat air patrol: patrol of fighters maintained over the task force to destroy enemy aircraft which might threaten the force (See CAP)

Frag—(See Frag Order)

Fragged—Mission directed by fragmentary operational order from higher headquarters

Frag Order—A fragmentary operations order; the daily supplement to standard operations orders governing the conduct of the air war in Southeast Asia; directs a specific military mission

Freedom Train—Nickname for JCS-directed USAF strikes against targets in North Vietnam as far as 20° N latitude during the period 6 Apr–7 May 1972; replaced by Linebacker I

Fresco—North Atlantic Treaty Organization designator for the MIG–17

Friendl(ies)(y)—Aircraft belong to, or held by, one's own forces or the forces of an allied nation

Front—The individual in the front seat of the F–4; the aircraft commander

Ftr—Abbreviation for fighter

G—Unit of acceleration (32.2 ft/sec^2): unit of force applied to a body at rest equal to the force exerted on it by gravity

G—Gunner; or specifically in this work, a B–52 gunner

Gaggle—Slang term for a number of aircraft operating in close proximity but not necessarily in any semblance of formation

Gate—To fly at maximum possible speed or power (full afterburner power); also refers to Range Gate, an indication on F–4 radar of the distance between the target and the interceptor

GCA—Ground-controlled approach

GCI—Ground-controlled intercept

Gen—Abbreviation for General, often in combination with other abbreviations for different levels, e.g., Brig (Brigadier) Gen, Maj Gen, or Lt Gen

GIB—"Guy in Back;" the backseat crew member in fighter aircraft (See Back)

G-load—The force exerted upon a pilot (and his aircraft) by gravity or a reaction to acceleration or deceleration as in a change of direction (maneuvering)

Growl—(See Missile tone)

Guard—Emergency UHF radio channel usually monitored by all aircraft and ground stations as a secondary frequency, in addition to primary tactical frequencies

Guide—With respect to an air-to-air missile: to follow the course intended when fired

Hard turn—A planned turn in which the intensity of the turn is governed by the angle-off and range of the attacking aircraft

Heat—Armament switch setting for using infrared missiles

HEI—High explosive incendiary

High-G—Status of having the G-load increased during aircraft maneuvering

Home(d)—Of a missile: to direct itself toward the target by guiding on heat waves, radar, echoes, radio waves, or other radiation emanating from the target

Home plate—Nickname for base of origin

Hos(ed) (ing)—To direct an intense stream of gunfire toward the target, sometimes by pulling lead and allowing the enemy aircraft to fly into it

H-time—Hotel time; i.e., Zulu time plus 8 hours (See Z-time)

Hunter-Killer—An Iron Hand mission against targets of opportunity, flown by a flight of two specially equipped F–105's and two F–4's; (Earlier in the air war, flown by one F–105 and three F–4's, and called SAM Strike teams)

IAS—Indicated air speed

ID—Identification

IFF—Identification, friend or foe; aircraft transponding beacon receiving radar information distinguishing friend from foe

Immelmann—Maneuver in which the aircraft completes the first half of a loop and then rolls over to an upright position, thus changing direction 180° with a simultaneous gain in altitude (See p. 165)

Inactivate—1922–1959: To withdraw all personnel from an active unit and place the unit on the inactive list. 1960–: To transfer a discontinued unit from the active to the inactive list

Interlocks switch—A 2-position ("in" and "out") switch on the F–4 front cockpit missile control panel; "in" position prevents AIM–7's from firing until the FCS computer parameters are met

IP—Initial point; a well-defined point, usually distinguishable visually and/or by radar, used as a starting point for a bomb run to a target or for other tactical purposes, such as air refueling

IR—Infrared

IR missile—An infrared (heat-seeking) missile

Iron Hand—Nickname for a flight with special ordnance and avionics equipment, with a mission of seeking and destroying enemy SAM sites and radar-controlled AAA sites

JCS—Joint Chiefs of Staff

JCS target—A target appearing on the JCS target list

Jink (ed) (ing)—Constant maneuvering in both the horizontal and vertical planes to present a difficult target to enemy defenses by spoiling the tracking solution; a simultaneous change in bank, pitch, and velocity—at random

Joker—A term for fuel planning information: a particular fuel level usually selected to warn that bingo is approaching and further engagements should be avoided

Judy—Term used to indicate that the interceptor has contact with the target and is assuming control of the engagement

KCAS—Knots calibrated air speed

KIAS—Knots indicated air speed

Kill—An enemy airplane shot down or otherwise destroyed by military action while in flight

Kt—Knot (one nautical mile per hour)

KTAS—Knots true air speed

Lead—The lead aircraft in a flight or element, or the lead element of a flight; also a reference to a specific lead aircraft or its pilot

Lead angle—The angle between the line of sight to a moving target and the line of sight to the predicted position of the target at the time the projectile intercepts the target

Lead-pursuit curve—The path followed by an attacking aircraft when its guns are continually aimed so that the bullets will strike the target aircraft (i.e., leading the target)

Lethal envelope—The envelope within which parameters can be met for successful employment of a munition by a particular weapon system (See Envelope)

LGB—Laser-guided bomb

Linebacker—A series of JCS-directed USAF strikes against targets in North Vietnam; Linebacker I began 9 May 1972 and ended 22 Oct 1972; Linebacker II ran from 18 to 29 Dec 1972

Lock-on (lock-up)—To follow a target automatically in one or more dimensions (e.g., range, bearing, elevation) by means of a radar beam

Loose deuce—A term to describe fighter tactics in which two to four aircraft maneuver to provide mutual support and increased firepower

LtC—Lieutenant Colonel

LtCdr—Lieutenant Commander

Lufberry Circle—A circular tail chase, ascending or descending

M—Mach

Mach—The ratio of the aircraft's velocity to the velocity of sound in the surrounding medium

Maj—Major

Maximum power—Afterburner power

Maximum turn-rate—Turn rate at which the maximum number of degrees per second is achieved

mi—Mile

MIG—The name for the Mikoyan/Gurevich series of Soviet jet fighter aircraft

MIGCAP (or MIG cap)—Combat air patrol directed specifically against MIG aircraft (See CAP)

MIGSCREEN (or MIG Screen)—Mission wherein protection of a strike force is provided by placing fighters between the threat (MIG's) and the protected force in a specific area

mil—Milliradian; one mil=0.0573 degrees; one degree=17.45 mils; about one foot at 1,000 feet

Military power—Maximum unaugmented (no afterburner) thrust of the aircraft engine

Missile free—Authority to fire missiles unless a target is identified as friendly

Missile tone—Audio signal indicating an AIM–9 is locked on to an infrared source

mm—Millimeter, as in 20-mm

MR—Military Region; the Republic of Vietnam was divided into four military regions

M–61—Vulcan 20-mm cannon used on the F–105 and F–4 aircraft, either by itself or incorporated into SUU–16 or SUU–23 gun pods

M/Sgt-Master Sergeant

MSL—Mean sea level; used as a reference for altitude

Narrow Gate—Mode which can be selected on a radar missile which will allow it to home only on targets with a selected range of "rate of closure"

NAVAIDS—Navigational aids

Negative G—A G-force exerted upon the human body as a result of footward acceleration

Night Owl—Night strike mission(s)

NM (or nm)—Nautical mile: 6,076.1 feet

Noise—Unwanted sound or disturbances found in or introduced into a communication system, or appearing on a radar scope

NVN—North Vietnam

NVNAF—North Vietnamese Air Force

Orbit—A circular or elliptical pattern flown by aircraft to remain in a specified area

Organize—1913–1922: To designate a unit and bring it into

physical existence by assignment of personnel; 1960–: To bring an active unit into physical existence by assignment of personnel

Overshoot—To pass through the defender's flight path in the plane of symmetry

Overtake velocity—Sudden gain in speed to come up on another aircraft

P—Pilot

PACAF—Pacific Air Forces

Padlocked—Term meaning that a crew member has sighted bogies or bandits and has his vision fixed on them; looking away would risk losing visual contact

Pave Knife—Nickname for F–4's equipped for laser-guided bombing

Phantom—Nickname for F-4 type aircraft

Pip—(See Blip)

Pipper—A 2-mil diameter dot in the center of the optical sight reticle (gunsight)—a dot of light within a lighted ring—used for aiming

PIRAZ—Positive Identification Radar Advisory Zone

Pk—Probability of kill

Pod—Any one of several aerodynamically configured subsystems carried externally on fighter aircraft

Pod formation—A formation of two or more aircraft flown in such a way that ECM pods installed on each aircraft offer mutual and maximum protection

POL—Petroleum, oil, and lubricants

Pop-up—A climbing maneuver from a low-altitude position or other position of concealment, used to gain an advantageous position for weapons delivery; also a maneuver used by enemy aircraft which involved a steep climb from a low-altitude area of concealment to an inbound aircraft or flight of aircraft (See p. 167)

"Powdered"—Destroyed; caused it to disintegrate (with respect to aircraft)

PRF—Pulse recurrence frequency

Pulling lead—Act of aiming the nose of the aircraft ahead of an enemy aircraft; used primarily in a weapons firing maneuver

Pull-up—An act or instance of pulling up; a pullout, or recovery from a dive; to bring the nose of an aircraft up sharply, especially from a level attitude

Pylon—A projection under an aircraft's wing, designed for suspending ordnance, fuel tanks or pods

QRC–160—Quick reaction capability noise jamming ECM pod, developed to counter new radar threats

Radar (position)—One of three switch positions on the F-4 front cockpit missile control panel; used to select radar-guided missile (AIM-7's) as ordnance to be fired

Radar signature—Characteristics peculiar to different aircraft which are distinguishable when displayed on a radar scope

Range-analog bar—A part of the F-4 optical sight reticle which indicates the radar range to the target; does not appear on the reticle until a full-system lock-on has been achieved

Rd(s)—Round(s) (of ammunition)

Ready light—Light indicating a particular avionics/munitions system is operating and ready for use

Recce—Reconnaissance

Recon—Reconnaissance

Reconstitute—To return a demobilized or disbanded unit to the inactive list, thereby making it available for activation

Red—Term referring to the enemy, i.e., "Red" (Communist) North Vietnam

Red Crown—Voice call sign for the radar-equipped USS *Long Beach* (CLN–9), the USN's PIRAZ ship, stationed in the northern part of the Gulf of Tonkin, which performed GCI functions

Redesignate—To change the designation (name or name and number) of a unit

RESCAP—Rescue combat air patrol (See CAP)

Reticle—Optical sight reticle; a system of lines around a dot (pipper) in the focus of an optical gunsight that provides a reference for aiming and estimating range and distance to the target

RHAW—Radar homing and warning; on-board aircraft equipment to warn pilot of active enemy defenses

Ripple fire—Rapid sequential firing of two or more missiles

Rivet Top—Nickname for experimental EC-121M aircraft tested in SEA beginning in Aug 1967; equipped with advanced airborne radar

R-max—Maximum range

Roger—Term meaning "Message received and understood"

Rolling Thunder—Nickname for JCS-directed USAF air strikes against targets in North Vietnam; began as gradual reprisals rather than hard-hitting military campaigns, but gradually escalated into major air strikes as the war continued; phases of Rolling Thunder: Phase I, 2 Mar–11 May 1965; Phase II, 18 May–24 Dec 1965; Phase III, 31 Jan–31 Mar 1966; Phase IV, 1 Apr–24 Dec 1966; Phase V, 14 Feb–24 Dec 1967; and Phase VI, 3 Jan–1 Nov 1968

Rollout—Termination of a maneuver, or series of maneuvers, designed to place an aircraft in a position which would most optimally assure completion of the intended activity, e.g., airborne intercept, instrument approach

Route Package—One of seven geographical divisions of North Vietnam assigned for air strike targeting (RP 1 through 5, 6A, and 6B); Roman numerals sometimes used rather than arabic, such as RP–6A (See map, p. 9)

RP—(See Route Package)

RTAFB—Royal Thai Air Force Base

RTB—Return (ed) to base

Rudder reversal—A roll reversal using rudder only; normally used in maximum performance, high angle of attack maneuvering

RVN—Republic of Vietnam (South Vietnam)

RVNAF—Republic of Vietnam Air Force

SAM—Surface-to-air missile

Sandwich—Situation wherein an aircraft is positioned between two opposing aircraft

SAR—Search and rescue

SARCAP—Search and rescue combat air patrol, used to cover rescue operations; later changed to RESCAP (See CAP)

SA-2—Soviet-built surface-to-air missile system

Scissors—A defensive maneuver in which a series of turn reversals are executed in an attempt to achieve the offensive after an overshoot by the attacker (See p. 165)

SEA—Southeast Asia

2 AD—2nd Air Division

Separation—The distance between the interceptor and the target aircraft; can be lateral, longitudinal, or vertical

Separation maneuver—An energy-gaining maneuver performed with a low angle of attack and maximum thrust, to increase separation (extend) or decrease separation (close)

Shrike—Nickname for the AGM-45 air-to-ground radar-seeking missile

Sidewinder—(See AIM-9)

Sidewinder tone—(See Missile tone)

SIF—Selective identification feature; an electronic device with variable codes for identification

"S"-ing—Performing a series of "S" turns

Six—Six (6) o'clock position or area; refers to the rear or aft area of an aircraft

Slice(d)—A maximum performance, hard, descending, nose-low turn with more than 90° of bank

Slow CAP—Combat air patrol for slower aircraft such as the B-66, B-52 or EC-121, as opposed to fast CAP

"S" maneuver—A weave in a horizontal plane

Snap-roll(ed)—An aerial maneuver in which an aircraft is made to effect a quick, complete roll about its longitudinal axis; the act of putting an aircraft into a snap-roll

Snap-up—A rapid pull-up to establish a climb and gain altitude in order to launch a weapon against an enemy aircraft at a higher altitude.

Sparrow—(See AIM-7)

"S" Pattern—(See "S" maneuver)

Speedbrakes—Flaps designed for slowing down an aircraft in flight

Splash—Term meaning that destruction of the target has been verified by visual or radar means

Split-plane maneuvering—Aircraft or elements maneuvering in relation to one another, but in different planes and/or altitudes; for example, the defensive split

Split-S—180° rotation about the aircraft's longitudinal axis followed by a 180° change of heading in a vertical plane (a half loop starting from the top) (See p. 165)

Squawk—Term meaning to turn the IFF master control switch to "normal" position so that the IFF can respond to interrogation

SSgt—Staff Sergeant

Standard Arm—Nickname for the AGM-78 air-to-ground missile, anti-radiation type

Standdown—Term meaning that an aircraft stays out of the air, or refrains from air operations, for any number of valid reasons

Steering dot—(See Dot)

Stratofortress—Nickname for the B-52

Streamer(ed)—A parachute that does not open fully when deployed, but streams or trails backward

Strike—An attack upon a surface target, intended to inflict damage on or to destroy an enemy objective

Strike/CAP—Aircraft fragged for a primary strike role with a secondary air defense role; these aircraft are permitted to jettison strike ordnance and engage enemy aircraft only if they come under direct attack.

"S" turn—A turn to one side of a reference heading followed by a turn to the other side; provides a difficult tracking problem for ground radars

SUU-16—Gun pod containing the M-61 Vulcan 20-mm cannon used on F-4C aircraft

SUU-23—Gun pod containing the M-61 Vulcan 20-mm cannon used on F-4D aircraft

SW—Strategic Wing

Sweep—An offensive mission by several fighter aircraft, sometimes accompanied by fighter-bombers, over a particular area of enemy territory for the purpose of seeking out and attacking enemy aircraft or targets of opportunity; the action of flying over an area in making a search; the path flown in making a search; to clear the skies or other places of opposition

TAC—Tactical Air Command

Tac—Tactical

Tacair—Tactical air

TACAN—Tactical air navigation; an active electronic navigational system which locates the aircraft with respect to another installation

Tally-ho—Term meaning that the target has been visually sighted

TAS—True air speed (in knots)

TCA—Track-crossing angle; the angle between flight paths measured from the tail of the reference aircraft

TDY—Temporary duty; the status of being on TDY

Tet—Vietnamese lunar New Year

TFS—Tactical fighter squadron

TFW—Tactical fighter wing

Thud—Nickname for the F-105

Thud Ridge—Nickname for a mountain range beginning about 20 NM north-northwest of Hanoi and extending about 25 NM northwest, used for navigational and terrain masking; located in RP-6A (See map, p. 48)

Thunderchief—Nickname for the F-105

Tone—(See Missile tone)

Top Cover—(See Cover)

TOT—Time over target

Tracking—Term referring to the maintaining of the center of the field of view of search radars or airborne sensors on a target

Trail formation—Aircraft directly behind one another

Troll(ed)(ing)—Flying a random pattern by ECM aircraft to detect enemy electronic signals; flying a pattern in a specific area to detect signals of a suspected SAM or AAA site

TRW—Tactical reconnaissance wing

T/Sgt—Technical Sergeant

Tuck-under—A tendency of certain aircraft to drop its nose when flying at or near its critical mach number

Turn radius—A radial distance required to effect a 180° turn which varies according to the aircraft's speed and altitude

UHF-DF—Ultra high frequency direction finder

Unk—Unknown

Unload(ed)(ing)—To reduce the angle of attack (thus, the G-load) on an aircraft, primarily for the purpose of gaining speed

US—United States (of America)
USAF—United States Air Force
USMC—United States Marine Corps
USN—United States Navy
USSR—Union of Soviet Socialist Republics
Vc—Relative closing velocity; closure
Vector—A command which directs an aircraft to follow a specific heading
Vertical rolling scissors—A defensive, rolling maneuver in the vertical plane executed in an attempt to achieve an offensive position on the attacker (See p. 167)
VFR—Visual flight rules
VID—Visual identification
Wagon Wheel—(See Wheel)
Walleye—Nickname for the AGM-62 air-to-ground missile, anti-materiel type
Weapons system—Refers to the combination of aicraft, crew, ordnance, avionics, etc.
Weave—A formation in which the two elements of a flight or the two members of an element continuously cross each other's flight path, normally in the horizontal plane, to increase their visual coverage of each other's rear area; also provides a difficult tracking problem for ground radars
Wheel—Wagon Wheel or Cartwheel; an enemy defensive formation in which two or more aircraft circle in the horizontal plane while covering each other's rear area against attack (See p. 170)
Whifferdill—A maneuver used to change direction 180°. The nose is raised 30 to 60 degrees, then 90 degrees of bank is used to reverse direction of flight and to pull the nose down below the horizon
Wild Weasel—F-100F/F-105F aircraft equipped with RHAW and anti-radiation missiles, enabling them to home on SA-2 radar guidance signals and to mark the location of missile sites
Winchester—Term indicating that all ordnance has been expended
Wingman—Pilot (or aircraft) who flies at the side and to the rear of an element leader. In an aircraft flight, 02 is wingman to lead (01), and 04 is wingman to 03. Usually, more experienced pilots fly the lead and 03 positions in a flight, and these pilots initiate combat actions while their wingmen fly cover
WSO—Weapon systems officer; backseater in the F-4
Yaw—Rotation of an aircraft about its vertical axis so as to cause the longitudinal axis of the aircraft to deviate from the line of flight
Yo-Yo, High-Speed—An offensive tactic in which the attacker maneuvers through both vertical and horizontal planes to prevent an overshoot in the plane of the defender's turn (See p. 167)
Yo-Yo, Low-Speed—A dive for air speed and a pull-up for position closure or extension; also called an acceleration maneuver (See p. 167)
Zoom—An unloaded climb used to gain maximum altitude while dissipating minimum energy
Z-time—Zulu time; a term for Greenwich mean time.
Zulu—(See Z-time)

Index*

Aces
  crediting system: v–vi, 22
  first: vi, 20, 102–111
  ranking: 93
  U.S. Navy: vi
Advisors, assignment: 1
Aerial photography. See Reconnaissance operations
Aerospace Division, 818th: 143
Air Commands
  Strategic: 4, 16, 112
  Tactical: 143, 146–154, 155
Air crews, proficiency: 19–20
Air Defense Command: 4
Air defenses. See Antiaircraft defenses and weapons; Missiles; Radar systems
Air Divisions:
  2d: 22, 25–26, 118, 127–128, 132, 136, 142–143, 146, 152
  41st: 146
  831st: 142
  832d: 144
  835th: 142, 148
Air Forces
  Pacific: v, 3, 94, 141–146
  Seventh: v–vi, 12, 14–16, 35, 64, 66, 68, 73, 78, 96, 102, 109, 115, 142–144, 152
  Eighth: 142
  Thirteenth: 142, 144, 146, 148, 154
Air operations, vi, 1, 3–4
  advantages, USAF: 85
  advantages, enemy: 48, 85
  air-to-ground missions: 155
  bombing operations. See Bombing operations
  characteristics of combat: 160–161
  close-support missions: 155
  commencement: 19
  counter-air missions: 15
  enemy, general: 7, 22, 35–42, 83
  fighter operations. See Fighter operations
  first double kill: 44
  first kills: vi, 22–28, 90, 94
  first mission: 19
  first night action: 85
  first quadruple kill: 60
  formations. See Formations and maneuvers, combat
  gunners, kills by: 111–115, 117
  hunter-killer missions: 103, 108
  inertial-guidance system: 155
  instrument flight control: 155
  interdiction missions: 155
  kills distribution: 117–140, 155–157
  kills ratios: vi, 101, 160–161
  last kills: 115, 117
  limitations on: 7, 35, 48, 80, 117
  maintenance, supply and support forces: vi, 19–20, 37
  maneuvers, combat. See Formations and maneuvers, combat
  reconnaissance missions: vi, 4–5, 13–14, 43, 62, 68, 83, 101
  search-and-rescue missions, vi, 14, 30, 47, 51, 105
  sorties, number flown: 10, 17
  superiority, definition and attainment: 1
  support missions. See Escort and patrol missions
  suspensions and resumptions: 20–27, 44–45, 64–66, 80–85, 88–89, 97, 101, 111, 115
  tactics. See Tactics
  teamwork, importance in: 103, 110
Air speed, advances in: 19
Air superiority, definition and attainment: 1
Air-to-ground missions: 155
Air units, organizations, assignment and operations: 141–154
Aircraft carriers: 90
Aircraft types
  armament. See Armament, aircraft
  capabilities and deficiencies: 55, 155
  characteristics: 155–156
  characteristics, enemy: 157–160
  losses: 5, 7, 12, 14, 16–17, 19, 26, 32, 34, 48, 51, 64–66, 68–72, 74–76, 80, 84, 87–92, 94–97, 100–101, 105, 111
  losses, enemy: 5, 7–8, 11–12, 14, 16–17, 19, 26–27, 29–35, 38–73, 85–115, 117, 141–154, 160
  models employed: 155
  ranges: 155–156
  ranges, enemy: 160

*Photo captions are annotated pc.

179

speeds: 19, 155–156
A–1: 47
A–7: 16
B–17: 156
B–29: 111
B–52: 4, 14, 16–17, 85, 90, 111–115, 117, 125, 135, 138, 155–157
EB–66: 4, 7–8, 16, 30, 35, 37–42, 58, 72, 85, 91
EC–121: 4, 7, 12, 14, 16, 91
F–4: vi, 4–5, 7–12, 14–16, 29–44, 48–80, 84–111, 117–141, 155–158
F–5: 12
F–8: 19
F–100: 4, 7
F–104: 37–42
F–105: 4–5, 7–8, 11–12, 14, 16, 19, 22, 26–27, 29–44, 46–80, 94, 103, 108, 117–141, 155–158
F–111: 16
KC–135: 37
MIG: v–vi, 3–4, 7–16, 20–27, 35–42
MIG–15: 13, 19, 26, 52–53, 68, 83, 157
MIG–17: 7–10, 13, 19, 24, 26–27, 30–35, 44–48, 50–80, 83, 94, 117–140, 155–157, 159, 170
MIG–19: 13, 83, 90, 94–96, 103–111, 118, 123–124, 127, 129–134, 138, 155–157, 160
MIG–21: 7–14, 26, 28–29, 35, 38–49, 52–53, 57–58, 61–62, 65–80, 83, 85, 88–89, 91–115, 117–140, 155–157, 160
RB–66: 28
RC–121: 37
RF–4: 43
RF–101: 83
Aircraft warning systems. *See* Ground control intercept systems; Radar systems
Airfields, enemy (*see also by name*)
 construction and repair: 83
 strikes against: 11–12, 16, 106, 111
Anderson, Harold: 22–25, 26 pc
Anderson, Robert D.: 48–49 pc, 119, 127
Anderson, Ronald C.: 22, 25, 26 pc, 118, 127
Anderson, Wilbure E.: 22, 25, 26 pc
Antiaircraft defenses and weapons, enemy: vi, 4, 10, 13–14, 16–17, 19, 26, 43–44, 48–49, 61–62, 66, 68–71, 75, 80, 83, 88, 96, 105, 189. *See also* Missiles
Armament, aircraft
 bomb loads: 155–156
 bomb loads, enemy: 157
 caliber .50 guns: 155, 157
 computers in: 155–156
 enemy weapons: 157–160
 fire-control systems: 155
 high-explosive incendiary: 68, 105
 kills distribution: 157
 laser-guided bombs: 14, 16, 101
 missiles. *See* Missiles
 radars. *See* Radar systems
 rocket clusters: 7, 155
 rockets, enemy: 157, 160
 SUU–16 gun pod: 55, 60–61, 72, 77–79, 110, 150

 SUU–23 gun pod: 156, 158
 20–mm. guns: 10, 53, 55–57, 60, 62–63, 66, 71, 74–75, 79, 94–96, 104–105, 108, 118–140, 155, 157–158
 Vulcan gun: 53, 125
Aronoff, Joel S.: 77
Armor assaults, enemy: 14
Atlanta call sign: 129
Auto-acquisition of target: 102–103, 105
Autrey, Daniel L.: 105, 124, 127
Awards. *See* Decorations and awards

Bac Giang: 27, 29, 50, 62, 75
Bac Le: 58
Bac Mai: 13
Baily, Carl G.: 99–100, 100 pc, 123–124, 127
Baker, Doyle D., USMC: 72, 121, 127
Bakke, Samuel O.: 57, 120, 127
Ballot call sign: 129, 133
Balter call sign: 127, 132, 137
Barrel roll attack: 167
Barry, Phineas T.: 158 pc
Barton, Charles D.: 108, 125, 127
Basco call sign: 128, 130, 134–135
Basel, Gene I.: 69–71, 71 pc, 121, 127
Battista, Robert B.: 77, 122, 127
Beatty, James M.: 94–95, 123, 127
Beckers, Lyle L.: 94–95, 105, 123–124, 127
Bell, James R.: 94, 123, 127
Bettine, Frank J.: 102, 124, 127
Bever, Michael R.: 54, 120, 127
Bien Hoa Air Base: 149
Big Eye radar: 4, 22
Binh Long province: 14
Binkley, Eldon D.: 112, 125, 127
Bison call sign: 127
Black River: 73, 98
Blake, Robert E.: 27, 28 pc, 118, 127
Bland, David F.: 109
Blank, Kenneth T.: 32, 118, 128
Bleakley, Robert A.: 29, 30 pc, 118, 128
Bodenhamer, Howard L.: 47–48
Bogoslofski, Bernard J.: 75, 122, 128
Bokshar, William B.: 158 pc
Boles, Robert H.: 77, 122, 128
Bolo operations: 11, 35–42
Bomb loads: 155–156
Bomb loads, enemy: 157
Bombing operations: 3–14, 16–17, 27, 29, 31–35, 44–45, 48–80, 85, 88, 89–115, 117, 155–156. *See also* Close air support
Bombing operations, enemy: 13
Bongartz, Theodore R.: 68, 121, 128
Borchik, Albert S., Jr.: 75
Brenda call sign: 131, 133, 137
Brestel, Max C.: vi, 44–45, 119, 128
Bridges, strikes against: 5, 19, 27, 29, 32–34, 62, 69, 72–73, 75, 96, 102, 105
Broadcast stations, strikes against: 16, 111
Brown, Frederick W.: 110–111, 125, 128

180

Brown call sign: 138
Brunson, Cecil H.: 108, 125, 128
Brunson, James E.: 113, 125, 128
Bucket call sign: 127, 137
Buick call sign: 20–22, 127–129, 131, 133, 135–136
Buffer zones: 5, 7, 11
Burgess, Ray M.: 78–79
Burr, Daniel S.: 58
Buttell, Duane A., Jr.: 31–32, 32 pc, 118, 128
Buttrey, Ronald W.: 104 pc

Cactus call sign: 135, 137
Cadillac call sign: 127, 130
Cahill, Robert V.: 78
Cairns, Douglas B.: 64
Call signs
    Atlanta: 129
    Ballot: 129, 133
    Balter: 127, 132, 137
    Basco: 128, 130, 134–135
    Bison: 127
    Brenda: 131, 133, 137
    Brown: 138
    Bucket: 127, 137
    Buick: 20–22, 127–129, 131, 133, 135–136
    Cactus: 135, 137
    Cadillac: 127, 130
    Chevrolet: 129–130
    Chevy: 128, 131, 134, 138
    Chicago: 49, 127, 133, 135, 139
    Crab: 131, 135, 137, 139
    Crafty: 132–133
    Crossbow: 53, 137–138
    Date: 134, 137
    Dodge: 130, 136
    Drill: 52, 131, 136
    Eagle: 127–129, 134, 138
    Elgin: 58, 127, 129, 132–133, 136, 138–139
    Falcon: 132–134
    Finch: 127, 131, 136
    Flamingo: 133, 135
    Ford: 38, 40, 129, 131, 133–134, 136, 139
    Galore: 129, 132
    Gambit: 127, 131–132, 136
    Gopher: 127, 130, 133, 135
    Hambone: 133, 139
    Harlow: 129–130
    Harpoon: 127, 131, 133, 138
    Honda: 128
    Icebag: 135–136
    Iceman: 128, 131
    Kangaroo: 128
    Killer: 130, 139
    Kimona: 137
    Kingfish: 132, 138
    Lark: 132, 136
    Leech: 136
    List: 130, 134
    Nash: 132, 134–135, 138
    Nitro: 132, 138
    Oakland: 135
    Olds: 128–131, 134–139
    Opal: 133, 136, 138
    Otter: 129–131, 137, 139
    Oyster: 129–130, 133–134, 136
    Panda: 47–48, 130
    Papa: 135, 138
    Parrot: 129, 132
    Paula: 129, 136
    Pistol: 127, 132, 137, 139
    Rambler: 128–131, 137
    Random: 135–136
    Rattler: 50, 133
    Robin: 129, 134, 137, 139
    Ruby: 135
    Sapphire: 134, 137
    Snug: 127, 130
    Speedo: 129, 131, 138
    Spitfire: 131
    Stinger: 129, 138
    Tampa: 128–129, 132, 135, 138
    Unknown: 127–134, 136–138
    Vega: 20–22, 134–135, 139
    Wander: 138–139
    Wildcat: 136
Cam Pha: 108
Cam Ranh Bay Air Base: 158
Cambodia: 1, 14
Cameron, Max F.: 27, 28 pc, 118, 128
Canal des Rapides: 69
Cannon Air Force Base, N.M.: 153
Cao Nung: 77
Carroll, R.: 87
Cary, Lawrence E.: 41–42, 42 pc, 119, 128
Cat Bi airfield: 37
Catton, Ronald E.: 54
Cease-fire declared: 115
Chap Le: 13
Cherry, Edward D.: 89, 123, 128
Chevrolet call sign: 129–130
Chevy call sign: 128, 131, 134, 138
Chicago call sign: 49, 127, 133, 135, 139
Chief of Staff, U.S. Air Force. *See* McConnell, John P.; Ryan, John D.
China, Communist. *See* People's Republic of China
Christiansen, Von R.: 97–98, 123, 128
Christmas truces: 7, 11–12
Chute, Clarence W.: 114
Clark, Arthur C.: 22, 25, 26 pc, 118, 128
Clark Air Force Base, Philippines: 151, 153
Clements, Donald F.: 158 pc
Cleveland, Edward Y.: 103
Clifton, Charles C.: 38, 119, 128
Close-support missions: *See also* Bombing operations; Fighter operations
Clouser, Gordon L.: 108, 125, 129

Coady, Thomas J.: 103
Cobb, Lawrence (Larry) D.: 53, 68–69, 121, 129
Coe, Richard E.: 106, 124, 129
Combat Crew Training Wing, 4453d: 150–151
Combies, Philip P.: 40–41, 60, 60 pc, 119, 121, 129
Computers, combat use: 155–156
Cooney, James P.: 94, 123, 129
Couch, Charles W.: 53, 120, 129
Counter-air missions: 155
Crab call sign: 131, 135, 137, 139
Crafty call sign: 132–133
Craig, James T., Jr.: 56 pc, 56–57, 120, 129
Crane, Dale A.: 89
Crews, Barton P.: 90, 123, 129
Croker, Stephen B.: 59, 60 pc, 121, 129
Crossbow call sign: 53, 137–138
Crosson, Gerald J., Jr.: 78
Cunningham, Randy: vi

Da Nang: 28, 35
Da Nang Air Base: 143–144, 146–147, 151, 153, 158
Dai Loi: 67, 73
Dalecky, William J.: 105
Dalton, William M.: 73–74, 122, 129
Dap Cau: 32–34, 76
Date call sign: 134, 137
Davis-Monthan Air Force Base, Ariz.: 149–151
Dawson, Leland: 32 pc
DeBellevue, Charles B.: vi, 20–22, 93, 98–100, 100 pc, 103–105, 104 pc, 105 pc, 123–124, 129
Deception. See Ruses, application of
Decorations and awards: 26
Demilitarized Zone: 13–14, 87
Democratic People's Republic of Korea. See North Korea
Democratic Republic of Vietnam. See North Vietnam; North Vietnam Air Forces; North Vietnam Army; North Vietnam Navy
DeMuth, Stephen H.: 55–56, 56 pc, 120, 129
Dennis, Arthur F.: 50, 120, 129
Dickey, Roy S.: 35, 119, 129
Diehl, William C.: 109–110, 125, 129
Diem, Ngo Dinh: 1
Dien Bien Phu: 1
Dilger, Robert G.: 51–52, 52 pc, 120, 129
Disco radar: 14, 20–22, 85–87, 98–99, 106, 108
Distinguished Flying Cross awards: 26
Documents, capture and exploitation: 14
Dodge call sign: 130, 136
Dong Dau: 75
Doom Club: 35
Dowell, William B. D.: 29, 29 pc, 118, 129
Drew, Philip M.: 73–74, 122, 130
Drill call sign: 52, 131, 136
Driscoll, William: vi
Dubler, John E.: 114–115, 125, 130
Dudley, Wilbur R.: 30, 118, 130
Dunnegan, Clifton P., Jr.: 41–42, 42 pc, 119, 130
Dutton, Lee R.: 40–41, 119, 130

Eagle call sign: 127–129, 134, 138
Easter offensive, 1972: vi
Eaves, Stephen D.: 93, 123, 130
Eden, Douglas W.: 97
Eglin Air Force Base, Fla.: 146, 148–149
Eisenhower, Dwight D.: 1
Ejections: 46, 65
Electronic countermeasures systems: 4, 11, 14, 16–17, 30, 37, 43, 75, 85, 97, 155–156
Electronic countermeasures systems, enemy: 26
Electronic warfare crews: vi
Elgin call sign: 58, 127, 129, 132–133, 136, 138–139
Enemy aircraft claims evaluation boards: v, 66, 73, 102, 109, 115
Escort and patrol missions: 4, 8, 12, 14–16, 22, 27–32, 35, 37, 43, 47, 51–55, 57–58, 60, 62–80, 85–88, 90–115, 161–165
Escort and patrol missions, enemy: 44
Eskew, William E.: 47, 119, 130
Ettel, Michael J., USN: 101, 124, 130
Evans, Bob C.: 37, 37 pc
Evans, Robert E.: 27, 28 pc, 118, 130

Faison, James E.: 158 pc
Falcon (AIM–4) air-to-air missile: 63–64, 69, 72, 75–77, 79, 122, 127, 129, 131–133, 135–137, 156–157
Falcon call sign: 132–134
Feezel, Tommy L: 93
Feighny, James P., Jr.: 79, 122, 130
Feinstein, Jeffrey S.: vi, 89, 95–96, 99–100, 100 pc, 102, 109, 109 pc, 123, 124, 125, 130
Ferguson, Alonzo L.: 53
Fighter operations: 4, 8–17, 19–73, 85–111. See also Close air support; Napalm strikes; Tactics
Fighter-Interceptor Wing, 51st: 154
Finch call sign: 127, 131, 136
Fire-control systems: 155
Flamingo call sign: 133, 135
Fluid-four formation: 22, 91–92, 97, 165
Ford call sign: 38, 40, 129, 131, 133–134, 136, 139
Formations and maneuvers, combat: 164
  barrel roll attack: 167
  escort and patrol missions: 4, 8, 12, 14–16, 22, 27–32, 35, 37, 43, 47, 51–55, 57–58, 60, 62–80, 85–88, 90–97, 115, 161–165
  escort and patrol missions, enemy: 44
  fluid-four: 22, 91–92, 97, 165
  high- and low-speed yo-yo: 167
  Immelmann turn: 165
  loose-deuce: 24
  Lufbery circle: 45, 47, 170
  pop-up maneuvers: 167–170
  scissors maneuver: 165–167
  split-S: 165
  strike formations: 91–92
  tactics of. See Tactics, combat
  vertical rolling scissors: 167
  wagon wheel: 57, 63, 78, 95, 170
France: 1
Freedom Train operation: 14–16

Frye, Wayne T.: 92, 94, 123, 130
Funk, Carl: 110

Galore call sign: 129, 132
Gambit call sign: 127, 131–132, 136
George Air Force Base, Calif.: 143, 150–152
Gast, Philip C.: 44–45, 53, 120, 130
Geneva conferences: 1
George, S. W.: 27, 28 pc, 118, 130
Gia Lam International Airport: 12, 37, 71–72
Giap, Vo Nguyen: 1, 14
Gilmore, Paul J.: 27–29, 29 pc, 118, 130
Givens, Billy R.: 66
Glynn, Lawrence J.: 41–42, 42 pc, 119, 131
Golberg, Lawrence H.: 30, 31 pc, 118, 131
Gopher call sign: 127, 130, 133, 135
Gordon, William S., III: 68–69, 121, 131
Gossard, Halbert E.: 29, 29 pc, 118, 131
Graham, James L.: 73–74, 122, 131
Green, Stanley C.: 97
Griffin, Thomas M.: 105, 124, 131
Ground control intercept systems: 4, 7, 12, 14, 16, 22, 38, 41, 44, 52, 55, 66, 78, 101
Ground control intercept systems, enemy: 4–5, 7, 12–13, 39, 83, 94
Grond crews. *See* Maintenance, supply and support forces
Guam: 4
Guerrilla operations, enemy: 1–3
Gulf of Tonkin: 3–4, 14, 58–59, 85, 90
Gullick, Francis M.: 63, 121, 131
Gunners, kills by: 111–115, 117

Ha Dong: 55, 60
Ha Gia: 76
Ha Tinh: 10
Haeffner, Fred A.: 54, 120, 131
Haiphong: 6, 10, 12, 16, 83, 88, 111
Hall, John A.: 69
Hall, Richard: 22–24, 26 pc
Hambone call sign: 133, 139
Hamilton, Albert T.: 69
Han Phong causeway: 50
Handley, Philip W.: 96–97, 123, 131
Hanoi: 5, 10, 12, 16, 48–49, 60, 69–71, 75, 88, 90, 94, 96–99, 104, 109, 111, 113
Hanoi Circle: 11
Harden, Kaye M.: 97–98, 123, 131
Hardgrave, Gerald D.: 30, 31 pc, 118, 131
Hardy, Richard F.: 98, 123, 131
Hargrove, James A., Jr.: 55–57, 56 pc, 120, 131
Hargrove, William S.: 104, 106, 124, 131
Harlow call sign: 129–130
Harpoon call sign: 127, 131, 133, 138
Harris, David L.: 87
Harris, Hunter, Jr.: 3, 3 pc
Hartfield, Lonnie J.: 158 pc
Heat-seeking home device: 25
Height finders, enemy: 4

Hendrickson, James L.: 110, 125, 131
Higgins, Harry E.: 50, 120, 131
High- and low-speed yo-yo: 167
Hill, Robert G.: 76–77, 122, 131
Hilliard, Michael A.: 106
Hirsch, Thomas M.: 43, 119, 131
Ho Chi Minh: 1, 3
Ho Chi Minh Trail: 1–3
Hoa Binh: 90
Hoa Lac airfield: 12, 35, 45, 48, 52, 61
Hodgdon, Leigh A.: 85, 122, 132
Holcombe, Kenneth E.: 22–25, 26 pc, 118, 132
Holland, Michael T.: 90
Holloman Air Force Base, N.M.: 144, 151, 153
Holtz, Robert L.: 109–110, 125, 132
Homestead Air Force Base, Fla.: 149, 151
Honda call sign: 128
Host, John F.: 158 pc
Howerton, Rex D.: 79, 122, 132
Howman, Paul D.: 115, 125, 132
Hudson, Sidney B.: 94
Huneke, Bruce V.: 76, 122, 132
Hunt, Jack W.: 47, 119, 132
Hunter, Harris: 3. *See also* Pacific Air Forces
Hunter-killer missions: 103, 108
Huntley, Robert R.: 73–74
Huskey, Richard L.: 75, 122, 132
Huwe, John F.: 94, 123, 132

Icebag call sign: 135–136
Iceman call sign: 128, 131
Identification, friend or foe: 12
Identification, friend or foe, enemy: 97
Imaye, Stanley M.: 100–101, 124, 132
Immelmann turn: 165
Incendiary ammunition: 68, 105
Indochina. *See* North Vietnam; Republic of Vietnam
Inertial-guidance system: 155
Instrument flight control: 155
Intelligence operations and reports: vi, 113. *See also* Reconnaissance operations
Interdiction missions: 155

James, Daniel: 37, 37 pc, 38, 39–40
Jameson, Jerry W.: 32–33, 32 pc, 118, 132
Janca, Robert D.: 58, 120, 132
Jasperson, Robert H.: 108, 125, 132
Jenkins, Gordon: 50
Jettisons: 7, 10–12, 24, 26, 28, 30–31, 33, 35, 49, 51, 58, 60, 65, 73–74, 76, 88–89, 108, 113
Johnson, Harold E.: 46–47, 119, 132
Johnson, Lyndon B.: vi, 3, 4, 7, 12–13, 13 pc, 80, 88, 93, 117
Joint Chiefs of Staff: 3, 10–11, 13–14, 17, 48. *See also* Moorer, Thomas H.
Jones, Keith W., Jr.: 90, 123, 132

Kadena Air Base, Okinawa: 147, 150, 153
Kangaroo call sign: 128

183

Keith, Larry R.: 20, 29, 30 pc, 118, 132
Kelly, Alexander D.: 78
Kennedy, John F.: 1
Kep airfield: 11–12, 35–37, 48, 60, 71, 77, 94–95, 99, 105–106, 109, 113
Khe Sanh: 12
Kien An airfield: 12, 159
Killer call sign: 130, 139
Kills
  distribution by aircraft and weapon: 117–140, 155–157
  first: vi, 22–28, 90, 94
  first double: 44
  first quadruple: 60
  by gunners: 111–115, 117
  last: 115, 117
  ratios: vi, 101, 160–161
Kimball, Wesley D.: 78–79
Kimona call sign: 137
Kingfish call sign: 46, 132, 138
Kinh No: 57
Kirchner, Peter A.: 100
Kirk, William L.: 54, 59, 67–68, 67 pc, 120–121, 133
Kisinger, Vernon E.: 158 pc
Kissinger, Henry A.: 16–17
Kittinger, Joseph W., Jr.: 85–87, 87 pc, 122, 133
Kjer, Fred D.: 48, 49 pc, 119, 133
Klause, Klaus J.: 34 pc, 35, 119, 133
Knapp, Herman L.: 41
Kontum province: 14
Korat Royal Thai Air Force Base: 30, 33, 35, 62, 65, 78, 97, 146–147, 150–151, 153, 158
Korean War comparison: 111
Krieps, Richard N.: 31, 32 pc, 118, 133
Kringelis, Emants: 30, 118, 133
Kullman, Lawrence W.: 115, 125, 133
Kunsan Air Base, Korea: 147, 151
Kurz, Harold E.: 103
Kuster, Ralph L.: 62–63, 63 pc, 121, 133
Kutyna, Don: 126

Lachman, Jerald L.: 89
Lafever, William D.: 52, 120, 133
Lafferty, Daniel L.: 60, 60 pc, 121, 133
Lam airfield: 35
Lambert, Robert W.: 57, 120, 133
Lang, Alfred E., Jr.: 77–78, 122, 133
Lang Lau: 72
Laos: 1–3, 13–14, 85–89, 105
Lark call sign: 132, 136
Larson, George: 22, 24
Laser-guided bombs: 14, 16, 101
Latham, Wilbur J., Jr.: 34 pc, 35, 119, 133
Lavoy, Alan A.: 68, 121, 133
Leach, Thomas: 101
LeBlanc, Lewis E.: 112
Leech call sign: 136
Leonard, Bruce G., Jr.: 95, 123, 133
Lesan, Thomas C.: 50–51, 120, 133

Levy, Stuart W.: 78
Lewinski, Paul T.: 98, 123, 133
Lincoln Air Force Base, Neb.: 143
Linebacker operations: 14–17, 89–92, 94–103, 106–115
Lines of communication, strikes against: 45, 101
List call sign: 130, 134
Locher, Roger C.: 85, 90, 92–93, 122, 123, 133
Lodge, Robert A.: 85, 90–93, 122–123, 134
Logeman, John D., Jr.: 68–69, 121, 134
Logistical support: 37
Logistics system, strikes against: 101
Loose-deuce formation: 24
Lucas, Jon I.: 103, 124, 134
Lufbery circle: 45, 47, 170
Luke Air Force Base, Ariz.: 149, 154

Maas, Stuart W.: 88–89, 122, 134
MacDill Air Force Base, Fla.: 148, 151, 153
Madden, John A., Jr.: 103–106, 108–109, 124, 125, 134
Maddox, USS: 3
Madison, Thomas M.: 46
Magill, William S.: 90
Mahaffey, Michael J.: 106, 124, 134
Maintenance, supply and support forces: vi, 19–20, 37
Malaney, James: 110
Malloy, Douglas G.: 103, 112, 124, 134
Maltbie, Robert M.: 97
Maneuvers, combat. *See* Formations and maneuvers, combat; Tactics
Markey, Ronald L.: 75
Markle, John D.: 93, 123, 134
Martin, Ronald G.: 31, 32 pc, 118, 134
Massen, Mark A.: 101–102, 124, 134
Maurer, Maurer: 141
McConnell, John P.: 3. *See also* Chief of Staff, U.S. Air Force
McConnell Air Force Base, Kan.: 143–144, 149–151, 153
McCoy, Frederick E., II: 68, 121, 134
McCoy, Ivy J., Jr.: 110–111, 125, 134
McGrath, Joseph E.: 67 pc
McKee, Harry L.: 114–115, 125, 134
McKinney, George H., Jr.: 71–74, 121–122, 134
McNamara, Robert S.: 3, 10
Mesenbourg, John L.: 102
Meteorologists: vi
Meyer, John C.: 112 pc. *See also* Strategic Air Forces
Middleton, James H., Jr.: 51
MIGCAP. *See* Escort and Patrol missions
Mincer, Gary P.: 158 pc
Mining operations: 14, 89
Missile systems, air-to-air: 37
  Falcon AIM-4: 63–64, 69, 72, 75–77, 79, 122, 127, 129, 131–133, 135–137, 156–157
  kills distribution: 156
  Shrike AGM-45: 7, 31, 46, 58, 71
  Sidewinder AIM-9: 5, 8–10, 19, 22, 25, 27–33, 35, 38–41, 43, 47–48, 50, 52–55, 57–62, 64, 78, 89, 95, 98–99, 104–106, 110–111, 118–140, 156–158, 170
  Sparrow AIM-7: 5, 10, 19, 22–24, 27, 32–33, 35, 40–41, 43,

49, 51–52, 54–59, 63–65, 68–69, 73, 77–79, 85, 88–96, 98–111, 113, 115, 118–140, 155–158
Missile systems, air-to-air, enemy: 12, 26, 35, 61, 65, 92, 95, 98, 103, 105, 156–157, 160
Missile systems, air-to-ground
    Walleye AGM–62: 76, 160
Missile systems, surface-to-air
    Talos: 13, 80
Missile systems, surface-to-air, enemy: vi, 5, 7, 10, 13–14, 16–17, 19, 26, 44, 48–49, 52, 55, 58, 61–62, 64–66, 68–71, 75, 80, 83–85, 88, 96–97, 100, 103, 111–112, 155, 159
Momyer, William W.: 10–11, 10 pc, 64. *See also* Seventh Air Force
Monitoring systems, enemy: 87
Monsees, James H.: 68, 121, 134
Monsoons. *See* Weather, effect on operations
Moore, Albert E.: 114, 125, 135
Moore, Joseph.: 25–26
Moore, Joseph D.: 73–74, 122, 135
Moore, Rolland W.: 49, 119, 135
Moorer, Thomas H.: 17. *See also* Joint Chiefs of Staff
Moss, Randy P.: 77–78, 122, 135
Motor vehicles, strikes against: 96
Mountain Home Air Force Base, Idaho: 144, 151
Muldoon, Michael D.: 75, 122, 135
Murphy, Terrance M.: 105
Murray, James E., III: 38, 119, 135

Naha Air Base, Okinawa: 153–154
Nakhon Phanom Air Base: 142
Nash call sign: 132, 134–135, 138
Naval operations: 3
Navigation systems: 16
Nichols, Stephen E.: 94, 123, 135
Night actions, first: 85
Nitro call sign: 132, 138
Nixon, Richard M.: 13–14, 16, 17, 83, 89, 111, 115
North Korea armed forces: 10–11
North Vietnam, aggression by: vi, 1–3, 14, 87, 111
North Vietnam Air Force: 3, 10–11, 13, 26–27, 37, 41, 71, 83, 117, 170
North Vietnam Navy: 3
Northeast Railway: 99
Northwest Railway: 102
Norton, William A.: 58
Norwood, George: 109
Null, James C.: 89, 123, 135

Oakland call sign: 135
O'Brien, Michael B.: 103
Ogilvie, James W.: 115
Olds, Robin: vi, 35–42, 42 pc, 52–53, 59–60, 60 pc, 62–64, 66, 119, 120, 121, 135
Olds call sign: 20–22, 128–131, 134–139
Olmsted, Frederick S., Jr.: 87–89, 122, 135
Opal call sign: 133, 136, 138
Organization, air units: 141–154

Osan Air Base, Korea: 147
Osborne, Carl D.: 53–54, 120, 135
Otter call sign: 129–131, 137, 139
Oyster call sign: 129–130, 133–134, 136

Panda call sign: 47–48, 130
Pankhurst, John E.: 64, 121, 135
Papa call sign: 135, 138
Pardo, John R.: 59–60, 60 pc, 120, 135
Paris conference: 13
Parrot call sign: 129, 132
Pascoe, Richard M.: 43, 64–65, 65 pc, 119, 121, 135
Patrol missions. *See* Escort and patrol missions
Paula call sign: 129, 136
Peace negotiations: 5, 7, 13, 16–17, 83
Penney, Forrest: 102
People's Republic of China: 1–5, 24, 30, 64, 71, 74, 85
Petroleum-oil-lubricants, strikes against: 7
Pettit, Lawrence H.: 93, 96, 108–109, 123, 125, 135
Phan Rang Air Base: 143–144, 151
Photography, aerial. *See* Reconnaissance missions
Phu Tho: 93, 99, 102, 113
Phu Cat Air Base: 151, 153, 158
Phuc Yen airfield: 3–4, 11–12, 22, 35–38, 40–41, 43, 49, 52, 67–68, 72, 76, 78–79, 99, 103–106, 108, 111
Pickett, Ralph S.: 113, 125, 135
Pilots, training and efficiency: 14, 16, 160–161
Pilots, enemy, training and efficiency: 4–5, 8–12, 14, 26–27, 44–45, 64, 71, 97
Pistol call sign: 127, 132, 137, 139
Pop-up maneuvers: 167–170
Port facilities, strikes against: 16, 89
Positive Identification Radar Advisory Zone Ship. *See* Red Crown radar ship
Power plants, strikes against: 11, 16, 49, 75, 102, 111
Priester, Durwood K.: 64, 121, 135
Prisoners of war: 14, 17
Profitt, Glenn A.: 111
Proximity fuze: 89

Quang Binh province: 83
Quang Lang airfield: 106
Quang Tri province: 14, 87

Rabeni, John J., Jr.: 34 pc, 35, 119, 136
Radar jamming operations. *See* Electronic countermeasures systems
Radar operators, proficiency: 20
Radar systems: 4, 7, 12, 14, 16, 20–22, 24–25, 156
Radar systems, enemy: 4, 7, 13, 19, 22, 85, 157
Radeker, Walter S.: 38–39, 119, 136
Radio call signs. *See* Call signs
Radio transmission, typical: 20–22
Railways, strikes against: vi, 4–5, 7, 11, 16, 38, 50, 53–54, 58–59, 65, 67, 71, 73, 75–77, 99, 102, 111, 114
Rambler call sign: 128–131, 137
Random call sign: 135–136
Raspberry, Everett T., Jr.: 39–40, 42, 42 pc, 63, 119, 121, 136

Rattler call sign: 50, 133
Rauscher, Forrest L.: 10 pc
Reconnaissance missions: vi, 4–5, 13–14, 43, 62, 68, 83, 101
Red Crown radar ship: 14–16, 20–22, 85, 87–88, 90, 93, 96, 98–101, 108–115
Red River and Valley: 28, 30, 37, 44–45, 65, 71–72, 90, 101, 106
Refueling operations and units: vi, 22, 91
Republic of Vietnam
    military assistance to: 1–3
    training and equipment: 13
RESCAP. *See* Search-and-rescue missions
Retterbush, Gary L.: 105, 108, 124–125, 136
Rhine, Kimzey W.: 114
Richard, Lawrence G., USMC: 101, 124, 136
Richter, Karl W.: 33 pc, 33–34, 118, 136
Rilling, Robert G.: 53–54, 120, 136
Ritchie, Richard S.: vi, 20–22, 93, 96, 98–100, 100 pc, 102–104, 104 pc, 123–124, 136
Roberts, Thomas S.: 22–25, 118, 136
Roberts, William E., Jr.: 58, 120, 136
Robin call sign: 129, 134, 137, 139
Rocket clusters: 7, 155
Rockets, enemy: 157, 160
Rogers, Danny R.: 100
Rolling Thunder operation: 3–14, 37, 101
Rose, Douglas B.: 32–33, 32 pc, 118, 136
Rotation system: vi
Route Packages
    1 and 2: 80
    3: 80, 115
    5: 14
    6: 97, 101, 113
    6A: 14, 72
Ruby call sign: 135
Rubus, Gary M.: 110, 125, 136
Ruses, application of: 11, 37, 43–44
Russell, Donald M.: 67, 67 pc, 121, 136
Russia. *See* Soviet Union
Rutherford, Robert L.: 76
Ryan, John D.: vi. *See also* Chief of Staff, U.S. Air Force
Ryan, John D., Jr.: 72, 121, 136

Sandy call sign: 47–48
Sapphire call sign: 134, 137
Saudi Arabia: 142
Scissors maneuver: 165–167
Scott, Robert R.: 44–45, 119, 136
Screen missions: 27, 31
Search-and-rescue missions: vi, 14n 30, 47, 51, 105
Sears, James F.: 49, 119, 137
Seaver, Maurice E., Jr.: 54–55, 55 pc, 120, 137
Seventh Fleet: 3
Seymour, Paul A.: 47, 54
Seymour Johnson Air Force Base, N.C.: 149
Sharp, Jerry K.: 38, 119, 137
Shaw Air Force Base, S.C.: 145
Sheffler, Fred W.: 101–102, 124, 137
Shields, George I.: 106, 124, 137

Shipping, strikes against: 96
Sholders, Gary L.: 112–113, 125, 137
Shrike (AGM–45) air-to-air missile: 7, 31, 46, 58, 71
Sidewinder (AIM–9) air-to-air missile: 5, 8–10, 19, 22, 25, 27–33, 35, 38–41, 43, 47–48, 50, 52–55, 57–62, 64, 78, 89, 95, 98–99, 104–106, 110–111, 118–140, 158–168, 170
Silver Star awards: 26
Simmonds, Darrell D.: 71–72, 121, 137
Simonet, Kenneth A.: 76, 122, 137
Slaughter Alley: 10
Slay, Alton D.: 11, 91
Smallwood, John J.: 96–97, 123, 137
Smith, Wayne O.: 76, 122, 137
Smith, William T.: 27, 118, 137
Sniegowski, Greg E.: 158 pc
Snug call sign: 127, 130
Sorties flown, number: 10, 17
Southeast Asia Treaty Organization: 1
Soviet Union: 1, 4, 11, 85, 97, 156–157
Sparrow (AIM–7) air-to-air missile: 5, 10, 19, 22–24, 27, 32–33, 35, 40–41, 43, 49, 51–52, 54–59, 63–65, 68–69, 73, 77–79, 85, 88–96, 98–111, 113, 115, 118–140, 155–158
Speedo call sign: 129, 131, 138
Spencer, Robert V.: 77–78
Spitfire call sign: 131
Split-S maneuver: 165
Squadrons. *See* Tactical Fighter Squadrons
Squier, Clayton K.: 75, 122, 137
Stearman, Ralph W.: 73
Steel plants, strikes against: 44
Sterling, Thomas J.: 46
Stinger call sign: 129, 138
Stone, John B.: 40–41, 119, 137
Storage facilities, strikes against: 16, 96, 111
Strasswimmer, Roger J.: 43, 119, 137
Strategic Air Command: 4, 16, 112. *See also* Meyer, John C.
Strategic Wing, 307th: 111, 125, 135, 138, 141, 142
Strike formations: 91–92
Sumner, James M.: 94–95, 123, 137
Supply depots, strikes against: 55, 57, 88, 96, 111
Supply forces. *See* Maintenance, supply and support forces
Support forces. *See* Maintenance, supply and support forces
Support missions. *See* Escort and patrol missions
Surprise, application of: 4
Suzanne, Jacques A.: 53, 120, 137
Sweeny, Allan R.: 78
Swendner, William J.: 31–32, 32 pc, 118, 137

Tactical Air Command: 143, 148–153, 155
Tactical Fighter Squadrons
    4th: 98, 100, 123–125, 127, 131–133, 137, 139, 144, 145
    13th: 99, 121–125, 127–136, 138–139, 144
    34th: 32, 118, 121, 124–125, 127–129, 132, 134, 138–139, 144
    35th: 123–125, 127, 131–132, 134, 136–137, 143, 146, 147
    44th: 120, 137, 146, 147
    45th: 19, 22, 118, 127–128, 132, 136, 146, 147

58th: 96, 101, 123–124, 130–131, 136–137, 146, 147
307th: 125, 131, 136, 148, 149
333d: 118–122, 129, 131, 133, 135–137, 139, 148
336th: 101, 124, 134, 137, 148, 149
354th: 119–121, 127–130, 132, 138, 148, 149
357th: 119–120, 122, 129–132, 138–139, 148, 149
389th: 119–121, 127, 132–133, 135–137, 139, 150, 151
390th: 54, 118, 120, 129–130, 133, 138, 150, 151
421st: 118, 136, 150, 151
433d: 54, 119–122, 127–133, 135, 137–138, 150, 151
435th: 75, 121–122, 130, 133–135, 137, 139, 150, 151
469th: 97, 119, 121, 123–124, 128–129, 131, 134, 137, 139, 152, 153
480th: 31, 35, 118–121, 127–131, 133–138, 152, 153
523d: 123, 125, 128, 134–135, 138, 152, 153
555th: 27, 29, 32, 61–63, 85, 92–96, 98, 106, 118–125, 127–139, 154
Tactical Fighter Training Wing, 58th: 154
Tactical Fighter Wings
  3d: 146, 148
  4th: 148
  8th: 11, 35, 43, 51–54, 57–58, 62, 67, 71, 75, 77, 85, 101, 118–122, 124, 127–139, 142, 143, 148, 150, 154
  12th: 146, 150, 152
  15th: 146, 150
  18th: 144, 146
  23d: 148, 150
  27th: 152
  31st: 148
  33d: 144, 146
  35th: 118, 128, 130, 133–134, 137, 142, 143, 150, 152
  37th: 150, 152
  347th: 144, 150
  355th: 34, 37, 44–45, 50, 52, 67, 118–122, 127–133, 135–139, 142, 143, 147, 149–151, 153
  366th: 34, 37, 48–49, 54–55, 57, 100, 119–121, 123–124, 127, 129, 131–133, 135–139, 144, 145, 146, 151, 153
  388th: 30, 33, 35–37, 44, 53–54, 62, 65–67, 94, 98, 103, 105–106, 108–109, 118–121, 123–125, 127–129, 131–134, 136–139, 141, 144, 145, 146, 150, 152, 158
  401st: 148
  405th: 152
  457th: 150
  4531st: 150
  6234th: 150, 152
  6251st: 148
  6252d: 150
  6441st: 146
Tactical Reconnaissance Wing: 432d: 72, 85, 90–92, 94–96, 99, 101, 109–110, 115, 121–125, 127–139, 144, 145, 146, 148, 150, 152, 154
Tactics: 5–8, 11, 16, 19, 22–73, 85–111, 160–170. *See also* Formations and maneuvers, combat
Tactics, enemy: vi, 1–3, 5, 10–14, 16, 22, 24–26, 29, 31, 34–42, 44–45, 48–80, 97–111, 170
Taft, Gene E.: 100–101, 124, 137
Takhli Air Base: 34, 69, 143–144, 146–147, 149–152
Talley, James T.: 56–57, 56 pc, 120, 138
Talos surface-to-air missile: 13, 80
Tampa call sign: 128–129, 132, 135, 138
Tan Son Nhut Air Base: v, 142
Target acquisition systems: 16, 102–103, 105. *See also* Ground control intercept systems; Radar systems
Tax, Cal W.: 71
Taylor, Reggie: 103, 104 pc
Teamwork, importance of: 103, 110
Tet offensive: 12
Thai Nguyen: 44, 76, 96, 108, 110, 114
Thailand: 1, 4, 7, 80
Thanh Hoa: 4, 19
Thibodeaux, James L.: 64
Thies, Mack: 51–52, 52 pc, 120, 138
Tho, Le Duc: 17
Thorsness, Leo K.: 46–47, 119, 138
Thud Ridge: 38, 49, 58, 63–66, 69–72, 78–79
Tibbett, Calvin B.: 104, 106, 124, 138
Tien Cuong: 73
Titus, Robert F.: 58, 60, 120–121, 138
Tolman, Frederick G.: 47, 119, 138
Torching: 71
Torrejon Air Base, Spain: 149
Tracy, Fred L.: 30–31, 118, 138
Troops, withdrawal: 83
Truman, Harry S: 1
Trung Quang: 75
Tuan Quan: 105
Tuck, James E.: 34 pc, 35, 119, 138
Turner, Samuel O.: 111–112, 112 pc, 125, 138
Turner Joy, USS: 3

Ubon Royal Thai Air Force Base: 22, 32, 51, 58, 62, 65, 77, 109, 142, 148–149, 152, 154
Udorn Royal Thai Air Force Base: 25, 30, 87–89, 91, 105, 145–146, 149, 152–154
United States Air Force: v, 7, 16, 80, 141
United States Air Forces in Europe: 142
United States Marine Corps: 12, 72, 101
United States Navy: 4–5, 7, 13–14, 16, 19, 40, 48, 51, 67, 69, 80, 85, 90, 101, 155–156
Unknown call sign: 127–134, 136–138
U-Tapao Royal Thai Air Force Base: 111, 143

Vahue, Michael D.: 89, 123, 138
Vandenberg, Hoyt S., Jr.: 52 pc
Vega call sign: 20–22, 134–135, 139
Vertical rolling scissors maneuver: 167
Viet Tri: 73, 102, 109–110
Vietnamization program: 13, 83
Vinh: 13, 96, 106
Vinh Yen: 53
Voigt, Ted L., II: 79, 122, 138
Vojvodich, Mele: 97
Volloy, Gerald R: 87–88, 122, 138

Wagon-wheel formation: 57, 63, 78, 95, 170
Waldrop, David B., III: 65–66, 121, 138

Walleye (AGM) air-to-ground missile: 76, 166
Wander call sign: 138–139
Watson, George D.: 108, 125, 138
Wayne, Robert E.: 111
Wayne, Stephen A.: 54, 59–60, 60 pc, 120, 138
Weapon systems, aircraft. *See* Armament, aircraft; Missile systems
Weapon systems, enemy aircraft: 156–157
Weather, effect on operations: vi, 7, 11–12, 16, 27, 37–38, 41, 43–45, 77, 80, 165
Weather men. *See* Meteorologists
Webb, Omri K., III: 106, 124, 139
Wells, Norman E.: 43, 64–65, 65 pc, 119, 121, 139
Weskamp, Robert L.: 45
Western, Robert W.: 40, 42 pc, 119, 139
Westphal, Curtis D.: 109, 125, 139
Wetterhahn, Ralph K.: 38, 119, 139
Wheeler, William H.: 73–74, 122, 139
White, Sammy C.: 102, 124, 139
Wiggins, Larry D.: 62–63, 63 pc, 121, 139
Wildcat call sign: 136
Williams, David O., Jr.: 79, 122, 139
Williams, Lee: 101
Wilson, Fred A., Jr.: 33 pc, 34, 118, 139
Wings. *See* Fighter-Interceptor Wing; Strategic Wing; Tactical Fighter Training Wing; Tactical Fighter Wings; Tactical Reconnaissance Wing
World War II comparison: 58–64

Xuan Mai: 45, 47

Yen Bai airfield: 10, 22–24, 65, 90, 92–94, 98, 106, 110, 113
Yen Vien: 53–54, 65
Yokota Air Base, Japan: 147, 153
Yunnan province: 30

Zimer, Milan: 58, 60, 120–121, 139